The American Liberal
Tradition Reconsidered

American Political Thought
Wilson Carey McWilliams and Lance Banning
Founding Editors

The American Liberal Tradition Reconsidered

The Contested Legacy of Louis Hartz

Edited by Mark Hulliung

University Press of Kansas

Published by the University Press of Kansas (Lawrence, Kansas 66045),
which was organized by the Kansas Board of Regents and is operated and
funded by Emporia State University, Fort Hays State University, Kansas
State University, Pittsburg State University, the University of Kansas, and
Wichita State University

Library of Congress Cataloging-in-Publication Data

The American liberal tradition reconsidered : the contested legacy
of Louis Hartz / edited by Mark Hulliung.
  p.   cm. — (American political thought)
  Includes bibliographical references and index.
  ISBN 978-0-7006-1708-1 (cloth : alk. paper)
  1. Hartz, Louis, 1919-1986. 2. Liberalism—United States
  I. Hulliung, Mark.
  JC251.H37A44 2010
  320.510973—dc22   2009052227

British Library Cataloguing-in-Publication Data is available.

Printed in the United States of America

10 9 8 7 6 5 4 3 2 1

The paper used in this publication is recycled and contains 30 percent
postconsumer waste. It is acid free and meets the minimum requirements
of the American National Standard for Permanence of Paper for Printed
Library Materials Z39.48-1992.

To Amy, first and last

Contents

Preface   ix

Introduction: Louis Hartz, His Life and Writings   1
   —Mark Hulliung

PART ONE. HARTZ IN CONTEXT
1. Louis Hartz, His Day and Ours   11
   —Mark Hulliung

PART TWO. HARTZ'S ARGUMENT REAPPRAISED
2. Understanding the Symbiosis of American Rights and
   American Racism   55
   —Rogers M. Smith
3. *Requiescat in Pacem*: The Liberal Tradition of Louis Hartz   90
   —James T. Kloppenberg
4. Capitalism, Democracy, and the Missing State in
   Louis Hartz's America   125
   —Desmond King and Marc Stears

PART THREE. YESTERDAY: EPISODES IN AMERICAN HISTORY
5. Louis Hartz and Study of the American Founding: The Search for
   New Fundamental Categories   149
   —Alan Gibson
6. Change We Already Believe In? The Liberal Tradition and the American
   Left   184
   —Marc Stears

PART FOUR. FROM YESTERDAY TO TODAY

7. The Liberal Tradition in an Age of Conservative Power and
   Partisan Polarization   207
   —Richard J. Ellis
8. The Case against Arrested Development: Hartz's Liberal Tradition in
   America Revisited   237
   —Carol Nackenoff

Afterword: What's Living, What's Dead, in the Work of Louis Hartz   267
   —Mark Hulliung

About the Contributors   275

Index   277

Preface

When I published a book in 2002, a number of scholars and graduate students responded by asking whether my project was one of resurrecting Louis Hartz's *The Liberal Tradition in America.* After publishing another book in 2007, the same question came my way. While the plain truth is that Hartz was not on my mind when I wrote either book, the queries did whet my appetite for an opportunity to express my views on Hartz.

I have recruited seven distinguished scholars to join me on this quest. On this occasion I wish to thank all of them and to express my sorrow that Hartz's devoted student Paul Roazen died shortly before the commencement of this project. Paul's absence from this book is regrettable.

If the essays included in this volume are frequently quite critical of Hartz, it is nevertheless undeniable that his book continues to generate specific scholarly questions, some raised within the pages of this volume. More generally, we may suggest that although many scholars of our time have abandoned Hartz's method of analysis, his concern for the fate of "liberal society" is still with us.

Our ties to Hartz have frayed but not entirely disappeared. We still wish, as he did in wielding his notion of a "liberal society," to understand America by studying it in comparative terms. We continue to insist, moreover, upon studying the extent to which America both has and has not lived up to its liberal professions. Finally, an examination of the vicissitudes of liberalism in America is immediately meaningful in our day—a time when the Republicans have so successfully stigmatized the word "liberal" that even the Democrats run away from it, in a dramatic reversal of a previous era when Herbert Hoover accused Franklin Delano Roosevelt of usurping the coveted label "liberal."

Whatever the contemporary standing of Hartz's book, we cannot escape from addressing his topic: the triumphs, failures, trials, and tribulations of liberalism in America.

Louis Hartz, His Life and Writings

Mark Hulliung

The Liberal Tradition in America, the book Louis Hartz published in 1955, figured from the outset as a highly influential work, a stimulus to further research, and a focus of keen controversy. A year after its publication the American Political Science Association bestowed upon Hartz its coveted Woodrow Wilson Prize; two decades later Hartz's famous study won the Lippincott Prize in recognition of its enduring interest. Even Hartz's numerous critics, it seems safe to say, must admit that the only study of liberalism since his book that has received comparable attention is the philosopher John Rawls's *A Theory of Justice* (1971). Among twentieth-century historical studies of America, possibly only the works of Charles Beard and the Progressive historians have elicited similarly sustained and impassioned attention.

A veritable cottage industry of studies of Hartz's famous book has flourished for decades and has yet to fade into the past. A number of his students, all of whom testify to his mesmerizing presence in the classroom, continue to hold professorships at leading institutions of higher learning. Especially in departments of political science *The Liberal Tradition in America* remains essential reading, most notably so in graduate courses on "American political development." The contributors to the present volume wish to offer their own respective understandings of the significance of *The Liberal Tradition in America* in the worlds of yesterday and today.

Hartz's career may be likened to a meteor that burst upon the scene, burned with extraordinary intensity, and then abruptly disappeared from the horizon. In 1940, at the age of twenty-one, he published his precocious essay "Seth Luther: The Story of a Working-Class Rebel."[1] In 1948, well before his thirtieth birthday, Hartz published his first book, *Economic Policy and Democratic Thought: Pennsylvania, 1776–1860.* Then, having advanced only to his mid-thirties, he brought forth his most noteworthy book, *The Liberal Tradition in America: An Interpretation of American Political Thought since the Revolution*. By his mid-forties, in the year 1964, he was ready to publish his third book, *The Founding of New Societies: Studies in the History of the United States, Latin America, South Africa, Canada, and Australia.*

No one in the 1960s could have guessed that Hartz's flourishing career was all but over—that by 1974 his attachment to Harvard University would be severed—and that Louis Hartz would spend the rest of his life wandering the world, never again to publish a book. Born on April 8, 1919, Hartz died on January 20, 1986, at the age of sixty-six. We are left to wonder how much more he might have accomplished had his career not been cut short by the illness that plagued him from the early 1970s to his death.

Hartz's life outside the academy was one of travel in an endless quest for personal growth and insight. Born in Youngstown, Ohio, he was raised in Omaha, Nebraska, and, with the assistance of a scholarship financed by the *Omaha World Herald,* he matriculated at Harvard. Upon completing his undergraduate studies, he spent a year abroad in 1940, the first of his journeys outside the United States, the last voyage coming many years later, ending with his death on the streets of Istanbul, Turkey. Unwilling to be confined to an American perspective, Hartz eventually found the entire Western world too constricting. He died believing that the quest for knowledge could never be fulfilled unless sought on a genuinely global scale.

Each of Hartz's books was more comprehensive, expansive, and ambitious than its predecessor. How very intent he was upon painting on a large canvas may already be seen in his first book, which dealt with Pennsylvania. On the face of it Hartz was dealing with only one state, but his readers were bound to be impressed by his grand narrative arc, which began with the Revolution and did not halt until he reached the Civil War. Of equal or even greater importance, his specific message in *Economic Policy and Democratic Thought* was one that had implications for all of American history, including his own day. Against the conservatives of the post–World War II era who bemoaned the loss of the good old days of laissez-faire, Hartz proved that regulation had flourished in antebellum state governments. Thus the federal regulations and "mixed economy" initiatives of the New Dealers were extensions rather than denials of long-established American practice.

Bold though his first book might be, his second book on "the liberal tradition in America" was written on a much larger scale. "An interpretation of American political thought since the Revolution" was his daunting objective, an endeavor that was bound to fail, in his view, unless the investigator reached well beyond the confines of the United States. He understood that to comprehend the political culture of America, and to draw any conclusions as to the existence and nature of "American exceptionalism," nothing less would suffice than a sustained comparative analysis with Europe. Accordingly Hartz sprinkled his book on America with constant allusions to the histories of France and England. One of the courses Hartz regularly taught at Harvard was on European political thought in the nineteenth century, a course in which he assigned readings from primary sources and recommended such secondary sources as Élie Halévy's *The Growth of Philosophic Radicalism* and Guido de Ruggiero's *The History of European Liberalism.* Of course, the European writer to whom Hartz owed most was Alexis de Tocqueville, who had traveled to America the better to understand France, which inspired Hartz to travel to Europe to understand America.

The link between *Democracy in America* and *The Liberal Tradition in America* is explicit. When readers open Hartz's book, the first words they encounter are a quotation from Tocqueville's classic study: "The great advantage of the Americans is that they have arrived at a state of democracy without having to endure a democratic revolution; and that they are born equal, instead of becoming so." Less certainly but quite possibly, Hartz's next book, *The Founding of New Societies,* may have drawn inspiration from Tocqueville's other renowned study, *The Old Regime and the French Revolution.* For in the notes of *The Old Regime* Tocqueville briefly suggested the kind of investigation that Hartz was to undertake a century later: the study of what happened to various "fragments" of European political culture when transplanted to other lands in colonial settlements.

Specifically, Tocqueville commented briefly on French Canada. "The physiognomy of governments," he noted, "can be best detected in their colonies, for there their features are magnified. . . . When I want to discover the spirit and vices of the government of Louis XIV, I must go to Canada." It was excessive political centralization and the resulting diminution of civic life that Tocqueville spied in France's Canadian possessions, where, unlike in France proper, the Church and local notables were too weak to thwart the will of the royal administrators. By contrast, the English colonies in America were, he remarked, "almost democratic republics" and marvels of self-rule. "In Canada," he concluded, "equality was an accessory of absolutism; in the British colonies it was the companion of liberty."[2]

Intentionally or not, *The Founding of New Societies* took up where Tocqueville left off. In what proved to be his final work Hartz assembled a team of scholars, each an expert on one of various European colonial settlements that had transmuted over time into independent modern nations: South Africa, Canada, Australia, and Latin America, with Hartz himself providing the chapter on the United States and also the three crucial theoretical and comparative chapters that framed the volume. The four chapters written by four experts on four areas of the world other than America stand as contributions in their own right, but the overall project remained unquestionably the offspring of Louis Hartz.

Hartz's argument in *The Founding of New Societies* was a direct extension of that set forth in *The Liberal Tradition in America*. If, as he asserted in 1955, it was the European middle class that settled in America, then in Australia, he added in 1964, it was the lower class that had broken off from Europe; and if "the United States enshrines Locke," then Australia enshrines "the spirit of the Chartists and of Cobbett."[3] Every one of the "new societies" could be understood, Hartz held, by pointing to its European class origins and then designating the corresponding European class ideology that became an unchallenged national faith in its new setting: national liberalism in the case of America, national radicalism in that of Australia.

Both Latin America and French Canada were fragments from feudal Europe; hence their political cultures took social hierarchy for granted, observed Hartz. By contrast, the United States, English Canada, and Dutch South Africa were bourgeois, liberal fragments speaking in slightly different accents. As for Australia and English South Africa, they were radical fragments in the manner of the working-class, non-Marxist, radicalism of England in the early nineteenth century. No matter how much these countries located across the world differed from one another, they had at least one element in common: just as Hartz had earlier held in *The Liberal Tradition* that virtual ideological unanimity in America had blocked the creation of creative political theory,[4] so now he generalized his finding for all of the colonial settlements: "It is no accident that none of the fragment cultures . . . produced a major tradition of social philosophy."[5] In the absence of alternative ideologies, the reigning ideology of each country assumed the status of self-evident truth needing no thoughtful defense—or so Hartz maintained.

When treating the all-important topics of slavery and race, Hartz drew a strong contrast between feudal Latin America, on the one side, and liberal America, on the other. Shockingly, doctrines of slavery were harsher, he suggested, in "Enlightenment cultures" than in "feudal cultures," for in the latter the humanity of the slave did not have to be denied, whereas a country awash in a liberal beginning could only justify slavery by reducing its victims to property. Feudal societies, with their sense of hierarchy, could place the slave at the bottom of the social ladder, whereas a country practicing "liberal slavery" had to transform the slave into a thing, a possession pure and simple.[6]

Since the publication of Hartz's books, scholars have frequently expressed sympathy for what he said about slavery but rarely have they sided with his views on the consequences of abolition. The flip side for Hartz, but not for his successors, of the exceptionally vicious "liberal" defense of slavery was that "once humanity is conceded, the liberal ethic is more compulsively generous, since it demands completely equal treatment."[7] For the next generation of scholars, influenced by the New Left of the late 1960s or the New Politics of the Democratic Party in the 1970s, it was obvious that the abolition of slavery was only the beginning of the struggle to end racism in America. Hartz himself, his admiring student Paul Roazen reported in 1990, "once said to me that he regretted neglecting the role of race in his *The Liberal Tradition in America*."[8]

Continuing in his final years to pursue investigations on an ever-larger scale, Hartz worked with uncertain success on a volume tentatively titled *A Synthesis of World History*. Only a handful of persons, it seems, know much about this final, unpublished volume, and those few who approach it do so in a spirit of tact and diplomacy. Hartz's student Benjamin Barber has remarked, briefly, that "in this synthesis Europe with its principles of rational technology and domination, and the non-Western world with its more pliant intuitive cultures and its saving devotion to inner values, were to be reconciled."[9] Patrick Riley, who wrote his dissertation under the direction of Hartz, has made a noble effort in a journal article to find traces of rhyme and reason in a manuscript that seems to testify to the mental instability of Hartz's declining years. Despite Riley's best efforts, the final effort of Hartz appears to be an exercise in extreme psychological reductionism, wherein thinkers, religions, and cultures are deemed interchangeable, except that some are more active, others more passive. It is difficult to escape the conclusion that Hartz's final thoughts are best ignored.[10]

The focus of the essays on Hartz written for the present volume is on *The Liberal Tradition in America,* the book that is without question his most influential work, the one to which students of American political culture have found themselves returning time and again over the last several decades. This does not mean, of course, that his other writings will be completely neglected in our presentations. His first book on economic policy and democratic thought in Pennsylvania is fair game for contributors who wish to discuss it as a forerunner of his most famous book or, alternatively, as an offering distinctly different in approach from his approach in *The Liberal Tradition*. Likewise, *The Founding of New Societies* is pertinent insofar as it may shed additional insight into Hartz's undertaking in his second book. There are also several scattered articles written by Hartz that our scholars will avail themselves of as they see fit.

One final source is the volume published in 1990 by Paul Roazen, *The Necessity of Choice: Nineteenth-Century Political Thought,* which consists of the notes of students enrolled in one of the courses Hartz taught repeatedly over a period of some twenty-five years. Because this course was dedicated to an examination of European thinkers and events, it arguably provides useful background for understanding his European references and his comparative method in *The Liberal Tradition in America.*

Whatever conclusion one draws about *The Liberal Tradition in America,* whether one wishes to agree with Hartz, reject him, or revise him, there is no denying the importance of his book. Our eight contributors make no pretense to seeing eye to eye in their assessments of Hartz; they have differing and perhaps conflicting answers to the question of the value of *The Liberal Tradition* for fostering understanding of the American past or for throwing light on the present; different judgments to offer as to the worth or limitations of Hartz's method of analysis. But they are as one in their conviction that, more than half a century after its publication, there is still much to be gained from settling our accounts with *The Liberal Tradition in America.*

We shall begin with an essay that places Hartz in historical context and prepares the way for part 2, containing three essays attempting overall assessments of Hartz's argument. This will be followed by a third part wherein two scholars will test the worth of Hartz's analysis when applied to specific historical events and movements, to wit, the Founding and the history of American radicalism. Then, in part 4, two scholars will inquire whether Hartz's interpretations are of use in helping us understand contemporary America. Finally, the volume will close with a brief afterword.

NOTES

1. Louis Hartz, "Seth Luther: The Story of a Working-Class Rebel," *New England Quarterly* 13, no. 3 (September 1940): 401–418.

2. Alexis de Tocqueville, *The Old Regime and the French Revolution,* trans. Stuart Gilbert (New York: Anchor, 1983), 253–254.

3. Louis Hartz et al., *The Founding of New Societies* (New York: Harcourt, Brace & World, 1964), 4, 11.

4. Louis Hartz, *The Liberal Tradition in America* (New York: Harvest, 1955), 10, 141.

5. Hartz, *The Founding of New Societies,* 23.

6. Ibid., 17, 50, 55.

7. Ibid., 17.

8. Paul Roazen, introduction to *The Necessity of Choice: Nineteenth-Century Political Thought,* by Louis Hartz (New Brunswick, N.J.: Transaction Books, 1990), 14.

9. Benjamin R. Barber, "Louis Hartz," *Political Theory* 14, no. 3 (August 1986): 358.

10. Patrick Riley, "Louis Hartz: The Final Years, the Unknown Work," *Political Theory* 16, no. 3 (August 1988): 377–399.

PART ONE

Hartz in Context

CHAPTER 1

Louis Hartz, His Day and Ours

Mark Hulliung

It is a matter of indisputable fact that Louis Hartz's *The Liberal Tradition in America* was one of the most influential books on American history published in the twentieth century, equaled in notoriety only by the works of the Progressive historians at the beginning of the century and perhaps by those of Arthur M. Schlesinger Jr. or Richard Hofstadter during the middle years. Ever since the release of Hartz's book in 1955 political theorists and historians, occasionally joined by the aficionados of other disciplines such as sociology and literary studies, have passionately devoted themselves to assessing and reassessing *The Liberal Tradition*. Pro and anti *The Liberal Tradition in America: An Interpretation of American Political Thought Since the Revolution* has long been, and perhaps still is, a favorite topic of intellectual debate within and sometimes beyond the academy.[1]

Not least among the reasons why the stands taken for and against Hartz are fascinating and refuse to die out is that the protagonists often directly contradict one another on what Hartz did or did not argue. Some intellectuals, frequently quasi-Marxist and almost always leftist in inspiration, have accused him of paying attention to ideas only, to the detriment of economic considerations and discussions of class conflict, while other intellectuals have charged that Hartz's book is no different from Daniel Boorstin's *The Genius of American Politics*, published two years earlier, which took all the ideas out of American politics, past and present—which is to say, scholars have had trouble deciding the fundamental question of whether Hartz was underscoring or denying the role of ideas in the history of the United States.

Every time that Hartz's book is pronounced dead and buried or demoted to the status of a relic from a bygone age, it threatens to come back from the grave. In the 1970s J. G. A. Pocock announced that his approach to early American history, based on the themes of classical republicanism, civic virtue, and fear of modernity, "altogether replaces" that of Hartz.[2] Today, it seems fair to say, it is Pocock's approach that has fallen out of favor, and with the fading of his "republican" interpretation, Hartz's fate once again becomes an open question. Since the 1970s historians such as Joyce Appleby have discerned a ferocious capitalist mentality within the ranks of early American farmers, a finding that Hartz would have welcomed but that poses a major threat to Pocock's vision of would-be civic humanists, haunted by a "dread of modernity"[3] and convinced that market society and political corruption go hand in hand.[4]

Pocock seemed confident that his contemptuous dismissal of Hartz in the 1970s marked the end of the reign of *The Liberal Tradition in America.* In fact, however, the ensuing debate over the next several decades took the form of "republicanism versus liberalism"—hardly a promising formula for forgetting Louis Hartz, even on those occasions when those social scientists engaged in the controversy sided with the republican interpretation. All the more so would Hartz inevitably return to mind when, in more recent years, a number of scholars have reinstated with a vengeance the prominence of John Locke, natural rights, and the social contract at the time of the Revolution, the Founding, and possibly long thereafter. So strong has been the resurgence of Locke in our understanding of American political thought that today the question is no longer, will Hartz withstand the "republican" onslaught? Rather, it is, does the return of Locke signify a belated vindication of Hartz or does the most recent scholarship bear only an incidental similarity to the Hartzian viewpoint?

In this essay my intention is, eventually, to address the question of whether the scholarship of our day is leading us back to Hartz, or, instead, to something that bears merely an accidental likeness to his famous book. Along the way, we shall also find time to confront the issue of whether contemporary efforts to put the ideas back into American history are a reprise of Hartz or whether they, instead, constitute an alternative to his manner of studying American political culture.

Another question we shall confront is whether Hartz's scholarship was, as he believed, a thoughtful adaptation of Alexis de Tocqueville's, or whether *The Liberal Tradition in America* was the betrayal of *Democracy in America,* as many scholars of our day have suggested or implied. The difference between the Tocqueville of the 1950s and Tocqueville now tells us much about both Hartz's day and ours.

Before seeking out the meaning of *The Liberal Tradition in America* for our day, I believe we should examine Hartz in his day, his context, the 1950s especially. Only by studying him historically can we hope to appreciate his ambitious intellectual enterprise and earn the right to criticize his breathtaking account of American history. Many of Hartz's critics have spoken past him; we must speak to him, no matter whether we ultimately agree or disagree with him.

LOUIS HARTZ AND HIS DAY

All of us are inevitably the children of our age, Louis Hartz along with everyone else. What mattered to him from the beginning of his career and was conspicuously evident in his pre-1955 writings was the New Deal, especially its social initiatives, which he thought long overdue, such as the inclusion of labor unions in national politics, provisions for social security, and related programs to combat poverty and offer a modest but meaningful redistribution of wealth. Later, in *The Liberal Tradition,* his concern for Franklin Delano Roosevelt and the legacy of the New Deal was still evident but had to share the spotlight with Hartz's new preoccupation with the evils of McCarthyism and the question of how America would exercise the power of its newly prominent place in international politics. Hartz's world as a mature scholar was that of a New Dealer struggling to come to terms with the Cold War, both domestically and internationally.

Hartz's earliest publication, "Seth Luther: The Story of a Working-Class Rebel,"[5] saw the light of day in 1940, when, at the tender age of twenty-one, he wrote about the life and thought of an antebellum labor organizer and reformer. Fully fifteen years before the appearance of *The Liberal Tradition,* the budding scholar was already hinting at what would prove to be a lifelong commitment to the idea that America must learn to treat its working class with dignity and respect. Hartz ended his journal article on Seth Luther with a call for further studies of "the development of labor ideas from the Revolution to the Civil War, a field all too much neglected by historians today."[6] So restrained is his language that anyone unfamiliar with his subsequent thought might fail to recognize that everything Hartz said about the plight of the labor movement of 1840 was motivated by his preoccupation with the workers of 1940.

Eight years later, in 1948, Hartz published his first book, *Economic Policy and Democratic Thought: Pennsylvania, 1776–1860.* Here the New Dealer was far more outspoken about his political purpose. With painstaking labor Hartz set out to deflate "the myth of laissez-faire" in revolutionary and ante-bellum America. No doubt it is true, he conceded, that the national government intervened relatively little in economic affairs before the late nineteenth century or thereafter, but, he insisted, at the level of the states nothing was more common than governmental oversight.

Much later in his career Hartz bluntly stated, in reference to himself, "Our central preoccupation . . . is the [positive] role of the state in attaining a free society."[7] In hindsight, then, his early book on Pennsylvania was a major first step in what would prove to be a lifetime plan of arguing, as a New Dealer, for the affirmative uses of government. In 1948 he held that the states had done for governmental regulation of business in antebellum times what the national state of the New Dealers was doing in the modern age. Thus, despite the persistence of the myth of laissez-faire, the conviction of New Dealers that government should be used to foster social justice was deeply rooted in the American past.

By the time we reach the publication date of *The Liberal Tradition in America,* Louis Hartz had undergone a transformation forced upon him by the events of the 1950s. While the old focus on New Deal domestic reforms remained intact, he had found it necessary to add other topics to his agenda. One of Hartz's new preoccupations can be seen with perfect clarity in his final chapter, "America and the World." After World War I America had returned to isolationism, shrugging off its international responsibilities. During that war, moreover, the very Progressive voices with whom Hartz wanted to identify had failed miserably to understand the larger world: "Wasn't [Woodrow] Wilson smashing the Austro-Hungarian Empire into bits much as he would an American trust?"[8] he asked. The most enlightened souls in the United States had justified going to war by arguing naively and ethnocentrically that the world should be saved for democracy, American style.

Throughout their history, argued Hartz, Americans had indulged themselves in "a curiously Hebraic kind of separatism,"[9] occasionally supplanted by a brief, inevitably futile effort to remake the world in their own image. Completing the vicious circle, a disillusioned America, its dreams repudiated on the international stage, soon resumed with enhanced obstinacy its customary delusional withdrawal from the rest of the world.

To Hartz it was obvious that post–World War II America held great power. Whether that power would be wielded wisely or unwisely was the only question. Rather than withdraw from or impose itself upon the world, Hartz would apparently have the United States practice balance-of-power politics and "containment" in the manner of George Kennan. Rather than judge the emerging countries of the Third World according to our standards, Hartz longed for the United States to sanction "the principle of [cultural and ideological] diversity"[10] abroad that it unfortunately lacked at home. At the end of his book Hartz was raising the question of whether his findings gave him any reason to hope that the Americans of the 1950s, in their relationships with the rest of the world, could transcend their past. Could they finally and belatedly learn to understand other peoples, other cultures? Could they open their minds to new experiences and accept the new challenges posed by the turbulent and complicated relations between nations in the postwar era?

If America's situation in the world was one of Hartz's two new concerns in the *Liberal Tradition,* the other was McCarthyism at home. Abroad, Americans were locked in a struggle with real Communists; at home, McCarthy initiated a purge of unreal Communists and in the course of doing so rode roughshod over civil liberties and human decency. Again and again in his book, Hartz returned to the phenomenon of McCarthyism, and each time he took up the topic, he portrayed it as a recurring rather than a unique phenomenon. Repeatedly Hartz reminded his readers of the Red Scare, the Palmer Raids, and similar incidents that had taken place in the wake of World War I and on earlier occasions when external events shocked Americans.

Exploiting the advantages of hindsight, one might say that Hartz, a devoted liberal, was struggling to face up to the problem of McCarthyism without adding his name to the growing list of Cold War liberals who were ready to transfigure "the people" of democratic legend into "the masses." *The Liberal Tradition in America* was published at the very moment when the concept of "totalitarianism" was becoming a major preoccupation of the liberals inhabiting the academy. At almost the same time that Hartz published his book, Carl J. Friedrich and Zbigniew K. Brzezinski published *Totalitarian Dictatorship and Autocracy.* One of their primary findings was that "totalitarian dictatorship is historically unique and *sui generis,*" different from all previous dictatorships and autocracies in that it is "a logical extension of certain traits of our modern industrial society."[11] Hannah Arendt had led the way in 1951, whether for better or for worse, with her *The Origins of Totalitarianism.* In her view totalitarianism was effect; "mass society" was cause—and by "mass society" she meant the decline of the old social classes and the rise of the bourgeoisie she hated, whose philosopher, she would have us believe, was Thomas Hobbes because he "gives an almost complete picture, not of man but of bourgeois man." The democratization of the modern world was for Arendt, as for her teacher Martin Heidegger, the road to nihilism.[12]

During the terrible years of the early 1950s when Senator Joseph McCarthy played the role of arch-demagogue, the onlookers in the academy were sorely tempted to view him through the lenses provided by the literature on totalitarianism. Even those among the Cold War liberals who had flirted as adolescents with Marxism took to writing in the 1950s about "working-class authoritarianism."[13] J. L. Talmon's *The Rise of Totalitarian Democracy* (1952) was emblematic of the age. And although Heidegger and the European Right were beyond the pale, the same argument, that the advance of democracy in modern society was the source of a new despotism, can be found in the works of many nineteenth-century European liberals whose writings in English translation were avidly devoured by mid-twentieth-century American liberal intellectuals disturbed by McCarthyism.

One example of a nineteenth-century European liberal whose disgust with America did not prevent Cold War liberals from flocking to his banner was Jacob Burckhardt. Noted Swiss historian, erstwhile confidant of Friedrich Nietzsche, Burckhardt was both an ardent liberal and an archenemy of democracy, which he held responsible for all the ills of the modern world. In the 1950s his lectures were commonly quoted in America, not only his attacks upon Hegel's power state but more frequently his warnings that the democratization of modern society was responsible for the excesses of the French Revolution, the advent of the masses, hyperideological politics, excessive political centralization, militarism, and unprecedented despotism.

Even without another Napoleon the situation was hopeless, Burckhardt contended. For him the ultimate test of a society was its willingness to recognize beauty, which led him to despair of his century, in which "skilled and famous artists descend to illustrating the reading-matter of Philistia."[14] Nothing, he thought, could be worse than "the present-day devastation of the mind by newspapers and novels."[15] Burckhardt's fear was that in Europe "everything [might] turn into big business, as in America."[16] His liberalism was aristocratic through and through, but that did not prevent his writings from being frequently cited favorably by American Cold War intellectuals, who were fearful that mass society in the United States made their country a prime candidate for degeneration into totalitarianism via McCarthyism.

The same might be said of Ortega y Gasset's *The Revolt of the Masses* (1930). Again there is the embrace of the word "liberal" in "liberal democracy"; again the denunciation of democracy on the grounds that it fosters illiberalism. Ortega blamed mass society for the triumph of Mussolini,[17] and he spoke with disdain of America: "It is not altogether by chance that lynch law comes from America, for America is, in a fashion, the paradise of the masses."[18] Yet Cold War liberals in America heartily approved of his reissued work and gave it a place of honor on their reading lists.

Even Tocqueville sometimes was transformed into a Cold War liberal. His worries about "the tyranny of the majority," his strongly stated belief that democratic society could easily generate a novel form of despotism, his bleak closing chapters in volume 2 of *Democracy in America*, were more than enough to convince some Cold Warriors that his position was no different from Burckhardt's or Ortega's. Tocqueville, too, could be understood as a theorist of mass society and totalitarianism.[19]

Louis Hartz was one liberal of the 1950s who refused to join the ranks of the Cold Warriors. Notions of mass society do not figure in *The Liberal Tradition in America*; Burckhardt and Ortega are not his heroes; his Tocqueville is not an antidemocrat; nowhere does he suggest that liberalism must be saved from democracy. Louis Hartz sought a way to transcend the limitations of his day and found it, as we shall eventually see, in the comparative method.

MYOPIA OF THE POLITICAL THEORISTS AND HISTORIANS

To see beyond one's age is always extremely difficult and was especially so for the intellectuals whose unfortunate fate it was to write while suffering from the profoundly stultifying effects of the Cold War on American cultural and intellectual life.[20] Louis Hartz did his best to distance himself, quietly but effectively, from the new brand of liberalism served up by his colleagues in the 1950s—antidemocratic, frightened, defensive, narrow, emaciated.

Hartz knew a thing or two about the history of French liberalism and had some idea of how much harm François Guizot had done to the liberal cause by insisting upon the most narrowly conceived definition of the suffrage.[21] Unlike the Cold War liberals, Hartz was the critic rather than the admirer of the conservative and antidemocratic liberals of nineteenth-century Europe, Guizot, Pierre Royer-Collard, Thomas Babington Macaulay, and the like. Anyone who thinks otherwise should consult the lecture notes for his course on nineteenth-century European political thought, *The Necessity of Choice*, collected and edited by his student, Paul Roazen. If the liberal Louis Hartz went to Europe, it was not to bring European liberalism to America.

The two intellectual disciplines to which Hartz turned in his quest for an escape clause from the limitations of his day were political theory and history. Neither, however, offered an immediate solution; far from it: both disciplines often seemed more the aggravation of the problematic Cold War mentality than its solution.

To begin with the political theorists of Hartz's day, often they seemed more intent on driving the Cold War frenzy to fever pitch than on seeking a cure. Book after book, from the 1950s through the early 1960s, sought to uncover the seeds of Adolf Hitler or Joseph Stalin in a classic text written ages before "totalitarianism" became a reality. Philosopher Karl Popper most famously and notoriously published *The Open Society and Its Enemies.* Volume 1 he subtitled *The Spell of Plato,* and dedicated it to sustaining the thesis that Plato's program could, he thought, "be fairly described as totalitarian." Soon thereafter a lesser-known political theorist came out with a book under the title *Plato: Totalitarian or Democrat?* no matter that liberal democracy hailed from the nineteenth century, totalitarianism from the twentieth. Arendt, Brzezinski, and Friedrich had insisted that totalitarianism was a novel, unprecedented evil, but that did not stop the political theorists from discovering it in the minds of the greatest thinkers 2,300 years ago.[22]

To his credit, Hartz never paid the slightest attention to the efforts of political theorists to walk up and down the centuries, on the lookout for the first totalitarian. Nor did he join the ranks of those political theorists who wanted to answer the challenges of the Cold War by reaffirming the natural law philosophies of classical and medieval times. The same year Hartz published his book, the renowned journalist Walter Lippmann launched a campaign in *Essays in the Public Philosophy* to resist "the doctrine of popular sovereignty" and offset the influence of "the recently enfranchised voters," all for the sake of evading the menace of populist McCarthyism. Lippmann's ploy was to marshal a mountain of quotations culled from the classics that supposedly advocated a natural law philosophy and taught the evils of impassioned radical democracy. Students in the universities, the future leaders of America, were to be exposed to these great texts and their conservative messages of self-restraint. No more than anyone else, however, did Lippmann succeed in proving that his time-honored truths were absolute or universal, and at the close of his book, he revealingly admitted that "what is necessary . . . is that [these notions] shall be *believed* to be right," not that they were right, all of which smacked of the Pragmatism of his youth.[23]

As far back as 1918 Oliver Wendell Holmes Jr. had commented that those "who believe in natural law seem to me to be in that naïve state of mind that accepts what has been familiar and accepted by them and their neighbors as something that must be accepted by all men everywhere."[24] Undeterred, in 1952 philosopher Mortimer J. Adler published the series Great Books of the Western World and thus began a crusade to place the classics at the forefront of the curriculum, so that students could imbibe the "perennial wisdom" contained in the most famous texts, namely, the message that the natural moral law had been professed by one and all of the great thinkers throughout the ages. Anyone who pointed to the ethnocentrism of the ensuing wisdom[25] or the emptiness of the generalizations or the pluralism of Western traditions was accused of the sin of "relativism" and scolded for upholding a form of nihilism that would inevitably lead to totalitarianism.[26]

Only in the cramped and nervous atmosphere of the 1950s could anyone take seriously this plea for absolutes that made its case by an argument about consequences rather than truth. And only in the 1950s could anyone embrace an argument suggesting that the outcome of a contest between constitutional and totalitarian forms of government in the larger world hinged on whether academic intellectuals believed in natural law. As was his wont, Louis Hartz wisely sidestepped this foolish debate about "perennial wisdom."

Whenever the political philosophers of the 1950s were not dogmatists, they were logical positivists, whose skeptical outlook led Peter Laslett to announce that "for the moment, anyway, political philosophy is dead."[27] Analytical philosopher T. D. Weldon's *The Vocabulary of Politics* (1953) amounted to a wake for political theory. Insofar as Plato and the other great thinkers had attempted to settle matters such as "What is justice?" their texts were a waste of time, Weldon argued, because truth pertains strictly to matters of fact or questions of logic. Possibly Plato's *Laws* merits serious study, for that work might contain some empirical truths, but as for the highfalutin *Republic*, it is quite worthless.[28]

In the background of Weldon's book there lurked, once again, the Cold War. No message was more prominent in *The Vocabulary of Politics* than Weldon's insistence that there is no rational basis for deciding that one regime is better than another—democracy better than totalitarianism, for instance. Hence we should abjure the dangerous ideological struggles of the day, devoting ourselves, instead, to piecemeal, modest, and safe political measures.[29] "Ideological wars have no tendency whatever to prove that one answer is right and another wrong."[30]

The political theory of his day offered Hartz nothing attractive. Hence he donned his other hat, that of historian, but not without encountering a new set of difficulties. Louis Hartz was a man on a mission, intent on asking and answering big questions. Alas, the historians of his day were of little use to him in his ongoing quest, for their work was usually period-specific whereas he wished to move across the entire landscape of American history. And then there was the predilection of historians for burrowing one or another tunnel into the past, whether it be in economic history, political history, or intellectual history, while ignoring the larger picture.[31] Finally, although his heart was solidly on the side of the Progressives, Louis Hartz knew there was something fundamentally wrong with the Progressive histories of Charles Beard, Vernon Parrington, J. Allen Smith, and Frederick Jackson Turner—to which list we perhaps should add the later name of Progressive Arthur M. Schlesinger Jr.[32]

In the end Louis Hartz opted for investigating the possibilities offered by comparative history. Transcendence, he knew, could not come in the form of knowledge of the law of nature or any other scheme based on the pretense that the investigators could elevate themselves above history and then pontificate *sub specie aeternitatis*. Nevertheless, it might be possible for us to cast off the blinders of nationalist prejudices—Hartz believed—if we learn how to approach America from the outside, especially from Europe. Perfect "objectivity" might be an illusion, but by broadening our perspective we can hope for a less subjective understanding of our own culture. Despite the many intellectual failures of the 1950s, in spite of all the obstacles, to be of one's day but not trapped by it might yet prove possible.

LOUIS HARTZ AND THE COMPARATIVE METHOD

As he embarked on his ambitious effort to understand America by way of comparing it with Europe, Hartz was cheered by the thought that his undertaking was not unprecedented. Arguably the single most famous book ever written on America was a sweeping comparative study, Alexis de Tocqueville's *De la démocratie en Amérique.* Just as Tocqueville had gained insight into France by studying it alongside America, Hartz sought to deepen his understanding of America by comparing it with England and France. Faced with the problem of finding a strategy for rising above the limitations of the Cold War mentality that afflicted his peers, Louis Hartz decided to enroll in the school of Tocqueville.

From our perspective today we can look back on Hartz and note the affinities of his comparative analysis not only with Tocqueville's in the nineteenth century but with Montesquieu's in the eighteenth, and in Hartz's own day with Raymond Aron's in France and Stanley Hoffmann's in America.[33] Hartz obviously was not without distinguished forerunners and contemporaries.

Admittedly the line of continuity from Montesquieu to Tocqueville to Hartz may be clearer in retrospect than it was to the actors themselves. Neither the author of *Democracy in America* nor the author of *The Liberal Tradition in America* displayed a thorough understanding of *The Spirit of the Laws*. Tocqueville, for instance, gets Montesquieu wrong, exactly wrong, when he writes, "Montesquieu, in attributing a peculiar force to despotism, did it an honor which, I think, it did not deserve. Despotism by itself can maintain nothing durable."[34] In fact, from *The Persian Letters* in 1721 through *The Spirit of the Laws* in 1748, Montesquieu's constant message was that despotism is self-destructive, its omnipotence in theory belied by its impotence in practice.[35] Tocqueville "corrected" Montesquieu by unknowingly duplicating Montesquieu's position.

Yet despite such occasional misunderstandings, Tocqueville accurately drew upon Montesquieu when the topic was how, under the Old Regime, the powers of monarchs claiming to rule by divine right were offset by the "intermediary bodies," that is, the privileged orders. Again, by way of a second influence of Montesquieu on Tocqueville, it may not be an accident that Tocqueville's depiction of America bears a family resemblance to Montesquieu's portrait of England as a commercial, free, and fluid society, no longer under the sway of a feudal nobility: some of what Tocqueville accomplished by comparing America with France was foreshadowed fully a century in advance by Montesquieu's comparison of post-feudal England with the Old Regime of continental Europe.[36] What is certain is that every now and again Tocqueville stopped to acknowledge, however briefly, his debt to Montesquieu's pioneering investigations.

Louis Hartz was pleased to acknowledge the inspiration he derived from *Democracy in America.* For the epigraph of *The Liberal Tradition in America* Hartz quoted Tocqueville's saying that the Americans were born equal rather than having to endure the turmoil of a democratic revolution to become so.[37] As for Montesquieu, his name rarely appears in the writings of Louis Hartz,[38] and even on those rare occasions when we come across a reference to *The Spirit of the Laws,* there is no awareness that the style of comparative analysis employed in *The Liberal Tradition* runs exactly parallel to that developed by Montesquieu two centuries earlier. When Hartz wrote that "the feudal factor is the mother factor of modern life,"[39] he apparently did not realize he might as well have been quoting from *The Spirit of the Laws.*

There is no point in claiming that the line of descent from Montesquieu to Tocqueville to Hartz runs clean and smooth. In the cases of both Tocqueville and Hartz, Montesquieu does not always get his due, Hartz being especially deficient in this regard. We cannot comment on a Montesquieu/Tocqueville/Hartz "school of thought," if by that term one means a perfectly self-conscious intellectual tradition refurbished time and again across the centuries, so as to answer problems newly arisen. On our own initiative, however, we can fill in the missing spaces between Montesquieu and Hartz, and there is good reason to do so. The kind of comparative thinking in which Hartz was engaged can be better appreciated, its strengths and weaknesses made to stand out in sharper relief, by taking a brief look at the pathbreaking work of Montesquieu.

In *The Spirit of the Laws* Montesquieu presented his rationale for viewing the concept of feudalism as the key to unlocking the secrets of past and present. It was feudalism, he believed, that distinguished royal absolutism in the West from its Oriental counterpart, and it was feudalism, again, that tied the various Western nations to one another and rendered them amenable to comparative analysis. Aristotle's *per genus et differentiam* was the implicit logic of Montesquieu's comparisons, with feudalism figuring as the differentiating factor when he discussed West versus East and as the generic factor when he compared one Western nation to another.

"Oriental despotism" was royal absolutism minus feudalism, which is to say, minus the "intermediary bodies," the clergy and nobility, the first and second estates of France or Spain. Absolutism, then, was the generic form and feudalism the differential separating out the Western variety of absolutism and accentuating its distinctiveness. Within the West, a feudal backdrop was what the nations of Europe shared; it was the generic factor assuring the comparability of the units. Occidental countries had feudalism as their starting point, and not even the long passage of time from feudal childhood to the contrasting Old Regimes of Montesquieu's time could hide the underlying feudal commonality of European nations.

The countries of Europe, in Montesquieu's conception, had evolved in different directions from their similar feudal commencement. Hungary and Poland, with their weak kings, enormous peasantries, and unruly nobles acting as local tyrants, were reminders of what France had been like in the Middle Ages. Spain, by contrast, had over the centuries developed a centralized government under an absolutist monarchy, but because its nobles and clergy remained powerful, it was an economically backward country and a center of religious inquisition. England, unlike Spain, was an economically progressive and politically free country, the first postfeudal nation, no longer burdened by either of the two regressive "intermediary bodies," the feudal nobility and the Catholic Church. The English, wrote Montesquieu, "are the people who have best availed themselves at the same time of these three great things: [Protestant] religion, commerce and liberty."[40] Montesquieu's hope was that France might become more like England; his fear was that it might move in the direction of Spain.[41]

Louis Hartz's account of his comparative method reads as if it were an updated version of Montesquieu. His analysis, he wrote, "at the same moment [that] it stresses the absence of the feudal factor in America, stresses its presence abroad."[42] When comparing America with Europe, feudalism is the differentiating factor; when comparing the nations of Europe with one another, it is the generic factor.

Although Hartz himself did not write a comparative history of Europe, he did remark on how unfortunate it was that "with the crystallization of national states, the European nations have been studied almost as independently as America." Because of nationalist passions, the underlying European cultural unity provided by feudalism has been forgotten. "The result is that many of the most primitive correlations among the European countries have not been made. But if the 'medieval unity' is found actually to be a decisive factor in the epoch that followed it, the basis for these correlations automatically appears."[43] Whereas Montesquieu's grand tour from western to eastern Europe was a voyage from the new regime of England or the old regime of France back along a path to an earlier feudal disunity in eastern Europe, a follower of Hartz might envision the same itinerary, in a later age, as one from more liberal Western regimes to more authoritarian eastern European ones.

We shall never know for certain, of course, what Hartz might have argued had he written a comparative history of Europe. All his emphasis as a comparativist was on coming to terms with America, a nation different from Europe, as he never tired of saying, precisely in that its inhabitants had left the feudal heritage behind them when they embarked on their ships to cross the Atlantic. Europe, with its feudal past, was the land of disruptive transitions from Old Regime to revolution to liberal constitutional regimes; not so America, where "we are confronted by a kind of inverted Trotskyite law of combined development, America skipping the feudal stage of history as Russia presumably skipped the liberal stage."[44] When C. Vann Woodward in 1968 invited a group of leading scholars to write about *The Comparative Approach to American History*, R. R. Palmer, Ray Allen Billington, George W. Pierson, and David A. Shannon were numbered among the scholars who underscored the importance of the missing feudal tradition in America.[45]

Defining America or any country by pointing to what is *absent* is not sufficient to attain a fully realized historical understanding and can even lead to major misunderstandings if unaccompanied by an inquiry into what is *present*. Montesquieu surely failed to do justice to Turkey and China when, after stressing that feudalism was not part of their experience, he filled the void in his knowledge of the non-Western world with imaginative improvisations on what Plato and Aristotle had written about ancient tyranny. To his credit Louis Hartz did not repeat Montesquieu's mistake in his treatment of

America. Near the beginning of his book Hartz made clear his deliberate intent to reach beyond the language of "minus," "absent," and "missing": "We are actually dealing with two factors," he explained, "the absence of feudalism and the presence of the liberal idea."[46]

Hartz's insistence on pinning the label of "liberalism" on what is present in American political culture was probably the most momentous decision he made in writing his book. Although he certainly was interested in democracy in America, it was not Tocqueville's preemption of the title *Democracy in America* that accounted for Hartz's choice of the title *The Liberal Tradition in America*. Everything was at stake when Hartz chose the title of his book, everything, that is, relating to his efforts to counteract the scholarship of the Cold War liberals.

If Hartz could make the "liberal" label stick, he would have pulled off a major intellectual coup or what might be called a great reversal. As opposed to the Cold War liberals and their nineteenth-century liberal predecessors, Hartz portrayed not a world in which democracy ("mass society") threatened to undermine liberalism but, rather, a history of America wherein liberalism oversaw the growth of democracy and was itself democratic. Liberalism, he argued, was the American democratic faith, the American creed, the American way of life, a set of cultural convictions so compulsive that although John Locke, the godfather of liberalism, had taught the virtues of rationalism, his American children were "irrational Lockians."[47]

It was incumbent on Hartz to cite evidence of American addiction to liberalism, and he did his best to meet the challenge. Good liberals, he knew, believed that power corrupts and absolute power corrupts absolutely. Were not Americans, then, the purest of liberals? For, historically, they had not trusted their elected rulers, nor did they always trust themselves. Montesquieu's checks and balances were to be found not in England, with its parliamentary government, but in America, where the capacity of one governmental body to frustrate another was so marked that, as Progressives had complained, government could not always govern. Afraid of themselves and their own propensity to abuse power, the supposedly "sovereign people" permitted the practice of judicial review that the less democratic regimes of England and the Continent rejected. In America alone were liberal formulas treated with unquestioning reverence.[48]

McCarthyism was, so to speak, the test case for Hartz's scheme of interpretation. He had to explain the McCarthy era and similar earlier experiences without abandoning his hypothesis of a liberal American political community. "When a liberal community faces militant and ideological pressure from without it transforms eccentricity into sin," he explained. While this may at first glance sound like Tocqueville's "tyranny of the majority," Hartz saw things otherwise. The basic ethical problem of a liberal society, he postulated, is "not the danger of the majority which has been its conscious fear, but the danger of unanimity, which has slumbered unconsciously." A society in which everyone is a liberal or a liberal manqué is vulnerable to "violent moods of . . . mass Lockianism." There is, however, no reason to despair, no reason to join with the Cold War liberals in their search for devices to make liberal democracy less democratic. A liberal society can be saved from its worst excesses by its own self-corrective mechanisms: "Given the individualist nature of the Lockian doctrine, there is always a logical impulse within it to transcend the very conformitarian spirit it breeds."[49]

Hartz, as we have seen, cited as much evidence as he could garner to build the strongest possible empirical case for the proposition that liberalism in America was not one ideology among several but, rather, a national liberalism. Still not satisfied, he set forth a version of comparative analysis allowing him to argue that no other outcome was possible in America than the domination of liberalism. It was the sociology of knowledge he called upon to set forth this bold theoretical argument, particularly the version articulated in Karl Mannheim's *Ideology and Utopia,* published in German in 1929, translated into English in 1936, and widely read in the intellectual circles of the 1950s. When Hartz said that feudalism was the mother factor of modern life, he may have begun in an intellectual world inhabited by Montesquieu and Tocqueville, but for better or worse Mannheim quickly moved to the forefront of his influences whenever Hartz discussed ideology, and it was under Mannheim's direction that Hartz spelled out the consequences of feudalism for the modern world.[50]

Mannheim, a student of European politics, believed ideologies were inseparable from the social classes whose interests they championed, conservatism being the ideology of the aristocracy, liberalism the ideology of the middle class, and socialism that of the proletariat. Hartz embraced Mannheim's scheme but not without criticizing Marx, lest the stress on social class in *The Liberal Tradition* be confused with Marxism. "One of the places where Marx went wrong in his historical analysis," wrote Hartz, lay in his "attributing as he did the emergence of socialist ideology to the objective movement of social forces. . . . It is not accidental that America which has uniquely lacked a feudal tradition has uniquely lacked a socialist tradition. The hidden origin of socialist thought everywhere in the West is to be found in the feudal ethos."[51]

As Hartz read history, the old class structure of the ancien régime lived on in modern Europe. The aristocracy did not exit after the French Revolution; hence the prominence of conservative ideology in England and France; hence also the need of the middle class to expound a liberal ideology attacking the parasitism of the privileged class while simultaneously fending off the upward thrusts of the dregs of society; hence, finally, the anarchist and socialist ideologies professed by lower classes composed more of old-fashioned peasants and artisans than of modern proletarians in France. Such, with the help of Mannheim, was Hartz's understanding of the class and ideological makeup of western Europe.

While Mannheim's focus was strictly on Europe, Hartz directed his inquiry to the implications of *Ideology and Utopia* for America. If the peasant of Europe was the independent farmer of America; if the aristocrat was nonexistent on American soil; if, as Tocqueville said, Americans had originally hailed from the middle class of England;[52] and if, as Hartz added, all Americans throughout the history of their country identified themselves as middle-class, then the consequence was clear. Liberalism, the ideology of the middle class, was the one and only ideology of America.

In Hartz's own day the Democratic Party represented the outlook of New Deal liberalism; the Republican Party hankered for the old liberalism of Herbert Hoover but followed Dwight Eisenhower in reluctantly accepting the legislation passed under FDR and Harry S. Truman. This situation of the 1950s, one of Tweedledum-and-Tweedledee liberalism, Hartz read back across the entire American past: all ideological battles in America, he contended, had always been between different variations on a single liberal theme, never between liberalism and another ideology. When the dust stirred up in the course of the various American historical conflicts dissipated, liberalism was always left standing because it was the only contender. Ironically, because liberalism is omnipresent and unchallenged on this side of the Atlantic, Americans have been slow to recognize their liberalism. "There has never been a 'liberal movement' or a real 'liberal party' in America: we have only had the American way of life, a nationalist articulation of Locke."[53]

Or so Hartz would have us believe. Eventually we may wish to quibble or perhaps quarrel outright with his position. For now, however, it suffices to observe that he was remarkably successful at turning the tables on the Cold War liberals. They had contended that the problem was one of too little liberalism in the 1950s; he answered, in effect, that there was too much liberalism. The American problem sprang from its liberalism rather than its democracy. Where liberalism is embedded monolithically in the political culture, the liberal commitment to the principle of diversity is endangered. Liberalism, so to speak, was both its own best friend and its own worst enemy in America.

STRENGTHS AND WEAKNESSES
OF HARTZ'S COMPARATIVE ANALYSIS

In 1968 C. Vann Woodward lamented that "the recent vogue of [departments of] American studies, encouraging national boundaries to the study of culture, has probably had the effect of enhancing the subjective and inward tendency [of historical studies]."[54] The reason Professor Woodward in 1997 reissued his edited 1968 volume *The Comparative Approach to American History* was not because the original book was so successful but precisely because it was not. Provisionally suppressing his doubts, he voiced his cautious hope that, on the eve of the millennium, the scholarly community might finally be ready to look beyond American borders when studying the United States.

C. Vann Woodward's comments give us reason to be amazed that Louis Hartz as early as 1955 had insisted that America could only be understood if studied in comparative historical perspective. The method of comparison was the central feature of Hartz's thought, and it was what made his contribution distinctive and innovative. To what extent did his daring and pioneering comparative approach bear fruit? Where did he fall short?

On the old question of American "exceptionalism," Hartz the comparativist could justly claim superiority over his predecessors. To Marxists, America was distressingly exceptional in that, although it was the most advanced capitalist country, it had little to show in the way of a socialist ideology. Hartz readily countered the Marxists with his argument that nineteenth-century ideologies were the product of the retention of the old feudal class structure rather than the expression of new economic forces. Nonfeudal America, for all its capitalism, lacked a working class that identified itself as a proletariat. Hence there was no equivalent in America of the German Social Democratic Party or even of the British Labour Party. The United States was different because the class consciousness of Americans was virtually nonexistent. Either Americans, despite extreme differentials of wealth, obstinately refused to think about their country in terms of class, or they all proclaimed themselves middle-class.

The Progressives were as mistaken as the Marxists. If Hartz effectively criticized the Marxists for failing to understand the nature of American exceptionalism, he was equally insistent that his comparative analysis forced the conclusion that the Progressive historians were wrongheaded in their denial that American experience was exceptional. Progressives such as Charles Beard had invoked an industrialization thesis to argue that America was no different from Europe. Another way they had likened America to Europe, Hartz observed, was by going "back to the origins of American history, splitting it up into two warring camps, discovering a 'social revolution' in the eighteenth century."[55] Everywhere they looked in the American past the Progressives had unearthed mighty struggles between conservative villains and radical heroes that reminded one of European ideological struggles.

"Here there is an interesting paradox," Hartz noted, "for one of the advances that the Progressives thought they were making lay in the explosion of the old nationalist history." Yet, with the advantage of comparative insight, it is evident that the Progressives were not exempt from the rule that "the American historian at practically every stage has functioned quite inside the nation." Although the Progressives saw themselves as iconoclasts breaking away from the old self-congratulatory histories of the likes of George Bancroft, they shared more than they knew with previous American historians. About European history they knew little or nothing, and in the end they repeated the hackneyed self-congratulatory pieties of their predecessors. "Actually there was amid all the smoke and flame of Progressive historical scholarship a continuous and almost complacent note of reassurance. A new Jefferson would arise as he had always arisen before. The 'reactionaries' would be laid low again."[56]

"Our progressive historians, one is tempted to say, have not produced a study of American political thought: they have produced a replica of it,"[57] Hartz complained. "What is really wrong with the Progressive analysis . . . is not that it is Progressive but that it is American."[58] None of their conservatives even vaguely resembles Edmund Burke or Joseph de Maistre; none of their radicals brings to mind Marx or Mikhail Bakunin. In a country lacking a feudal tradition both the right wing and the left speak in tones that Europeans would recognize as different dialects of the same language of liberalism. During the late nineteenth century, when the Progressive movement took root, the "radicals" of the day were in reality liberal reformers, while the so-called conservatives were champions of liberal laissez-faire in all matters political and economic, save the tariff. Throughout all of American history, Hartz generalized, the outstanding battles had been between different kinds of liberals, who, in the absence of an aristocracy or a proletariat and because of the consequent default of genuine conservatism and radicalism, were not compelled to recognize their own credentials as liberals.[59]

A prime example of Hartz's use of the comparative method may be seen in his treatment of the coming of universal suffrage for white males in the age of Jackson. Tocqueville had handled this matter rather peremptorily; he simply remarked on the "irresistible lowering of voting qualifications"[60] in a "democratic society" and was done with the matter. Hartz's far richer explanation was grounded in the class and ideological framework he adapted from Mannheim.

In Europe, where manhood suffrage came late, it was the liberals, Hartz observed, who led the opposition. Hemmed in by aristocrats on one side and peasants or proletarians on the other, the liberals were intensely class conscious. James Mill in England wrote that "there can be no doubt that the middle rank . . . gives to science, to art, and to legislation itself their most distinguished ornaments, and is the chief source of all that has exalted and refined human nature."[61] Votes for the upper middle class were therefore mandatory, just as it was essential that the unwashed many be denied the suffrage. Much the same sentiments may be found in the ranks of the French liberals, also of the upper middle class, and convinced that the progressive path of history was a record of the rise of the Third Estate from the Middle Ages to modern times.[62] English liberals wished to go no further than the extremely limited suffrage reform of 1832; French liberals in 1830 were certain that civilization would break into bits if the lower classes were granted the vote.

For a long time the liberals had their way, because the class divisions of Europe allowed them to play a game of what Hartz accurately called "*divide et impera*"—divide and rule. "When the English Whigs and the French Liberals fought the aristocratic order of Europe, they became liberal heroes, rallying behind them the workers and small property owners both of England and France. When, on the other hand, they insisted on excluding their supporters from the suffrage—the workers from the Reform Act and both the workers and the petit-bourgeois from the July Charter—they became conservative heroes."[63]

America, of course, had its own upper middle class, which nursed fears of democracy during the first and second party systems. But in a country lacking the class structure bequeathed by feudalism, these American counterparts of European liberals quickly capitulated to the pressure for extending the vote to all white males. "Here there are no aristocracies to fight, and the Federalists and Whigs are denied the chance of dominating the people in a campaign against [the upper class]. Here there are no aristocracies to ally with, and they cannot use their help to exclude the people from political power. Here there are no genuine proletarian outbursts to meet, and they cannot frighten [anyone] into fleeing from [the lower classes]."[64]

Hartz might have halted at this point. He might have been satisfied with his case for having discovered *a cause* of the exceptionally early march to universal suffrage for white males in America. Instead, he pushed forward. Rightly or wrongly, he tried to advance his argument to the point where, using something akin to John Stuart Mill's "method of difference,"[65] he could claim that the explanation he had offered designated not *a cause* but *the decisive cause.* All other explanations, he contended, fell short when subjected to the test of comparative analysis. "Turner's frontier thesis breaks down because frontiers are to be found in other lands. An emphasis on urban industrialism . . . breaks down even more, since industrialism was farther advanced in England. . . . But if we assert that the quick emergence of democracy was inherent in the American liberal community, we advance a proposition that comparative analysis cannot destroy."[66]

Hartz's argument is illuminating, but the insistence upon conferring a privileged status upon his "liberal society" explanation is dogmatic. To see how far his causal language overshoots the mark, it suffices to take a closer look at his comments about the frontier. True enough, a number of other societies with frontier experiences did not extend the vote as rapidly as the Americans; but he failed to notice how different the frontiers of other lands were from their American counterpart. Where there are so many differences, the method of difference cannot be decisively applied.

In Australia, for instance, the physical climate was inhospitable to American-style family farming but highly compatible with large-scale cattle farming and sheep grazing, which required the investment of considerable capital. In consequence the typical Australian frontiersman was a wageworker, not an independent farmer. Physically, socially, culturally, and politically, the Australian frontier had little in common with the American, despite the missing feudal factor in both countries. After studying the frontiers of several countries, historian Ray Allen Billington concluded that "the uniqueness of the American experience is emphasized in the studies of comparative frontiers."[67]

Whence it follows that while Hartz may have succeeded in disproving Frederick Jackson Turner's claims that the frontier in American history was everything, he did not prove that his "liberal factor" had reduced the frontier thesis to relative insignificance. His causal argument was much too strong; it is not obvious that we must choose between Turner and Hartz or rate one superior to the other.

Why Hartz overshot the mark is an intriguing question. Neither Montesquieu nor Tocqueville attempted to press his comparative findings beyond reasonable limits. Hartz did go too far, which is perhaps less surprising if we once again think of him in terms of his day. By way of departmental affiliation he was housed with the political scientists, far away from the pesky, generalization-killing historians. One of the characteristics of the political scientists of the 1950s was their addiction to a positivist mind-set: if political science could not be behaviorist, it would at least be behavioralist, the extra syllable saving the day for social scientists envious of the elevated status of the natural scientists. Quantification was highly prized in the atmosphere of the 1950s and later; hence the proliferation of numbers-friendly voting studies. Taking note that economists boasted of econometrics, some political scientists sought respect by talking of "polimetrics."

The differences between historical periods and the cultural divides within a period that impressed historians were cast aside by the political scientists of the 1950s because such niceties stood in the way of grand generalizations. Were not Thucydides and Hans Morgenthau speaking about exactly the same thing, the balance of power? Hartz the political scientist made causal arguments that were too sweeping but quite in keeping with the company he kept. John P. Roche may have been on to something when he remarked in passing that Hartz had employed "a variety of political physics."[68]

Unfortunately, Hartz never offered his readers anything more than a few fragmentary remarks concerning his thoughts on methodology. Such scattered comments as we do find in his works are, however, not without interest since they suggest he was not consistently under the spell of positivism. In *The Necessity of Choice* he sometimes sounds more like, say, Wilhelm Dilthey or Max Weber than Auguste Comte or Émile Durkheim. "A variety of interpretations can be right,"[69] he conceded. His purpose in these lectures was to go "through history to reconsider the preconceptions that were critical when people considered the problem of personal freedom and state control." There was, he realized, "an arbitrary element in our making central the problem of the state in promoting a free society." That, however, did not mean we must authorize "an anarchy of possible interpretations." "We are not reduced to the subjectivistic conclusion that any viewpoint is as good as any other. Interpretations are capable of checking one another, and factual data do threaten certain possible outlooks."[70]

So far as we can tell, Hartz probably did not spend a great deal of time pondering the writings of philosophers of social science.[71] If he had grappled with the methodological essays of Max Weber, translated into English in 1949,[72] he might have effected a synthesis between limited causal arguments and the interpretive understanding of German historicism. Instead, he clumsily and indecisively juxtaposed positivism and historicism in his writings. In *The Liberal Tradition in America* the positivist in him, as we have

seen, made causal arguments that went too far. It is important to add, however, that in the same text he also urged that the point of his work was to foster what the children of Hegel had always sought in their studies of the past,
not so much causal reasoning as self-knowledge.

Near the end of his famous book Hartz stated the purpose of his research: "What is at stake is nothing less than a new level of consciousness, a
transcending of irrational Lockianism, in which an understanding of self
and an understanding of others go hand in hand." His final paragraph is
equally insistent upon the crying need for Americans to achieve self-
knowledge: "Can a people 'born equal' ever understand peoples elsewhere
that have to become so? Can it ever understand itself?"[73] The ghosts of
Hegel and Dilthey hover above the page.

Hartz never moved beyond an amalgamation of positivism and historicism to a higher theoretical synthesis. In his actual scholarly practice he
nevertheless could have arrived at the same result simply by diluting his
overstated causal claims while continuing to adhere to the elements in his
thought that smacked of German historicism. This is precisely what happened eight years later, in 1963, when he published an essay entitled "The
Rise of the Democratic Idea." Here he seemingly granted far more to previous historians than he had in *The Liberal Tradition*. "The concept of a liberal
tradition," he wrote in conclusion, "if it modifies Turner and Beard, puts
them on a stronger ground. . . . Actually all the major analyses of American
democracy, from Bancroft's nationalism to Beard's proletarianism, seized
on lasting insights. I believe that the idea of a liberal society puts these insights into a meaningful relationship to one another."[74] His wording is not
entirely decisive, but interpretive charity suggests that he was moving toward a more nuanced position.

USES OF TOCQUEVILLE IN HARTZ'S DAY AND OURS

A promising strategy for discerning the significance of Hartz's thought for
both his day and ours is to contrast the portraits of Tocqueville frequently
painted in the 1950s with those drawn in ours and then to note how different from either are Hartz's graven images of the famous Frenchman. The
Tocqueville of Hartz was not the Cold War liberal of his contemporaries.
Neither, however, was his Tocqueville someone who cared whether we
"bowl alone," in Robert Putnam's image; nor in all likelihood would Hartz
have accepted the notion that the fulfillment of *Democracy in America* was in
the "faith-based initiatives" of George W. Bush.

The Cold War liberals of the 1950s invoked the Tocqueville who reminded them of themselves, a man dedicated to liberalism but frightened by democracy. Their Tocqueville—as we have previously noticed in passing—was among the first to proclaim that the age of the masses could easily lead to the advent of a new and especially deleterious form of tyranny. At the outset of his two volumes Tocqueville indicated that *Democracy in America* had been "written under the impulse of a kind of religious dread," and in the gloomy closing pages of volume 2 he struggled to avoid succumbing to despair. "Despotism is particularly to be feared in ages of democracy," he warned his contemporaries. A century before Hannah Arendt, he wrote that "the type of oppression which threatens democracies is different from anything there has ever been in the world before." "Such old words as 'despotism' and 'tyranny' do not fit. The thing is new." "The past throws no light on the future, and the spirit of man walks through the night."[75] How could the academic liberals of the 1950s fail to find themselves in the pages of Tocqueville?

In their retreat from democracy the Cold War liberals were more than happy to applaud rule by competing "elites," again claiming Tocqueville as their forerunner. Well-known political sociologist Seymour Martin Lipset approved "Tocqueville's concern for a pluralistic political system" wherein "conflict between one organization and another" prevents any one group from monopolizing state power.[76] "The American Medical Association and the unions within the AFL-CIO are dominated by self-perpetuating oligarchies, but the heads of these bodies take sharply conflicting stands." The larger picture is that the "many internally oligarchic organizations help to sustain political democracy in the larger society."[77] Lost along the way in Lipset's account was the pleasure Tocqueville took in observing that associations in America were far less oligarchic than those in Europe.[78]

Lipset chose to call his scheme "the elitist theory of democracy," but it is perfectly obvious that his point was to revisit the old European liberal idea of saving freedom by minimizing democracy. "Pluralism" to Lipset and his comrades meant checks and balances between multiple economic-interest groups, with no one such group having enough power to dominate the entire political system, and with each major group mighty on this or that issue but not on the full array of issues. Theirs was in reality an elitist theory of liberalism, not democracy.

Only coincidentally did Hartz ever say anything that could link him to the Tocqueville of the Cold War or the so-called elitist theory of democracy. He did, of course, believe in "democratic pluralism" and thought it an appropriate substitute in the modern world for what he termed "feudal pluralism" or "old corporate pluralism."[79] Nowhere, however, does he defend an elitist theory of democracy or try to present the limitations of European and American democracies as if their shortcomings were their finest features. The concern expressed in his essay "Democracy: Image and Reality," published in the early 1960s, was that the citizenry might demand more of democracy than it can deliver; might unrealistically expect the democracies to be as democratic in practice as they are in their official ideals; and they might, in consequence, become disillusioned and abandon the good fight.

In any event, the pluralism that aroused his passions was less economic than cultural. Hartz admired the cultural pluralism that was present in Europe because of its feudal past, its multiple social classes and contrasting class ideologies; he regretted that the American blessing of being spared a feudal background entailed the curse of cultural uniformity. Throughout *The Liberal Tradition* he wondered aloud whether the exposure of the Americans of his day to the larger world might at last give them the appreciation of diversity that had been denied them by their monolithic political culture.[80] The Tocqueville who may have been relevant to Hartz's diagnosis was the one who wrote, "I know no country in which, speaking generally, there is less independence of mind and true freedom than in America."[81] Both Tocqueville and Hartz feared that, for all the different social and economic groups in America, culturally there was only one all-encompassing group.

Nowadays nothing is more common than to hear someone charge Hartz with failing to understand Tocqueville, champion of associational activities, proponent of political participation—and sometimes this argument is extended to the point of suggesting that Tocqueville understood America, and Hartz did not.[82] A much fairer assessment is that Hartz's two overriding concerns when he addressed the eras of Thomas Jefferson and Andrew Jackson were largely the same as Tocqueville's, the difference being that Hartz stressed one of these, and Tocqueville the other. Hartz found "two national impulses" in antebellum America, "the impulse toward democracy and the impulse toward capitalism."[83] Tocqueville agreed, focusing most of his attention on democracy whereas Hartz was more intent on dealing with capitalism.

Hartz was by no means unaware of, nor was he hostile to, the American record of popular involvement in civic affairs. He remarked with evident approval that "the American had a genius for political participation" and tipped his hat to the "political activism of the American public." Often, admittedly, "the slogans of democratic liberalism" were crude, but who could complain, considering that these frequently crass messages "produced a type of political participation which kept the people continuously in the public arena."[84] About the last thing Hartz wanted was to join ranks with the Cold War liberals, some of whom were so eager to remove the many from politics that they praised political apathy and low voter turnout as signs of political health. One political scientist in 1954 went so far as to suggest that "many of the ideas connected with the general theme of a Duty to Vote belong properly to the totalitarian camp." As he saw matters, apathy was "a more or less effective counterforce to the fanatics who constitute the real danger to liberal democracy." As much as possible, citizens should be encouraged "to devote themselves to their gardens."[85]

Presumably Hartz might have answered the Cold Warriors by citing Tocqueville's theme that democratic "association" and political participation were the answer to the threat posed by "totalitarianism." But why should Hartz bother when he was never swayed by the argument that America was especially vulnerable to a totalitarian mass movement? Moreover, had not Hartz demonstrated in *The Liberal Tradition* the futility of "Whiggish" efforts to keep the "people" out of public life? The new academic "Whigs" of the 1950s, he knew, would have no more success than their nineteenth-century predecessors in stemming the democratic tide.

Hartz turned his attention to the passages in *Democracy in America* that he believed really mattered, namely, those in which Tocqueville had shown how a "democratic society" fostered a great outpouring of economic productivity. France's backward peasantry had no counterpart in America: "The Americans," wrote Tocqueville, "never use the word 'peasant'; the word is unused because the idea is unknown." Instead of peasants, in the United States there were commercial farmers, each caught up in the mania for getting ahead. "In democracies," Tocqueville generalized, "nothing has brighter luster than commerce; it attracts the attention of the public and fills the imagination of the crowd."[86]

Other than the absence of feudalism, the theme Hartz most of all shared with Tocqueville is that of the inevitable triumph of democratic capitalism in America. Even in the earliest days of the Republic, affirmed Hartz, when some wealthy Americans still yearned for a deferential social order, "they were forced almost everywhere, even in George Washington's Virginia, to rely for survival upon shrewd activity in the capitalist race."[87] Once again Hartz pressed an argument by utilizing his favorite conceptual tool, class analysis: "Where the aristocracies, peasantries, and proletariats of Europe are missing, . . . virtually everyone, including the nascent industrial worker, has the mentality of an independent entrepreneur."[88]

The critical moment, Hartz continued, was the presidential election of 1840, for it was then that the Whigs learned to copy Jacksonian campaigning techniques, calling on slogans ("Tippecanoe and Tyler Too!") and such homely symbols as hard cider and a faux log cabin to make their candidate William Henry Harrison look like everyman. It was then, too, that the Whigs learned to combine their capitalist dream with "the Jeffersonian concept of equal opportunity." After 1840, everyman was henceforth a capitalist, sometimes on a grand scale, other times on a small scale, and virtually no one admitted to being a worker or proletarian, certainly not on a permanent basis.[89]

Both Tocqueville and Hartz were ambivalent about the buoyant commercialism of America, but their reasons for having misgivings were not the same. For Tocqueville the way to offset the threat of despotism in democratic society was to foster the vibrant civic and associational life that he witnessed in America. In earlier societies—Tyre, Florence, England—commerce had proven highly compatible with freedom.[90] The United States was different, however, because in America commerce dictated all tastes, interests, and culture, giving him reason to worry that perpetually busy Americans would eventually decide that political democracy takes too many evenings. "In times of democracy private life is so active and agitated, so full of desires and labor, that each individual has scarcely any leisure left for political life."[91] Commerce in modern times begins by fostering freedom but may end by destroying it, Tocqueville feared.

The difference between Hartz's and Tocqueville's responses to democratic capitalism was the difference between a New Deal centralizing liberal and a French decentralizing liberal. Tocqueville's nightmare was that the coming of democratic society in France—the breakup of the old corporate order—would isolate individuals and enable an overbearing state to impose its will from above on an impotent populace. In America's case, he realized that the federal government, indeed the Union itself, was not yet secure and might in fact be growing weaker.[92] But the state governments were quite another matter: "In America the legislature of each state is faced with no power capable of resisting it. Nothing can check its progress, neither privileges, nor local immunities."[93] Hence his praise of local participation in public affairs.

For Hartz and for all New Deal liberals, in direct contrast, the time had finally come to call upon the resources of the federal government to advance the cause of social justice. In Hartz's words, "The ideal would be an active state, intensely flexible within, operating inside a plural society."[94] Securing the economic well-being of the working classes and all Americans through the positive use of government was the issue weighing on Hartz's mind in

1955,[95] when he dwelled on the problem of social justice. Very soon New Deal liberals would also be thinking about racial injustice, and the more they paid attention to the horrors of racism in America, the more they again were forced to turn to the federal government—for deliverance of blacks from the tender mercies of their neighbors. Localism and New Deal liberalism have not been natural allies.

Hartz would no doubt have been perplexed had he lived long enough to see scholars demoting him in the name of Tocqueville. The civic theme of *Democracy in America* has been placed in the spotlight in recent times; the theme of democratic capitalism in Tocqueville's work has been forgotten. Political scientist Robert Putnam has called himself a thinker of "neo-Tocquevillian bent" in the course of bemoaning the breakdown of "the networks of civic engagement."[96] Putnam does not mention the extent to which his work is an updating of the New Left's theme of "participatory democracy." Richard John Neuhaus and Peter Berger were more forthcoming about their ideological credentials, as neoconservatives,[97] when the American Enterprise Institute published their pamphlet in 1976 titled *To Empower People: The Role of Mediating Structures in Public Policy.* Liberals, they charged, with their stress on the federal government, had grown oblivious to the moral significance of neighborhood, family, church, and voluntary association. Burke was one of the heroes of Neuhaus and Berger, but even better than Burke was Tocqueville, under whose auspices an alliance might be forged with New Lefters at the expense of the "liberal establishment."[98] Finally, there were the "communitarians" who did not always know whether they were on the left or the right, only that they were against the liberals and in favor of localism. Not surprisingly, they too claimed Tocqueville as their godfather.[99] In sum, the New Left, the New Right, and the left-and-right communitarians, from the 1960s to the present day, have all been critics of New Deal liberalism and have all proudly enrolled Tocqueville in their ranks. Hartz has no place in their world.

If Hartz has faded in our day at the same time that Tocqueville's star has risen to perhaps unprecedented heights, it is only fair to point out that the demise of *The Liberal Tradition* is frequently more the result of a change of political outlooks than the outcome of a compelling critique. All too often what is presented as a telling repudiation of Hartz's interpretation of American history is little more than a reading back into the past of the present-day ideologies of the New Left or their neoconservative detractors, or of various other liberal-baiting ideologies.

Hartz can no longer speak for himself, but it is not impossible to imagine how he might have answered his Tocqueville-quoting critics. Surely he would ask his detractors to consider for a moment why he, a New Dealer, paid so much attention to Tocqueville's themes of the absence of feudalism and the presence of unchallenged capitalism. Hartz wanted to show just how difficult it was in America, where the working class did not think of itself as working-class, to build a viable welfare state. An uphill battle had been won by Franklin Delano Roosevelt. Nothing was more important to Hartz than to cherish and safeguard the belated victories won by New Dealers.

Tocqueville's concern, as a Frenchman, was to cut down to size the oversized bureaucratic apparatus of his country. Hartz's concern, as a New Deal American, was to build a national state adequate to the tasks of realizing social justice. His comment in his first book about the government of Pennsylvania is revealing: "What was needed, given the great scope of economic policy, was a stable and expert administrative system. It did not develop."[100]

Why, Hartz might have asked in dismay, would the New Left of a later day want to assist the right wing in dismantling the legacy of the New Deal? Why return to localism, so tardily overcome? Why join in on the right wing's standard bashing of "big government"? Why ignore the positive uses of government? The post-Hartzian and anti-Hartzian revival of Tocqueville probably would have struck him as a distressing confirmation of his fundamental argument that Americans rarely display a willingness to transcend their past.

THE ROLE OF IDEAS IN AMERICAN HISTORY

In our day the study of ideas in American history is flourishing. As much as ever, perhaps more than ever before, historians and political theorists are writing about the important role political doctrines have played in the history of the United States. Not least among the topics currently being addressed are the significance of John Locke, natural rights, and theories of the social contract. From our perspective the question that inevitably arises is whether this amounts to a return to Hartz.

The answer may well hinge on whether Hartz was accentuating or downplaying the role of ideas in American history. Alas, thoughtful commentators have flatly contradicted one another in this matter. Paul Roazen did not doubt that "Hartz was . . . emphasizing the powerful historical role of the life of the mind."[101] Upholding the opposite view was J. G. A. Pocock, who lumped together Louis Hartz and Daniel Boorstin, attributing to both the view that "there was no ideology in America."[102] To settle the matter, insofar as is within our means, we shall have to conduct our own investigation.

Isaiah Berlin in 1949 wrote that "the world is today stiff with rigid rules and codes and ardent, irrational religions." He despised "the great ideological wars of our time" and yearned for "less Messianic ardour, more enlightened scepticism, more tolerance of idiosyncrasies."[103] The Cold War liberals of the 1950s followed in Berlin's footsteps, with the likes of Daniel Bell, Seymour Martin Lipset, and others gleefully announcing "the end of ideology," even as Daniel Boorstin was doing them one better by declaring it had never started in the United States.

Louis Hartz would undoubtedly have been perplexed that Pocock and many others confused his position with Boorstin's or Bell's. Never did he deny the existence and importance of ideology in American history or make the mistake of declaring it over and done with, a thing of the past. His constantly repeated theme, after all, was the all-important dominance of liberal ideology in the American past and present.

The "end of ideology" thesis of the 1950s shows clearly that the Cold Warriors had their own reasons, different from Hartz's, for stealing some pages from Mannheim's *Ideology and Utopia*. With one major revision, Bell, Lipset, and company accepted Mannheim's thesis of 1929 that with the admission of the working classes to full citizenship, the curtain had finally come down on the age of ideologies.[104] Much as Mannheim had forecast decades earlier, the coming of the welfare state during and after World War II meant—the Cold War liberals contended—that there was no longer an oppressed social class with a vested interest in ideological politics. Their revision of Mannheim was, however, as unmistakable as their general acceptance of his argument: whereas the German sociologist depressingly concluded that the progressive history of higher utopian aspirations had also ended and that humans would be robbed of their humanity,[105] the American academic liberals were delighted that politics was destined henceforth to be more about mundane "means" than grandiloquent "ends."[106] They had witnessed more than enough of the fanatical ideological politics of totalitarian regimes.

Louis Hartz, as we have seen, derived much of the framework of his comparative analysis from Mannheim, yet he never wrote, as Bell did, about "the exhaustion of political ideas in the fifties." So far as Hartz could see, American politics had always been ideological and might always continue to be so, with the twist that, in contrast to Europe's, America's political battles were all waged within the outlook of a single ideology, liberalism. In America the workers had not at long last become middle-class and liberal; they had always been such, unlike in Europe, where not so long before they had posed a challenge to the liberals. Hartz used Mannheim to point out how suffocating ideology was in America, rather than to declare its demise.

Although Daniel Boorstin's *The Genius of American Politics* (1953) was related to Bell's *The End of Ideology*, it remained quite distinct from it. Bell and
Lipset had applied their argument to Europe and America, arguing that
both abroad and at home ideology had once been but thankfully was no
more. Boorstin, by contrast, viewed ideological politics as a misfortune limited to "our sick friends in Europe."[107] There had never been any ideas in
American politics, Boorstin contended; there had only been the continuity
provided by the antitheoretical common law. It was no accident that "the
marvelous success and vitality of our institutions" stood juxtaposed to "the
amazing poverty and inarticulateness of our theorizing about politics."[108]
This lack of political theory, reaching even into the academy, where every
other topic was better studied,[109] accounted for the wonderful continuity of
American history, so unlike the disruptions the Europeans had endured.

There was at least one similarity between Hartz's position and Boorstin's.
Much like Boorstin, Hartz wrote that "law has flourished on the corpse of
philosophy in America."[110] Appearances, however, can be deceiving, for
Hartz was as disheartened by "the sterility of our political thought"[111] as
Boorstin was cheered by the same. Boorstin was the self-anointed apologist
of American political culture, and Hartz its stern critic. Against the "end of
ideology" Cold Warriors and the equally conservative liberalism of Boorstin, Hartz insisted that American politics was in fact ideological but sadly
one-dimensionally so, and that because the liberal ideology of Americans
reigned unchallenged, liberalism in the United States had unfortunately
never been forced to rise to the intellectual heights of anything vaguely resembling political philosophy. Only in America were liberal values regarded
as "self-evident" truths.

Why was Hartz's book wrongly conflated with Boorstin's? One explanation is that, beginning with the advent of the New Left, commentators had
a strong ideological interest in reducing *The Liberal Tradition in America* to
Boorstin's rather simplistic understanding of the American past and
present.[112] Another reason, a better one, was that Hartz arguably invited
misunderstanding. On the one hand, he stated quite clearly in his book
that he meant to underscore "the crucial significance of ideology."[113] As to
the content of ideology in America, it was overwhelmingly Lockean: "Locke
dominates American political thought, as no thinker anywhere dominates
the political thought of a nation. He is a massive national cliché."[114] On the
other hand, he later admitted that in his account Locke was merely "a symbol" and that "there is no need to overemphasize his significance."[115] We
find ourselves puzzling over the problem of what it means to underscore
Lockean ideology and yet dismiss the significance of John Locke.

Our chances of understanding Hartz, without necessarily defending him, are improved if we think about his way of approaching the slippery word "ideology." In *The Liberal Tradition* Hartz spoke of America's Lockeanism as "irrational," and in his essay "The Rise of the Democratic Idea," he said, "Fundamentally we are dealing with a psychic matter."[116] On the several occasions when Hartz bemoaned the absence of political philosophy in America, he sounded like Tocqueville[117] or any of a number of other European visitors who searched in vain for an American Hegel or Mill. Hartz's true interest, however, was in ideology, ideas in action, not in formal philosophy, and he decided in advance that ideologies could only matter insofar as they figured as weapons in sociopolitical conflicts, never because they said anything thoughtful about the political universe.[118] The opening sentence of Hartz's essay "Democracy: Image and Reality" reads: "The system of democracy works by virtue of certain processes which its theory never describes, to which, indeed, its theory is hostile." Locke, for example, was a hindrance to an appreciation of political parties, and the only reason his talk about a state of nature was tolerable was because "no polemical instrument less powerful could have shaken the rigidities of the group structure" of the old social order.[119] Locke said much that was useful in ideological combat but nothing that was true.

It is one thing to investigate and then decide whether political theory has been present or absent in American political culture; it is another to study American thought, as Hartz did, in such a manner that one rules out in advance the possible existence of political theory. Following Mannheim's example, Hartz reduced all ideologies to the social conditions underlying them.[120] In his world it is always social class that is the actor: the Enlightenment, for example, is incomprehensible to Hartz without "the rise of the middle class."[121] Everything comes back to social class in his analysis; a social determinism, never fully acknowledged, is at work. Ideas are inadvertently cheated by Hartz, even as he touts the great importance of ideology.

The negative consequences of Hartz's fixation on social classes and their corresponding class ideologies were not limited to an unfair a priori conclusion that there has been no political theory worth speaking of in America. Because he saw the world exclusively in terms of European class ideologies, Hartz paid the additional price of missing the formidable currents of American thought that fell outside liberal ideology. In particular, despite his personal commitment to liberal causes, he missed the illiberal patterns of thought and culture that are the shame of American history.[122] *The Liberal Tradition* was not the only important historical study released in 1955; another was John Higham's *Strangers in the Land: Patterns of American*

Nativism, 1860–1925. In our day we take it for granted that racism, nativism, and other forms of bigotry are central, not accidental, features of the historical record. The example of Higham's book proves that Hartz in his day could have come face-to-face with illiberal America, were he not blinded by his insistence upon approaching political reality solely through the lens of class analysis.

By and large it was also Hartz's preoccupation with class analysis that was responsible for his inadequate treatment of religion in American history. After noting that religion was itself revolutionary during the American Revolution, he was done with it. The continuing story of the intersection of religion and politics was missing from his story of America. Ethnicity, too, counted for little or nothing in his book; women, likewise, played no role in his account of the American past. And although he was attentive to slavery, Hartz did not deal adequately with post–Civil War racism.

There were problems not only with what was omitted from *The Liberal Tradition* but also with the strands of thought the volume did address. In Mannheim's view a given thinker was never anything more than a mouthpiece of conservative, liberal, or socialist ideology, never a figure whose thought merited in-depth analysis. When Hartz followed Mannheim's dubious example, the result was that he was sometimes guilty of serious misunderstandings of a particular person or political movement.

One may well question, for instance, whether Hartz's account of the Progressives was all it might have been. "The contention of Croly that there was a great and 'fundamental difference' between the New Freedom and the New Nationalism can hardly be defended,"[123] wrote Hartz. Not if Hartz was right in claiming that both branches of Progressivism were dedicated to "trust-busting" and a return to the past. Unfortunately, he was not right. The New Nationalists accepted the trusts while insisting on governmental regulation of business. Neither Croly nor Theodore Roosevelt, on this issue, hesitated to call Woodrow Wilson a reactionary.[124] Perhaps the deepest conceptual problem here was that Hartz's mode of analysis led to an arbitrary assumption of continuity across the ages. He assumed, falsely, that because Louis Brandeis and Woodrow Wilson embraced Jefferson and Jackson, so did Herbert Croly and Teddy Roosevelt. The liberal scheme of analysis discouraged recognition of change and historicity; it fostered the mistaken notion that American thought and culture were preformed.[125]

To do justice to Hartz, there was one occasion at least in *The Liberal Tradition* when Mannheim's ghost did not prevent him from setting forth a rich appreciation of Americans engaged in meaningful, thoughtful political debate. Even today Hartz's two chapters on "the feudal dream of the South" make for rewarding reading. Under attack from the North, spokespersons for the South dared question the self-evident truths. Their writings constituted "one of the great and creative episodes in the history of American thought"; "this was the great imaginative moment . . . , the moment when America almost got out of itself."[126] In spite of the despicable cause they represented, the Southern thinkers "had gotten hold of a relevant point: the real nature of social oppression. Considering the superficiality of the Jeffersonian and Jacksonian traditions on this score, their achievement can hardly be dismissed."[127]

Just how much this Southern discovery of the fact of social oppression meant to Hartz can only be appreciated by reading *The Necessity of Choice*. In that volume of lectures his theme is that instead of dreaming, Lockean style, of regaining our freedom in the state of nature, we should search for ways within the established social order to build a "fluid liberal plurality." All societies are oppressive, some more, some less than others, so it is only by coming to terms with the inevitability of unfreedom that we can salvage a measure of freedom. Unlike the communitarians of a later day, Hartz insisted that "the liberty of the individual does not lie in his ability to form an association, but in his capacity to leave it."[128]

In the end Hartz's foray into Southern thought did not lead him to reconsider his thesis that all American thought was merely an articulation of one and the same cultural imperative, the liberal ethos. George Fitzhugh may have broken out of the liberal stranglehold, but no one in the North deemed his telling critique worthy of a response. John C. Calhoun had actually paid homage to liberalism with his overwrought constitutional gimmickry, and other Southerners were cousins of Adam Smith in their championing of free international trade. "After the Civil War they were soon forgotten and they all but forgot themselves."[129]

Even if Hartz had wanted to take ideas seriously in *The Liberal Tradition*, Mannheim's sociological determinism and exclusive focus on social class stood in his way. A better place in the corpus of Hartz's writings to look for a discussion of lively, multidimensional political debates, with ideas playing an active role, is his first book, *Economic Policy and Democratic Thought: Pennsylvania, 1776–1860*. To all appearances, Hartz had not yet encountered *Ideology and Utopia* in 1948. At this early moment in his career, he was not tempted to push all American thought into a single, possibly prefabricated, formula. He had not yet begun the process of reducing each thinker into an unconscious mouthpiece of a one-dimensional cultural imperative.

Although the famous name of Thomas Paine is occasionally raised in his book on antebellum Pennsylvania, Hartz insisted that the ideas in question "were developed mainly by men whose names have been forgotten"; it was in the speeches and journalism of these now anonymous public figures "that the substance of the original American conception of the legitimate sphere of governmental action in economic life is to be found."[130] Far more compellingly than in his later, more famous book, where John Locke was only a symbol, Hartz demonstrated how important the *Second Treatise of Government* was to ordinary citizens engaged in important debates over the regulation of charters, banks, corporations, factories, and other institutions. Among the many disputes that Hartz unearthed and brought to the attention of the reader were the following: debates over "first principles" and the implications of the doctrine of popular sovereignty, discussions of the possible conflict between generational autonomy and the chartering of self-renewing "monopolies," claims that the children of workers in factories would never understand the terms of the social contract unless fundamental social reforms were initiated, and an expanding definition of natural rights to encompass social rights.[131]

One can spy in the book on antebellum Pennsylvania a very promising line of research that Hartz chose not to pursue further in *The Liberal Tradition in America*. Not only did he seem to be unearthing past philosophical battles when writing his first book, but he also proved that these struggles dealt with issues that aroused many citizens and that the stakes in these conflicts were articulated by spokespersons drawn from the common ranks.

On the other hand, on reading *Economic Policy and Democratic Thought*, we can also surmise that Hartz was ready to go off at a moment's notice in a different direction, one far less sympathetic to the role of ideas, even before his fateful encounter with the thought of Mannheim. In his first book he was too preoccupied with finding precursors of postbellum uses of natural law arguments by corporate America to see much more than empty bellowing in antebellum debates about natural rights and social contracts.[132] Implicitly he suggested that ideas were one thing, reality another. The true point of his book was to show that government had been remarkably active in antebellum America but was frustrated in execution by a primitive administrative apparatus. "Democratic thought," despite its appearance in the title, was of secondary interest at best.

THE STUDY OF POLITICAL IDEAS TODAY

Today Locke is no longer relegated in American history to the status of a mere symbol or an unthinking, conditioned reflex. Studies of Locke, natural rights, and different theories of the social contract have come into their own and have offered many insights into the Revolution and the Founding, the great debates of the antebellum period, and much more.[133] But Hartz has had little or nothing to do with the new research because, for all his ostensible emphasis on ideology, the true key to *The Liberal Tradition* is the concept of social class—in America's case, the middle class to which everyone aspires and the liberal ideology it has unthinkingly sponsored.

The preliminary results of the new research reveal that, Hartz notwithstanding, political philosophy is not foreign to the American tradition. There have been great debates over alienable versus inalienable rights, a social contract signed once and for all versus a contract that must be renewed with each generation, and the sovereign people as the people of the various states versus the people of the nation—to name only a few of the noteworthy intellectual battles. And these debates of yesteryear were not merely "academic." Far from it; we now appreciate more than ever before that, thanks to the efforts of journalists, public officials, preachers, and pamphleteers, "political theory" was a preoccupation of the public over the course of much of American history, antebellum America especially but by no means exclusively. These debates, moreover, included the voices of women, blacks, workers, and land reformers—all the groups important to social historians. Under the new dispensation social and intellectual historians, who parted company after the 1960s, have much to say to one another.

Hartz's insistence that America be understood by looking beyond its boundaries remains a vital concern of historians and political scientists, if on terms he might not recognize. John Locke's political writings that fared poorly in the England of 1688 were successfully transplanted to America during the revolutionary era. "Atlantic crossings," we now know, showed up on later occasions as well—the Progressive era for example, when European ideas and examples were imported by Americans—which raises questions about Hartz's assumption that American thought was consistently insular.[134] On the matter of comparative studies, then, as on the emphasis on Locke, natural rights, and social contracts, contemporary scholarship sometimes sounds like Hartz but in reality takes a distinctive approach.

The difference between Hartz yesterday and the scholars of our day can be seen in shorthand by considering their contrasting visions of the American Revolution. Hartz declared the Revolution a nonrevolution, in this following the views of such Europeans as Marx on the left, Tocqueville in the middle, and Friedrich Gentz on the right,[135] for all of whom a revolution had to be a social revolution. What the new scholarship does quite consistently is to make a powerful case for the proposition that the American Revolution was indeed a revolution, because of its revolutionary ideology, its insistence on putting the doctrine of the sovereignty of the people into effect by means of the invention of constitutional conventions, its transformation of the rights of Englishmen into universal human rights, and related ideas. Ideas hatched in England but scuttled there became established practice in America and eventually were shipped back to Europe, where they influenced the French Revolution. Among other things, the Declaration of Independence was the direct forerunner of the Declaration of the Rights of Man and Citizen.[136]

The Liberal Tradition in America is a great book, a work fully deserving the attention it has received, and worthy of the vigorous controversies it has ignited. It is also a book that like all books—even the most remarkable—had sooner or later to yield ground to new interpretations, new perspectives. One can admire Hartz's originality, his daring, and his brilliance and yet arrive at the conclusion that his day is no longer ours. We cannot accept his view that "the liberal tradition in America" is a given or that it is the sole American tradition. We cannot accept an account of American history that lacks a sense of time, change, and history. Whatever triumphs liberalism achieved in the past were the result of active struggle and intense debate, not of preformed inevitability, and the same is true of the present and the future: whether there is and will be a liberal tradition in America is our burden, our calling, and our quest, rather than our predetermined fate.

NOTES

1. One indication that Hartz's work reached beyond the academy is that journalist Tom Wicker wrote an introduction to the 1991 reprint of *The Liberal Tradition in America.*

2. J. G. A. Pocock, *The Machiavellian Moment: Florentine Political Thought and the Atlantic Republican Tradition* (Princeton, N.J.: Princeton University Press, 1975), 509.

3. J. G. A. Pocock, "Virtue and Commerce in the Eighteenth Century," *Journal of Interdisciplinary History* 3 (1972): 122. Cf. Gordon Wood, *The Creation of the American Republic, 1776–1787* (Chapel Hill: University of North Carolina Press, 1969), 59: "Republicanism as the Americans expressed it in 1776 possessed a decidedly reactionary tone."

4. Joyce Appleby, *Capitalism and a New Social Order: The Republican Vision of the 1790s* (New York: New York University Press, 1984); Appleby, *Liberalism and Republicanism in the Historical Imagination* (Cambridge, Mass.: Harvard University Press, 1992).

5. Louis Hartz, "Seth Luther: The Story of a Working-Class Rebel," *New England Quarterly* 13, no. 3 (September 1940): 401–418.

6. Ibid., 418.

7. Louis Hartz, *The Necessity of Choice: Nineteenth-Century Political Thought* (New Brunswick, N.J.: Transaction Books, 1990), 73.

8. Louis Hartz, *The Liberal Tradition in America: An Interpretation of American Political Thought since the Revolution* (New York: Harcourt, Brace, 1955), 296; hereafter cited as *LTA*.

9. Ibid., 37.

10. Ibid., 142.

11. Carl J. Friedrich and Zbigniew K. Brzezinski, *Totalitarian Dictatorship and Autocracy* (1956; reprint, New York: Praeger, 1961), 3, 5.

12. Hannah Arendt, *The Origins of Totalitarianism* (1951; reprint, New York: Meridian, 1963), 139, 308, 316–318.

13. Seymour Martin Lipset originally published his essay on "Working-Class Authoritarianism" in 1959. It is reprinted in Lipset's book *Political Man: The Social Bases of Politics* (New York: Doubleday/Anchor, 1963), chap. 4.

14. Jacob Burckhardt, *Reflections on History* (Indianapolis, Ind.: Liberty Classics, 1979), 211.

15. Ibid., 49.

16. Ibid., 266.

17. José Ortega y Gasset, *La rebelión de las masas* (1930); reprinted in English as *The Revolt of the Masses* (New York: Norton, 1993), 122.

18. Ibid., 116.

19. For example, see William Kornhauser, *The Politics of Mass Society* (Glencoe, Ill.: Free Press, 1959), 25, 26, 86, 87, 121, 126, 127, 132, 133, 135, 136.

20. See Stephen J. Whitfield, *The Culture of the Cold War* (Baltimore: Johns Hopkins University Press, 1991); Richard H. Pells, *The Liberal Mind in a Conservative Age: American Intellectuals in the 1940s and 1950s* (New York: Harper & Row, 1985); Neil Jumonville, *Critical Crossings: The New York Intellectuals in Postwar America* (Berkeley: University of California Press, 1991).

21. On Guizot and French liberalism, see Vincent E. Starzinger, *Middlingness: Juste Milieu Political Theory in France and England, 1815–1848* (Charlottesville: University Press of Virginia, 1965); and Mark Hulliung, *Citizens and Citoyens: Republicanism and Liberalism in America and France* (Cambridge, Mass.: Harvard University Press, 2002), chap. 5. Starzinger's book was based upon the doctoral dissertation that I believe he wrote under the supervision of Hartz.

22. Karl Popper, *The Open Society and Its Enemies*, vol. 1, *The Spell of Plato* (Princeton, N.J.: Princeton University Press, 1962), 87; Thomas Landon Thorson, *Plato: Totalitarian or Democrat?* (Englewood Cliffs, N.J.: Prentice-Hall, 1963).

23. Walter Lippmann, *Essays in the Public Philosophy* (1955; reprint, New York: Mentor, 1956), 36–38, 137.

24. Oliver Wendell Holmes Jr., "Natural Law," in *The American Intellectual Tradition*, ed. David H. Hollinger and Charles Capper, 2nd ed. (New York: Oxford University Press, 1993), 2:128–130.

25. Note, for instance, the incomprehension of the Japanese officials placed on trial by the victorious powers after World War II and charged with violating the law of nature. Judith Shklar, *Legalism: An Essay on Law, Morals, and Politics* (Cambridge, Mass.: Harvard University Press, 1964), 179–190.

26. For example, see Leo Strauss, *Natural Right and History* (Chicago: University of Chicago Press, 1953). Even the influential left-wing thinker Erich Fromm held that all the great writers, Western and Eastern, had taught the same doctrine of natural law, which happened to coincide with his own. "Relativists" struck back with an equally implausible argument that the dogmatism of absolutism was conducive to authoritarian politics. For example, see Hans Kelsen, "Absolutism and Relativism in Philosophy and Politics," *American Political Science Review* 42 (1948): 906–914.

27. Peter Laslett, ed., *Philosophy, Politics and Society* (Oxford: Blackwell, 1956), vii.

28. T. D. Weldon, *The Vocabulary of Politics* (Baltimore: Penguin, 1953), 15.

29. Ibid., 15, 39, 57, 168, 178–179, 191, 192, and the comments on the dust jacket.

30. Ibid., 159.

31. For a critique of "tunnel" history, see J. H. Hexter, *Reappraisals in History* (New York: Harper, 1963), 194–195.

32. Arthur M. Schlesinger Jr., *The Age of Jackson* (Boston: Little, Brown, 1945), *The Age of Roosevelt,* 3 vols. (Boston: Houghton Mifflin, 1957–1960).

33. Note Raymond Aron's identification with Montesquieu and Tocqueville, at the expense of Auguste Comte and Karl Marx, in the first volume of *Main Currents in Sociological Thought* (New York: Doubleday/Anchor, 1968). Stanley Hoffmann has frequently acknowledged his debt to Aron and sided with the approach of Montesquieu and Tocqueville.

34. Alexis de Tocqueville, *Democracy in America* (New York: Harper, 1988), 94.

35. Mark Hulliung, *Montesquieu and the Old Regime* (Berkeley and Los Angeles: University of California Press, 1976), 38–46.

36. This is a major theme of my book on Montesquieu.

37. Tocqueville, *Democracy in America,* 509.

38. *LTA,* 44, 153. The references to Montesquieu in Hartz, *The Necessity of Choice,* 36, 37, 39, 40, 45, 71, 95, 112, 132, 158, 166, are more numerous but display no awareness of the nature of Montesquieu's labors in comparative history and politics.

39. *LTA,* 24.

40. Montesquieu, *De l'esprit des lois,* book 20, chap. 7.

41. I am paraphrasing my more extended analysis of Montesquieu's comparative method and findings in Hulliung, *Montesquieu and the Old Regime,* esp. 77–88.

42. *LTA,* 24.

43. Ibid., 25–26.

44. Ibid., 3.

45. C. Vann Woodward, ed., *The Comparative Approach to American History* (New York: Basic Books, 1968; reprint, New York: Oxford University Press, 1997), 53, 76, 117, 248.

46. *LTA*, 20.

47. Ibid., 10, 30, 308 on irrational Lockeanism ("Lockianism" in Hartz's spelling) and "irrational liberalism."

48. Ibid., 9, 137, 281 on judicial review; 85, 134 on checks and balances.

49. Ibid., 11–12.

50. Mannheim appears several times in Hartz's thought;, e.g., see *LTA*, 24, 150; *The Necessity of Choice*, 78, 81. Although Hartz never stops to explain how important Mannheim was to him, one can see the German sociologist whenever Hartz discussed ideology. All the intellectuals of Hartz's day took Mannheim seriously, especially, as we shall see, those who participated in the "end of ideology" debate.

51. *LTA*, 6.

52. Tocqueville, *Democracy in America*, 34, 39.

53. *LTA*, 11.

54. Woodward, *The Comparative Approach to American History*, 11.

55. *LTA*, 29.

56. Ibid., 28–32.

57. Ibid., 28.

58. Ibid., 101, 28.

59. Hartz could not, within the limits of his book, discuss the Progressive historians in detail. A fully realized account may be found in Richard Hofstadter, *The Progressive Historians* (New York: Knopf, 1968).

60. Tocqueville, *Democracy in America*, 58.

61. James Mill, *An Essay on Government* (Indianapolis, Ind.: Bobbs-Merrill, 1977), 90.

62. For example, see the works of Augustin Thierry (1795–1856).

63. *LTA*, 19, 92.

64. Ibid., 93.

65. John Stuart Mill, *A System of Logic* (1843; reprint, London: Longmans, Green, 1949), book 3, chap. 8.

66. *LTA*, 95–96, 22–23.

67. Ray Allen Billington, "Frontiers," in Woodward, *The Comparative Approach to American History*, 90. Cf. 80: "Elsewhere neither physical conditions nor cultural traditions were properly combined to create the same social environment that existed in the successive American Wests."

68. John P. Roche, ed., *Origins of American Political Thought* (New York: Harper Torchbooks, 1967), 59.

69. Hartz, *The Necessity of Choice*, 212.

70. Ibid., 74.

71. Ibid., 126, 132, for evidence that he did know something about Karl Popper's writings on the philosophy of science and social science.

72. Edward A. Shils and Henry A. Finch, eds., *Max Weber on the Methodology of the Social Sciences* (Glencoe, Ill.: Free Press, 1949).

73. *LTA*, 308, 309.

74. Louis Hartz, "The Rise of the Democratic Idea," in Roche, *Origins of American Political Thought,* 77. Reprinted from Arthur M. Schlesinger Jr. and Morton White, eds., *Paths of American Thought* (Boston: Houghton Mifflin, 1963).

75. Tocqueville, *Democracy in America,* 12, 695, 691, 703.

76. Lipset, *Political Man,* 7, 8.

77. Lipset, introduction to *Political Parties: A Sociological Study of the Oligarchical Tendencies of Modern Democracy,* by Robert Michels (New York: Free Press, 1962), 35, 36.

78. Tocqueville, *Democracy in America,* 194–195.

79. Louis Hartz, "Democracy: Image and Reality," in *Democracy Today: Problems and Prospects,* ed. William H. Chambers and Robert H. Salisbury (New York: Collier, 1962), 33, 37.

80. For example, see *LTA,* 14, 57, 142.

81. Tocqueville, *Democracy in America,* 254–255.

82. James T. Kloppenberg, a contributor to the present volume, figures prominently among those scholars who believe they must save Tocqueville from Hartz.

83. *LTA,* 89.

84. Hartz, "The Rise of the Democratic Idea," 63, 64, 65, 69, 70.

85. W. H. Morris Jones, "In Defence of Apathy: Some Doubts on the Duty to Vote," *Political Studies* 2, no. 1 (1954): 25–37.

86. Tocqueville, *Democracy in America,* 303, 553, 554.

87. *LTA,* 52.

88. Ibid., 89.

89. Ibid., 110–112.

90. Tocqueville, *Democracy in America,* 539.

91. Ibid., 671.

92. Ibid., 384.

93. Ibid., 89.

94. Hartz, *The Necessity of Choice,* 210.

95. See, however, the essay by Desmond King and Marc Stears in the present volume.

96. Robert Putnam, "Bowling Alone," *Journal of Democracy* 6, no. 1 (January 1995): 65–77.

97. The neoconservatives of the 1970s, opponents of New Left populism, had originally been Cold War liberals hostile to the populism of the "radical Right"—McCarthy in the 1950s, Barry Goldwater in the early 1960s. More recently, the term "neoconservative" has been captured by the radical Right.

98. Richard Neuhaus and Peter Berger, *To Empower People: The Role of Mediating Structures in Public Policy* (Washington, D.C.: American Enterprise Institute, 1976).

99. For example, see Michael Sandel, *Democracy's Discontent: America in Search of a Public Philosophy* (Cambridge, Mass.: Harvard University Press, 1996), 27, 314, 320, 347, 348.

100. Louis Hartz, *Economic Policy and Democratic Thought: Pennsylvania, 1776–1860* (Cambridge, Mass.: Harvard University Press, 1948), 293; see also 263, 292.

101. Paul Roazen, introduction to Hartz, *The Necessity of Choice,* 7.

102. Pocock, *The Machiavellian Moment,* 509.

103. Isaiah Berlin, "Political Ideas in the Twentieth Century" (1949), in *Four Essays on Liberty* (New York: Oxford, 1969), 37–39.

104. For a collection of the relevant sources, see Chaim I. Waxman, ed., *The End of Ideology Debate* (New York: Funk & Wagnalls, 1968).

105. "The disappearance of utopia brings about a static state of affairs in which man himself becomes no more than a thing." Karl Mannheim, *Ideology and Utopia* (New York: Harvest, 1968), 262–263.

106. Daniel Bell, *The End of Ideology: On the Exhaustion of Political Ideas in the Fifties* (Glencoe, Ill.: Free Press, 1960); Seymour Martin Lipset, "The End of Ideology?" in *Political Man,* chap. 13.

107. Daniel Boorstin, *The Genius of American Politics* (Chicago: University of Chicago Press, 1953), 183. In fairness to Boorstin, I should say that he is all too often judged by this book, by far his worst.

108. Ibid., 8.

109. Ibid., 17.

110. *LTA,* 10.

111. Ibid., 141.

112. For example, see James O'Brien, *America the Beautiful: An Essay on Daniel Boorstin and Louis Hartz* (Ann Arbor, Mich.: Radical Education Project, n.d. [late 1960s]).

113. *LTA,* 231. See also Louis Hartz, "The Problem of Political Ideas," in *Approaches to the Study of Politics,* ed. Roland Young (Evanston, Ill.: Northwestern University Press, 1958), 78–86.

114. *LTA,* 140.

115. Hartz, "The Rise of the Democratic Idea," 68.

116. Ibid., 69.

117. For Tocqueville's comments on the antitheoretical bias of Americans, see *Democracy in America,* 256, 285, 301, 429.

118. An ideology succeeds in unmasking opponents, never in offering anything positive and insightful. "Its image of itself is a negation of what it seeks to destroy." Hartz, "Democracy: Image and Reality," 26.

119. Ibid., 25, 31–32.

120. "All arguments are linked to the existence of social forces." Hartz, *The Necessity of Choice,* 181.

121. Ibid., 33. For my own, I think very different, view of the Enlightenment, see Mark Hulliung, *The Autocritique of Enlightenment: Rousseau and the Philosophes* (Cambridge, Mass.: Harvard University Press, 1994).

122. Possibly Hartz meant to offset this deficiency in *The Founding of New Societies: Studies in the History of the United States, Latin America, South Africa, Canada, and Australia* (New York: Harcourt, Brace & World, 1964). Here he argued that the settlement colonies hailing from the most "enlightened" countries of Europe were the worst when it came to slavery. In order to justify so vile an institution, they had

to reduce the slave to a thinglike property. Against this view David Brion Davis argued that the practice of slavery was equally bad in all these nations, whatever their European origin. Davis, *The Problem of Slavery in Western Culture* (Ithaca, N.Y.: Cornell University Press, 1966).

123. *LTA*, 230.

124. Theodore Roosevelt, *An Autobiography* (1913; reprint, New York: Da Capo, 1985), 437, 597; Herbert Croly, *Progressive Democracy* (1914; reprint, New Brunswick, N.J.: Transaction Books, 1998), 15–19.

125. For more on Hartz's view of the Progressives, see his essay "The New Individualism and the Progressive Tradition," in *Innocence and Power: Individualism in Twentieth-Century America*, ed. Gordon Mills (Austin: University of Texas Press, 1965), 72–91.

126. *LTA*, 147, 176.

127. Ibid., 184.

128. Hartz, *The Necessity of Choice*, 94, 171.

129. *LTA*, 172.

130. Hartz, *Economic Policy and Democratic Thought*, 3.

131. Ibid., 199, 223, 247, 252, 306.

132. Ibid., 70, 78, 121, 167, 174, 180, 315–316.

133. Daniel T. Rodgers, *Contested Truths: Keywords in American Politics since Independence* (New York: Basic Books: 1987), chap. 2; Isaac Kramnick, *Republicanism and Bourgeois Radicalism: Political Ideology in Late Eighteenth-Century England and America* (Ithaca, N.Y.: Cornell University Press, 1990); Michael P. Zuckert, *Natural Rights and the New Republicanism* (Princeton, N.J.: Princeton University Press, 1994); Zuckert, *The Natural Rights Republic: Studies in the Foundation of the American Political Tradition* (Notre Dame, Ind.: University of Notre Dame Press, 1996); Hulliung, *Citizens and Citoyens*; Hulliung, *The Social Contract in America: From the Revolution to the Present* (Lawrence: University Press of Kansas, 2007). Although J. G. A. Pocock tried to claim for his cause Bernard Bailyn's *The Ideological Origins of the American Revolution* (Cambridge, Mass.: Harvard University Press, 1967), the book actually contains ample evidence of the great significance of natural rights doctrines.

134. Daniel T. Rodgers, *Atlantic Crossings: Social Politics in a Progressive Age* (Cambridge, Mass.: Harvard University Press, 1998).

135. A leading theorist of the counterrevolution was Friedrich Gentz, author of the influential pamphlet *The French and American Revolutions Compared* (Chicago: Gateway, 1955).

136. If there was a book in Hartz's day that pointed the way to where we are—or ought to be—today, it is, in my judgment, the first volume, published in 1959, of R. R. Palmer's *The Age of the Democratic Revolution* (Princeton, N.J.: Princeton University Press, 1959–1964).

PART TWO

Hartz's Argument Reappraised

CHAPTER 2

Understanding the Symbiosis of American Rights and American Racism

Rogers M. Smith

If Louis Hartz's "liberal society" thesis was the dominant interpretation of American political culture, at least in political science, for roughly a quarter of a century after its 1955 publication in *The Liberal Tradition in America*, and if that thesis faced a range of critiques in the ensuing quarter century (with this writer among the critics), many scholars are now exploring important issues previous debates have left unresolved.[1] In this essay, I assess the state of play on some undecided questions that show the continuing value of grappling with Hartz's account. These questions might be construed broadly to center on how to understand the historical intertwining of American liberalism with American racism, though to bracket temporarily controversies over the term "liberalism," I cast the issue here as to how to understand the relationships of doctrines, institutions, and practices of individual rights with inegalitarian racial doctrines, institutions, and practices in the United States, historically and today. For brevity, I focus primarily on discourses and ideas, though in ways attentive to their interrelationships with institutions and practices.

No one from Hartz to the present has ever denied that American political discourses, institutions, and practices have long expressed both advocacy of "the rights of man" and assertions of the existence of distinct races that should not be assigned identical rights. Different analysts have, however, given those elements of American political culture very different emphases and interpretations. If we hope either to adjudicate among or to improve on those accounts, a number of more specific questions about the coexistence

in American political culture of individual rights and racial inequalities have
to be answered. Here, I focus on four such interrelated questions:

1. Should the coexistence in America of individual rights doctrines,
    institutions, and practices and inegalitarian racial doctrines,
    institutions, and practices be conceived as a historical contingency, or
    have these elements somehow been necessarily connected, so that
    neither could have existed without the other?
2. Have either the individual rights elements or the racially inegalitarian
    elements been historically more central to and definitive of American
    political culture and American political development, and if so, in
    what ways?
3. Have their relationships been static historically, or have they evolved
    significantly, and if so, how and why?
4. Perhaps most importantly, but also most complexly: if we do interpret
    individual rights and racial inequalities as deeply interconnected in
    America, how should we conceive of those interconnections—as
    fundamentally conceptual or philosophical? As economic? As
    psychological? As political? If more than one of these, which ones and
    why, and what have been the mechanisms of their interconnections?

In this paper I categorize the main answers to these questions that I discern in current scholarship, highlighting some strengths and weaknesses.
Seeing the jury as still out on most of these issues, I also seek to identify
what inquiries must be pursued to move analyses forward. Better answers
are significant for grasping the fundamentals of American political culture
and its development and for understanding what political options may be
open to Americans and others, today and in the future.

SOME PRELIMINARIES

For many engaged with these issues, the starting point remains Hartz's famous argument that the United States is a "liberal society," one that in some
sense began with the political values of "liberalism," used "in the classic
Lockian sense," and one that has stayed with those values with remarkable
"moral unanimity," displaying the "universality" or indeed the "tyranny" of
"the liberal idea" and the "liberal tradition" throughout its history.[2] But
Hartz did not define "liberalism," the "liberal idea," or the "liberal tradition,"
and many of the debates his work has spurred have centered on whether or
how we should understand those terms.

In a seminal discussion of this essay's topics, Jennifer Hochschild contended in 1984 that liberalism "asserts the unique value of all persons, political equality of all citizens, liberty of all humans."[3] In perhaps the most influential effort to adapt and extend Hartz, David Greenstone argued that Hartz's "liberal consensus" theory "holds that Americans are committed to . . . the basic values of private property, individual freedom, and government based on popular consent."[4] In an effort to test Hartz's claims, I interpreted him to define liberalism as "government by consent, limited by the rule of law protecting individual rights, and a market economy, all officially open to all minimally rational adults."[5] In building on but critiquing these predecessors, Carol Horton has defined American liberalism as prioritizing "the value of individual rights and liberties, limited and representative government, private property and free market, and constitutionalism and the rule of law."[6] And in arguing for a return to Hartz, Marc Stears has more recently interpreted Hartz's liberalism as involving "a commitment to individualist ethics, widespread hostility to the power of the state, a pervasive skepticism toward social elites, and an intense sense of social equality."[7]

Similar as these definitions are, note that Greenstone and Horton speak only of "individual freedom" and "individual rights" without any specification of whether all or only some individuals are entitled to freedom and rights, much less equal freedom and rights. The other definitions are more overtly inclusive and egalitarian. In 1964, Hartz also went further. He contended, "Once humanity is conceded . . . the liberal ethic is . . . compulsively generous, since it demands completely equal treatment."[8] But if we define liberalism as insisting that all humans are entitled to completely equal treatment in terms of basic human rights and that all citizens are entitled to equal political rights, then we constrain the possible linkages between doctrines of individual rights and racial inequalities, at least at the conceptual level. If we define liberalism as not including those stipulations, we may stack the deck the opposite way. Either way, we appear to settle much of the issue of the relationship of (liberal) rights to racial inequalities by definitional fiat. Here I therefore postpone debating the proper definition of liberalism and focus simply on different ways of conceptualizing the relationships between individual rights and racial inequalities in America, relationships that lie at the heart of the liberalism-and-racism debate. Since all definitions of liberalism give some place to individual rights, I nonetheless draw on scholars' discussions of "liberalism" in discerning how they perceive American relationships of rights and race.

I also postpone a second question raised by Hartz's framework: in what sense, if any, should we speak of a "liberal tradition" in America? John Gunnell has argued that Hartz's "liberal tradition" is not an actual "historically autonomous tradition" that can be "historically investigated." It is "basically a rhetorical metaphor," a Weberian "ideal type," or a Wittgensteinian "perspicuous representation," a "model or typification that captured the essence or underlying meaning of the phenomenon in question."[9] Gunnell acknowledges that many of Hartz's successors, both defenders and detractors, have nonetheless assumed that there really was and is such a historical tradition. And not without reason, because Hartz did, "maybe less than entirely self-consciously," contribute "to the construction of an emerging vision of liberalism" by "social theorists, particularly in the field of political science," as "something involving Locke and representing an actual tradition" that "explained, for better or worse, the condition of modernity and the character of American politics."[10] Edmund Fong has similarly contended that, rather than being "a historian of American political culture," Hartz should be viewed "as attempting to divine the mythological structure of American liberalism and how it has shaped the possibilities of the American political imaginary," though Fong also believes Hartz ultimately fell "prey to the very liberal mythology he attempted to render apparent."[11]

I have suggested as well that Hartz's "liberal tradition" appears to be more a scholarly construction than a tradition that, prior to the twentieth century, was "openly viewed as such by most of those whom we might reasonably identify as participants in or bearers of that tradition."[12] But many disagree, so again rather than, or at least prior to, debating what a "tradition" is and whether America displays a "liberal tradition," it seems most productive to focus here on how we might understand the undeniable copresence in American political culture of both individual rights and racial inequalities.

In regard to racism, few scholars dispute that we can identify American scientific as well as religious discourses of racial inequality whose contributors, including figures like Thomas Jefferson, Josiah Nott, Josiah Strong, Madison Grant, and today Charles Murray, have consciously seen themselves as part of a shared, unfolding intellectual endeavor or tradition. But scholars disagree over whether their views count as political "ideologies" and, especially, over whether such discourses have been as significant in fostering racial inequalities as more emotional and often unconscious prejudices, anxieties, and stereotypes.[13] And whether they see American racist discourses as more ideological or more emotional, scholars also differ on their relationship to rights doctrines.

One final preliminary is key. Many modern scholars have followed Hochschild in terming the coexistence in America of advocacy for individual rights and for systems of racial inequality a "symbiosis," and as the title of this essay indicates, I regard that usage as apt. But I do so in part because the definition of the term "symbiosis" is itself disputed. Some insist that in biology, it means a close association of two animal or plant species "to their mutual benefit," relationships termed "mutualist symbiosis." The strongest such symbiosis would occur when neither species could exist without its relationship to other. Hochschild used "symbiosis" in something like this sense, saying it means that "liberal democracy and racism in the United States are historically, even inherently, reinforcing," having their "foundation in racially based slavery" and continuing to thrive today "only because racial discrimination continues."[14] The last phrase implies that American systems of rights would actually collapse if racial inequalities were to end.

But symbiosis often is used for more mildly mutually beneficial partnerships, and many scholars extend the term still further. They hold that "symbiosis" also includes "commensalist" relationships, in which one organism benefits and the other is neither much helped nor harmed, and "parasitic" relationships, in which one species predominantly benefits and the other is predominantly harmed.[15] Even these three categories do not exhaust the logical possibilities. We can also imagine symbiotic partnerships in which there are complex mixes of mutual harms and benefits that make it difficult to judge whether either party is better or worse off than it would be without the symbiosis, though both survive. And we can conceive of relationships that, over time, shape the evolution of both partners so that it is hard to know what standards to use to judge benefit or harm, since both have become something other than what they once were. Rather than simply using the umbrella term "symbiosis," then, I offer categories that specify the types of American rights/race partnerships that scholars have depicted.[16]

OPTIONS FOR UNDERSTANDING RIGHTS AND RACE IN AMERICA

Though logically there are many more possibilities, I see current scholarship as featuring four categories of responses to the coexistence of individual rights and racial inequalities in the United States, all of which have important variants: *anomaly* theories; *strongly reinforcing partnership* theories; *multiple liberalisms* theories; and theories of *contesting, contingent political partnerships*. All but the first endorse some sort of symbiosis between individual rights and inegalitarian racial doctrines (and even the first can be read to

do so). All but the last include versions presented as basically in accord with
Hartz, though often with modifications significant enough to make this
claim debatable.

Anomaly Theories

The type of account that is probably most politically palatable and widely
held in modern America is one that gained prominence in the mid-
twentieth century and to which Hartz's *Liberal Tradition* contributed. But as
Hochschild observed, it is most identified with Gunnar Myrdal's 1944 classic *An American Dilemma,* even though that sprawling, multiauthored work
also contains contrary arguments and evidence. Myrdal contended that in
the course of their revolutionary struggle, Americans elaborated and embraced an "American Creed" advancing ideals of the "dignity of the individual human being, of the fundamental equality of all men, and of certain inalienable rights to freedom, justice, and a fair opportunity." This
"equalitarian creed" then became the enduring "national *ethos*" that historically drove racial reforms, reforms that were, he averred, well on the road to
completion.[17] In contrast to the creedal commitments to equal rights,
which were "valuations preserved on the general plane" that Americans saw
as "morally higher," Myrdal thought inegalitarian racial doctrines, institutions, and practices expressed "*valuations on specific planes of individual and
group living,*" where American outlooks were dominated by "*personal and
local interests; economic, social, and sexual jealousies; considerations of community
prestige and conformity; group prejudice against particular persons or types of people;
and all sorts of miscellaneous wants, impulses and habits.*"

Myrdal nonetheless suggested that to some degree, America's endorsement of individual rights helped generate American racist ideologies, a
phenomenon that might be seen as a limited form of symbiosis. Myrdal said
that, whenever circumstances compelled Americans to focus on the conflicts between their racial injustices, rooted in specific interests, passions,
and prejudices, and their general creedal values, the American creed "calls
forth" doctrines of racial inequality to try to rationalize those inconsisten-
cies. But he laid far less stress on these intellectual doctrines than on white
prejudices and self-interest as sources of support for racial inequalities.[18]

For Myrdal, then, principles of equal individual rights, but not racial
doctrines, were at the core of American political culture. Individual rights
doctrines were relatively unchanging. They had no necessary, inextinguish-
able relationship to the persistence of racial inequalities but, instead, had
worked throughout American history to eliminate racial injustices. Myrdal

did see a historical linkage between American doctrines of rights and Americans' occasional elaborations of racial theories to explain away denials of those rights, but he did not proclaim the existence of any deep, mutually beneficial, "symbiosis." Instead, he presented racial ideologies as more ephemeral things, thin rationalizations generated by the clash between Americans' enduring egalitarian values and their unfortunate but corrigible racial prejudices and practices. Thus, in Myrdal's account, American racism was a regrettable, consequential, but still contingent anomaly, an "excrescence on a fundamentally healthy liberal democratic body," in Hochschild's words, that was gradually being excised—not a defining or permanent feature of American core values and institutions.[19]

In *The Liberal Tradition in America,* Hartz took a similar view, deeming the scientific racism of the antebellum American school of ethnography "one of the most vicious and antiliberal doctrines of modern times" and calling late-nineteenth-century doctrines of Anglo-Saxon racial superiority "basically alien to the national liberal spirit," while dismissing them as "the prejudice of loose elements" amid "the massive and uniform democratic faith" of the American "liberal community."[20] Many distinguished scholars have since written in similar veins.[21] And though some have modified their views in light of later critiques of Hartz, others, such as the historian Philip Gleason, explicitly reiterate that the American Creed has been more fundamental than doctrines or practices of racial inequality and that "historical experience has given us a deeper and more comprehensive understanding of our fundamental national values and what they require in practice."[22]

But scholarly critics of this fairly optimistic "anomaly" view of the relationship of individual rights doctrines to American racial inequalities are now numerous. Most see some kind of deeper symbiotic partnership in operation, though views on the nature of that partnership vary greatly.

Strongly Reinforcing Partnership Theories

The strongest "symbiosis" views see the ideas and institutions of individual rights and racial inequality in the United States as in fact so intimately connected as to make the metaphor of "symbiosis" almost inappropriate. These analysts see racism and rights advocacy not as two distinguishable entities but as ultimately two dimensions of one phenomenon, which some term "liberalism," some "modernity." In a representative statement, Richard Iton suggests that we should perhaps recognize "liberalism's need for the other and the compatibility of the liberal and ascriptive traditions, their dynamic interplay, and perhaps, at least in the American context, their practical and effective identity."[23] Most scholars stressing "symbiosis" agree that in America, race and rights have been, if not practically and effectively identical as Iton suggests, at least strongly mutually reinforcing. Yet many of their arguments actually seem to suggest something more like "commensalist" or "parasitic" symbioses, with significant differences on which has been the parasite and which has been the host.

Conceptualist theses.—Perhaps the most extreme imaginable versions of this "strongly mutualist symbiosis to the point of identity" position are ones that see individual rights as ineradicably linked to racial inequalities at the conceptual level. Yet though many writers suggest such views, particularly those employing postmodern approaches, it is hard to find fully elaborated defenses of these claims. Building on Michel Foucault's notion of "biopower" as well as on the works of Toni Morrison, Jane Flax, for example, contends that "race/gender based inclusions and exclusions, are internal to individualism and democratic republicanism." From the start of U.S. history, "the modal American citizen, the liberal individual, was in fact white and male," because notions of individual "autonomy" were defined in opposition to slavery and female dependence. If "overt legal or cultural support" for this "ascriptive material internal to individualism and citizenship" is ever "(temporarily) withdrawn from such subject formation," she maintains, it must somehow be reestablished, or "the alienation that is intrinsic to modern liberal culture" will be "more evident." Yet though such reassertions are liberal prerequisites, they should not be too explicit, because "liberal and democratic republican ideas . . . require a homogeneous, universal individual as rights bearer" and cannot acknowledge "the inescapable race/gender specificity of all modern subjects."[24] Hence the symbiosis: racial inequalities are legitimated by abstract individual rights doctrines, while the proponents of those doctrines need stabilizing support for their ascriptive racial and gender identities.

Arguments like Flax's gain credibility from the reality that historically, full American citizenship was long denied to those who were not white or were not male. It is not clear, however, that she is making the sort of "strongly reinforcing" symbiosis view to which Hochschild referred, because those accounts must show that individual rights doctrines and inegalitarian racial precepts are *mutually* beneficial. Flax's account, like many others, focuses only on why individual rights doctrines need stabilizing ascriptive boundaries. She does not argue explicitly that ascriptive and race/gender-based doctrines, which she says have often had "overt" legal and cultural support, have also needed legitimation by universal individual rights doctrines to exist or persist. Nor does she make clear whether the inegalitarian discourses conceptually require or imply the "universal individual" rights doctrines they explicitly reject. Flax's arguments suggest instead that, at least at the conceptual level, individual rights doctrines may exist in "commensalist" symbiosis, with racial inequalities benefiting from them but not much helping or harming them, if they are not actually parasitic upon them, needing them for stabilization but also challenging them.

The character and strength of the conceptual linkages she perceives are also unclear. No scholar has shown that conceptually, notions of individual rights bearers *must* be defined in opposition to an "other" that is not white or not male. Rather, arguments that suggest, as Judith Shklar did, that the "value" of having standing as a full civic rights–bearer in early America "derived primarily" from denials of this standing "to slaves, to some white men, and to all women" seem more contingently contextual, social psychological, and political.[25] Shklar saw the narrow early definitions of American rights-bearers as political efforts by the more privileged to secure their "social standing" in a context of preexisting racial and gender hierarchies, efforts she thought were not "not easily reconciled" with egalitarian rights doctrines.[26] She interpreted ensuing struggles for equal rights as political efforts to break down "barriers to recognition," to social standing; and though she saw those struggles as continuing into the present because the unequal conditions to which they responded "have not disappeared," Shklar did not argue for any unalterable, permanent linkages between rights doctrines and race (or gender) inequalities.[27] Historic associations alone did not imply for her either philosophic necessity or political destiny.

Uday Mehta is perhaps the scholar who has most carefully made the case for close conceptual connections between doctrines of individual rights and racial subordinations and exclusions. In an important essay and two books, he argues for the existence of "a theoretical space from within which liberal exclusion can be seen as intrinsic to liberalism." If not quite "a theoretically dictated necessity," exclusion is not "merely an occasional happenstance of purely contingent significance."[28] Most pertinent to Hartz's claims about American "Lockianism," Mehta argues that for Locke, all individuals are indeed born free, and equally so. But this natural freedom provokes anxiety in Locke, a fear that persons will act in anarchic ways that violate what he presents as rational natural laws. Locke believes that the only practical response is for people to be educated, to have their rationality developed, in at least general accord with the "complex constellation of social structures and conventional norms" that constitute the societies in which they live, including those norms deemed appropriate to their social status.[29] The result can be to stifle many forms of individuality and, worse, to embrace

invidious forms of social hierarchy and to deny the rationality and entitle-
ment to political inclusion of those conventionally deemed inadequate or
even simply unfamiliar within prevailing social contexts.[30]

Mehta's reading of Locke shows well why the unsettling implications of
broad doctrines of individual rights and liberties might prompt even those
who subscribe to such doctrines to seek to bound them through cultivating
senses of rationality that express and respect many of the structures and customs of their communities. But though Mehta says his focus is on "theoretical" linkages between rights and social inequalities, his emphasis on the
"anxiety" of freedom suggests this quest can be understood in emotional or
psychological terms, and it might also be seen as expressing political judgments about how principles of natural liberty can best be realized in particular contexts. Thus read, Mehta's account reinforces the psychological and
political theses discussed below. Because it leads us to expect doctrines of individual rights to be elaborated differently in different social contexts, it is
also consonant with accounts stressing multiple and evolving "liberalisms."

As Mehta states, he does *not* show any conceptual "necessity" for linkages
between rights doctrines and racial inequalities specifically or, I would add,
any "strongly mutually reinforcing" form of rights/race symbiosis. His symbiosis is again more one-sided. He depicts psychological and political pressures to render rights doctrines less threatening to deeply entrenched inegalitarian social conditions. He does not claim that the inegalitarian
conditions reciprocally require embrace of Lockean conceptions of natural
rights and freedom. Those conceptions are presented as dangers, not sup-
ports, for social conditions like American systems of racial inequality; that is
why they must be bounded. And though it is undeniable that in America,
rights doctrines have in fact long been bounded in ways that have permitted the persistence of deeply entrenched racial inequalities, more historical
investigation is required before we can conclude that Americans have had
no other way to settle anxieties stirred by rights doctrines than by embracing racial hierarchies, or that denials of appropriate rationality to African
Americans, among others, were ever intellectually coherent, even according to the standards of the day. If they were not, their subordination in
America cannot be said to follow necessarily or indeed consistently from a
Lockean stress on the need for rationality in all citizens.

Nor, without more support, does Mehta's argument about the "theoretical opening" that rights doctrines create give us reason to affirm Hartz and
to assert that those "liberal" doctrines have been more fundamental to or
more definitive of American political culture than its racial conditions,
much less that they have been the source of racial inequalities. Because its

thrust is to suggest that rights doctrines generally must be limited by preexisting inegalitarian conditions that they otherwise challenge, it rather implies that those inegalitarian conditions are most fundamental. If liberal rights doctrines can survive only if they do not endanger organic parts of their social hosts too much, they seem to be more in "parasitic symbiosis" with preexisting hierarchical structures than to be the conceptual or ideological centers of the societies that adopt them. Rather than supporting those who believe that Hartz's "liberal idea" of individual rights has lain "underneath" racial doctrines and practices in America, Mehta's account, like Flax's, makes it seem more the other way around: racial doctrines and practices have lain "underneath" rights doctrines.[31] And supporters of inegalitarian conditions seem to have experienced this overlay more as burden than benefit.

Economic theses.—We would reach different conclusions, however, if doctrines, institutions, and practices of individual rights appeared to have helped generate America's conditions of racial inequality. Thus, reflection on the implications of Mehta's analysis for "strongly reinforcing partnership" claims compels us to examine how inegalitarian racial conditions originated in the United States. The undisputed starting points are the British American colonial practices of displacing the native tribes and imposing chattel slavery on (primarily) Africans. Scholars overwhelmingly agree that the colonists involved saw these measures as economically advantageous, if not necessary, and that notions of "white" superiority, in civilization and perhaps in nature, soon proliferated in response to the unequal conditions the colonists established.[32] Many of the settlers who came to label themselves "white" also eventually decided that they could further their economic interests by embracing developing bourgeois conceptions of property rights.

Some analysts, particularly those writing in Marxian traditions, therefore suggest that the rise and maintenance of unequal racial conditions in America can be traced back to specifically capitalist notions of individual property rights, as well as to the material interests they served. On such views, British and more generally European imperial expansion arose out of emergent market capitalist interests and ideologies; when European imperialists encountered distinct populations in Africa and the Americas, they then sought to exploit their resources and labor, and the competitive market systems they crafted then generated continuing pressures for economic acquisitions that were served by varying forms of racial discrimination and exploitation. On such views, capitalist doctrines of individual economic rights and inegalitarian racial ideologies are all expressive of, and limited by, the material interests of the groups who propagated them. Racial discourses, in particular, are one way in which, in Immanuel Wallerstein's words, "historical capitalism" resolves one of its "basic contradictions," its "simultaneous thrust for theoretical equality and practical inequality." [33] So while there *are* theoretical contradictions between individual rights doctrines and racial inequalities, these are superficial. The rights doctrines and the inequalities are both rooted in and strongly linked at the level of economic activity, "strongly reinforcing" each other in their symbiotic service to the economic interests of those propagating them.

Though plausible in general outline, such economic symbiosis arguments require much elaboration and evidence if they are to be fully convincing. Important issues of timing, sequence, and causality need clarification. Did individual rights doctrines actually *drive* European imperial ventures? That seems unlikely, since monarchies claiming absolute power launched many of those ventures, and they predate much economic writing in the "liberal tradition," however defined. It is more credible to assert that capitalist rights doctrines, like racist doctrines, were elaborated later to express and justify still emergent economic interests. But if so, these doctrines may appear epiphenomenal to economic factors in ways that many analysts find unduly reductive and deterministic, erroneously denying the constructed character of both economic and racial statuses and relationships. [34] Yet if capitalist imperatives did not actually mandate the propagation of doctrines of race and individual rights, were either or both those doctrines, much less their recurrent intertwining, really economically required, or were they simply politically convenient?

In any case, which came first in America—rights doctrines and capitalist economic arrangements, or racial doctrines and racially unequal economic structures? Or did they arise together? Answers here are important for those who, like Hartz, contend that "liberal" economic rights doctrines, institutions, and practices have *always* been more fundamental to American political culture than racial ones. If so, economic rights doctrines cannot have arisen later. Whether or not they did, what about subsequent material racial inequalities in U.S. history: did all stem from policies and practices that actually furthered capitalist economic interests, or were many—such as the public carrier segregation laws that most transportation companies opposed—neither economically efficient by capitalist standards nor consistent with capitalist conceptions of economic rights, but, rather, merely satisfying to white racists? Those answers are important for those who contend that doctrines of individual rights and unequal races have necessarily been paired in America for economic reasons.

And because the historical sequencing and relationship of racial and capitalist economic doctrines are in dispute, because it is also not clear how far America's structures of racial discrimination were actually economically optimal even for white capitalists, it is unclear that the answers to these still unresolved questions will fully support "strongly reinforcing" economic accounts. Instead of providing thoroughgoing defenses of such claims, many recent scholars stressing economic interests have concluded that economic factors cannot do the whole job of explaining American racial inequalities. They agree that accounts of economic interests must be supplemented by acknowledging that whites, especially poorer whites, have received what W. E. B. Du Bois called a "psychological wage" of higher social standing. This psychological benefit accounts for whites' support of inegalitarian policies that were *not* in their economic best interests.[35] Though no one who has considered the relationships of rights and race doctrines in America has claimed that the service of racial ideologies to systems of economic inequality has been historically unimportant, scholars are now giving considerable attention to psychological linkages.

Psychological theses.—Derrick Bell is perhaps the most prominent scholar to have long stressed that a "major function of racial discrimination is to facilitate the exploitation of black labor" but whose arguments for the probable permanence of racial inequalities rest even more on psychological grounds. Bell contends that "even those whites who lack wealth and power" are willing to accept such disadvantages so long as they are "sustained in their sense of racial superiority" by receiving "priority over blacks and other people of color for access to whatever opportunities are left."[36] Bell believes that racism is thoroughly "internalized and institutionalized" in American society, so that progress for blacks can come only when their interests converge with those of whites—and white commitments to sustaining their relatively superior position over blacks, even at some cost to their overall economic well-being, suggests that white and black interests can never converge fully enough to realize "racial equality goals."[37] Though Bell has often written in more traditional Marxian and Hartzian terms that depict American racial inequalities as rooted in its capitalist economic relations, in passages like these he suggests that America's racial order is even more fundamental to American society than its economic order, and obviously deeper than inclusive principles of equal rights.

But how are we to understand the benefits to whites of this "sense of racial superiority"? Do they amount to no more than the prerogative to be ahead of nonwhites in the queue for restricted economic opportunities? Many scholars offer less materially centered interpretations. Using somewhat different interpretive routes, Margaret Kohn and Laura Janara have both found in the writings of Alexis de Tocqueville and his friend Gustave de Beaumont "extra-economic," psychological arguments connecting the spread of democratic rights to American racism in ways that resemble Shklar's arguments about historical concerns with "standing" and Mehta's contentions about the anxieties generated by notions of individual rights more generally.[38] By challenging the "fixed hierarchies and categories," the "familiar forms of social differentiation" that "stabilized relationships in aristocratic times," both scholars suggest, democracy creates "uncertainty . . . flux . . . anxiety" that foster a "covert companion desire for the comforts and predictability of hierarchy."[39] Since British Americans had in the colonial era already labeled the indigenous peoples as "uncivilized" and Africans as fit for slavery, whites in the early Republic could maintain a sense of secure social status only by believing they sat atop a racial hierarchy. Those beliefs were so important to white Americans' psyches as to make "U.S. racism and democracy . . . mutually constitutive," and to render whites prone to explosive violence if their whiteness or white privileges were threatened.[40]

Again, these claims are plausible, but more work is needed to determine how far we should take them and how much they explain. Do they mean that systems of democratic rights can *never* exist without something like racial hierarchies, so that if they had not existed, they would have had to be invented? Did American racial hierarchies, in turn, somehow need or require the spread of democracy? The answers to both must be yes to uphold the strongest sorts of "mutually reinforcing" symbiosis claims. Or is it that preexisting racial hierarchies did not foster democracy but, given their presence, democracy could not be sustainable unless it accommodated them? That account appears, again, to present democracy as more "parasitic" on or at least in "commensalist" symbiosis with continuing racial inequalities.

Either way, just how permanent is this American partnership of democracy and racism? Are these "psychopolitical" linkages ineradicable or sufficiently weak that Americans can eventually break them and have democracy without unequal racial statuses?[41] Might it even have been psychologically possible for Americans to democratize in the past *without* strengthening racist commitments, although they failed to do so? Since they failed to do so, should America be seen historically as a political community whose identity is defined essentially by commitments to democratic rights, among other individual rights, in Hartzian fashion? Or have its unequal racial conditions been more constitutive and definitive? Many of these issues are interpretive ones that will remain subject to legitimate dispute even with more-thorough historical and empirical work. But it should be possible to clarify via evidence how far such psychological explanations can account for phenomena that conceptual and economic explanations cannot, and whether American history displays patterns and developments that support or challenge the strongest versions of these "mutually reinforcing" psychological theses of symbiosis.

Political theses.—In any case, psychological arguments, like conceptual and economic ones, are often elements in more fundamentally political theses about how doctrines of rights and race have partnered, and perhaps necessarily partnered, in American experience. As Hochschild noted, the historian Edmund Morgan argued that in colonial Virginia, Bacon's Rebellion in 1676 stirred patrician fears that poorer whites might align with slaves against the privileged classes. Morgan saw the elites' "answer" to this political problem, "gradually recognized," as the elaboration of "racism, to separate dangerous free whites from dangerous free blacks by a screen of racial contempt."[42] This political strategy continued later when Virginia tobacco plantation owners refrained from swallowing up small white planters and instead allowed them "not only to prosper but also to acquire social, psychological, and political advantages" over African slaves and free blacks.[43] And ultimately, Virginia patricians won poorer whites' support for their own revolution against Britain by promising them equal rights in a republic in which most labor would be done by slaves who would have no rights.[44]

We might conclude, then, that American revolutionary doctrines of equal individual economic and political rights and American doctrines of racial inequality both arose from the political needs of colonial elites to win poorer whites' support for the systems of economic production and political governance that elites favored and that favored elites. This is clearly a "strongly reinforcing" symbiosis account—but how strong? Does it imply that racial inequalities were politically *necessary* for the creation of American systems of rights, and vice versa? Morgan was more cautious: "This is not to say that a belief in republican equality had to rest on slavery, but only that in Virginia (and probably in other southern colonies) it did."[45] Still, once it did, states arose that threatened not to accept a common constitution unless it countenanced slavery; and scholars have long debated whether America's constitutional system could have been created without acceding to many of their demands. Perhaps, then, in America's historical context, the protection of rights within a national republic would have been *politically* impossible without acceptance of slavery and other forms of racial inequality, and the development of that constitutional system, in turn, assisted the spread of slavery and discourses and institutions of racial inequality at least up to the Civil War.[46]

None have defended this "strongly reinforcing" political symbiosis thesis more ardently than Joel Olson. Citing the arguments of Morgan, Bell, and others, he writes, "Racial oppression makes full democracy impossible, but it has also made American democracy possible. Conversely, American democracy has made racial oppression possible, for neither slavery nor segregation nor any other form of racial domination could have survived without the tacit or explicit consent of the white majority."[47] Olson maintains that "there is no *necessary* contradiction" between doctrines of democratic individual rights and a privileged status for whites, because while logically, "absolute equality and privilege conflict," when "equality is reserved only for some . . . it can co-exist with privilege."[48]

Focusing not so much on American "democracy" as on the construction of nationality, citizenship, and the federal state in America, Lauren Basson has also concluded that "racialized assumptions" have been so thoroughly interwoven into American identity that in order to be politically successful, "political activists" across "the entire political landscape" have had to employ different kinds of "racialized discourse" in which "race played a crucial role in the definition of nation and state."[49] She contends that in the political processes of constituting the American nation and state, "liberal, republican and ascriptive strands became inextricably intertwined and impossible to recognize as conceptually distinct approaches," so that treating them as separate traditions masks the "often silently shared assumptions among discourses," especially the racial assumptions of American liberalism.[50] Her use of the adverb "inextricably" suggests that Basson sees this strong symbiosis as unbreakable, but she does not develop this claim. Instead, she maintains that in America, "whiteness gained its meaning through" political "contestations" and that "policymakers, government officials, and other professionals" continually adjusted "the meaning of whiteness in order to best serve their interests" in their contexts.[51] She leaves it unclear whether they might ever find it politically possible and in their interests to do so in ways that would promote genuine racial equality.

These political theses have great force. There can be no denying that American citizenship, nationality, state structures, and political institutions have been historically structured in ways that long protected slavery and that for much longer have protected many entrenched forms of white advantage. There is also no doubt that through most of American history, most American whites with voting rights have exercised them in ways that sustained their advantages. It is indeed plausible to say that at the political level, the systems of individual rights that Americans created and the systems of racial inequalities they created have often worked to sustain each other in "mutualist symbiosis" fashion.

Still, important questions must be answered before we can affirm either the strongest possible symbiotic claims or Hartzian interpretations of what this political intertwining of rights and race means for characterizations of American political culture. Did America's revolutionary leaders and constitutional framers *need* to make such extensive concessions to slaveholders and champions of racial inequality as they did in order to succeed? Even if they did, can this legacy be overcome—can Americans ever separate the fulfillment of democratic ideals from racial discriminations? Bell expresses great doubt; Basson suggests doubt too while taking no definitive stance; but Olson explicitly departs from the strongest versions of political symbiosis by arguing that Americans can do so.[52] Though he says there is no necessary contradiction between democratic ideals and white privilege, he recognizes that this is true only if we depart from Hartz and bestow the term "democracy" on systems in which "equality is reserved only for some" of those deemed citizens.[53] He thinks it possible for American notions of rights to evolve, that Americans can choose a far more "full" democracy that abolishes racial inequalities, so democratic rights and racism are not "inherently" reinforcing on a permanent basis. It would nonetheless be wrong to read Olson or any of these other proponents of political symbiosis theses as suggesting that American racism has been somehow an anomaly that can be overcome without radically transforming America. Instead, their portraits of the American political symbiosis of race and rights suggest, contrary to Myrdal and Hartz, that commitments to racial orderings have been as much or more constitutive of American political culture as have egalitarian versions of democracy, because they have successfully limited the scope of democratic rights and the breadth of egalitarian themes in political discourses.

Multiple Liberalisms Theories

Other scholars express variants of a third general position, distinct from both "anomaly" theses and the various "strongly reinforcing partnership" theses. They accept that there are some conceptual, economic, psychological, and particularly political linkages between American doctrines of individual rights and racial inequality, though most do not address whether any of these types of linkages should be given priority. But more firmly than the advocates of most "strongly reinforcing partnership" theories, they reject the notion that rights and racism are inherently and permanently necessary to each other. They affirm the historical existence of nonracist rights doctrines, along with racist ones. They differ over whether racism or individual rights have been the dominant partner in the historical linkages they observe.

Racism as subordinate partner theses.—Some "multiple liberalisms" writers explicitly resist any claim that inegalitarian racial discourses, institutions, and practices have been more fundamental in or definitive of American political culture than individual rights doctrines. They contend that something like Hartz's 1964 argument is correct: racial inequalities in the United States have generally been defended in terms of liberal and democratic conceptions of rights, because these conceptions are Americans' core values. Racism in their view has not been the anomaly it was for Myrdal or for Hartz in 1955, but it is nonetheless the lesser partner in what must still be deemed a basically liberal democratic society.

To make this case, most modern Hartzians have felt compelled to reject two features of Hartz's understanding of liberal doctrines of individual rights, while emphasizing a third more than he did. They abandon his insistence that liberalism holds that all who are recognized as human must receive "completely equal treatment" in terms of basic rights and his view that American doctrines of individual rights have been relatively static and unchanged in U.S. history. And they stress more than Hartz did the presence of "illiberalism" in America, including inegalitarian racial discourses, though they depict these as having subordinate or marginal statuses.

J. David Greenstone's *The Lincoln Persuasion,* which sees in U.S. history both "humanist liberalism," protective of "negative" liberties, and "reform liberalism," aimed at more active empowerment, is a seminal text for "multiple liberalisms" theories.[54] But Greenstone did not deal extensively with inegalitarian racism, so more pertinent here are the works of two of his students, David Ericson and Carol Horton. Ericson defines as "liberal" those discourses that "appeal to personal freedom, equal worth, government by consent, and private ownership of property," but he does not think equal worth implies equal treatment or equal rights.[55] His central claim in favor of "liberal consensus" views is that not just antislavery critics but also antebellum defenders of slavery "offered predominantly liberal arguments" on behalf of the most illiberal institution in U.S. history—all the more so over time. They did so, Ericson believes, because they found that liberal arguments worked best to persuade "other Americans" even of slavery's legitimacy.[56] On this account racial inequalities seem parasitic on America's liberal rights doctrines, because they have been sustainable only when defended in such terms.

Ericson's work is exemplary in focusing on the sorts of historical evidence that can deepen our understanding of the relationships of rights discourses and racial inequalities in American experience. Still, his interpretations are debatable. He usefully canvasses many defenses of racial inequities, more than can be considered here. But he especially stresses as proof of the increasing "liberalism" of proslavery discourses the frequently noted transition from early justifications of slavery as a "necessary evil" to late antebellum celebrations of slavery as a "positive good." Slavery was deemed good in part because blacks were increasingly portrayed as people who could flourish best, and whose worth would be best realized, if they remained slaves for the foreseeable future.[57] Ericson concludes that proslavery rhetoric increasingly focused on rights and on blacks as having "equal worth," in liberal fashion. Yet the same evidence also shows that inegalitarian racial discourses denying that blacks could benefit from equal rights rose in prominence during the antebellum period, and that proslavery forces more explicitly subordinated rights doctrines to them. It is debatable whether this pattern proves that liberal rights rhetoric became more prevalent than inegalitarian racial discourses. Even if so, it is also unclear whether this shows that American racism was a subordinate partner in a fundamentally "liberal consensus" society, whether rights arguments were tools used for racially inegalitarian purposes in a fundamentally "white supremacist" one, or whether both descriptions are one-sided.

Ericson's account of the rise to predominance of liberal views of individual rights ends with the Civil War, so he does not consider the surge of inegalitarian racial intellectual and political discourses in the late nineteenth century, after the era in which he believes political rhetoric became still more liberal. In *Race and the Making of American Liberalism,* Carol Horton does so, but in ways that vary from Ericson's analysis. Though she also does not define liberalism as requiring fully equal rights, she does think it must accord "the most elemental rights" to all, and she sees in American political culture some "nonliberal racial ideologies" that have denied blacks even very basic rights.[58] Like Ericson, however, she believes that these ideologies "have generally occupied a relatively small corner of the American political landscape."[59] She sees late-nineteenth-century America as rejecting the "anti-caste," more egalitarian "liberalism" of the antislavery movement in favor of "Darwinian liberalism," whose adherents "paired ideologies of white supremacism and laissez-faire liberalism" but remained fundamentally liberals because they believed blacks were entitled to basic economic rights.[60]

Yet Horton also says that these Darwinian liberals were "usually willing to violate these minimal guarantees," supporting Jim Crow restrictions on economic rights, and that as those laws spread, Darwinian liberalism was "largely eclipsed by the even more violent politics of white nationalism," in which both African and Chinese Americans "were deemed inherently incapable of assuming the rights" of citizenship.[61] Her evidence suggests, then, that even her inegalitarian Darwinian liberalism, along with more egalitarian versions, came to be subordinated for a long stretch of U.S. history to "nonliberal" discourses of racial inequality; though Horton herself concludes merely that "liberalism" had become fully "racially exclusive," in a way that violates her definition of liberalism.[62] It is again debatable whether these patterns demonstrate that "liberal" doctrines of "elemental rights" have been more politically fundamental throughout the history of American politics than inegalitarian racial discourses denying African Americans rights, so that all these positions should be deemed forms of "liberalism" in Horton's sense.

Liberalism as subordinate partner.—The philosopher Charles Mills has long argued powerfully for a more conceptualist "multiple liberalisms" view that rejects the Hartzian relationship of discourses of racial inequality and liberal rights that Ericson and Horton defend. He contends that "liberal" doctrines of individual rights and racial inequality "have been intertwined for hundreds of years" in the United States and elsewhere, because "the same developments that brought liberalism into existence . . . also brought race into existence as a set of restrictions and entitlements governing the application" of rights doctrines.[63] Those developments were "European expansionism, and the conquest and expropriation of indigenous peoples," as theorists of economic symbiosis argue.[64] Mills sees social contract doctrines as central to modern liberal philosophy, and he contends that the most influential versions of social contract theory, crafted in the context of this exploitative European expansionism, have been "racial contracts," in which only white males were conceived as capable contractors.[65]

Mills insists, moreover, that these racial limitations should not be seen as "prejudices" or unconscious assumptions. Racism has been "*a normative system in its own right*" that has been "symbiotically related" to individual rights doctrines in social contract theories and, particularly, in American political experience.[66] But though Mills sees liberal rights doctrines as in fact massively "racialized" historically, he does not believe this has occurred "as a matter of conceptual necessity."[67] So he does not endorse the strongest conceptualist versions of symbiosis theories, in which liberal rights doctrines and racial inequalities cannot be separated. Mills instead sees, with

Michael Dawson, historical forms of "black liberalism," among others, that have challenged white supremacist liberalism in America, and he calls for pursuit of "the promise of a nonracial liberalism and a genuinely inclusive social contract."[68]

Like Ericson and Horton, then, Mills depicts the existence of multiple racist and nonracist forms of liberalism. But unlike them, he argues, "Actually racism *is* the dominant tradition" in the United States historically and more broadly in the European-crafted "philosophy of modernity."[69] Though nonracial liberal rights doctrines are historically discernible, thus far they have been marginal to what Mills calls the "hybrid system" of "white-supremacist" or "racial liberalism" in America and elsewhere.[70] Mills's choice of "liberalism" as the noun and "racial" as the modifier may seem to place him still in the Hartzian camp. However, Mills, like Mehta and others, suggests that, rather than racial inequalities being sustained by the liberal defenses acceptable in a liberal consensus society, in America and many other "modern" contexts, rights doctrines have been acceptable only when crafted to serve rather than endanger racism.

Like some proponents of stronger conceptual versions of symbiosis, however, Mills does not explain why Americans and other participants in "modernity" have often chosen to deploy universalistic, egalitarian rights doctrines instead of just explicitly confining rights to white males. On his account, it cannot be because they felt politically compelled to persuade believers in a Hartzian liberal consensus. His view is probably best understood as reliant on economic theses holding that racialized economic rights doctrines have served the material interests of European imperialists and the governors of many of their former colonies. Like the final set of authors, he also suggests that conceiving of rights as racialized served the political goals of those who advanced them.

Theories of Contesting, Contingent Political Partnerships

Scholars in this fourth category, myself among them, interpret America's historical symbiosis of rights and race as more purely a political partnership than any of the preceding accounts. Most of us analyze these partnerships as dimensions of elite-led efforts at nation and state building and as aspects of the coalition building involved in creating and sustaining political parties and social movements. The content of culturally available ideas, prevailing and emerging economic interests, and psychological needs provide the contexts for these nation, party, and movement building political endeavors, and so all these factors help us understand why political actors make

the choices they do and why some efforts have had much better chances of
success than others. These positions also contend as strongly as any other
that the political discourses, institutions, and practices that have prevailed
historically in the United States have embodied intertwined rights doctrines and inegalitarian racial ones as constitutive features.

But on these accounts, the constituting of America as a blend of individual rights and racial inequalities has not been *necessitated* by the conceptual
presuppositions of rights, by economic conditions, or by the psychological
and political anxieties characteristic of American "liberalism" or "democracy."[71] Those circumstances made such blends politically potent and contributed to their success, but both efforts to extend and efforts to deny
rights in racially inclusive ways have always been contested, and the fluctuat-
ing historical patterns of rights and race in different regions and different
eras suggest that the outcomes have always been to some degree contingent. And if we accept their claims for contestation and contingency, then
these views imply that it is not inevitable that rights in the United States will
continue to be constructed in ways that perpetuate racial inequalities. It is
simply politically probable, at least for the foreseeable future.

Analysts in this camp agree that the historical result of contingent, contested processes of nation, party, and movement building in the United
States has been to shift the laws of the nation, the policies of the parties,
and the agendas of successful movements more in the direction of the sorts
of egalitarian individual rights doctrines that Hartz defined as "liberal." But
none would agree with Hartz that doctrines of individual rights have had
fundamentally the same content throughout American history and across
most of the spectrum of American politics. Instead, these scholars see substantial shifts in the content of dominant American political ideologies over
time that constitute important forms of American political development.
They differ over whether it is most important to stress the complicity of liberal ideas in racial inequalities to grasp the power and place of racial inequalities in American history, or whether that focus ends up still unduly
minimizing racial ideologies, eclipsing them behind an all-encompassing
liberalism.

Multiple traditions theses.—Along with others, I take the second view.[72]
Since the late 1980s, I have argued that early America's ideational and economic contexts were more varied than Hartz's "liberal idea" account indicated. They included distinguishable conceptions of civic republicanism,
and especially doctrines, institutions, and practices of racial and gender
hierarchies that structured the resources, constraints, and indeed the
senses of identities and interests available to American political actors. I

have contended in particular that in their efforts to "forge a revolutionary people," American colonial elites felt compelled to move beyond their vulnerable claims of rights under the British Constitution to defenses of their cause in terms of natural rights, but that at the same time, most judged it infeasible if not undesirable to extend such rights equally to the African Americans, Native Americans, and women in their political communities. Still, some revolutionaries contested such exclusions, and in any case, political rhetoricians can rarely pause to detail and justify all the qualifications to their appeals for broad support. So revolutionary political discourses and documents often used universalistic, egalitarian language, even when laws, policies, and practices explicitly included forms of racial and gender subordination. As a result, I have portrayed the early American nation and state as constituted by "multiple traditions"—some doctrines of universalistic, egalitarian individual economic and political rights, some exclusionary doctrines in ways that were in logical tension but that were successful in building political coalitions broad enough that the Revolution could be won and new governments constituted. In the altered political, economic, and cultural contexts thus created, I have argued, "almost all political leaders" and "political parties" and movements "relied on congenial aspects" of "liberal, republican, and ascriptive" racial and gender conceptions that they "mixed" in different ways to "gain political leverage against their opponents."[73]

Subsequently, Philip Klinkner and I argued that Americans had made systems of racial inequality so pervasive in their national life that building coalitions in support of substantial egalitarian reforms has proven impossible outside of times of intense external threats and domestic political pressures. We identified three such periods: the Revolutionary War, incubating gradual emancipation in the North; the Civil War, ending slavery throughout the country; and the World War II/Cold War era, which made possible the ending of Jim Crow segregation. But we saw racial inequalities as so deeply entrenched that in between those reform eras, Americans rebuilt new, if on the whole lesser, forms of racial hierarchy, so that much of American history displays stagnation and partial retreats in struggles for racial progress.[74] Desmond King and I have added that the periods between reform eras have been politically structured via rival coalitions formed around certain battleground issues that have defined those epochs—slavery in the antebellum period, Jim Crow from the end of Reconstruction to the 1960s, and today, conflicts over whether public policies and institutions should be "color-blind" or race conscious.[75] In these works, we have portrayed all the political actors, organizations, and coalitions involved as continuing to blend ideas of race and individual rights in distinct ways. And we

have argued that as matters of contingent but reconstitutive political struggles, political forces championing more extensive (but still far from full) racial equality have come to predominate in American life.

In sum, multiple traditions analyses adopt milder versions of the accounts of conceptual, economic, and psychological linkages between
American doctrines of rights and racial inequalities, stressing that these
doctrines have been neither unitary nor easily harmonized logically, but
that American leaders, parties, and movements have adopted versions of
both in order to build coalitions capable of forging and sustaining a political community and support for their governance within it. These views can
be read as seeing American racism and rights as two dimensions of one phenomenon, but that phenomenon is not best described as "liberalism," "democracy," or "racism." It is better described as "the American political tradition," understood as the politics of building the American nation and state
and the organizations and coalitions that can gain power within it. It is
"American political culture," "American political development," and
"American governance" that should be seen as politically combining all
these elements historically as constitutive. And rather than depicting
American politics as a struggle between these elements—"liberalism" versus
"democracy" or "liberalism" versus "racism"—a multiple traditions approach suggests we must analyze American politics as involving clashes
between the ideologies and policies of competing political parties such as
Jeffersonians and Federalists, Jacksonians and Whigs, Republicans and
Democrats; between social movement organizations such as the National
Association for the Advancement of Colored People and the Ku Klux Klan;
and between broader racial alliances such as proslavery and antislavery coalitions. All of these can be expected to advance distinct, often novel blends
of the ideas available to them to define purposes and win support in their
varying and evolving political contexts.[76]

Liberal complicity theses.—To many scholars, even those who stress political
linkages and do not see the American symbiosis of race and rights as necessary and inescapable, such "multiple traditions" accounts still fail to capture
just how deeply and broadly inegalitarian racial discourses have structured
American politics. Though these scholars do not depict the United States as
a "liberal consensus" society, they argue that it is particularly important to
recognize how what they see as liberal ideas, including ideas of individual
rights, have contributed to American racial inequalities—especially because such ideas now predominate in the United States, whether or not
they have always done so.

Exemplary here among many outstanding analysts is Catherine Holland, who argues that American political development does display "a variety of competing and often *il*liberal traditions" that are "historical products of founding and refounding an American nation" and that still "shape civic activity."[77] Like those who argue for a still stronger symbiosis on conceptual and psychological grounds, Holland suggests that modern liberal democracies involve "the dissolution of the palpable markers of certainty that undergirded the cosmic sense of place" in earlier societies in ways that can "generate collective anxieties," provoking reassertions of orders attributed to characteristics of human bodies.[78] This means that "complex countertendencies and traces of archaic political and ideological commitments . . . inhabit both American liberalism and modern political thought more generally."[79] But though Holland believes inegalitarian commitments "inhabit" American liberalism, she analyzes their presence as products of the processes of American political development and does not argue that they can never be eradicated. Like other "contingent, contesting political partnerships" accounts, hers leaves open the possibility that under some circumstances, political actors and institutions might construct more egalitarian racial identities and statuses. But like many others, Holland nonetheless contends that this presence of inegalitarian values, including racial ones, within American liberalism is obscured if we define liberalism so that it is analytically wholly distinct from racism.[80]

Stephen Skowronek has advanced a related but different concern. Using the example of Woodrow Wilson, he contends that in responding to the challenges of their political contexts, American political figures have sometimes creatively reconstituted the ideas available to them to create new political ideologies. Skowronek argues that Wilson, a southern man attached to states' rights in part for racial reasons, reconfigured those ideas to formulate a new internationalist vision embracing rights of national self-determination that took on "a life of its own" as a new kind of inclusive liberalism, even though for Wilson it really only applied to "advanced" democracies.[81]

Skowronek's account is convincing, but he does not define liberalism, so it is hard to judge just how "new" he thinks Wilson's "internationalist liberalism" was. That omission is pertinent here, because Skowronek suggests that a multiple traditions framework requires us to treat traditions as fundamentally unchanging, and so it cannot grasp how political actors might creatively recombine ideas in ways that can generate genuine political development.[82] Multiple traditions analyses therefore miss, again, just how deeply intertwined inegalitarian ascriptive ideas and notions of individual

rights have been in American life. To judge whether this is a real difference between Skowronek's approach and a multiple traditions framework,
Skowronek's standards for what is required to deem a position "still liberalism but a new liberalism" would have to be clarified. In any case, Skowronek's argument remains one in which political figures exercise agency
by drawing on political ideas available in their contexts to craft policies
and principles that can win support for their purposes, so it too falls in the
family of "competing, contingent partnership" explanations. His example
also suggests that, even against the intentions of their proponents, the new
political perspectives leaders forge can work toward more racially egalitarian ends.

CONCLUSION

At a minimum, the preceding discussion should persuade most readers
that there is a range of relatively plausible views on the relationships of individual rights and inegalitarian racial doctrines in the United States, and
many questions about those relationships still to be answered. Scholars
differ on how closely connected race and rights are, some holding that
they have been necessarily and ineradicably intertwined, in America, in
modernity, even in their very conceptual foundations; others, that their
linkages have been less universal, more contingent, and more alterable.
Some scholars particularly stress conceptual linkages; others stress economic, psychological, and/or political ones. And scholars also differ on
whether rights and racism have been largely mutually reinforcing;
whether racism has instead been parasitic on fundamental rights doctrines; whether rights doctrines, institutions, and practices have been parasitic on racial ones; or whether their reciprocal effects have been too
multivalent and shifting over time for any of these simpler descriptions to
be sustainable. And though some writers see the core ideas of race and
rights in America, at least, as relatively unchanging, others stress how substantial their reconfigurations and transformations have been over time.
Some, finally, continue to see racial doctrines as fundamentally anomalies
within an otherwise overwhelming "liberal consensus" society.

   Not all the alternative understandings appear equally credible. Anomaly accounts, while still widely defended, are clearly embattled. I have also
suggested here that advocates of the strongest versions of "strongly reinforcing" symbioses have much more work to do if they are to demonstrate
that doctrines of rights and racial inequality actually require each other

conceptually, economically, psychologically, or politically, or that rights and race doctrines have largely been mutually reinforcing throughout U.S. history, in ways that have not significantly changed. Their own arguments as well as historical evidence indicate instead that many formulations of rights doctrines have often been seen as threatening by proponents of inegalitarian racial systems. And most scholars also agree that more-egalitarian rights and race doctrines have become more influential in American political life over time, reducing racial hierarchies.

There is, on the other hand, considerable *agreement* among all these positions that the propagation of individual rights doctrines in the United States, including doctrines of capitalist property rights and democratic political rights, has fostered economic, social psychological, and political contexts that in various ways have led many of those deeming themselves white to insist on racial limits on who could claim full and equal rights. And there is virtual unanimity that many if not virtually all the American political actors, parties, and movements that have won much support historically have done so in part by blending rights doctrines with some sorts of racialized assumptions, often explicitly inegalitarian racial doctrines. But there is much work to be done to clarify the precise economic, psychological, and political linkages that have operated historically and to judge their relative weight, their interactions, and their contingency.

Those results, in turn, may help us make progress on the debate started by Louis Hartz, about whether it makes sense to see America as a "liberal consensus" society and if so, in what sense. Doing so will inevitably return us to the tasks I have not undertaken here, of deciding whether there is a historically recognizable "liberal tradition" throughout U.S. history and how its contours should be defined. Neo-Hartzians generally have adopted definitions that allow for multiple liberalisms, but as Marc Stears has pointed out, if everything can be counted as a form of liberalism, "the very idea of liberalism will cease to add any analytic value to our search for political explanations."[83] Yet if with Hartz we define liberalism more narrowly, as in principle opposed to racial inequalities, we must at a minimum attend to the variety of ways that ideas he deemed "liberal" have been elements of American political ideologies that have defended such inequalities—something critics believe "multiple traditions" accounts cannot do. To decide whether or not that is so, we should probably focus, as Ericson does, on comparing how persuasively different approaches analyze actual political actors, parties, movements, and contests in U.S. history, even if interpretive battles will remain.

And whatever definition of liberalism we adopt, we still face the task of judging whether America's racisms have rested on liberal foundations thus defined, whether the liberalism or liberalisms we see have rested on racial foundations, or whether it is wrong to privilege either component as more definitive of American politics as a whole. The many scholars who stress, rightly in my view, that American ideas have been combined and recombined in distinct and often novel ways over time must also be open to the possibility that our answers to that question should vary in different periods. In some eras racial doctrines and practices may have predominated; in others, more inclusive doctrines of individual rights have prevailed. Here, further careful historical empirical investigations may particularly shed light.

These last issues are especially pertinent now, for another point on which there is broad agreement is that in the course of American political development, political ideologies defending more egalitarian doctrines of individual rights have gained political predominance, even if scholars differ on how contingent or predictable this development has been and on how much change it really represents. Whatever may be true of America's past, today most analysts see explicit doctrines of white supremacy as politically marginal in the United States. Modern debates over racial issues often involve issues of whether "color-blind" doctrines that focus on individual rights without regard to race, in recognizably Hartzian liberal fashion, are working to alleviate America's surviving racial inequities, or whether these versions of modern liberalism are instead operating as the chief contemporary ideological defenses for the nation's still entrenched systems of racial inequality. Desmond King and I contend that in fact these disputes, which can plausibly be seen as contests between different versions of liberalism that rely on different conceptions about race, define the issues around which rival racial alliances are formed in our time.[84] If so, that reality underscores the fact that Americans are still struggling with the symbiosis of race and rights that, many analysts concur, has been so central to American national experience. And if Americans are still engaged in those struggles, then despite the daunting empirical and interpretive tasks they pose to us, we scholars should not cease to do any less.

NOTES

My thanks to Chloé Bakalar for excellent research assistance on this essay.

1. For example, see Stephen Skowronek, "The Reassociation of Ideas and Purposes: Racism, Liberalism, and the American Political Tradition," *American Political*

Science Review 100 (2006): 385–401; Alan Gibson, *Understanding the Founding: The Crucial Questions* (Lawrence: University Press of Kansas, 2007); Marc Stears, "The Liberal Tradition and the Politics of Exclusion," *Annual Review of Political Science* 10 (2007): 85–101; Edmund Fong, "Reconstructing the 'Problem' of Race," *Political Research Quarterly Online First,* October 2, 2008, doi:10.1177/1065912908324588, http://prq.sagepub.com/cgi/content/short/1065912908324588v1. A more recent version was also published in *Political Research Quarterly* 61, no. 4 (2008): 660–670.

2. Louis Hartz, *The Liberal Tradition in America* (New York: Harcourt, Brace, 1955), 3–4, 6, 8, 10.

3. Jennifer L. Hochschild, *The New American Dilemma: Liberal Democracy and School Desegregation* (New Haven, Conn.: Yale University Press, 1984), 2.

4. J. David Greenstone, *The Lincoln Persuasion: Remaking American Liberalism* (Princeton, N.J.: Princeton University Press, 1993), 48.

5. Rogers M. Smith, *Civic Ideals: Conflicting Visions of Citizenship in U.S. History* (New Haven, Conn.: Yale University Press, 1997), 507n5.

6. Carol A. Horton, *Race and the Making of American Liberalism* (New York: Oxford University Press, 2005), 5.

7. Stears, "The Liberal Tradition and the Politics of Exclusion," 85. In another recent effort to defend Hartz that seeks to show that a "liberal society" account best explains the liberal reforms of the 1960s, Philip Abbott follows Hartz in not defining liberalism; see Philip Abbott, "Still Louis Hartz after All These Years: A Defense of the Liberal Society Thesis," *Perspectives on Politics* 3 (2005): 93–109. Abbott does not dispute that racism played a role in earlier periods of illiberal reforms, those that created "legal toleration of racism," but he sees no significant racial elements in the "liberal Thermidor" reaction against civil rights reforms and the Great Society (102–104). For a different reading, see Philip A. Klinkner with Rogers M. Smith, *The Unsteady March: The Rise and Decline of Racial Equality in America* (Chicago: University of Chicago Press, 1999), 242–316.

8. Louis Hartz, *The Founding of New Societies: Studies in the History of the United States, Latin America, South Africa, Canada, and Australia* (New York: Harcourt, Brace & World, 1964), 17.

9. John G. Gunnell, "Louis Hartz and the Liberal Metaphor: A Half-Century Later," *Studies in American Political Development* 19 (2005): 197, 198, 203, 204.

10. Ibid., 203, 199.

11. Fong, "Reconstructing the 'Problem' of Race," 7. In a related but distinct book-length argument, Brent Gilchrist contends that Hartz was correct "that liberalism has been the only significant political ideology in America," but he believes that Hartz overlooked the way political culture contains "a matrix of ideology, religion, and myth," not just ideology. Gilchrist, *Cultus Americanus* (Lanham, Md.: Lexington Books, 2006), 3. Gilchrist thinks racism and other "non-liberal expressions" are "myths" that are "not ideological" (10). Gilchrist follows Ernst Cassirer and Sheldon Wolin in defining political ideology as a "uniquely modern degradation of political philosophy" aimed at supplying "belief and conviction," not "knowledge and

84 *Rogers M. Smith*

wisdom," to "political mass movements" (30). Gilchrist does not discuss American racial views in detail and does not explain why they are not ideological in this sense. He does contend that the fact that many Americans "pretended" that "scientific racialism" justified the subordination of blacks as "unfit for civil society" served to "satisfy the needs of liberal argument" (141). It is unclear how Gilchrist knows American racist arguments were a pretense, or why the desires of many Americans to make, and their success in making, arguments he regards as "non-liberal" support the claim that they and other Americans were ideological liberals in his sense.

12. Rogers M. Smith, "Liberalism and Racism: The Problem of Analyzing Traditions," in· *The Liberal Tradition in American Politics*, ed. David F. Ericson and Louisa Bertch Green (New York: Routledge, 1999), 14–15. John G. Gunnell, "The Archaeology of American Liberalism," *Journal of Political Ideologies* 6 (2001): 124–145, provides considerable further evidence and arguments for this characterization.

13. Gilchrist, *Cultus Americanus*; see also Gunnar Myrdal, *An American Dilemma* (New York: Harper & Brothers, 1944), 443; Klinkner with Smith, *The Unsteady March*, 24, 32, 95, 113–14, and 335–339.

14. Hochschild, *The New American Dilemma*, 5.

15. Definitions derived from *Wikipedia*, s.v. "Symbiosis," subhead "Commensalism," http://en.wikipedia.org/wiki/Symbiosis#Commensalism (accessed June 10, 2009).

16. My "multiple traditions" argument is sometimes contrasted to "symbiosis" views; see, e.g., Michael W. Combs and Gwendolyn M. Combs, "Revisiting *Brown v. Board of Education*," *Howard Law Journal* 47 (2003–2004): 632–633; Charles W. Mills, "Modernity, Persons, and Subpersons," in *Race and the Foundations of Knowledge*, ed. Joseph Young and Jana Evans Braziel (Champaign: University of Illinois Press, 2006), 216. This contrast is correct if symbiosis is taken to mean that doctrines of individual rights and racial inequalities are strongly mutually beneficial or even require each other. It is not correct if symbiosis is understood to include the possibility that doctrines of race and rights, while pervasively intertwined in American experience, have been only partly "mutualist" and partly destructively "parasitic."

17. Myrdal, *An American Dilemma*, 4, 6–7, 52.

18. Ibid., 89, 1021.

19. Hochschild, *The New American Dilemma*, 5.

20. Hartz, *The Liberal Tradition in America*, 167–169, 291–292. In 1964 Hartz modified his view, seeking to place racial inequalities within the ideological confines of his American liberal tradition. He contended that European liberal ideas lay "beneath the surface" of American racial attitudes, pushing Americans to regard racial minorities either as nonhuman "property" or as full equals. Hartz, *The Founding of New Societies*, 16–17, 58–61. Hartz acknowledged that even so, "in fact" American law long assigned blacks intermediate statuses in which possession of rights was "a matter of degree," but he insisted these statuses were unstable because "the moral issue does not change" and "cannot be a matter of degree." Hartz thought he had thereby laid bare the source of "the civil rights struggles of the present moment" (62). But

Hartz did not seek to explain how or why notions of race emerged in America's "liberal fragment" of society or why Americans were so long able to sustain "in fact" statuses that "cannot be" in such a society; so his revised account must be seen as at best not fully developed for the issues examined here.

21. I discuss a number of proponents of the anomaly thesis in Smith, *Civic Ideals*, 14–15, 27–28, including Philip Gleason, Samuel Huntington, and Michael Walzer. In a book published that same year, Thomas G. West argues somewhat as Myrdal does that the founders knew slavery violated their principles of human rights but felt compelled to make "concessions to passions and interests they could not tame" that subsequently set the stage for the rise of racist doctrines they would have rejected and that Americans ultimately overthrew; Thomas G. West, *Vindicating the Founders: Race, Sex, Class, and Justice in the Origins of America* (Lanham, Md.: Rowman & Littlefield, 1997), 1–10, 32–36.

22. Philip Gleason, "Sea Change in the Civil Culture of the 1960s," in *E Pluribus Unum?* ed. Gary Gerstle and John Mollenkopf (New York: Russell Sage Foundation, 2001), 112. Samuel Huntington later explicitly revised his view in *Who Are We? The Challenges to American National Identity* (New York: Simon & Schuster, 2004), 46–49.

23. Richard Iton, "The Sound of Silence: Comments on 'Still Louis Hartz after All These Years,'" *Perspective on Politics* 3 (2005): 113.

24. Jane Flax, "Can There Be Citizenship without Race and Gender?" Insitut für die Wissenschaften vom Menschen (IWM) Working Paper no. 11 (Vienna: IWM Publications, 1999), 4, 7, 16–17.

25. Judith N. Shklar, *American Citizenship* (Cambridge, Mass.: Harvard University Press, 1991), 16.

26. Ibid., 2.

27. Ibid., 3, 64.

28. Uday S. Mehta, "Liberal Strategies of Exclusion," *Politics and Society* 18 (1990): 430.

29. Uday S. Mehta, *The Anxiety of Freedom* (Ithaca, N.Y.: Cornell University Press, 1992), 170; cf. Mehta, "Liberal Strategies of Exclusion," 435–439. David Theo Goldberg contends somewhat similarly that Locke's "empiricist antiessentialism" led him to rely on conventional understandings about what constituted rational capacities in ways that permitted Locke to endorse racial inequalities. Goldberg, *Racist Culture: Philosophy and the Politics of Meaning* (Oxford: Blackwell, 1993), 28. Through such arguments, Goldberg contends, liberalism historically legitimated racial categories, while modern liberalism treats race as morally irrelevant, failing to recognize and address continuing racial inequities. Thus, Goldberg believes "liberalism serves to legitimate ideologically and to rationalize politico-economically prevailing sets of racialized conditions and racist exclusions." Goldberg, *Racist Culture*, 1, 6–7; see also Goldberg, *The Racial State* (Oxford: Blackwell, 2002), 4–5. Goldberg's view is thus a very "strongly reinforcing partnership" one, but it is less tightly argued than Mehta's. Goldberg fails to recognize, for example, that when Locke argues that an English child might conclude that "*a Negro is not a Man,*" Locke is criticizing that judgment. Cf. Goldberg, *The*

Racial State, 28; and John Locke, *An Essay Concerning Human Understanding* (Oxford: Clarendon Press, 1975), 607.

30. Mehta, "Liberal Strategies of Exclusion," 438–439; Mehta, *The Anxiety of Freedom*, 171–174.

31. Uday S. Mehta endorses Hartz's claim in regard to British racial imperialism; see Mehta, *Liberalism and Empire* (Chicago: University of Chicago Press, 1999), 16.

32. For example, see Barbara Jeanne Fields, "Slavery, Race, and Ideology in the United States of America," *New Left Review* 181 (1990): 101–116.

33. Immanuel Wallerstein, "The Construction of Peoplehood: Racism, Nationalism, Ethnicity," in *Race, Nation, Class*, ed. Etienne Balibar and Immanuel Wallerstein (New York: Verso, 1991), 84.

34. For example, see Horton, *Race and the Making of American Liberalism*, 8.

35. Richard Delgado and Jean Stefancic, eds., *The Derrick Bell Reader* (New York: New York University Press, 2005), 27–28; see also, e.g., Hochschild, *The New American Dilemma*, 6–8; David R. Roediger, *The Wages of Whiteness* (New York: Verso, 1991); Michael Omi and Howard Winant, *Racial Formation in the United States* (New York: Routledge, 1994), 24–35; Loïc Wacquant, "Deadly Symbiosis: When Ghetto and Prison Meet and Mesh," *Punishment and Society* 3 (2001): 95–134; Joel Olson, *The Abolition of White Democracy* (Minneapolis: University of Minnesota Press, 2004), xxiv–xxix.

36. Derrick Bell, "White Superiority in America: Its Legal Legacy, Its Economic Costs," and "Racism Is Here to Stay: Now What?" both in Delgado and Stefancic, *The Derrick Bell Reader*, 27, 88.

37. Ibid., 86–87, 89.

38. Margaret Kohn, "The Other America: Tocqueville and Beaumont on Race and Slavery," *Polity* 35 (2002): 191; Laura Janara, "Brothers and Others: Tocqueville and Beaumont, U.S. Genealogy, Democracy, and Racism," *Political Theory* 32 (2004): 778.

39. Kohn, "The Other America," 190–191.

40. Ibid., 189–190; see also Janara, "Brothers and Others," 776, 783.

41. Janara, "Brothers and Others," 776.

42. Edmund S. Morgan, *American Slavery—American Freedom* (New York: Norton, 1975), 328; see also Hochschild, *The New American Dilemma*, 5–6.

43. Morgan, *American Slavery—American Freedom*, 344.

44. Ibid., 380.

45. Ibid., 381.

46. See, e.g., West, *Vindicating the Founders*, 1–35; cf. Akhil Reed Amar, *America's Constitution* (New York: Random House, 2005), 87–98.

47. Olson, *The Abolition of White Democracy*, xv; see also Kohn, "The Other America," 187.

48. Olson, *The Abolition of White Democracy*, xvi.

49. Lauren L. Basson, *White Enough to Be American?* (Chapel Hill: University of North Carolina Press, 2008), 2–4, 179–180.

50. Ibid., 14–15, 178.

51. Ibid., 20.

52. Olson, *The Abolition of White Democracy*, 125–145.

53. Ibid., xvi.

54. Greenstone, *The Lincoln Persuasion*, 53–54, 59–60.

55. David F. Ericson, *The Debate over Slavery* (New York: New York University Press, 2000), 14.

56. Ibid., 10. As Stears points out in "The Liberal Tradition and the Politics of Exclusion," 91–92, both Laura J. Scalia, in *America's Jeffersonian Experiment* (DeKalb: Northern Illinois University Press, 1998), and Desmond S. King, in *In the Name of Liberalism* (New York: Oxford University Press, 1999), stress how "a variety of liberal tropes" were politically deployed in American experience for racially inegalitarian purposes. Scalia, like Ericson, argues that these patterns confirm the centrality of "Lockian liberalism" in America, a view also defended carefully in Michael Foley, *American Credo* (Oxford: Oxford University Press, 2007), esp. 393–422.

57. Ericson, *The Debate over Slavery*, 23, 94, 116, 130–31. Ericson also counts the most prevalent defenses of slavery, religious arguments usually based on biblical exegeses, as liberal; Ericson, *The Debate over Slavery*, 19, 101, 130–131. Relying on secondary sources, he dismisses antebellum scientific racism as "marginalized" (178n24), so he does not analyze their writings, and he also gives limited attention to their leading political champion, John C. Calhoun.

58. Horton, *Race and the Making of American Liberalism*, 5–6.

59. Ibid., 5.

60. Ibid., 37–38, 44–46.

61. Ibid., 57, 81.

62. Ibid., 59.

63. Charles W. Mills, "Racial Liberalism," *PMLA* 123 (2008): 1394.

64. Ibid., 1388.

65. Charles W. Mills, *The Racial Contract* (Ithaca, N.Y.: Cornell University Press, 1997); Mills, "Modernity, Persons, and Subpersons."

66. Mills, "Modernity, Persons, and Subpersons," 213, 215–216.

67. Ibid., 216.

68. Mills, "Racial Liberalism," 1382–1383, 1394.

69. Mills, "Modernity, Persons, and Subpersons," 216.

70. Charles W. Mills, "Under Class Under Standings," *Ethics* 104 (1994): 863; Mills, "Racial Liberalism," 1380, 1382.

71. As noted above, scholars like Goldberg and Olson similarly stress the politics of building modern, putatively democratic states in understanding the relationships of race and rights, but they present the two as more necessarily linked than writers in this fourth category.

72. For related but distinct "multiple traditions" accounts, see, e.g., Karen Orren, *Belated Feudalism* (New York: Cambridge University Press, 1992); Catherine A. Holland, *The Body Politic* (New York: Routledge, 2001), discussed below; Gary

Gerstle, *American Crucible* (Princeton, N.J.: Princeton University Press, 2001); James T. Kloppenberg. "From Hartz to Tocqueville," in *The Democratic Experiment,* ed. Meg Jacobs, William J. Novak, and Julian E. Zelizer (Princeton, N.J.: Princeton University Press, 2003), 350–380; Rodney Hero, "Multiple Theoretical Traditions in American Politics and Racial Policy Inequality," *Political Research Quarterly* 56 (2003): 401–408; Deborah J. Schildkraut, "Defining American Identity in the Twenty-first Century," *Journal of Politics* 69 (2007): 597–715; Gibson, *Understanding the Founding,* 130–174; Dowell Myers, *Immigrants and Boomers* (New York: Russell Sage Foundation, 2007), 154–155.

73. Smith, *Civic Ideals,* 39.

74. Klinkner with Smith, *The Unsteady March.*

75. Desmond S. King and Rogers M. Smith, "Racial Orders in American Political Development," *American Political Science Review* 99 (2005): 75–92; King and Smith, "Strange Bedfellows? Polarized Politics?" *Political Research Quarterly Online First,* September 29, 2008, doi: 10.1177/1065912908322410, http://prq.sagepub.com/cgi/content/short/1065912908322410v1. A more recent version was also published in *Political Research Quarterly* 61, no. 4 (2008): 686–703.

76. The framing of American political development in terms of the interaction of contrasting multiple traditions embodying different political "ideal types" for the nation and its citizenry does have deficiencies. It has led many to conclude that it indeed requires us to place political actors, parties, and movements as entirely within one tradition and to interpret political struggles as contests between proponents of single, wholly distinct traditions. Instead, it is meant to map the ideational ingredients that all American actors, parties, and movements have interwoven more to gain political success than to create internal consistency. These mappings can help both describe and explain their distinctive, never unmixed principles, policies, and purposes. But the analytically distinguishable ideas themselves are not political actors, as the framework may seem to imply.

77. Holland, *The Body Politic,* xv. Note that Basson also analyzes American political discourses in terms of their role in nation and state building, but she suggests more strongly that all American traditions have been "inextricably" racialized; see Basson, *White Enough to Be American?* 178.

78. Holland, *The Body Politic,* xvii–xviii.

79. Ibid., xvi.

80. Other significant arguments that the multiple traditions position understates liberal complicity include, e.g., Ira Katznelson, "Review: Civic Ideals," *Political Theory* 17 (1999): 568–569; Bonnie Honig, *Democracy and the Foreigner* (Princeton, N.J.: Princeton University Press, 2001), 11–12; Barbara Arneil, *Diverse Communities* (New York: Cambridge University Press, 2006), 211–212; Mark Kessler, "Free Speech Doctrine in American Political Culture," *Connecticut Public Interest Law Journal* 6 (2007): 214–218.

81. Skowronek, "The Reassociation of Ideas and Purposes," 388–398.

82. Ibid., 386–387. Unsurprisingly, I think the accounts of changing party ideologies and the broader transitions in early twentieth-century American political thought depicted in my *Civic Ideals* show this suggestion to be unwarranted. But I also see Skowronek's call for us to attend to how ideas are intermixed to create new political perspectives as correct and valuable.

83. Stears, "The Liberal Tradition and the Politics of Exclusion," 98.

84. King and Smith, "Racial Orders in American Political Development"; King and Smith, "Strange Bedfellows? Polarized Politics?"

CHAPTER 3

Requiescat in Pacem: *The Liberal Tradition of Louis Hartz*

James T. Kloppenberg

Louis Hartz died on January 29, 1986, at age sixty-six. Less than a year after his death, many of Hartz's former Harvard students and colleagues gathered in Cambridge, Massachusetts, on January 23, 1987, for a conference devoted to his work. Although the circumstances of Hartz's death in Istanbul remained a mystery, it seemed to many in attendance an almost inevitable culmination of his tragic decline. After the breakdown that had precipitated his retirement from Harvard in 1974, only eighteen years after the American Political Science Association had awarded the Woodrow Wilson Prize to *The Liberal Tradition in America,* Hartz had slid into mental illness.

The poignant and reverential tone of the scholars at the conference surprised and impressed me. Hartz's former students spoke movingly about his undisputed brilliance as a teacher. The passion and intelligence of his lectures and seminars had left a deep and lasting mark. It is hard not to admire anyone capable of leaving such a legacy.[1] But again and again those in attendance went on to characterize Hartz as a peerless analyst of American culture and to describe *The Liberal Tradition in America* (hereafter cited as *LTA*) as the most incisive book ever written about America.[2]

That reverence seemed to me misplaced. As a historian of American thought I had become accustomed to historicizing *LTA*, reflecting on its significance as a document from the 1950s rather than as a useful guide to American political culture. I considered it a provocative but mistaken and misleading book, all the principal arguments of which had been shown by a generation of historians to be profoundly flawed. Throughout the day of the conference I and a few other skeptics (notably the Harvard political theorist Judith Shklar) tried, both during the proceedings and between sessions, to inquire how a book wrong in each of its particular claims could still be right overall.[3] At last one exasperated political theorist, as oblivious to the circularity of his claim as are those who rely on notions of repression and hegemony, announced that our evident failure to grasp the nature of American liberalism showed only the depth of our entanglement in the irrational assumptions that Hartz had so brilliantly laid bare.

Perhaps. I came away from that conference, however, more impressed with Hartz as a teacher and more firmly convinced of the shortcomings of *LTA*, a conviction that has grown in the last two decades as I have continued to study the history of American and European political thought and political practice. Despite the weaknesses of Hartz's argument, which I will outline in this essay, *LTA* established him as one of the most influential figures in American political science. That influence needs to be explained, and the renewed attention being paid to the historical analysis of the American social sciences by a rising generation of scholars may eventually illuminate the reasons for Hartz's rise to prominence. Although recent scholarship points in that direction, so far no one has provided the richly textured study that would enable us to locate Hartz in the sociological and institutional dynamics of the Harvard Government Department in particular and American political science more generally. Until that work is done, locating *LTA* in the sociology of knowledge of postwar American will be impossible.[4]

In this essay I advance two arguments that skirt questions about Hartz's personal history and his place in the discipline of American political science. First, whatever its importance as a historical document, whatever its merits as a piece of political theory, and whatever its value as a meditation on American culture and politics, *LTA* advances an argument about American history that is too flat and too static to be convincing. Because Hartz focused on issues of economics and psychology, he overstated their significance and missed the constitutive roles played by democracy, religion, race, ethnicity, and gender in American history. He therefore misunderstood (as thoroughly as did his predecessors and progressive bêtes noires Charles Beard, Frederick Jackson Turner, and Vernon Louis Parrington, whose work he sought to replace) the complicated and changing dynamics of the democratic struggle that has driven American social and political conflict since the seventeenth century. Hartz's analysis must be understood in the context of the early post–World War II era rather than treated as a source of timeless truths about America. Second, acknowledging the inaccuracies of *LTA* is important, because the widespread acceptance of its argument has had consequences unfortunate for the study of American political thought and poisonous for political debate. The time has come to refocus our attention away from Cold War era controversies over liberalism and socialism, and away from late twentieth-century squabbles over liberalism and republicanism, and turn our attention toward democracy.

Of course, such liberal ideas as individual autonomy, representative government, and toleration of diversity remain important to the study of American culture. I want only to insist that liberalism historically has included just such ideals (which I have elsewhere called "the virtues of liberalism") and cannot be reduced to the self-interested assertion by individuals of the right to own property. Important as liberal ideas have been in American history, they have coexisted and interacted with others drawn from quite different religious, ethnic, and political traditions. In short, liberalism has been one among a number of strands in American public life.

Nor do I propose to replace a one-dimensional conception of liberalism with an equally unsatisfying one-dimensional conception of democracy; to the contrary, democracy provides an attractive analytical framework precisely because it highlights the ceaseless wrangling—the deep disagreements over procedures as well as principles—that has marked American history. Focusing on democracy need not imply any particular teleology. Although it is true that early twentieth-century progressive historians tended to lionize "the people" and demonize "the interests," such a simple Manichean model distorts the more complex historical reality these essays in this volume illuminate. Neither the masses nor the monied have played the parts written for them in such simpleminded morality tales. Instead, the combatants in American public life fought, and continue to fight, sometimes in quite unexpected ways and sometimes by forging odd alliances, as bitterly over rules as over results. The most radical and profound truth of popular sovereignty—one of the core principles of democracy—is that it puts everything up for grabs. The temporary outcomes of political struggles have generated not only endless challenges from the defeated but sometimes preemptive strikes from winners who feared the outcome of the next battle. Although I insist in this essay on the inadequacy of the idea of a "liberal consensus," I do not seek to put in its place an equally creaky notion of "democratic conflict" premised on assumptions about class, race, or gender antagonisms. The historical record is more complicated—and more fascinating.

In part from dissatisfaction with fractured narratives and in part from a yearning to understand those on the right or the left who have been dismissed as "un-American" by scholars or by popular perception, American historians are returning to the study of politics. In part from dissatisfaction with behaviorism and rational choice theory and in part from a yearning to understand the relation between institutions and individuals, political scientists likewise are returning to the historical study of American politics. Historians need not, and most do not, resist theory as antithetical to our work. Many of the essays in this volume implicitly or explicitly draw on theoretical frameworks derived from social science; historical study surely need not be antitheoretical. But the human sciences are empirical disciplines, and only by continuing to test our theories against evidence can we keep them supple. The ideas Hartz advanced in *The Liberal Tradition in America* have become too brittle to be of further use.[5]

Hartz's thesis, although advanced by means of a rhetorical strategy calculated to dazzle his readers, was simple and elegant. He conceded that his approach could be characterized as a "'single factor' analysis" with two dimensions: "the absence of feudalism and the presence of the liberal idea."[6] Because America lacked a feudal tradition, it lacked both a "genuine revolutionary tradition" and a "tradition of reaction." America contained instead only "a kind of self-completing mechanism, which insures the universality of the liberal idea" (5–6). In order to grasp the contours of this all-encompassing liberal tradition, Hartz argued, we must compare America with Europe. Only then can we understand not only the absence of socialism and conservatism but the stultifying presence and "moral unanimity" imposed by "this fixed, dogmatic liberalism of a liberal way of life." Moreover, the "deep and unwritten tyrannical compulsion" of American liberalism "transforms eccentricity into sin," an alchemy that explains the periodic eruption of red scares (9–12). In short, "the master assumption of American political thought" is "the reality of atomistic social freedom. It is instinctive in the American mind" (62).

Hartz advanced his interpretation by contrasting, in a series of chronologically arranged chapters, the nation's continuous history with the convulsions of European revolutions and restorations. He insisted that Americans' shared commitment to Lockean (or, as he spelled it, "Lockian") liberalism enabled them to avoid upheavals at the cost of enforcing conformity. He used "Locke" as a shorthand for the self-interested, profit-maximizing values and behaviors of liberal capitalism, against which he counterposed, on the one hand, the revolutionary egalitarian fervor of Jacobins and Marxian socialists and, on the other, the traditional hierarchical values of church elites and aristocrats under various European ancien régimes. Unfortunately, however, because Hartz never paused to explain exactly how he understood feudalism or precisely what he meant by

"Locke" or "liberalism," the meaning of his terms remained vague and his central claims somewhat fuzzy.[7]

It was an arresting argument, though, especially coming so soon after Senator Joseph McCarthy's anticommunist crusade and during a time of national self-congratulation, and Hartz's reviewers immediately acknowledged its persuasiveness. Historians as well as political scientists hailed the book. In the *American Historical Review* George Mowry called it "an extremely able and original interpretation." In the *William and Mary Quarterly* Arthur Mann credited Hartz with resisting the boosterism that had replaced critical analysis in postwar America. In the *Journal of the History of Ideas* Ralph Henry Gabriel applauded Hartz for showing how the Federalists and Whigs adopted the image of Horatio Alger to create an ideology of "Americanism" that proved impervious to the lure of socialism. In *Comparative Studies in Society and History* Marvin Meyers agreed with Hartz that Alexis de Tocqueville provided a more promising path toward understanding America than did Hartz's progressive predecessors.[8]

But unlike the many political theorists who still revere the book as an almost sacred text, historians also registered their misgivings about *LTA*. Mowry found "bewildering" Hartz's "claim for scientific analysis" and his reliance on "such terms as 'the democratic psyche' and a national 'Oedipus complex.'" Mann sounded the historian's call to Wilhelm Dilthey's hermeneutics: "The historian must somehow get *inside* the men of the past and recreate the world as they saw it" rather than criticizing them, as Hartz did repeatedly, for failing to see the deeper unanimity buried beneath their strident but shallow quarrels. "Political theory does not exist in a vacuum," Gabriel complained; Hartz's vague and imprecise analysis did to American thinkers what Walt Disney had done to Davy Crockett. Meyers noted that whereas Tocqueville did indeed stress the absence of feudalism in America, he also emphasized the importance of religion, the legacy of English law and liberty, the fact of slavery, the uniquely elevated status of women, the distinctive pattern of decentralized settlement in North America, a set of sturdy political institutions and wise founding documents, and other sociocultural, geographical, and demographic factors that together constitute the history of the United States.

The genre distinction between history and political theory helps to account for the divergence in assessments of *LTA*. The historians thought Hartz was flying too high to see clearly the details necessary for understanding the American historical record; political theorists, as Hartz's student Paul Roazen put it, instead appreciated that "Hartz had little interest in the study of political ideas as a scholastic exercise but rather wanted to use

Locke as a symbol for a brand of political thought that could illuminate political reality."[9] Responding to Meyers and to equally stinging critiques delivered by Leonard Krieger and Harry Jaffa, Hartz ascended for refuge to the sanctuary of high theory: "Comparative analysis," he instructed his slow-witted historian-critics, "is destined to produce disturbing results. In the American case it seems suddenly to shrink our domestic struggles to insignificance, robbing them of their glamour, challenging even the worth of their historical study." Moreover, and here Hartz cut to the heart of the difference between the historian's interest in the particular and the social scientist's quest for the universal, "the comparative approach to American history is bound in the end to raise the question of a general theory of historical development."[10]

Again, perhaps, but perhaps instead the historians were right to scrutinize such general theories and measure them against evidence. Historians always "qualify" and "pluralize" the grander claims of social science, Krieger pointed out, and when we undertake that task with *LTA* we find that the fundamental comparison between the United States and Europe is misconceived. Had Hartz compared apples with apples, nations with nations, Krieger argued, he could have arranged European national traditions geographically and discovered that liberty, equality, and democracy have mattered rather less the further east one goes. National differences within Europe would loom as large as those Hartz had identified. Every national tradition is distinctive.[11] Adrienne Koch, reviewing Hartz in the *Mississippi Valley Historical Review,* put the same point more bluntly: Hartz's method

> produces no substantial documentation or analysis, but proceeds rather to pick up one name after another and freeze its arbitrarily selected essence to support the author's historical intuition. Individuality, chance, and the complex, specific coloration of a thinker's outlook are rudely sacrificed. . . . The net result of this "comparative method," which the author recommends as a means to make history "scientific," is to repeat and reaffirm what he is obligated to establish in the first place.[12]

Almost two decades after the publication of *LTA,* writing in response to yet another historian's critique of his cavalier treatment of evidence and failure to recognize the deep conflicts in American history, Hartz skirted the issue of evidence and reiterated his earlier proclamation of American uniqueness: "The United States is distinctive as against Europe, and its distinctiveness derives from the fact that the *Mayflower* left behind in Europe the experiences of class, revolution, and collectivism out of which the European socialist movement arose."[13] The facts of history should be seen to flow from the framework Hartz provided, not vice versa. In his spirited defense of *LTA,* Roazen too invokes the genre distinction. He concedes the inaccuracies that critics have identified in Hartz's treatment of individual thinkers and historical incidents, then explains that "Hartz was all along basically using history for the sake of eliciting answers to some theoretical queries in connection with the nature of a free society; and those fundamental issues remain with us today."[14]

Those issues do indeed remain with us,, which is why an accurate understanding of the nature of American political thought and experience remains important. Before embarking on a detailed account of the particular arguments of *LTA,* I want at least to note in passing the almost complete absence from Hartz's analysis of four issues that now seem to us American historians essential to understanding our nation's past: race, ethnicity, gender, and religion. To indict Hartz for overlooking issues that escaped the attention of most historians until recently seems unfair; such blindness surely typified most scholarly writing until the 1960s and still typified much—including my own—until even more recently. Even so, if one is trying to assess the persuasiveness of Hartz's analysis from the perspective of 2010, acknowledging that American public life has revolved around crucial battles over race, ethnicity, and gender has become inescapable.[15]

The same is true of religion, which Hartz examined briefly in *LTA* but dismissed for reasons that merit discussion. Hartz contended that because religion in eighteenth-century America generated neither iconoclasm nor anticlericalism, it was of only minor significance. Colonial religious diversity "meant that the revolution would be led in part by fierce Dissenting ministers." In Europe, "where reactionary church establishments had made the Christian concept of sin and salvation into an explicit pillar of the status quo, liberals were forced to develop a political religion—as Rousseau saw it—if only in answer to it." But American liberals, "instead of being forced to pull the Christian heaven down to earth, were glad to let it remain where it was. They did not need to make a religion out of the revolution because religion was already revolutionary" (40–41).

These passages reveal two important characteristics of Hartz's analysis. First, because the standard continental European—or, more properly, French and Italian—division between an anticlerical Left and an entrenched Church hierarchy generated cultural and political warfare and American religious divisions did not, Hartz concluded that religion in America could safely be fitted within the liberal consensus. Second, Hartz did not realize how corrosive to his argument was his concession that

American "religion was already revolutionary," perhaps because, like many secular Jewish intellectuals in the middle of the twentieth century, he either failed to see or refused to acknowledge the pivotal role of Christianity in shaping American public life.[16]

Hartz did not understand that in America religious identity (like racial and ethnic identity and gender identity) has not been merely epiphenomenal, simply an analytical category separable from the *real* class identity at the core of all social life, but has instead been a central, constitutive component of American culture from the seventeenth century to the present. Almost all Americans' "structures of meaning," to use an apt phrase of David Hall's, have derived from an unsteady blend of religious and secular, elite and popular, male and female, white and nonwhite cultures. For that reason religion does not shrink to insignificance but exerts a powerful force shaping individual decisions, interpretations of experience, and social interactions.

The diversity of Americans' religious commitments prevented the emergence of a state church, as Hartz noted, but the depth and persistence of those commitments undermined the simple, straightforward Lockean attachment to self-interested property seeking that Hartz defined as the essence of America. Locke himself was no Lockean, at least in Hartz's sense of the word, because of the depth of his Calvinist convictions. Similarly, Americans from the seventeenth century onward have struggled—as Tocqueville and Max Weber saw much more clearly than Hartz did—not merely for riches but also for salvation as they understood it. That quest has carried them toward a variety of goals not reducible to the simple maximizing of self-interest that drove and defined Hartz's liberal tradition.[17]

The opening page of *LTA* contained a minor but telling error that makes clear why we must broaden our analytical focus from Hartz's version of liberalism to a nuanced and dynamic conception of democracy. Seeking to replace the progressive historians' focus on conflict with a focus on unanimity, Hartz adorned his book's title page with an epigraph taken from Tocqueville's *Democracy in America*: "The great advantage of the Americans is, that they have arrived at a state of democracy without having to endure a democratic revolution; and that they are born free, instead of becoming so." Unfortunately for Hartz, and for his readers' understanding of American culture, Tocqueville had written that Americans were born *equal,* rather than free. The mistake, noted initially by errata slips and corrected in later editions, is less trivial than Hartz's defenders have claimed. Had Hartz more carefully examined the passage in Tocqueville, he might have noticed its appearance at the end of a chapter preceded by Tocqueville's profound insight into the differences between the ancient vice of egoism and the modern, democratic tendency toward individualism. He might also have noticed that the passage was followed by Tocqueville's even more arresting claim that Americans "have used liberty to combat the individualism born of equality, and they have won."[18]

Although Hartz invoked Tocqueville repeatedly and criticized historians for neglecting the implications of his analysis, his own argument rests not on a simple, understandable error of transcription but on a deeper misunderstanding of Tocqueville's point. Tocqueville understood the consequences of the absence of feudal traditions and corporate institutions, and he warned that in a democracy "each man is forever thrown back on himself alone, and there is danger that he may be shut up in the solitude of his own heart." But he then pointed out—immediately after the passage Hartz misquoted for his epigraph—that participation in the "free institutions" of American democracy in fact mitigates these potentially anomic consequences. "Local liberties, then, which induce a great number of citizens to value the affection of their kindred and neighbors, bring men constantly into contact, despite the instincts which separate them, and force them to help one another."[19]

Whereas one might expect Tocqueville to have concluded—as Hartz indeed did—that self-interest leads democratic citizens away from the public interest and to lament the ways in which freedom (or, as the corrected versions of *LTA* properly have it, equality) erodes concern for others, Tocqueville made exactly the opposite point: "I have often seen Americans make really great sacrifices for the common good, and I have noticed a hundred cases in which, when help was needed, they hardly ever failed to give each other trusty support." Because the penultimate paragraph of that crucial chapter so directly challenges the heart of Hartz's argument and points toward the alternative interpretation I advance in this essay, I will quote it at length:

> The free institutions of the United States and the political rights enjoyed there provide a thousand continual reminders to every citizen that he lives in society. At every moment they bring his mind back to this idea, that it is the duty as well as the interest of men to be useful to their fellows. Having no particular reason to hate others, since he is neither their slave nor their master, the American's heart easily inclines toward benevolence.[20]

As that passage makes clear, Hartz flattened Tocqueville's rich conception of American democracy by eliminating the crucial significance of participation in civic life. Such participation, Tocqueville insisted, prevented Americans from ignoring each other and nourished in them the animating and distinctive ethic of reciprocity that manifested itself prototypically in jury deliberations and implicitly in the broader culture of democracy. Although Tocqueville—like many members of the culture he was describing—did find it problematic that democratic citizenship was limited to white male property holders, he had identified the logic that eventually drove the United States to extend the privileges and duties of citizenship to all adults. That logic, like the ethic of reciprocity and the culture of participation, eluded Hartz entirely.

From the perspective of 2010, the historical errors of *LTA* only begin with the title page. As I examine the principal arguments Hartz advanced, I will very briefly compare his characterizations of (1) the American Revolution, (2) antebellum American politics, (3) the progressive era, (4) the New Deal, and (5) the culture of the post–World War II United States with the findings of more recent historical scholarship. It would be pointless to criticize Hartz for failing to see what it has taken half a century of historical scholarship to make clear. But it is equally pointless to claim, as some of Hartz's bolder champions continue to do, that *LTA* nevertheless remains a reliable guide to the history of American public life. For reasons I will outline in my conclusion, the stubborn persistence of belief in an American liberal tradition of the sort Hartz described obscures both our understanding of our nation's past and our ability to envision strategies toward a more democratic future.

Hartz laid out the heart of his analysis in the provocative opening chapter of *LTA,* "The Concept of a Liberal Society." Although he admitted the presence of some conflict in America, its shallowness prevented the development of political theory. "America represents the liberal mechanism of Europe functioning without the European social antagonisms" (16). That claim reveals his blinkered vision. Because American social antagonisms operated on fault lines different from those of European revolutionaries confronting landed and titled aristocracies, or from those of later European socialists confronting an entrenched, antidemocratic bourgeoisie, Hartz denied the existence of significant conflict and significant political thought in the United States. More recent commentators, more alert to the depth and persistence of disagreements over the fate and place of, say, Indians, blacks, Asians, Jews, Slavs, and Hispanics; more alert to the gender wars that divide generations, families, and coworkers; and more alert to the implications for political and social life of other fundamental cultural or religious differences, have put the problem in a different framework. In the combative words of Richard J. Ellis, one of the political scientists who dissents from the view that has prevailed in his profession since the publication of *LTA,* "Political conflict in the United States has been and continues to be animated by fundamentally different visions of the good life. . . . That all sides appeal to terms such as equality or democracy or liberty should not conceal from us the fundamentally different meanings these terms have in different political cultures." Even the most casual glance at scholarship from the last three decades dealing with race, ethnicity, gender, or religion would suffice to confirm Ellis's judgment.[21]

The American Revolution, to begin where Hartz did, was from his perspective no revolution at all. Compared with the French Revolution, which served as his standard of measurement, what happened in the War for Independence merely codified what had previously been taken for granted in English North America. If Americans disestablished the Anglican Church, abolished primogeniture, and confiscated Tory estates, they were merely bringing to fruition processes already under way.[22] If they separated the powers of government, further divided authority by establishing a federal republic, and provided for judicial review of legislative and executive decisions, those mechanisms merely testified to their deep, preexisting agreement on fundamentals. The scholarship of the last three decades has obliterated this aspect of Hartz's argument, not only—to cite the most obvious challenges—by demonstrating the centrality and force of republican and religious rhetoric and ideals, but even more centrally by showing the creativity of the democratic mechanisms adopted to deal with the genuine conflicts invisible to Hartz.

The significance of the American Revolution lay not so much in the founders' liberalism, which was complicated by its mixture with republican and religious values, as in their commitment to nourishing the seeds of a democratic culture. They constructed or altered institutions that made possible continuous mediation, the endless production of compromises, a system deliberately calculated to satisfy some of the aspirations of all citizens and all of the aspirations of none. From the declarations of independence adopted by towns, counties, and states in the spring of 1776 through the ratification of the U.S. Constitution and the Bill of Rights, Americans authorized their representatives to gather together and deliberate on the form they wanted their government to take. Precisely because they could not agree once and for all on their common principles, they agreed to make all their agreements provisional and to provide, for one of the few times in human history, a range of escape hatches for dissent, ranging from a free press to the separation of church and state, from judicial review to provisions for amending the Constitution. It is true that such comfort with compromise did indeed distinguish the American founders from later Jacobins and Bolsheviks. But it is crucial to see that they emphatically did not agree to codify atomistic individualism, because that idea appealed to practically no one—neither Federalists nor Anti-Federalists—in late eighteenth-century America. Although the sobersided John Adams has attracted more attention than most of his like-minded contemporaries, both his doubt that republican virtue would eradicate sin and his disdain for profiteering resonated widely in the new republic. He and his contemporaries were not trying to make a world safe for bankers—whose work Adams described acidly in a letter to Jefferson as "an infinity of successive felonious larcenies"—but were seeking instead to create a liberal republic safe for worldly ascetics, a "Christian Sparta" in the phrase of Samuel Adams, where even those who failed to reach that lofty ethical ideal might not only survive but thrive. Codifying the procedures of democracy was their means to that end.[23]

Hartz's conviction that property holding and profit making exhausted the ambitions of eighteenth- and nineteenth-century Americans guided even his explicit analysis of state involvement in the economy in his first book, *Economic Policy and Democratic Thought: Pennsylvania, 1776–1860.* There Hartz argued that even though laissez-faire did not exist in early America, the activity of state governments served only to facilitate economic activity. The same assumption also drove his interpretation of antebellum America in *LTA*. Among the most explicit and convincing recent challenges to that analysis are the distinct but complementary writings of William J. Novak and Elizabeth J. Clark. Novak has demonstrated both the pervasive regulation, in myriad domains, of economic activity in antebellum America and, even more directly challenging Hartz, the equally pervasive reliance of courts on the principle of *salus populi,* "the welfare of the people," as the rationale used to justify that regulation.[24] Clark has shown the presence and explosive power of a different set of ideas missing from Hartz's account, ideas of sympathetic identification with slaves and other oppressed Americans, derived from diverse religious and secular sources, that motivated antebellum reformers and eventually coalesced in a sensibility that helped generate passionate loyalty to the Union cause.[25]

From Hartz's perspective, the quarrels between Whigs and Democrats betrayed "a massive confusion in political thought" that stemmed from both sides' refusal to concede their shared commitment to liberal capitalism. Whereas Whigs really should have become Tories, and Jacksonians really should have become socialists, instead they all mutated into the "American democrat," a "pathetic" figure "torn by an inner doubt," "not quite a Hercules but a Hercules with the brain of a Hamlet" (117–119). To

Hartz's champions such writing is brilliant, but it masks a strategy that Hartz himself lampooned when he saw it in others. For example, Orestes Brownson was, in Hartz's words, "a classic intellectual"; in his disenchantment with America he "did not blame his theory: he blamed the world." Likewise Hartz, when confronting Whigs who advocated reform in a language of self-discipline and harmony and Jacksonians who spoke in terms of equality and democracy, refused to admit that antebellum Americans saw themselves, each other, and their culture in terms quite different from his. Rather than modifying, abandoning, or "blaming" his theory, Hartz merely "blamed the world" of American history. He lamented the "veritable jig-saw puzzle of theoretical confusion" generated by Americans who might have pretended to disagree over slavery, temperance, education, Indian removal, and a hundred other issues when, viewed from his vantage point, "the liberal temper of American political theory is vividly apparent" beneath all their disputes (140). The "confusion," though, is Hartz's rather than theirs, for it springs from these Americans' refusal to play their scripted roles as aristocrats and proletarians. Instead, they enacted an altogether different drama, inventing subtly nuanced and strangely amalgamated characters impossible to reduce to European types. The richness and complexity of the American historical record reveals the poverty of one-dimensional theory when it confronts that world.

Hartz conceded the anomalous quality of some southerners' defense of slavery, but he presented it as the exception that proved his liberal rule. Careful analysis of nineteenth-century America shows instead that within as well as between North and South, Americans differed on many fundamental issues. Only the culture and institutions of democracy (as Jefferson, James Madison, and Tocqueville all saw) provided ways to mediate those deep disagreements over issues as diverse as free speech, slavery, Sabbatarianism, temperance, polygamy, and the legitimacy of using the authority of government—local, state, and national—to regulate the behavior of individuals. John Stuart Mill looked to the United States for examples of government regulation antithetical to the conception of liberal freedom he articulated in *On Liberty*.[26] Only the election of Abraham Lincoln, who insisted that the principle of popular sovereignty must be yoked to the principle of autonomy for all Americans, made manifest that on one issue compromise had at last become impossible. Lincoln's election did not augur "the triumph of a theory of democratic capitalism" (199), as Hartz contended; it signaled instead, as Lincoln's second inaugural made plain, the finally irresistible tug of Augustinian Christianity and republican ideals away from the evil of slavery, the deepest of all the divisions within the "liberal tradition" that Hartz imagined marching uninterrupted through American history.[27]

If Andrew Carnegie and Horatio Alger were "the children of Lincoln's achievement" (199), as Hartz argued to explain Americans' purportedly unanimous embrace of laissez-faire after the Civil War, whence sprang the populists or Knights of Labor, Jane Addams or Lillian Wald, John Dewey or Herbert Croly, Richard Ely or Walter Rauschenbusch, Charlotte Perkins Gilman or W. E. B. DuBois? For that matter, how do we explain Theodore or Franklin Delano Roosevelt? Hartz understood progressivism, as did many of his contemporaries, including of course Richard Hofstadter, as Woodrow Wilson's futile yearning for a lost world of small towns and small businesses, an exercise in nostalgia with no political or economic consequences. But historians today must disagree.

Diverse and incompatible as their strategies were, progressives nevertheless constructed from the materials they inherited a new order in governance, law, business, social organization, and culture. Louis Brandeis lost his battle against bigness. Yet the government regulation of private enterprise remains a permanent fact of life, rising and falling with public enthusiasm for, say, automobile safety or environmental protection. The National Association for the Advancement of Colored People failed to enact all of the program announced when it formed in 1909–1910, yet the civil rights movement, launched as *LTA* appeared, employed not only rights-talk but images of deliverance and salvation from Exodus and Matthew rather than Hartz's language of the main chance. The crusade for women's rights reached only a limited fulfillment in the franchise, yet feminists have invoked a variety of ideals concerning moral autonomy, civic responsibility, and more egalitarian households equally incompatible with Hartz's framework. Finally, the more social-democratically inclined American progressives failed to achieve their goals of a more egalitarian structure for work or wages, yet, from the platforms of the Populist Party in 1892 and the Progressive Party in 1912 through the agendas of the New Deal and the Fair Deal, such ambitious plans were at the heart, rather than on the margins, of political debate. To underscore the point, all were utterly inconsistent with Hartz's notion of an American liberal tradition. Some Americans, such as the opponents of the Civil War amendments and the members of the New York bourgeoisie who sought to shrink the franchise, did defend the prerogatives of wealthy white males in terms that would fit within Hartz's framework. It is important to remember that they failed to hold back the tides of democracy they feared.[28]

Hartz, writing in the shadow of McCarthyism, expected that all the moderate reforms of the twentieth century would meet the same fate. "Where capitalism is an essential principle of life," he wrote, "the man who seeks to regulate it is peculiarly vulnerable to the waving of the red flag." Just as Hartz could concede the presence of regulation in antebellum America and dismiss its significance (209–210), so his magic wand made Addams, Dewey, Ely, Croly, Gilman, and DuBois—and all they stood for—disappear. Where, he asked, were the American analogs of the British collectivist philosopher T. H. Green and the "new liberal" publicist L. T. Hobhouse and of the French and German moderate social democrats Jean Jaurès and Edward Bernstein? Whereas such Europeans shared a "frank recognition of the need for collective action to solve the class problem," Americans missed the point. Wages and hours legislation and workmen's compensation were but the "loose marginalia" of the progressive movement. Croly's democratic nationalism dissolved into "practically unintelligible rhetoric" (230, 233). Progressives, in Hartz's words, wanted only "to smash trusts and begin running the Lockian race all over again. But even the pathetic hope of Brandeis was blasted with an outpouring of liberal irrationalism" that made any notion of organization likely to be "denounced as 'un-American'" (223). In *LTA* the religious or ethical impulses that drove the social gospel, the founders of social settlements, and the architects of social security vanish beneath a fog of liberal individualism. The progressives' enduring achievements, from the graduated income tax through regulation of the economy, not surprisingly never surface.

Hartz insisted that European progressive reformers such as David Lloyd George and Léon Bourgeois could flirt with, and even ally with, socialists such as Sidney and Beatrice Webb or Jaurès, but that path, he insisted, remained closed in America. As I have tried to make clear elsewhere, this analysis relies on a widespread but faulty understanding of the dynamics of reform in England, France, and Germany as well as in the United States during these crucial years. Moderate social democracy (sometimes designated "revisionism" or "Fabianism" to indicate its divergence from Marxism) in these European nations emerged for some of the same reasons and made possible the appearance of quite similar coalitions, as those behind the more social democratic American progressive reform measures. The disappearance of those coalitions, which Hartz attributes in the American case to the red scare orchestrated by A. Mitchell Palmer after World War I, had consequences just as dramatic in England and France as in the United States. The consequences in Germany, of course, were far deadlier.[29]

Why did Hartz miss the substantial similarities and that dramatic difference? The answer reveals another reason why his analysis is no longer convincing two decades after 1989. "The attitude toward socialism remains, however, the final test of Progressive 'Americanism'" (243). That standard of judgment, reasonable as it might have been at the time, no longer seems compelling. How many decades should historians wait before inverting Werner Sombart's question and asking, Why was there socialism in Europe? Given his Eurocentric framework, Hartz understandably placed the piecemeal, pragmatic New Deal, limited as it was by Roosevelt's ability to forge a consensus from the fractured pieces of his party's coalition, comfortably within the liberal tradition. "What emerges then in the case of the New Deal is a liberal self that is lost from sight: a faith in property, a belief in class unity, a suspicion of state power, hostility to the utopian mood, all of which were blacked out by the weakness of the socialist challenge in the American liberal community" (270). This interpretation of the limits of the New Deal has since become standard; only varying degrees of admiration (from the center) or contempt (from left and right) for FDR's moderation have distinguished the major studies written in recent decades.

Historians have paid surprisingly little attention to the New Deal's unfulfilled social democratic agenda. FDR's 1944 State of the Union Address called for a "second bill of rights" assuring all Americans access to education, a job with a living wage, adequate housing, medical care, and insurance against old age, sickness, accident, and unemployment. Never mind that such ideas had been percolating in Roosevelt's administration since his Commonwealth Club speech in 1932, that Roosevelt thought the ambitious proposals for social provision contained in England's Beveridge Report derived so directly from the plans of his own administration that it should have been called "the Roosevelt Report," that FDR campaigned—and was in fact reelected—on just such a platform in 1944, that Harry S. Truman made such proposals the centerpiece of his Fair Deal, or that such ideas were at the heart of the G.I. Bill. The components of this far-reaching legislative program, caught in the cross fire between an incipient Cold War aversion to anything resembling government activity and Southern Democrats' intensified animosity toward anything resembling or contributing to equal treatment of African Americans, went down to defeats so decisive in Congress that historians refuse to believe either FDR or Truman could have been serious about them. More consistent with Hartz's concept of a liberal individualist, antigovernment straightjacket than with the historical evidence, such treatments confirm—indeed, seem to rest on—Hartz's judgment: since the New Deal did not try to bring socialism to America, its reformism must have been tepid at best.[30]

But in 2010, perhaps we American historians should stop using socialism as the litmus test of reform in the United States. When Hartz was writing, the social democratic governments sweeping into power across Northern Europe had only recently traded in their comprehensive socialist economic programs for more limited agendas featuring mixed economies supplemented with more or less extensive welfare states. The Social Democratic Party of Germany continued to speak the language of Marxism until the Bad Godesberg program of 1959, but it was already getting lonely on the left. Elsewhere in Western Europe the coalitions of urban professionals, farmers, and industrial workers that supported postwar social democratic governments surrendered the apocalyptic rhetoric of revolution. As Claus Offe and, more recently, Herrick Chapman and George Reid Andrews have pointed out, the post–World War II welfare states of Northern Europe depended more on a democratic consensus than American democracy ever did. The intensified pressure of unprecedented immigration and the subsequent diversification of population have led to increasingly wary and ungenerous electorates everywhere; only in America did progressives ever dare to proclaim that they were building their coalitions, as FDR and Truman (and later Lyndon Johnson) did, on celebrations of such diversity. In Scandinavia, as in Britain and throughout northwestern Europe, voters backed social democratic parties that promised economic growth for their nations and members of their constituencies as enthusiastically as they promised greater security and increasing equality.[31]

From the perspective of the twenty-first century, it is easy for us to discern the steady transformation of European labor parties from revolutionary Marxism to varieties of reformist social democracy, a political position far less distant from the left wing of the twentieth-century American Democratic Party than were European socialist parties earlier in the century. Not only the styles but, more importantly, the policies embraced by the British Labour Party, the German Social Democratic Party, and the French Socialist Party bear striking similarities to those of progressives in the U.S. Democratic Party. Hartz, writing in the wake of right-wing repression at home, confronting a hostile communist presence in Eastern Europe and Asia, and pondering the prospect of anticolonial revolutions looming elsewhere, could not have anticipated that development. Writing in the wake of 1989, we should not continue to ignore it.

Despite that process of development, that emergence of a "third way" in fact prior to its announcement as an ideology in the 1990s, it would be an obvious error to exaggerate the appeal of social democratic agendas. In Europe as in the United States, forces with deep cultural roots opposed every aspect of that program; on both sides of the Atlantic they have succeeded in tapping into widespread and passionate commitments. Americans' long-standing fears of inflation and aversion to taxation and their attachments to localism and various social, religious, and cultural traditions combined to propel the conservative political movement that has dominated public life in recent decades. Although acknowledging the legitimacy of their opponents' claims to embody authentic American traditions has been difficult for social democrats, just as seeing egalitarianism as an aspiration with deep roots in American history has been difficult for the New Right, it is time to abandon shopworn stories about "the people" battling heroically against "the interests." Preferences for the local over the national, the familiar over the novel, and authority and hierarchy against racial, class, and gender equality are as old as the United States. Pretending such commitments betray rather than perpetuate American traditions obstructs our understanding of our nation's past and its present.[32]

Assuming that we scholars know Americans' deeper or more authentic aspirations has inspired a generation of scolding or wishful thinking masquerading as history, political science, or cultural studies—on both ends of the political spectrum. Individuals have different ideas about human motivation: Karl Marx's concept of false consciousness, Antonio Gramsci's concept of hegemony, and Michel Foucault's concept of power/knowledge remind some analysts of consent and consensus. Rather than presuming to identify genuine preferences beneath Americans' choices as voters or consumers and to discern deeper longings buried beneath behavior we dislike, it is more fruitful to examine the struggles that have shaped our nation from a different point of view: the perspectives of those who fought them. Many scholars have unwittingly adopted Noah Webster's creed: "For God's sake, let not falsehood circulate without disproof," seeking, in his words, "to *keep public opinion correct*" by showing the perfidy of power.[33] Historians of American politics should exchange that arrogance for the more modest task of coming to grips with the complex evidence we face.

Hartz worried about Americans' smug assumption that they had solved their own problems and that other nations, both emerging and established, should simply follow their lead toward a paradise of consumption and complacency. As he expressed his anxiety early in *LTA*, "Can a people that is born equal ever understand peoples elsewhere that have become so?" (66). From that stark question to the wrenching national debate over Vietnam is a very short distance; indeed, the terms of that debate helped confirm Hartz's book as a classic and helped establish him as a sage. Given the current discrepancy between, on the one hand, the enthusiasm toward the

United States expressed by the elites of many other nations and, on the other, the distrust often sliding toward contempt toward the United States expressed by many of the world's dispossessed peoples, Hartz's insight into the problematic nature of America's tendency toward self-satisfied provincialism remains perhaps the most incisive part of the book, as valuable today as it was in 1955.

For the two decades between the publication of *LTA* and Hartz's resignation from Harvard, admiration for the book and its author mushroomed. The oracular quality of Hartz's writing, which elicited awe during a period when European émigrés such as Karl Popper, Eric Auerbach, Hannah Arendt, Max Horkheimer and Theodor Adorno, and Leo Strauss were producing their masterworks, now rankles. Few historians or political theorists in our hyperhistoricist culture of irony adopt a similar tone of voice. Consider a typical example of Hartz's rhetorical style:

> American pragmatism has always been deceptive because, glacierlike, it has rested on miles of submerged conviction, and the conformitarian ethos which that conviction generates has always been infuriating because it has refused to pay its critics the compliment of an argument. Here is where the joy of a Dewey meets the anguish of a Fenimore Cooper; for if the American deals with concrete cases because he never doubts his general principles, this is also the reason he is able to dismiss his critics with a fine and crushing ease. . . . History was on a lark, out to tease men, not by shattering their dreams, but by fulfilling them with a sort of satiric accuracy. (59–60)

Although this is writing of rare eloquence—even brilliance—historians usually want clarity and evidence served alongside such rich turns of phrase. Yet Hartz repeatedly relied on allusions and epigrams when he needed to develop arguments. Readers must know what Hartz meant not only when he dropped relatively familiar names such as Robert Filmer and John Locke, Jean-Jacques Rousseau and Joseph de Maistre, Karl Marx and Auguste Comte, or John Dewey and James Fenimore Cooper, they must also know, because Hartz provided no clues to their identity, many more-obscure thinkers on whose significance the persuasiveness of his particular arguments rests. To choose only a small random sample—French figures whose last names begin with the letter *B*—how many readers could identify Gracchus Babeuf, Pierre Simon Ballance, Pierre Nicolas Berryer, Louis Blanc, Vicomte Louis Gabriel Bonald, Jacques Bénigne Bossuet, Louis Boudin, and Aristide Briand? Few American readers, today or fifty years ago, know the questions to which those names provide the answers. Although Hartz engaged in a so-phisticated form of intimidation, it was intimidation nonetheless: readers who fail to grasp the force of a comparison are left doubting their judgment in the face of Hartz's apparently effortless erudition.

Yet many of Hartz's allusions and comparisons—as in the case of eighteenth-century American revolutionaries and French philosophes, in the case of the early twentieth-century European progressives and social democrats for whom no American analogs are said to exist, or in the case of his comments on American pragmatism—fall flat when one is familiar with the individuals or incidents involved. Given Hartz's soaring flights of rheto-ric, applying standard rules of evidence to *LTA* can seem pointless. Apho-risms and witticisms are perhaps better judged on cleverness than verifiabil-ity. It is hard—even meaningless—to determine whether the sentences in, say, Friedrich Nietzsche's *Beyond Good and Evil* are "true." Yet, unlike Nietz-sche, Hartz made empirical claims, and when one applies the test of evi-dence, they fail as often as they succeed. Even within the genre of political theory, that is a serious problem.

Equally unsettling from our perspective in 2010 is Hartz's breezy implica-tion that the works of notoriously complex thinkers such as Locke, Rous-seau, Marx, Jefferson, Madison, or Lincoln have a unitary meaning. Since Hartz wrote, the scholarship on all these thinkers has developed to the point that such one-dimensional interpretations seem not only unconvinc-ing but simpleminded. Yet even a half century ago most political theorists and intellectual historians exhibited greater care when characterizing the ideas of complicated thinkers. In short, even when Hartz wrote, his bold style stood out, but his dazzling displays of erudition and his equally spark-ling prose bought him credibility.[34] These days, hanging arguments on per-sonal authority is out of fashion; we prefer the hermeneutics of suspicion. When we see Hartz offering an epigram or sliding over an inconvenient fact or discrepancy, we want to examine the evidence and reconsider the analy-sis. As Hartz might have put it, when his writing asks us to genuflect, we raise an eyebrow instead.

What can Hartz mean, for example, by "the joy of a Dewey" or "the anguish of a Fenimore Cooper" in the passage quoted above? Given Dewey's deep dis-satisfaction about the distance between his own radical democratic politics and his own educational theory and the more limited achievements of twentieth-century American reformers and so-called progressive educators, and given Cooper's indomitable, triumphalist nationalism, one might as eas-ily (and perhaps just as accurately) invoke "the anguish of a Dewey" and the "joy of a Fenimore Cooper." But in either case imagery plays Charlemagne to meaning, doing all the analytical work and leaving readers puzzled. All of us call attention to our writing sometimes, depending on shorthand or metaphor to do our work for us (as I did in the preceding sentence). *LTA* depends heavily on such sleights.

To continue this exercise with another example, if "miles of submerged conviction" lie beneath pragmatism and that conviction generates a "conformitarian ethos" that "has refused to pay its critics the compliment of an argument," why did Charles Sanders Peirce, William James, George Herbert Mead, and Dewey have to work so hard to explain and defend themselves against critics (and each other) from the moment Peirce tried to explain how we make our ideas clear? Scrutinizing the pragmatists' writings would have forced Hartz to confront their head-on challenge to his assumptions about Americans' thoroughgoing, unexamined individualism undergirding his argument. Like the religious language of eighteenth-century America or the more social democratic wing of American progressivism, pragmatism remained absent from *LTA*.

Finally, if history can "go on a lark," what would happen if it kept its shoulder to the wheel? In short, these sentences, like many others that glitter through *LTA*, disintegrate into nonsense when subjected to analysis. Given Hartz's intelligence, acid wit, and penchant for dramatic flourishes, he might perhaps have followed the course of other gifted writers such as Oscar Wilde and George Bernard Shaw, who dabbled in nonfiction as contributors to *Fabian Essays in Socialism* before turning their talents to the theater.

Instead, Hartz devoted himself after *LTA* to defenses and elaborations of his "fragment theory" of comparative cultural development and then, in the final years of his life, to rambling ruminations on the meaning of world history. In one of his most compelling pieces of writing, an essay published in 1960, "Democracy: Image and Reality," Hartz undertook to expand his argument in *LTA* to encompass contemporary debates over democracy. This essay shows his characteristic imagination and insight. In the end, however, it merely reframes Hartz's argument about American exceptionalism and again subordinates the untidy evidence of history to the spare elegance of his analytical scheme. The ideas and institutions of liberal democracy emerged, Hartz wrote in "Democracy: Image and Reality," against the world of "church, guild, and province," which compelled the democratic "system to define itself in terms of the one it seeks to undermine." Thus, democrats elevated reason, individualism, and equality, thereby creating a democratic myth to replace the myths propping up the ancien régime. But democracy after its triumph proved unable to sustain those values in practice. Disillusionment inevitably followed the discovery that elites could maintain their power by manipulating the irrational impulses of the masses. Hartz recommended patience rather than despair in the face of such knowledge because the disenchantment likely in communist nations, saddled with the weight of even loftier expectations, would eventually bring them down.

Hartz's conclusion in this essay appeared to point in a direction opposite to that of *LTA:* "It would be absurd to say, in light of all the popular social reforms of the last century, that democracy has not produced more decisions in the popular interest than the will of eighteenth-century aristocracies." In short, Hartz admitted, Bernstein was right: Liberal democratic states in Europe had managed to achieve what Marx judged impossible, and the revisionists' "faith in the ultimate universality of the democratic state was a sound one." But Europe remained the standard of comparison for Hartz's analysis, and liberalism remained the heart of the matter. "The truth is, intellectually we have only experienced *one* revolution in modern times, and that is the revolution of the Enlightenment. The negative idealism that liberalism forged in the fight against feudalism, with its images of individuality, rationality, and the popular will," provided both democrats and Marxists with the weapons they needed.[35]

As in *LTA,* however, Hartz presented a deviant American case spinning away from a West European norm. He was now contrasting America against an even more wildly divergent communist world, but the logic of his exceptionalist model remained intact. With Thomas L. Haskell, I believe we should dispense with such conceptions of America—whether exceptionalist or antiexceptionalist—and adopt what Haskell calls a "postexceptionalist" perspective that might enable us to follow the historical evidence without claiming "to have discovered in the uniqueness of national experience an explanatory key that unlocks all doors." Liberated from debates between exceptionalists and antiexceptionalists, we can "admit that sweeping claims and counterclaims about the similarity or difference of entire nations will forever elude empirical resolution." As historians, we might find that a postexceptionalist perspective prevents us from freezing our evidence into the static typologies that prevented Hartz, even at his best, from dealing with the particularities of different times and different nations.[36]

The posthumous publication of Hartz's final work, *A Synthesis of World History,* shows how the most troubling of Hartz's tendencies in *LTA* spun out of control in his later years. Hartz aspired in his last book to explain all the philosophical systems in world history by reducing them to the allegedly universal psychological tension between "action" and "quiescence," or "thrust" and "surrender." Political as well as religious ideas could be stretched across the same grid: in Christian theology he contrasted the "active" Thomas Aquinas to the "passive" Augustine, in China the "active" Confucians to the "passive" Taoists, in America—although of course ranged across a narrower spectrum, as appropriate for the liberal fragment Hartz had anatomized in *LTA*—the "active" Jeffersonians to the "passive" Whigs. The book shows all the ambition of Montesquieu, Georg Wilhelm Friedrich Hegel, or Max Weber, all the iconoclastic fervor of Voltaire, Friedrich Nietzsche, or Sigmund Freud, without the necessary subtlety and analytical precision to give it force:

> Now what is the distinctive genius of the thinkers? They are individually "great," intrinsically powerful. Yet each worked with the same issue of human action and quiescence, utilizing its characteristic essences, legislation and consensualism, atomism and symbiosis, worldliness and localism, mind and ardent belief. Indeed it is by no means too much to say that they can be made interchangeable by a manipulation of the categories of that issue as a mathematician converts form into form. Shift the metaphor, and they can be created out of one another as a chemist recreates compounds.[37]

Although Hartz's grip was clearly slipping when he wrote *A Synthesis of World History,* the tendencies toward too-rigid typology, psychological reductionism, and the simplification of complex thinkers to fit a brittle framework all echo, albeit in exaggerated form, the worst features of *LTA.* Both books reflect a common attitude toward the relation between theory and history and a common methodology that privileges the insights of the analyst and refuses to take seriously, on their own terms, the ideas, values, or lives of those being analyzed.

Why does Hartz's analysis of America's liberal tradition matter in 2010? Why can't we historians simply acknowledge the book's significance as a product of the 1950s and leave it at that? Unfortunately, Hartz's argument has proved so powerful and so resistant to critics' charges that its legacy has had serious consequences of two sorts in America since the 1950s, consequences that merit consideration.

First, Hartz persuaded many American political theorists that there is no reason to study American political thought. Because America had no social conflicts, he argued, Americans contributed "relatively little political thought at all." Given moral consensus, "political philosophy did not have to get going in the first place." As a result, undergraduates and graduate students interested in political theory have learned to grapple with the writings of Rousseau or Hegel or Marx, but most of them have learned little or nothing about the American intellectual tradition. Hartz himself seems to have focused most of his energies as a teacher on European thinkers, and the profession has followed his lead.[38]

Not only is it possible to earn a Ph.D. in a first-rate graduate program in political science without having studied American political thought, but few courses in the field exist. Few political scientists consider it worth studying. At least four distinct reasons can be offered to explain this odd phenomenon. First, political theorists usually concentrate on philosophers in the tradition of Plato and Aristotle, Hegel and Marx, who derived their politics from elaborate systems ranging from ontology to metaphysics. The American tradition has indeed produced few such thinkers. Second, the style of linguistic analysis that has dominated Anglo-American philosophy since the middle of the twentieth century has been inhospitable to issues of the sort discussed by earlier American political theorists. Although recent theorists, following the lead of John Rawls, have returned to such concerns, most of them have also followed the methodology of the early Rawls, concentrating on thought experiments and eschewing a historical approach. Third, the discipline of political science continues its curious obsession with what Donald P. Green and Ian Shapiro have fittingly termed the "pathologies of rational choice theory," a peculiar analytical approach that is antagonistic to the classic concerns of political theory. In the words of William Riker, a founding father of a way of thinking uneasy with the notion of "founding" because of its historical implications, political scientists should dispense with "traditional methods—i.e., history writing, the description of institutions, and legal analysis," because such work can produce at best only wisdom, not science. Finally, a large number of those who teach political theory in American universities are the students (or the students of students) of two influential scholars who agreed on little but the insignificance of American thought, Leo Strauss and Louis Hartz.[39]

Hartz's devaluing of American political thought has thus helped justify the failure of American political scientists to take seriously their own heritage, poor as it is in Aristotles and Hegels but rich in debates about what democracy is and what it should be. Ideas have been at the center of American popular political debates since the seventeenth century. Because citizenship in the English North American colonies was relatively widespread from the outset, writers of compacts, covenants, constitutions, laws, and (at least until fairly recently) court decisions in America have sought to communicate with a broad public in terms ordinary people could understand and endorse. For that reason, as Donald S. Lutz has demonstrated, students of

American political theory should examine the meanings of public texts rather than limiting their attention to a canon of abstract political philosophy.[40] From Plato onward, most of the writers of "great books" of political philosophy either never had to deal with the problem of implementing their ideas, or, when the opportunity presented itself, came up with schemes quite different from those suggested in their theoretical treatises. Locke, for example, dreamed up a semifeudal never-never land in response to his friend the earl of Shaftesbury's invitation to write a constitution for the colony of Carolina. Rousseau prescribed for Poland a constitution allowing room for aristocrats, serfs, and forms of representative democracy inimical to the republican forms he envisioned for his native Geneva or for unspoiled Corsica. Unlike Benjamin Franklin's observation about a hanging, such opportunities to turn the abstract into the concrete can wonderfully muddle the mind.

Most of America's most enduring theorists, by contrast, have been actively involved in the complexities of the political process. For that reason their writings show not only a distinctive engagement with the practical questions of democratic governance but an equally distinctive tensile strength that professors and students of political theory, hurrying to get from Locke and Rousseau to Mill and Marx and then on to Rawls and Jürgen Habermas, fail to grasp in their quick readings of *Federalist* Number Ten and John C. Calhoun's *Disquisition on Government*. Hartz's portrait of America's "liberal tradition," by denying the depth and seriousness of the issues addressed by those who have shaped America's political and legal traditions, helped authorize such unfortunate disregard, and the enduring respect of political theorists for *LTA* perpetuates it.   .

A second consequence of the widespread acceptance of Hartz's argument has been the tendency to assume that the only authentic, legitimate questions of American politics are those concerning self-interest, individual rights, and the sanctity of personal property. This astonishing assumption is shared across the political spectrum. As John Diggins has pointed out, there is a surprising congruence between Hartz's *LTA* and Herbert Marcuse's *One Dimensional Man*. Both books reduce Americans to a band of single- and simpleminded consumers who lack the personal or cultural resources to see beyond the appeals of corporate and/or mainstream political advertisements. Whereas free-market capitalists and conservative cultural commentators unanimously dismissed Marcuse's diagnosis as simplistic and his prescriptions for reform as proto-totalitarian, they have tended implicitly to endorse Hartz's analysis, perhaps because it led, as he admitted himself (33), only to a shoulder-shrugging acceptance of unthinking individualism and market "imperatives."[41]

The ready embrace by radical scholars of Hartz's portrait of a one-dimensional American tradition, which depends on ignoring or denying the significance of a continuing series of democratic reform efforts stretching from the seventeenth century to the present, ironically reinforces the assumptions such scholars intend to criticize and transform. For if property holding alone mattered to Americans in the past and matters in the present, and if frontal (i.e., socialist) challenges to the institution of private property alone can be judged genuinely radical, then perhaps America should be defined as nothing more than a culture of consumer capitalism (so too should Great Britain, Germany, France, Denmark, and Sweden). That way of thinking seems better suited to the interests of free-marketeers than to those calling for America to become more egalitarian, but a surprising number of leftist scholars in the fields of law, philosophy, political theory, and history have embraced it. Criticizing Hartz thus ruffles feathers across the contemporary political spectrum. Too many people, right and left, have too much invested in the idea of an American liberal tradition to surrender it without a fight.

By diminishing the significance of democratic thinkers, activists, and movements in American history, those who continue to endorse Hartz's notion of a liberal tradition—whether from the right or the left—consciously or unwittingly reinforce the claims of those who define as un-American any conception of radical democracy. Challenging hierarchies, reasoning from the logic of the principle "one citizen, one vote" to the conclusion that economic power should not extend into social and political power, has been a recurring theme in American history. But such battles never end: disagreement, deliberation, and provisional compromises that in turn generate new disagreements are the ineluctable dynamic of democracy.

The Liberal Tradition in America came to prominence just as John Dewey's ideas went into eclipse. Perhaps the recent renaissance of American pragmatism will help refocus attention on the potential harmonies that Dewey envisioned between our culture's commitments to open-ended scientific inquiry and his ideal of an open-ended, experimental, pluralist democracy. Only when viewed through the backward telescope of Hartz's liberal tradition do the struggles for a democratic culture that Dewey saw at the heart of American history shrink to insignificance. For the sake of historical accuracy as well as democratic renewal, we should widen our focus as scholars to the projects that Tocqueville identified, the sometimes successful efforts to build a democratic culture on an ethic of reciprocity, efforts blurred beyond recognition by Hartz's distorting lens.

Hartz was worried about America's relevance to a world of nations shaking themselves free from the bonds of colonialism. Today the United States seems not only relevant but, despite the recent return to older patterns of imperial bullying and the current economic crisis, in at least certain respects a model. Developed and developing nations alike are drawn toward our sturdy democratic political institutions and our troubled but still relatively stable state-regulated market economy. The enthusiasm of the early 1990s for unchecked market economies in the formerly communist nations of Eastern Europe has faded into a renewed appreciation of the fundamental importance of popular sovereignty and the rule of law. The business scandals of 2002 and the collapse of 2009 have shown Americans the perils of the cowboy capitalism that has been preached by many in the Republican Party since 1980. Skepticism about business lends renewed luster to the progressives' idea of a mixed economy overseen by a vigilant regulatory state. The systematic dismantling of the regulatory apparatus by the administration of George W. Bush has been almost universally credited with having made possible the worst economic crisis since the Great Depression. In the wake of September 11, 2001, public authority briefly demonstrated again not only its indispensability but its potential effectiveness when exerted with resolve in behalf of the common good. In the wake of Hurricane Katrina in 2005, the failures of laissez-faire and government by cronies were likewise painfully exposed. Especially when popular government is mobilized from the ground up rather than from the top down, it has enormous potential to address problems effectively. Since the eighteenth century it has been less the absence of feudalism than the presence of democracy—albeit imperfect, contested, and constricted but nevertheless slowly expanding—that has distinguished the United States from other nations, and that difference has shrunk as democracy has spread. It is democracy that now makes America attractive to nations shaking themselves free from bonds of other kinds.[42] During the last fifty years varieties of liberal democratic polities and mixed economies have become the rule rather than the exception in the developed world and prototypes for developing nations eager to enjoy more stable politics and to share the richer nations' prosperity. "Democracy will come into its own," Dewey predicted, "for democracy is a name for a life of free and enriching communion. It had its seer in Walt Whitman."[43]

We know too much now, both about the stubborn persistence of inequality in America and about America's unsettling tendency to assert its will globally, to share entirely Whitman's indomitable optimism, but we can at least attempt to recover the vibrant sense of democratic possibility that infused his *Democratic Vistas,* written in the bleak days after the Civil War:

America, filling the present with greatest deeds and problems, cheerfully accepting the past, including feudalism (as, indeed, the present is but the legitimate birth of the past, including feudalism,) counts, as I reckon, for her justification and success (for who, as yet, dare claim success?) almost entirely on the future. Nor is that hope unwarranted. To-day, ahead, though dimly yet, we see, in vistas, a copious, sane, gigantic offspring. For our New World I consider far less important for what it has done, or what it is, than for results to come. Sole among nationalities, these States have assumed the task to put in forms of lasting power and practicality, on areas of amplitude rivaling the operations of the physical kosmos, the moral political speculations of ages, long, long deferr'd, the democratic republican principle, and the theory of development and perfection by voluntary standards, and self-reliance.[44]

From the perspective of 2010, it is not the sober-minded Hartz but the democratic "seer" Whitman who appears the more reliable guide to and the shrewder analyst of American culture. Those who seek to understand the dynamics of liberal democracy in American history would do well to keep both of their perspectives in view.

NOTES

1. For testimony concerning Hartz's genius in the classroom, see the essays by Benjamin Barber and Paul Roazen in a volume consisting of Hartz's lectures that have been painstakingly pieced together by his former students: Louis Hartz, *The Necessity of Choice: Nineteenth-Century Political Thought*, ed. Paul Roazen, with a preface by Benjamin Barber (New Brunswick, N.J.: Transaction Books, 1990).

2. One still finds that lofty assessment of *LTA* as "the greatest book ever written about the American political tradition" repeated in odd places, such as in the opening paragraph of a book devoted to a thinker not even mentioned by Hartz, and whose life and writings stand as a direct challenge to everything about Hartz's argument: Bob Pepperman Taylor, *America's Bachelor Uncle: Thoreau and the American Polity* (Lawrence: University Press of Kansas, 1996), 1.

3. In a passage that expresses the spirit of her critical comments about *LTA*, Shklar later wrote, "I do not treat [American political thought] as a peculiarly local phenomenon, 'a poor thing but our own,' but as intrinsically significant. Apart from the early establishment of representative democracy and the persistence of slavery, which do give it a special character, American political thought is just an integral part of modern history as a whole." Judith Shklar, "A Life of Learning," in *Liberalism without Illusions*, ed. Bernard Yack (Chicago: University of Chicago Press,

1996), 277. Conversations with Shklar about Hartz, and about his approach to American political culture in *LTA*, helped me formulate several of the principal arguments in this essay.

4. This scholarship is large and growing rapidly. Instructive examples of the institutional and disciplinary analysis of mid-twentieth-century social science include S. M. Amadae, *Rationalizing Capitalist Democracy: The Cold War Origins of Rational Choice Liberalism* (Chicago: University of Chicago Press, 2003); Robert Adcock, Mark Bevir, and Shannon C. Stimson, eds., *Modern Political Science: Anglo-American Exchanges since 1880* (Princeton, N.J.: Princeton University Press, 2007); *The Cambridge History of Science*, vol. 7, *The Modern Social Sciences*, ed. Theodore M. Porter and Dorothy Ross (Cambridge: Cambridge University Press, 2003); David Engerman, Nils Gilman, Mark H. Haefele, and Michael Latham, eds., *Staging Growth: Modernization, Development, and the Global Cold War* (Amherst: University of Massachusetts Press, 2003); Joel Isaac, "Theories of Knowledge and the American Human Sciences, 1920–1960" (Ph.D. diss., Cambridge University, 2005); Isaac, "The Human Sciences in Cold War America," *Historical Journal* 50 (2007): 725–746; Duncan Bell, *Political Thought and International Relations: Variations on a Realist Theme* (Oxford: Oxford University Press, 2009); Bell, "Writing the World: Disciplinary History and Beyond," *International Affairs*, forthcoming; and Richard Tuck, *Free Riding* (Cambridge, Mass.: Harvard University Press, 2008).

5. Examples of the cross-fertilization of history and political science include Byron E. Shafer and Anthony J. Badger, eds., *Contesting Democracy: Substance and Structure in American Political History* (Lawrence: University Press of Kansas, 2001); and Meg Jacobs, William J. Novak, and Julian E. Zelizer, eds., *The Democratic Experiment: New Directions in American Political History* (Princeton, N.J.: Princeton University Press, 2003). This essay draws on my contribution to that volume, "From Hartz to Tocqueville: Shifting the Focus from Liberalism to Democracy in America," 350–380.

6. Louis Hartz, *The Liberal Tradition in America* (New York: Harcourt, Brace & World/Harvest, 1955), 20. All further page references, noted in parentheses in the text, are to this edition.

7. The reconsideration of Locke that emphasized the importance of his religious convictions began with Peter Laslett's introduction to his edition of Locke's *Two Treatises of Government* (Cambridge: Cambridge University Press, 1960) and matured with John Dunn, *The Political Thought of John Locke: An Historical Account of the Argument of the "Two Treatises of Government"* (Cambridge: Cambridge University Press, 1969). For an especially helpful account of Locke's "worldly asceticism," which enabled him to take seriously both his commitment to Protestantism and his commitment to property, which enabled Americans such as Thomas Jefferson and John Adams to take Locke seriously, and which distinguishes the historical Locke decisively from the one-dimensional, liberty-and-property-obsessed Locke of Hartz's account, see Joshua Foa Dienstag, "Serving God and Mammon: The Lockean Sympathy in Early American Thought," *American Political Science Review* 90 (1996): 497–511; and Dienstag, "Between History and Nature: Social Contract Theory

in Locke and the Founders," *Journal of Politics* 58 (1996): 985–1009. For a more recent account developing these themes, see Jeremy Waldron, *God, Locke, and Equality: Christian Foundations in Locke's Political Thought* (Cambridge: Cambridge University Press, 2002).

8. Reviews of Hartz, *LTA*, by George Mowry, *American Historical Review* 61 (1955): 140–141; Arthur Mann, *William and Mary Quarterly*, 3rd series, 12 (1955): 653–655; Ralph Henry Gabriel, *Journal of the History of Ideas* 17 (1956): 136–138; and Marvin Meyers, *Comparative Studies in Society and History* 5 (1963–1964): 261–268.

9. Paul Roazen, introduction to Hartz, *The Necessity of Choice*, 8.

10. Louis Hartz, "Comment," *Comparative Studies in Society and History* 5 (1963–1964): 279–284.

11. Leonard Krieger, review of *The Liberal Tradition in America, Comparative Studies in History and Society* 5 (1963–1964): 269–273. Hartz had attempted to preempt this criticism in *LTA*, 26–27, by pointing out how little intra-European comparative history had been done. Krieger was not persuaded.

12. Adrienne Koch, review of *The Liberal Tradition in America*, by Louis Hartz, *Mississippi Valley Historical Review* 43 (1955): 550–552.

13. Louis Hartz, "Reply," in *Failure of a Dream? Essays in the History of American Socialism*, ed. John H. M. Laslett and Seymour Martin Lipset, rev. ed. (1974; reprint, Berkeley and Los Angeles: University of California Press, 1984), 357–361. For Kenneth McNaught's critique of *LTA*, which emphasizes the significance of class divisions and democratic reform movements in American history, see *Failure of a Dream*, 345–356.

14. Roazen, introduction to Hartz, *The Necessity of Choice*, 20.

15. For evidence of the centrality of race and gender in contemporary scholarship, see, for example, three of the most widely read and celebrated works of the closing years of the twentieth century: Rogers M. Smith, *Civic Ideals: Conflicting Visions of Citizenship in U.S. History* (New Haven, Conn.: Yale University Press, 1997); Eric Foner, *The Story of American Freedom* (New York: Norton, 1998); and Linda K. Kerber, *No Constitutional Right to Be Ladies: Women and the Obligations of Citizenship* (New York: Hill & Wang, 1998).

16. On the paradoxical consequences of this dynamic for our understanding of America's "liberal tradition" as a cultural phenomenon distinct from its Christian origins, see David A. Hollinger, *Science, Jews, and Secular Culture: Studies in Mid-Twentieth-Century American Intellectual History* (Princeton, N.J.: Princeton University Press, 1996), esp. chaps. 2, 3, and 8. Hartz could be an acute analyst of religion and its critics. In *The Necessity of Choice*, chap. 2, he brilliantly examined the eighteenth-century French philosophes' reliance on a standard of "nature" rather than "science" once they realized that a thoroughgoing empiricism would require them to take seriously the religious experience of French Catholics. Whereas a similar insight drove William James, committed to a radical empiricism, to examine in detail the varieties of religious experience, Hartz, for reasons not altogether clear, chose instead simply to dismiss the political significance of religion in America. For antidotes,

see the essays in Mark A. Noll, ed., *Religion and American Politics* (New York: Oxford University Press, 1990), and *America's God: From Jonathan Edwards to Abraham Lincoln* (New York: Oxford University Press, 2002).

17. David D. Hall, *Worlds of Wonder, Days of Judgment: Popular Religious Belief in Early New England* (Cambridge, Mass.: Harvard University Press, 1990), 245. See more generally Hall, "Narrating Puritanism," in *New Directions in American Religious History*, ed. Harry Stout and D. G. Hart (New York: Oxford University Press, 1997), 51–83; and Stephen Innes, *Creating the Commonwealth: The Economic Culture of Puritan New England* (New York: Norton, 1995). For a fuller exposition of my argument concerning the role of religion in American political culture, see James T. Kloppenberg, "Knowledge and Belief in American Public Life," in *The Virtues of Liberalism* (New York: Oxford University Press, 1998), 38–58.

18. Alexis de Tocqueville, *Democracy in America*, ed. J. P. Mayer, trans. George Lawrence (Garden City, N.Y.: Doubleday/Anchor, 1969), 509, 511.

19. Ibid., 508, 511.

20. Ibid., 512. For my understanding of Tocqueville and discussion of the various uses American scholars and politicians have made of his work, see James T. Kloppenberg, "Life Everlasting: Tocqueville in America," in *The Virtues of Liberalism*, 71–81, "The Canvas and the Color: Tocqueville's Philosophical History and Why It Matters Now," *Modern Intellectual History* 3 (2006): 495–521, and "Tocqueville, Mill, and the American Gentry," *La Revue Tocqueville/The Tocqueville Review* 27, no. 2 (2006): 351–379.

21. Richard J. Ellis, *American Political Cultures* (New York: Oxford University Press, 1993), 151. This spirited book can be read as an extended essay devoted to demonstrating, in considerable detail, the inadequacy of Hartz's argument in *LTA*. Readers still persuaded by Hartz's interpretation should read *American Political Cultures*, which examines more fully many of the shortcomings in *LTA* that I can only highlight briefly here.

22. For a strikingly different interpretation emphasizing the genuinely democratic and revolutionary achievements of the American Revolution, likewise examined in a comparative framework, see the still rewarding masterpiece by R. R. Palmer, *The Age of the Democratic Revolution*, 2 vols. (1959; reprint, Princeton, N.J.: Princeton University Press, 1964), 1: 185–235.

23. John Adams quoted in Joseph J. Ellis, *Passionate Sage: The Character and Legacy of John Adams* (New York: Norton, 1993), 136; Samuel Adams quoted in Gordon Wood, *The Creation of the American Republic, 1776–1787* (New York: Norton, 1969), 407. On the distance separating John Adams in particular from Hartz's notion of a liberal tradition, see the penetrating essay by John P. Diggins, "Knowledge and Sorrow: Louis Hartz's Quarrel with American History," *Political Theory* 16 (1988): 355–376. For recent studies establishing the founders' commitment to democratic procedures and challenging the idea that they should be seen as champions either of atomistic liberalism or of classical republicanism, see especially Lance Banning, *The Sacred Fire of Liberty* (Ithaca, N.Y.: Cornell University Press, 1995); Bernard Bailyn,

Faces of Revolution: Personalities and Themes in the Struggle for American Independence (New York: Knopf, 1990); Robert E. Shalhope, *The Roots of Democracy: American Thought and Culture, 1760–1800* (Boston: Twayne, 1990); Gordon Wood, *Revolutionary Characters: What Made the Founders Different* (New York: Penguin, 2006); and Akhil Amar, *America's Constitution: A Biography* (New York: Random House, 2005).

24. Cf. Louis Hartz, *Economic Policy and Democratic Thought: Pennsylvania, 1776–1860* (Cambridge, Mass.: Harvard University Press, 1948); Oscar Handlin and Mary Flug Handlin, *Commonwealth: A Study of the Role of Government in the American Economy: Massachusetts, 1774–1861* (New York: New York University Press, 1947; rev. ed., Cambridge, Mass.: Belknap Press of Harvard University Press, 1969); and William J. Novak, *The People's Welfare: Law and Regulation in Nineteenth-Century America* (Chapel Hill: University of North Carolina Press, 1996), esp. 1–18, 84–88, 284–285. A common response to Novak's head-on challenge to the prevailing wisdom of American economic and legal historians is simple incredulity. Like the mountain of evidence for the language of republicanism that Gordon Wood presented in *The Creation of the American Republic*, however, Novak's evidence cannot be dismissed or explained away so easily; only extensive further research will confirm or challenge his interpretation. For a wealth of evidence further disputing Hartz's portrait of an uncomplicated, triumphant liberal ethos, presented within an explicitly comparative framework, see the fine essays in Peter Becker, Jürgen Heideking, and James Henretta, eds., *Republicanism and Liberalism in America and the German States, 1750–1850* (New York: Cambridge University Press, 2002).

25. Elizabeth B. Clark, "The Sacred Rights of the Weak: Pain, Sympathy, and the Culture of Individual Rights in Antebellum America," *Journal of American History* 82 (1995): 463–493. For other portraits of antebellum American culture utterly irreconcilable with Hartz's, see Thomas L. Haskell's "Capitalism and the Origins of the Humanitarian Sensibility" and "Convention and Hegemonic Interest in the Debate over Antislavery: A Reply to Davis and Ashworth," in *The Antislavery Debate: Capitalism and Abolitionism as a Problem in Historical Interpretation,* ed. Thomas J. Bender (Berkeley and Los Angeles: University of California Press, 1992), 107–160, 200–260; Daniel Walker Howe, *Making the American Self: Jonathan Edwards to Abraham Lincoln* (Cambridge, Mass.: Harvard University Press, 1997); Sean Wilentz, *The Rise of American Democracy: Jefferson to Lincoln* (New York: Norton, 2005); and Daniel Walker Howe, *What Hath God Wrought: The Transformation of America, 1815–1848* (New York: Oxford University Press, 2007).

26. In John Stuart Mill, *On Liberty* (1859), see esp. chap. 4. I am grateful to William Novak for reminding me of this point.

27. Recent studies emphasizing these themes include William Lee Miller, *Lincoln's Virtues: An Ethical Biography* (New York: Knopf, 2002); Ronald C. White Jr., *Lincoln's Greatest Speech: The Second Inaugural* (New York: Simon & Schuster, 2002); and Mark A. Noll, *The Civil War as a Theological Crisis* (Chapel Hill: University of North Carolina Press, 2006). Hartz's remarkable power as teacher and interpreter is apparent in the brilliant work of J. David Greenstone, whose analysis in *The Lincoln*

Persuasion: Remaking American Liberalism (Princeton, N.J.: Princeton University Press, 1993) shows the inadequacy of Hartz's "liberal tradition." Greenstone's admiration for his teacher Hartz prevented him from admitting that his own compelling analysis of the "bipolarity" of American political thought, which he thought was overcome by Lincoln and by some later Progressive reformers as well, was incompatible with Hartz's argument in *LTA*.

28. On these issues, see Michael Vorenberg, "Bringing the Constitution Back In: Amendment, Innovation, and Popular Democracy during the Civil War Era," in Jacobs, Novak, and Zelizer, *The Democratic Experiment*, 120–145; and Sven Beckert, "Democracy and Its Discontents," *Past and Present* 174 (2002): 116–157.

29. I have tried to make clear the similarities as well as the differences between these American and European theorists and reformers in *Uncertain Victory: Social Democracy and Progressivism in European and American Thought, 1870–1920* (New York: Oxford University Press, 1986). A more recent interpretation that places progressivism in a trans-Atlantic context is Daniel T. Rodgers, *Atlantic Crossings: Social Politics in a Progressive Age* (Cambridge, Mass.: Harvard University Press, 1998). An excellent study of progressive thought that emphasizes its ethical and religious dimensions is Eldon Eisenach, *The Lost Promise of Progressivism* (Lawrence: University Press of Kansas, 1994).

30. On the origin, development, and fate of these ideas, the light they cast on American politics, and historians' dismissal of their importance, see James T. Kloppenberg, "Deliberative Democracy and the Problem of Poverty in America," in *The Virtues of Liberalism*, 100–123; and Cass Sunstein, *The Second Bill of Rights: FDR's Unfinished Revolution and Why We Need It More than Ever* (New York: Basic Books, 2004).

31. Claus Offe, *Contradictions of the Welfare State* (Cambridge, Mass.: MIT Press, 1984); George Reid Andrews and Herrick Chapman, eds., *The Social Construction of Democracy, 1870–1990* (New York: New York University Press, 1995). See also Stein Ringen, *The Possibility of Politics: A Study in the Political Economy of the Welfare State* (Oxford: Oxford University Press/Clarendon Press, 1987); and Abram de Swaan, *In Care of the State: Health Care, Education and Welfare in Europe and the USA in the Modern Era* (New York: Oxford University Press, 1988).

32. See Meg Jacobs, *Pocketbook Politics: Economic Citizenship in Twentieth-Century America* (Princeton, N.J.: Princeton University Press, 2004); and the essays in Bruce Schulman and Julian Zelizer, eds., *Rightward Bound: Making America Conservative in the 1970s* (Cambridge, Mass.: Harvard University Press, 2008).

33. Noah Webster to Oliver Wolcott Jr., June 23, 1800, quoted by Joanne Freeman, "Explaining the Unexplainable: The Cultural Context of the Sedition Act," in Jacobs, Novak, and Zelizer, *The Democratic Experiment*, 28.

34. Robert Adcock and Mark Bevir accurately characterize the writing of Hartz and contemporaries such as Carl Friedrich and Leo Strauss as "epic." See Adcock and Bevir, "The Remaking of Political Theory," in Adcock, Bevir, and Stimson, *Modern Political Science*, 209–233. I have addressed Strauss's writings in James T. Kloppenberg, "The Place of Value in a Culture of Facts: Truth and Historicism," in

The Humanities and the Dynamics of Inclusion since World War II, ed. David A. Hollinger (Baltimore: Johns Hopkins University Press, 2006), 126–158.

35. Louis Hartz, "Democracy: Image and Reality," in *Democracy Today*, ed. William N. Chambers and Robert H. Salisbury (St. Louis, Mo.: Washington University Press, 1960), 13–29.

36. Thomas L. Haskell, "Taking Exception to Exceptionalism," *Reviews in American History* 28 (2000): 151–166. See also the contributions to this debate in Thomas Bender, ed., *Rethinking American History in a Global Age* (Berkeley and Los Angeles: University of California Press, 2002).

37. See Louis Hartz, *The Founding of New Societies: Studies in the History of the United States, Latin America, South Africa, Canada, and Australia* (New York: Harcourt, Brace & World, 1964); on Hartz's final work, *A Synthesis of World History*, which he had printed privately in Europe before his death, see the gentle but nevertheless devastating assessment by Hartz's former student Patrick Riley, "Louis Hartz: The Final Years, the Unknown Work," *Political Theory* 16 (1988): 377–399. The passage quoted appears on page 383 of Riley's essay.

38. Hartz, *The Necessity of Choice*, 178; see also Roazen's discussion of this issue in the introduction to that volume: "If, as Hartz believed, philosophizing exists only where there is fundamental social conflict, it is no wonder that American political thought, compared to what happened in Europe, never succeeded in getting off the ground" (5).

39. Donald P. Green and Ian Shapiro, *Pathologies of Rational Choice Theory: A Critique of Applications in Political Science* (New Haven, Conn.: Yale University Press, 1994); Jeffrey Friedman, ed., *The Rational Choice Controversy: Economic Models of Politics Reconsidered* (New Haven, Conn.: Yale University Press, 1996), which includes voices on all sides of the debate over rational choice; William H. Riker, *The Theory of Political Coalitions* (New Haven, Conn.: Yale University Press, 1962), viii. For a wide-ranging and thoughtful discussion of these issues, see Rogers Smith, "Science, Non-Science, and Politics," in *The Historic Turn in the Human Sciences*, ed. Terrence J. McDonald (Ann Arbor: University of Michigan Press, 1996), 119–159. Two comprehensive histories of the profession of political science are David M. Ricci, *The Tragedy of Political Science: Politics, Scholarship, and Democracy* (New Haven, Conn.: Yale University Press, 1984); and Raymond Seidelman and Edward J. Harpham, *Disenchanted Realists: Political Science and the American Crisis, 1884–1984* (Albany: State University of New York Press, 1985). For more recent studies that pay close attention to institutional dynamics, see the works discussed in note 4 above.

40. Donald J. Lutz, *A Preface to American Political Theory* (Lawrence: University Press of Kansas, 1992).

41. John Patrick Diggins, *The Proud Decades: America in War and Peace, 1941–1960* (New York: Norton, 1988), 255–256.

42. This is of course not the first time the United States has played such a paradoxical role, to the disgust and dismay of American dissenters, who have understandably questioned whether the nation should be seen as a symbol of democratic

promise. To cite just one example, Woodrow Wilson, although himself a racist and an imperialist, inspired democratic or anticolonialist movements in Egypt, India, China, Korea, and Indochina by proclaiming the principle of self-determination of peoples. See Erez Manela, *The Wilsonian Moment: Self-Determination and the International Origins of Anticolonial Nationalism* (New York: Oxford University Press, 2007); and Trygve Throntveit, "The Fable of the Fourteen Points: Woodrow Wilson and National Self-Determination," unpublished manuscript, Harvard University.

43. John Dewey, *The Public and Its Problems* (1927), in his *Later Works*, ed. Jo Ann Boydston, vol. 2, *1925–1927* (Carbondale: Southern Illinois University Press, 1984), 350. See also Robert B. Westbrook, *John Dewey and American Democracy* (Ithaca, N.Y.: Cornell University Press, 1991), 552.

44. Walt Whitman, *Democratic Vistas* (based on essays written for the *Galaxy* in 1867; originally published in 1871), in *Complete Poetry and Collected Prose*, ed. Justin Kaplan (New York: Library of America, 1982), 929.

CHAPTER 4

Capitalism, Democracy, and the Missing State in Louis Hartz's America

Desmond King and Marc Stears

The American state was almost entirely absent from Louis Hartz's *The Liberal Tradition in America*.[1] For Hartz, American politics was overwhelmingly shaped not by its formal political institutions, its methods of governance, or the means by which political power was exercised but, rather, by the existence of a set of nearly universally held political values that he called "the Lockian liberal tradition." Having truck with neither Karl Marx nor Max Weber, Hartz famously insisted that the course of American politics was determined by these popular beliefs, and especially by American citizens' commitment to individualist ethics, their pervasive skepticism toward social elites, and their intense sense of the importance of social equality. The contrast with scholarly contemporaries such as Karl Polanyi, whose account of the origins of industrialization renders the relationship between state power and market institutions pivotal, or Progressive and Marxist historians, who placed the American state's regulatory and other activities as functions of dominant interests, is striking and analytically consequential. As Hartz momentarily (and ideologically) triumphed over such opponents, his work shaped generations of scholarly endeavor. His "liberal tradition thesis" magnified a widespread methodological practice in American political science that minimized the role of state processes in American political, economic, and social development and directed attention instead to cultural understandings and popular beliefs.[2]

Recent years have witnessed two powerful assaults on this Hartzian orthodoxy. The first assault, led by critics including Eric Foner, Gary Gerstle, Carol

Horton, and Stephen Skowronek, has insisted that Hartz's account of the liberal tradition was both too static and too restrictive. American liberalism, these scholars contend, has always been much more malleable than Hartz appreciated. The history of the Republic shows that the fundamental ideas of the tradition have been employed to justify policy proposals from both the left and the right, sometimes being used to defend the status quo and at other times presaging dramatic political change.[3] The second critique insists, instead, that Hartz was wrong in his conviction that American political beliefs have always, or even predominantly, been shaped by a liberal tradition, however broadly understood. Scholars led by Rogers M. Smith have thus insisted that the United States has always possessed multiple traditions, with liberalism pitted against (often suppressed) alternatives including democratic republicanism and ascriptive (racist) inegalitarianism.[4]

Crucial though both of these intellectual correctives have been, neither directly addresses the question of the absent American state. These new scholarly positions do allow for a greater complexity in the ideological story of America, and they rightly figure prominently in the pages of this volume, but they have not paid much attention to the root causes of the state's absence from the previous orthodoxy. It remains unclear, therefore, exactly why the state was missing from Hartz's account, why scholars of American politics tolerated its absence for so long, and what consequences this absence has had for the broader study of American politics.

The literature on Hartz that does touch on these issues usually insists that he ignored the state because he believed that the liberal tradition was inherently capitalistic and that capitalism was necessarily antithetical to the existence of a large, bureaucratic state machine. On this account, Hartz ignored the state because he was convinced that Americans' economic commitments led them ineluctably to refuse to build a significant state machine. As James Kloppenberg famously put it, Hartz overlooked the American state because he "focused exclusively on issues of economics and psychology."[5]

But this was not Hartz's view. In this paper, we demonstrate what is wrong with this conventional view and provide an alternative explanation for Hartz's decision to exclude the state from his framework. This alternative begins with the recognition that Hartz's primary ambition in drawing attention to the liberal tradition in American politics was not simply to explain the dominance of capitalism in the United States. Rather, his intention was to make salient what he saw as the most worrying modern *noneconomic* threats to the liberties and equalities of American citizens. It was not the state that posed the most serious danger to these liberties and equalities, as many of Hartz's contemporaries on both the left and the right contended. Paradoxically, he believed this threat emanated from the social understandings and cultural practices inherent in Lockean liberalism.

Putting that another way, we argue that Hartz chose to downplay the state in his analysis precisely because he believed that the majority of American citizens exaggerated the state's significance for their lives and possibilities as citizens. We also show that this argument has had profound implications for both American political science and American political theory and that many of those implications have been directly contrary to the interests that Hartz hoped to serve.

WHAT HARTZ MISSED

The absence of the state from Hartz's picture of American political development is striking. In *The Liberal Tradition*, the state does not feature in his discussions of economic regulation, of social policy, or of international affairs. And this is despite the fact that the administrative apparatus of the American state had grown dramatically through World War I, the Great Depression, and World War II, sharply and distinctly affecting all areas of the American experience. In fact, almost all of the major parts of citizen experience had been reshaped in some way by state action in the fifty years previous to the publication of Hartz's masterpiece. Such action encompassed industrial and workplace interventions, programs of economic redistribution and social welfare, and regulations of large areas of social life. At times, there were even self-conscious efforts to promote "social purity." The impact of the American state, in other words, was felt throughout what might otherwise be thought of as the most private aspects of citizen's lives.[6]

Hartz's silence on the state is most surprising and disconcerting on segregated America. It is remarkable that a book published in the middle of the 1950s addressing the ideology of national values could be so innocent in its subject matter about the state's role in enforcing America's racial orders.[7] Yet Louis Hartz's book gives little indication of the pending explosion in civil rights demands about to confront the American state and already visible to the politically alert. The political consequences of this oversight were rapidly apparent.[8] Nor can it be said that Hartz missed these facts because such efforts were short-lived or infrequent. The American state has been for long periods of its existence a segregated state set upon entrenching enduring racial orders.[9] Between the 1890s (and especially after the 1896 *Plessy v. Ferguson* judgment) and the late 1960s or early 1970s the federal government or American state was central to the promotion and defense of segregated race relations throughout the federal bureaucracy and in the national programs it delivered.[10] The state was neither a mere reflection of society nor an impartial arbiter. It was an active segregator, and it was so even during periods usually associated with more "progressive" political ideologies.[11]

In his well-titled book *When Affirmative Action Was White*, Ira Katznelson provides an overview of the historical role of the American state in exactly these terms.[12] Focusing his attention on the New Deal social security legislation and emergency relief measures and extending through the Fair Deal, Katznelson builds an account of how a coalition of southern Democrats and northern Republicans structured federal programs disproportionately to advantage white over black Americans. During these decades, the 1930s to the 1950s, the American state's education and economic policies constituted a program "of affirmative action granting white Americans privileged access to state-sponsored economic mobility." By designing New Deal social policies to exclude those occupations in which African Americans predominated and agreeing to the delegation of administrative powers to the states, President Franklin Delano Roosevelt and the Democratic Congress rendered these programs into "a massive transfer of quite specific privileges to white Americans."[13]

Such policies that favored whites date from the end of the nineteenth century to the years of World War II. But segregated programs such as the New Deal also fed dramatically into the postwar years, as eligibility for the G.I. Bill was shaped by wartime service. This restriction severely limited the ability of African Americans to access this route into education and social mobility.[14] Not only did wartime segregation limit African Americans' opportunities for equal military service, but the "postwar benefits created an affirmative action for white soldiers that contributed to a growing economic chasm between white and black veterans."[15] This "chasm" between African American and white veterans has a deeper historical trajectory than simply the 1940s G.I. Bill. Segregated organizations for veterans and the erasure of African Americans' wartime participation from the public memory were crucial ways in which the segregationist order was entrenched. The segregated state did not simply make the economic and citizenship chasm deeper and firmer; it made the white supremacist racial order into a national standard and caused the legacies of this era to endure in contemporary American politics.

CAPITALISM AND THE ABSENCE OF THE AMERICAN STATE

The actions of the American state shaped multiple core aspects of the American experience, from the nineteenth century through the twentieth. If we are to understand the work of Louis Hartz, therefore, we need to understand why he chose to ignore the role that the state had played in crucial areas of American life. This question itself has been raised before. The most popular answer to it in the current literature begins with three assumptions: first, that Hartz prioritized analysis of economic affairs over that of any other issue domain; second, that he believed that Americans were, and had always been, capitalists at heart—a kind of instinctive capitalist breed; and third, that capitalism was incompatible with a bureaucratic state machine. It is necessary, therefore, for us to start our search for an answer to why the state was missing from Hartz with these three assumptions.

Originating with the mildly obsessive literature posing the question of "why there was no socialism in the United States," the view of the incompatibility of capitalism and state apparatus has remained central long after that debate has dropped away from scholarly attention.[16] According to such a perspective, Hartz's belief that the vast majority of Americans were committed to the ideals of a capitalist economic order explains his reluctance to examine the state's role in American life. For if Hartz believed that Americans have always been capitalists, the argument continues, he surely must have also believed that they were committed to economic laissez-faire, striving always to weaken rather than strengthen the American state in order to protect the operation of free markets and prevent the growth of regulatory power. The hugely popular tales of Horatio Alger, to which Hartz referred so frequently and reverentially in his text, were, after all, premised on faith in individual enterprise, the necessity of private property, and the sense that financial reward should follow from dedication to hard work, and not from a belief that public authorities should play a significant role in shaping the economic opportunities that faced the American people. Anyone can succeed, in this worldview, no matter his or her religion, class, gender, race, national background, or region.

There are undeniably elements of Hartz's account that lend credence to this account. Throughout *The Liberal Tradition in America,* his major work on this subject, Hartz insisted that Americans of all social strata had since the Founding been committed to the economic ideology of capitalism and to the belief that citizens should pursue self-improvement through participation in independent economic activity. Unlike Europe, he continually argued, the United States had never been a feudal society, both in the sense that it lacked an established and entrenched aristocracy and in the sense that all of its social groups were committed to the idea that economic life should never be shaped by anything other than the operation of the free market. In the United States, "virtually everyone, including the nascent industrial worker, has the mentality of an independent entrepreneur."[17] In such an environment, Hartz enthused, capitalism did not have to be foisted upon an unwilling American people as the Marxist and Progressive historians of the interwar years had claimed. Rather, it had always been the default option. It was favored by almost everyone, opposed only by politically insignificant philosophers and social critics, in Hartz's sweeping judgment.[18] Faith in capitalism was crucial to the "unity of American life," leaving Americans as "indifferent to the challenge of socialism" as they were "unfamiliar with the heritage of feudalism."[19]

Despite such support, this explanation of the absence of the state from Hartz's vision of America is, nonetheless, wrong. The mistake is to conclude that Hartz saw capitalism and state intervention in economic and social life as mutually incompatible. He did not. Although that dichotomized view of the relationship of capitalism and the state is indeed widespread among scholars of American politics, it was decidedly not Hartz's own.

Faith in capitalism and in its attendant concepts of private property, free markets, and reward through economic effort was central to Hartz's story, but he did not believe that such a faith was necessarily inimical to the growth of an administrative state nor to the exercise of significant legislative and executive power. Instead, Hartz argued throughout his career that it was perfectly possible for a capitalism to coexist with extensive public administration and a significant degree of state intervention in economic activity. Indeed, Hartz insisted that, far from being committed to a small state or to the idea of laissez-faire, in the period before the Civil War, most emerging manufacturing interests understood that the growth of their industrial concerns was dependent on significant support from the rapidly expanding, if still underdeveloped, administrative machines located in the state capitals. As Hartz himself put it, "the idea of governmental regulation of economic life persisted throughout the period from the Revolution to the Civil War."[20]

This argument about government involvement in economic development was central to Hartz's early intellectual reputation, providing the backbone of his first major work, *Economic Policy and Democratic Thought,* published in 1948. In this work, Hartz insisted that the support of the public authorities in the industrializing states was crucial to the development of

American capitalism for at least four reasons. First, it fell to public authorities in these states to create the transport and communication infrastructures necessary for the operation of free markets. Second, state governments also occasionally provided crucial venture capital, offering loans and other forms of investment for nascent industrial concerns in a way that America's various and underdeveloped banks were unable to do. Third, the same authorities also crafted an early, if modest, regulatory environment in order to initiate fair competition between private industries and sought too to guarantee that at least the most brutal of the social costs associated with rapid industrialization were offset. Fourth, and most crucially, several of the states moved beyond the regulation of private concerns and into a position of direct influence with some. States thus employed the mechanism of "chartering" in order to force mergers between firms, even creating state-sanctioned monopolies when they believed industries would benefit substantially either from protection from competition or from economies of scale. Combined, Hartz insisted, these four factors entailed that early industrial development in the United States was dependent on the closely coordinated joint activity of public authorities and private corporations.[21] Within the most industrially advanced of the states, Hartz went as far as to argue, "government assumed the job of decisively shaping the contours of economic life."[22]

Crucial though these measures had been in antebellum America, Hartz did not believe that this program of assistance, regulation, and intervention continued after the Civil War. It was at that this stage that what he called the "big capitalists" in the United States—by which he meant rapidly expanding manufacturing interests—began to believe that they were more likely to prosper in markets that were free from regulation, were not dependent on state financing, and were not subject to forced mergers or the creation of state monopolies; these industrialists thus turned against the expansion of public authority and toward a philosophy more akin to traditional laissez-faire. It was the post–Civil War boom combined with the increased maturity of industrial organizations themselves, Hartz contended, that persuaded large-scale capitalists of the benefits of this new order.

According to Hartz, therefore, after Reconstruction the administrative apparatuses that had been created at state level to oversee the economy were rapidly undermined and replaced not by an equivalent federal machinery but, rather, by a new rule of economic nonintervention, maintained by a Supreme Court willing to wield the Fifth Amendment alongside the new Fourteenth Amendment in an effort to enforce the new doctrine across the Union. "One can trace this process of spiritual conversion and dramatic flip-flop with a brilliant clarity," Hartz argued in *The Liberal Tradi-tion,* for, once the "interests who had originally demanded many public investments, especially in banking and transportation," decided they could live without them, they "proceeded to deride them, producing precedent after precedent for the laissez-faire constitutional law so famous in the later time."[23] This interpretation sees the American state as an instrument of economic interests, including the prevailing segregationist order, and not just a neutral apparatus.

It is only at this stage that the persuasive grip of the "liberal tradition" on the American citizenry enters Hartz's account. According to Hartz, therefore, because the vast majority of Americans possessed social and political values that were conducive the basic ideas of capitalism—especially to Lockean notions of private property, individual thrift, and the rewards due to hard work—they were willing to take the word of "big capitalists" when they began to argue that the era of state intervention had rightly passed. The move from an age of state-sponsored economic development to an ideology of laissez-faire—what Hartz called the switch from "Carey to Carnegie"—was, on this account, possible because smaller investors, farmers, and industrial workers could be persuaded that their deeply held Lockean ideals actually demanded that the state should withdraw from the economic life of the nation.

Such a process was eased, on Hartz's account, by the fact that these smaller capitalists and employees had been dubious as to the advantages of assistance from state authorities all along. After all, they had not been the recipients of state financing, nor had they directly benefited from the mergers and monopolies that the states had helped create. Hartz thus insisted that when the "big capitalists" began to argue that it was "state action" that was "the root of inequity," with public officials always seeking to take "away from one man and give to another," the mass of Americans were more than ready to believe it and to reject it.[24] The "big capitalists" did not have to engage in a war of "conquest," Hartz insisted, because ideologically they had already won.[25]

The limitation of such a view, of course, is that it was wrong! There was, indeed, a transformation in American capitalism in the second half of the nineteenth century. Many large American capitalist concerns did become more insistent on the need to guarantee free markets across the Union, they did move against regulation by state authorities, and they did grow resistant to the policy of chartering that had previously enabled states to drive mergers and create monopolies. But this transformation did not involve the disappearance of public authorities from the economic lives of American citizens. Far from it. Rather, the transformation transferred such authority from a state to a federal level in a transformation of American economic governance that itself required the extensive use of national state action. A whole range of federal initiatives were thus required to abolish localized regulation of commercial movement, to protect heavy industry by means of an industrial tariff, and to ensure financial stability by means of adherence to the gold standard.

Furthermore, contrary to Hartz's polemic that these moves were somehow uncontroversial, all of these endeavors in fact provoked extensive political contests, involving every actor on the American political scene. Of all the battles thrown up by this transformation, the most bitter of all concerned efforts to create a national market for goods and services: this required eradicating a host of localized regulations cited as inimical to such a market. Hostility to this proposal was deep and widespread across the United States, especially among groups of organized workers and smaller business concerns, whose interests were ill-served by nationwide competition.

It was precisely for this reason that emergent laissez-faire jurisprudence of the late-nineteenth-century Supreme Court was both so crucial to the country's economic development and so widely remarked upon. The Court was drawn into debates concerning the legitimacy of state economic regulation, not because its decisions reflected a broad and widely shared public consensus, as Hartz insisted, but because those debates were the most intractable and thus the least given to compromise in Congress. Its decisions were favorable to the interests of big capital, moreover, largely because the major political agent of the creation of a national market, the Republican Party, had managed to secure control of nominations to the body at the crucial moment.[26] In addition, the Court's new jurisprudence did not equate to the *withdrawal* of the American state from the lives of individuals; rather, it signaled a host of new regulations on different actors, of which particularly dramatic were the new restrictions on organized labor. Between 1880 and 1931, close to 2,000 injunctions were issued prohibiting industrial action.[27] The American state shaped the economic lives of American citizens in the late nineteenth century even more dramatically than it did before the Civil War.

The key questions, therefore, are how and why Hartz chose not to acknowledge this intervention, just as he chose to ignore the role of the state in accommodating and perpetuating racial segregation in American society. It could not have been because he was committed to the idea of America as an inevitably "weak" and "non-interventionist" state or because he held fast to a dichotomized view that emphasized the necessity of a choice between state and market. His description of antebellum America undermined that interpretation. Nor could it be simply because Hartz did not know that the economic transformations of the later part of the nineteenth century had required significant degrees of state involvement, for although the sophisticated accounts offered by scholars such as Richard Bensel, Gretchen Ritter, and Elizabeth Sanders were obviously not available in the 1950s, a good number of analysts, including many of the Progressive historians whom Hartz so disparaged, had spent time outlining the multiple ways in which the American state had been actively involved in the transformation of capitalism in the later part of the nineteenth century.

We attain, then, a quandary. Hartz was more than willing to accept and describe the role of public authorities in the United States when they had helped to promote industrial development, regulate the activities of relatively small-scale capitalists, and ameliorate the impact of economic expansion at a state level in the earlier part of the nineteenth century. But he was entirely unwilling to recognize the role of branches of the federal government insofar as they helped larger-scale capitalists assert their independence from local oversight, imposed tariffs on foreign trade, and repressed industrial workers who stood up against the impact of industrial expansion.

LIBERAL FEAR AND DEMOCRATIC CONFUSION

This tension deeply troubled some of the earliest, and often perceptive, critics of Hartz. When *The Liberal Tradition* was first published, for example, Richard Lively insisted that the "absence of the Federal government" from its discussions of late-nineteenth-century political economy was all but "inexplicable."[28] But while Lively and colleagues were right to identify the problem, their pessimism about the search for an explanation was misplaced. For there is a persuasive explanation of Hartz's unwillingness, the core of which lies in his desire to "rebalance" American public opinion and correct for what he saw as Americans' overly intensive fear of the state in American society at large.

The Liberal Tradition in America was written during a period of widespread antistatism across the ideological spectrum of American politics.[29] This context is fundamental to any reading of Hartz's arguments. That antistatism was occasioned most of all by a fear of authoritarianism that grew up in response both to the war on Nazism and by the onset of the Cold War. It was felt on both the right and the left of the political spectrum. On the moderate left, there was new and widespread anxiety about the siren appeal of communism and about the growing state entrenchment of what would become known as the military-industrial complex.[30] On the right and center, on the other hand, the state was no better thought of. Looking into western Europe, many Republicans and centrist Democrats increasingly considered the state a dangerous and misguided instrument of excessively ambitious social reform. State action, in this vein, was associated with ideologies of intervention such as communism and fascism, ideologies in danger of taking the United States further down the "road to serfdom."[31]

Hartz was convinced that this antistatism was a mistake. There was indeed something awry in the politics of the immediate postwar period, he felt, but it was not the state the Left or the Right should fear. Instead, something deeper in American political society was actually the problem.[32] Americans were at risk from "tyrannical compulsion," Hartz insisted, just as many worried, but the causes of that compulsion came not from the state but from a "deep and unwritten" set of social assumptions, cultural values, and practices of daily living. The constant anxiety about the state, moreover, blinded Americans to the force of this "real" danger and needed correction.[33] It is this central idea—the notion that Americans were wrong to blame the state for their ills and that there were far more serious threats to their rights and liberties than its governing power—that explains his desire to write the interventionist state out of his political theory. Hartz believed that Americans were obsessed with the state and that it was his job to direct their attention elsewhere. He did that by writing the state out of American history entirely!

This is a complex rereading of Hartz, and as such we will unpack the claim in detail in this and the next section of this chapter. The story begins with Hartz's understanding of the origins of American democracy. Hartz was inordinately fond of Alexis de Tocqueville's assertion that the United States had "arrived at a state of democracy without having to endure a democratic revolution."[34] Free of the revolutionary struggles that had accompanied the decay of the feudal order in Europe, the United States was, to Hartz's mind, a society within which very few had ever doubted the desirability of a widely distributed franchise and where most had always believed that ultimate political sovereignty rested with the citizen body at large. The cause of such democratic supremacy was, Hartz believed, social in origin. In Europe, small property owners and entrepreneurs had spent much of the seventeenth, eighteenth, and nineteenth centuries vacillating between support for and opposition toward democratic reform. Suspicion of aristocratic interests and especially a desire to bring an end to feudal property holdings and anticompetitive economic practices encouraged such small-scale capitalists in a democratic direction, Hartz insisted. But fear of redistributive demands

from a disgruntled proletariat also made them cautious about the possibilities of universal suffrage. Antidemocratic forces, thus, always stood a chance
in Europe. As long as a case could be made that the established order would
protect the interests of small-scale capitalists, aristocrats had a potential ally
in their fight against the erosion of their long-cherished political powers.

In the United States, however, no such argument against democracy
could ever be mustered, Hartz maintained. For although there might have
been a few large-scale capitalists who would have preferred to see political
power stay out of the hands of the majority of the population, the mass of
the American citizen body could see no significant interest in withholding
the vote (though, of course, this was a judgment made in respect of whites
only). There was, after all, no aristocracy capable of asserting an alternative,
traditionalist schedule of rule. Nor was there, for most of the nineteenth
century at least, an unruly, economically dispossessed proletariat capable of
threatening the small property–owning classes into abandoning democratic governance in protection of their own material interests.[35]

But despite the apparently unquestionable strength of democratic
interests in American public life, Hartz also insisted that the fate of democracy in America was not as straightforward as Tocqueville's portrayal implied. In particular, antidemocratic forces had achieved considerable success. Thus, although campaigns against white male suffrage had failed, a
host of other restrictions entailed that the constitutional system that
emerged after the Founding, after all, was not the sort of participatory,
democratic ideal that many might have imagined. It was, instead, a republic that qualified its democratic elements in several crucial ways, notably by
enshrining a continued role for social elites through indirect election to
the Senate and the presidency and by establishing a more thoroughgoing
system of checks on majoritarian rule than any European democrat would
have thought conceivable.[36]

This embrace of some antidemocratic mechanisms, in Hartz's view, provided the absolutely central paradox of American politics: although anti-
democrats lacked "an aristocracy to ally with" or a "mob to denounce," they
had somehow nonetheless managed to construct "a fantastic system" of
checks on the popular will, including most notably the division of executive
and legislative powers and the practice of judicial review.[37] A nation that
should have been thoroughly democratic had, in fact, first constructed and
then maintained a system that could only partially be described as democratic. "What must be accounted one of the tamest, mildest, and most un-
imaginative majorities in modern political history," Hartz complained, "has

been bound by a set of restrictions that betray fanatical terror." "The American majority," he still more colorfully bemoaned, "has been an amiable shepherd dog kept forever on a lion's leash."[38]

Hartz was not the first public intellectual, of course, to draw attention to such a paradox. The Progressive historians of the earlier part of the century, led by Charles Beard, Herbert Croly, George Soule, and Walter Weyl, had also drawn primary attention to the restrictions on popular sovereignty within the American republican system. As Walter Weyl strikingly put it, although "no King was set up to rule over America," the Constitution that replaced the British monarchy "was more subtly subversive of the popular interest than might have been a dozen Georges."[39] Despite his general desire to supplant the Progressive orthodoxy, Hartz paid due homage to these predecessors. They had been right in their analysis of the constraints on American popular democracy, he suggested, and especially in their condemnation of judicial review.

The intellectual break with the Progressives came when he spurned their efforts to blame the creation and maintenance of these restrictions on some sort of elite conspiracy that had drawn on the power of the American state in order to repress the majority of the American populations. While "our progressive historians often imply" that the constitutional order had been forced on the United States "by the subtle machinations" of elite interests, it had in fact, Hartz insisted, been initially adopted and later protected by those very sections of society who would have been expected to have resisted its restrictions most fiercely (though others given no voice in the Founding would no doubt also have resisted the creation of an oppressive system). This has been a "voluntary servitude," Hartz argued, designed by the "American democrat" himself, and not imposed upon him by outside forces.[40]

The origins of that "servitude," Hartz continued, lay in the Lockean liberal tradition. Lockean liberalism, he argued, had at its heart an undiluted European concern with the need to protect the rights of the individual from the potential threats of the mob, a concern that had survived in the United States despite the very different social and cultural circumstances: by implication the American state was an expression of popular will and should be applauded, not trammeled. Such a priority, he concluded, led vast swaths of the American citizenry to support powerful restrictions on majority power in the name of individual protections, and that, in turn, led to significant limitations on the powers of the elected legislative and executive branches of the American state. The average (presumably white)

American citizen, Hartz concluded, failed to understand that there was no significant threat to the "individualist way of life" in America and was complicit in the construction of an institutional order that provided the unnecessary protections they craved. The "very liberalism that restrains the majority," he summarized, "has given rise to a vast neurotic fear of what the majority might do," and it was that "false American fear" that produced a series of checks unknown elsewhere in the democratizing world, checks that in turn threw "a set of chains around" democratic practices in the United States, vastly limiting the possibilities of American politics, though within a democratic core.

This was, he bemoaned, "one of the strangest examples of political confusion and political collapse" on the historical record.[41] Liberalism in America was essentially antistatist, Hartz believed, while elsewhere in the world it was more rationally Janus-faced: sometimes looking at the state askance, sometimes welcoming its advantages in the name of well-intentioned reform.[42]

This thesis—the claim that American democrats themselves had always been misguidedly worried about democratic governance and thus sought to restrain majority power as a result—is an intriguing conjecture for many reasons. It is especially crucial for our argument, as it illustrates Hartz's central conviction that Americans had always misunderstood the primary source of the threats to their liberties. Whereas most had believed that such threats originated either in organized majorities or in the behavior of the state elites who drew their authority and their power from those majorities, Hartz was insistent that this was a mistake. Instead, the repression of individual freedoms in the United States was a consequence *not* of state power but of a combination of patterns of thought and of social and economic realities. It is to that final part of the argument that it is necessary to turn.

A "DEEP AND UNWRITTEN TYRANNICAL COMPULSION"

For too long, Hartz believed, Americans had sought to protect themselves from *political* power, when their own democratic practices and ideals should have encouraged them instead to turn actively to democratic politics to achieve their own common good. This, in itself, was a serious concern for him, and good reason enough not to remind people of the potential abuses of state power, abuses to which he thought Americans were already far too attendant. But the American obsession with the state had far worse consequences than that alone, Hartz believed. For while Americans were content with trying to restrict their state, they should, in fact, have been trying to free themselves from two other dangers, namely, the inequalities and hierarchies implicit in capitalist socioeconomic relationships and the bondage of intellectual conformity. The point of *The Liberal Tradition* was to alert his fellow citizens to these dangers and to begin a debate as to how they could be avoided.

The first danger for Americans, Hartz insisted, resulted from blindness to social and economic inequalities. Americans, he feared, had become extraordinarily self-congratulatory with regard to their economic success and thus incapable of detecting the vast injustices, inequalities, and erosions of individual freedoms that were actually going on all around them (though, it should be noted, he rarely included racial injustice in this pantheon of ills). In particular, although Americans were fiercely alert to any formalized political constraints—to the misdemeanors of "Parliaments, ministers, and Stampmasters," as he put it—they were almost entirely unable to see the difficulties facing Americans in the "social side" of life.[43] White Americans, he insisted, almost universally behaved as if the "atomistic social freedom" of Lockean theory were a "reality" in the United States, which of course it was not. This, he claimed, was the "master assumption" of American thought, and by making such an assumption, Americans refused to recognize the desperate obstacles to the realization of liberal ideals faced by most Americans most of the time.[44]

Nowhere was this conviction rendered more clearly present than in Hartz's extensive discussions of the social theory of the Confederacy, a subject that made up a significant part of *The Liberal Tradition* and to which Hartz continually returned in other work.[45] Hartz's interest in this otherwise neglected topic was motivated by his belief that thinkers such as George Fitzhugh, George Holmes, and Henry Hughes were the one "major group of American thinkers who had to challenge" the American sense that the full benefits of freedom were already enjoyed by the formally free citizens in the United States. Only these thinkers, he argued, "began to go behind the action of legislatures to the nature of society itself, to the drive within it for hierarchy and subordination," a move that was "bound to provide a set of new and fruitful insights."[46] Sadly, he continued, such "insights were injected into an atmosphere that was still unprepared to appreciate them," and, of course, they were also tied up with the most appalling justifications of slavery. For Fitzhugh and colleagues, the absence of a "real" freedom for the "formally free" meant that the "formally unfree" were not entitled to complain about their lot. Such a terrible misuse of the argument, Hartz conceded, enabled most Americans to ignore their efforts and to continue in their "obsession" with majoritarianism and "governmental" oppression to the exclusion of all others.[47]

The second danger in American society was more frightening still. This was what he called the "American absolutism": a "deep and unwritten tyrannical compulsion" that closed down political debate and disallowed contentious ideological dispute.[48] Those who cleaved to the "liberal tradition," Hartz insisted, were not only too restrictive in their understandings of democratic politics and too blind to the inequalities and injustices perpetuated in American social life. They were also desperately unwilling to accept any challengers. Since the Founding, he argued, the majority of Americans had acted in the "sober faith that their norms were self-evident," rather than controversial moral and political claims about the meanings and possibilities of collective life.[49] This, in turn, entailed that a deeply distasteful and potentially deeply troubling "conformitarian spirit" occupied the very center of American ideological life.[50] European countries, he contended, had never known such a force. The social developments there, and especially the contest over feudalism, had ensured that Europeans had grown comfortable with the idea of ideological dispute; politics, for them, was a continuing battle for control led by groups willing expressly to disagree with one another. But in America, there was no such history to provide safety. Instead, all major political groups made constant declarations of unswerving loyalty to the "liberal tradition" and were quickly and severely censured if they failed to do so.[51]

It was this paradoxical commitment to "liberal conformity," he believed, that posed the greatest threat to the American citizen. The only way such a tradition could maintain itself over time, he continued, was by some form of social repression. When adherents to the "liberal tradition" were faced with dissent, from the left or the right, they responded by "binding the individual down more and more," so that such individuals were eventually unwilling to challenge the established norms.[52] Such repression could, Hartz conceded, take the form of state action—as in A. Mitchell Palmer's and Senator Joseph McCarthy's red scares and in early-twentieth-century "Americanist" restrictions on immigration—but its root cause lay in a "hysterical" opposition to any political view that challenged the liberal orthodoxy. The real danger thus lay essentially in the everyday conversations of the "bourgeois gossip" who looked down on the "eccentric" and the oppositionist, in the widespread sense that only a particular kind of social and political conversation was "decent" or permissible, and in the vast array of informal social sanctions, stretching from discouragement to effective ostracism, that were employed against anyone who dared disagree.[53]

It was in this way that Hartz believed that the real core of "liberalism"—the freedom to experiment that it promised—was actually becoming "a stranger in the land of its greatest realization and fulfilment" in the early postwar years. For although Americans celebrated the reality of their own liberal freedoms, in fact the "compulsive power" of liberal expectations was becoming "so great" in the United States that it actually "posed a threat to liberty itself."[54] For too long Americans had worried about the state. They should instead have been worrying about their own intellectual limitations and conformities.

FROM A MISSING STATE TO A SAFE STATE

It is here that the full answer emerges to our question of why the American state fails to feature in Hartz's account. Hartz's intention in *The Liberal Tradition* was to persuade his audience that despite the widespread assumption to the contrary, the primary source of repressions, inequalities, and exclusions in the United States was essentially *not* political but social. The dangers that Americans actually faced did not come from the state, as they believed; they were grounded in the expectations, values, and beliefs of American citizens and not in the behavior and practices of its governing institutions or elites. For Hartz, the most deleterious impact of the liberal tradition on American life was not that it necessitated capitalism but that it encouraged Americans to "trace the origin" of inequalities, injustices, and repressions "to the action of the State": an idea that at the very best "put the cart before the horse."[55] The "real nature" of oppression in the United States, Hartz thus argued, was social, not political. His job was to reveal that fact. Hartz took the state out of the story of American political development, therefore, precisely because he thought that Americans had been too eager for too long to place it at the center of their understandings.

This conclusion casts Hartz's curious neglect of the American state in a more meaningful context. He did not ignore the state because he believed that America did not possess a state; he ignored it because he was convinced that the state was not as dangerous as his contemporaries all appeared to believe. Such an argument implies that if his first public intellectual priority was to disabuse Americans about the alleged dangers of the state, his second might have been to argue for the American state as an appropriate agent of social reform, civil rights, and race equity. Though we admit that this view may be taking hopefulness to unsustainable heights in Hartz's own case, what is clear, however, is that Hartz's work had precisely this effect. The refocusing of Americans' anxiety away from the state and to other issues contributed significantly to a widespread trend in American political thought away from the antistatism that characterized it in the immediate postwar period, toward an attitude that moved from benign neglect to actual support and encouragement.

As the 1950s gave way to the 1960s, that is, even those American political theorists who called themselves "liberal" began to contend that it was the job of the state to overcome the inequalities, injustices, and exclusions that they detected in American society at large. By the 1970s, the argument went one step further still. Within the work of John Rawls and his many followers, the state became a "neutral agent" for social justice, capable of righting the wrongs of American history and overcoming the limitations implicit in the behavior and attitudes of American citizens themselves.[56] The "missing State" of Louis Hartz had become the "safe State" for a new generation of American political thinkers, just as Hartz himself might have hoped—so much so that the term "liberal" itself ceased popularly to imply "antistatist" and began instead to be instinctively associated with "big-government" reform.[57]

Hartz himself would have been well satisfied with this transformation, although he would no doubt have been disappointed that the influence of this new attitude to the state did not often extend to the majority of American citizens themselves. But the implications of the change were far from uniformly positive. Although it is, no doubt, right that American political theorists need to be sensitive to the dangers inherent in the ideas and attitudes of the citizenry itself, Hartz and his followers achieved this only by writing the American state out of the story of American political development entirely. This view is deeply unfortunate because liberal Americans turning to the possibilities of state action after years of neglect failed to see the racialized character of American state policy in the existing expression. As such, they failed to grasp the ways in which the existing state was repressive itself, especially in respect to race inequality, and thus exhibited no understanding of dangers that are always inherent in the actions of the central state. By choosing not to investigate the state at all, American liberal political theorists became immune to its worst characteristics.

We have shown in this chapter that Louis Hartz neglected to discuss the American state not because he believed that all Americans were capitalists and that capitalism has always required a small or severely limited state. He did so because he believed that Americans had been captivated by the dangers of the state for too long. He wished to draw his fellow citizens' attention away from the threat posed by the state and direct it instead to the dangers inherent in American society, especially the dangers posed by an unquestioning allegiance to the "Lockian liberal tradition." In so doing, he began a transformation of American political thought, a transformation that opened up the possibility of American liberals invoking state power and calling for it to embrace its reforming potential. He also, though, helped blind too many American political analysts to the repressive history of state action, a blindness that scholars have only just begun to put right more than fifty years after the publication of *The Liberal Tradition*.

NOTES

1. Louis Hartz, *The Liberal Tradition in America* (1955; reprint, New York: Harcourt, Brace, 1991).

2. See Karl Polanyi, *The Great Transformation* (New York: Reinhart, 1944); Charles Beard, *The Economic Basis of Politics* (New York: Knopf, 1934), *An Economic Interpretation of the Constitution of the United States* (New York: Macmillan, 1913).

3. See Eric Foner, *The Story of American Freedom* (New York: Norton, 1998); Gary Gerstle, "The Protean Character of American Liberalism," *American Historical Review* 99 (1994): 1043–1073; Carol Horton, *Race and the Making of American Liberalism* (New York: Oxford University Press, 2005); Desmond King, *In the Name of Liberalism: Illiberal Social Policy in the USA and Britain* (Oxford: Oxford University Press, 1999); Stephen Skowronek, "The Reassociation of Ideas and Purposes: Racism, Liberalism, and the American Political Tradition," *American Political Science Review* 100 (2006): 385–401.

4. See Rogers M. Smith, "Beyond Tocqueville, Myrdal, and Hartz: The Multiple Traditions in America," *American Political Science Review* 87 (1993): 549–66; Smith, *Civic Ideals: Conflicting Visions of Citizenship in U.S. History* (New Haven, Conn.: Yale University Press, 1997). See too James Morone, *The Democratic Wish: Popular Participation and the Limits of American Government* (New Haven, Conn.: Yale University Press, 1991); Carol Nackenoff, "Locke, Alger, and Atomistic Individualism: Revisiting Louis Hartz's *Liberal Tradition in America,*" *Studies in American Political Development* 19 (2005): 206–215; Barry Shain, *The Myth of American Individualism: The Protestant Origins of American Political Thought* (Princeton, N.J.: Princeton University Press, 1994).

5. James T. Kloppenberg, "In Retrospect: Louis Hartz's *The Liberal Tradition in America,*" *Reviews in American History* 29 (2001): 460. See too Richard Ellis, "Radical Lockeanism in American Political Culture," *Western Political Quarterly* 45 (1992): 825–849; Samuel P. Huntington, "Paradigms of American Politics: Beyond the One, the Two, and the Many," *Political Science Quarterly* 89 (1974): 1–26; Seymour Martin Lipset, "Historical Traditions and National Characteristics," *Canadian Journal of Sociology* 11 (1986): 113–155; and Nackenoff, "Locke, Alger, and Atomistic Individualism." For an overview of the scholarship on this aspect of Hartz, see Philip Abbott, "Still Louis Hartz after All These Years," *Perspectives on Politics* 3 (2005): 93–109.

6. For examples, see Michael McGerr, *A Fierce Discontent: The Rise and Fall of the Progressive Movement in America* (Oxford: Oxford University Press, 2003), 118–278; David M. Rabban, *Free Speech in Its Forgotten Years* (Cambridge: Cambridge University Press, 1997); Stephen Skowronek, *Building a New American State: The Expansion of National Administrative Capacities, 1877–1920* (Cambridge: Cambridge University Press, 1982).

7. Hartz's idealized American citizens were also uniformly white, as explained in Charles W. Mills, *The Racial Contract* (Ithaca, N.Y.: Cornell University Press, 1997).

8. Douglas S. Massey *Categorically Unequal: The American Stratification System* (New York: Russell Sage Foundation, 2007).

9. Desmond S. King, postscript to *Separate and Unequal: African Americans and the US Federal Government* (New York: Oxford University Press, 2007).

10. See ibid., passim.

11. Desmond S. King and Rogers M. Smith, "Racial Orders in American Political Development," *American Political Science Review* 99 (2005): 75–92.

12. Ira Katznelson, *When Affirmative Action Was White: An Untold History of Racial Inequality in Twentieth-Century America* (New York: Norton, 2005).

13. Ibid., 21, 23. And see Robert Lieberman, *Shifting the Color Line* (Cambridge, Mass.: Harvard University Press, 1998).

14. Katznelson takes a dimmer view of the success of the G.I. Bill for African Americans than does Suzanne Mettler in her study *Soldiers to Citizens* (Cambridge, Mass.: Harvard University Press, 2005).

15. Katznelson, *When Affirmative Action Was White*, 112.

16. See Nackenoff, "Locke, Alger, and Atomistic Individualism."

17. Hartz, *The Liberal Tradition in America*, 89.

18. See ibid., 130.

19. Ibid., 6.

20. See Louis Hartz, "Laissez-Faire Thought in Pennsylvania, 1776–1860," *Journal of Economic History* 3 (1943): 69.

21. See too the excellent summary in Robert Lively, "The American System," *Business History Review* 29, no. 1 (1995): 81–96.

22. Louis Hartz, *Economic Policy and Democratic Thought* (Cambridge, Mass.: Harvard University Press, 1948), 289.

23. Hartz, *The Liberal Tradition in America*, 216.

24. Ibid.

25. Ibid., 130.

26. See Richard F. Bensel, *The Political Economy of American Industrialization, 1877–1900* (Cambridge: Cambridge University Press, 2000); Gretchen Ritter, *Goldbugs and Greenbacks: The Antimonopoly Tradition and the Politics of Finance in America* (New York: Cambridge University Press, 1997); Elizabeth Sanders, *Roots of Reform: Farmers, Workers and the American State* (Chicago: University of Chicago Press, 1999).

27. See Leon Fink, "Labor, Liberty, and the Law: Trade Unionism and the Problem of American Constitutional Order," *Journal of American History* 74, no. 3 (1987):

904–925; William Forbath, "The Shaping of the American Labor Movement," *Harvard Law Review* 102, no. 6 (1989): 1109–1256; David Montgomery, "Labor and the Republic in Industrial America, 1860–1920," *Le mouvement social* 111 (1980): 201–215.

28. See Lively, "The American System," 93.

29. For more details, see David Ciepley, *Liberalism in the Shadow of Totalitarianism* (Cambridge, Mass.: Harvard University Press, 2006); and Desmond King and Marc Stears, "The Missing State in Post-war American Political Thought," in *The Unsustainable American State*, ed. Lawrence Jacobs and Desmond King (New York: Oxford University Press, in press).

30. For the paradigmatic example, see C. Wright Mills, *The Sociological Imagination* (Oxford: Oxford University Press, 1959). Such views were not restricted to the Far Left. It was after all the president—Dwight Eisenhower—who warned of (and coined the phrase) the "military industrial complex" when he demitted office in 1960.

31. For examples, see Daniel Bell, *The End of Ideology: On the Exhaustion of Political Ideas in the Fifties* (Cambridge, Mass.: Harvard University Press, 1960); F. A. Hayek, *The Road to Serfdom* (Chicago: University of Chicago Press, 1944); Judith Shklar, *After Utopia: The Decline of Political Faith* (Princeton, N.J.: Princeton University Press, 1957). Some liberals employed both the arguments of the Right and the Left. See Arthur M. Schlesinger Jr., *The Vital Center: The Politics of Freedom* (New York: Riverside Press, 1949). For excellent commentaries, see Robert Booth Fowler, *Believing Skeptics: American Political Intellectuals, 1945–1964* (Westport, Conn.: Greenwood Press, 1978); Robert Westbrook, *John Dewey and American Democracy* (Ithaca, N.Y.: Cornell University Press, 1991).

32. See Hartz, *The Liberal Tradition in America*, 11–13.

33. Ibid., 12.

34. See Louis Hartz, "American Political Thought and the American Revolution," *American Political Science Review* 46 (1952): 321–342. It is, of course, a highly contentious claim. For a rival view, see Gordon S. Wood, *The Radicalism of the American Revolution* (New York: Random House, 1991).

35. See Hartz, *The Liberal Tradition in America*, 93.

36. See the discussions in James Bryce, *The American Commonwealth* (Indianapolis, Ind.: Liberty Fund, 1995; first published in 1888).

37. Hartz, *The Liberal Tradition in America*, 96.

38. Ibid., 129.

39. Walter Weyl, *The New Democracy* (New York: Macmillan, 1912), 317. See too Charles Beard, *An Economic Interpretation of the Constitution of the United States* (New York: Macmillan, 1913); Herbert Croly, *The Promise of American Life* (New York: Macmillan, 1090); George Soule, *The Future of Liberty* (New York: Macmillan, 1936).

40. Hartz, *The Liberal Tradition in America*, 129.

41. Ibid., 103. It is unclear whether Hartz believed that this favored and reasonable majority would have overturned Jim Crow, and since he seemed unwilling to review race at all, we have to assume not.

42. See, especially, Hartz, "American Political Thought and the American Revolution," 327.

43. Ibid., 324.

44. Ibid., 339.

45. See Louis Hartz, "The Reactionary Enlightenment: Southern Political Thought before the Civil War," *Western Political Quarterly* 5 (1952): 31–50; and Hartz, "American Political Thought and the American Revolution," 338–340. Hartz was not alone in this interest. For other uses of Confederate political thought in mid-twentieth-century America, see Skowronek, "The Reassociation of Ideas and Purposes," esp. 386–387.

46. Hartz, *The Liberal Tradition in America,* 184.

47. See ibid., 170–172.

48. Ibid., 12.

49. Hartz, "American Political Thought and the American Revolution," 336.

50. See Hartz, *The Liberal Tradition in America,* 11–13. This argument provided the basis for Murray Levin's once highly controversial but now sadly overlooked *Political Hysteria in America: The Democratic Capacity for Repression* (New York: Basic Books, 1971).

51. See Hartz, "American Political Thought and the American Revolution," 335.

52. Hartz, *The Liberal Tradition in America,* 185.

53. Ibid., 12.

54. Ibid., 11.

55. Ibid., 184.

56. See John Rawls, *A Theory of Justice* (New York: Oxford University Press, 1971). For commentary on this trend and its critics, see Marc Stears, "Liberalism and the Politics of Compulsion," *British Journal of Political Science* 37 (2007): 505–531.

57. For discussion of this transformation, see Marc Stears, "The Liberal Tradition and the Politics of Exclusion," *Annual Review of Political Science* 10 (2007): 85–101; and for historical context, see Alan Brinkley, *Liberalism and Its Discontents* (Cambridge, Mass.: Harvard University Press, 1998).

PART THREE

Yesterday: Episodes in American History

CHAPTER 5

Louis Hartz and Study of the American Founding: The Search for New Fundamental Categories

Alan Gibson

But after all is said and done Beard somehow stays alive, and the reason for this is that, as in the case of Marx, you merely demonstrate your subservience to a thinker when you spend your time attempting to disprove him. The way to fully refute a man is to ignore him for the most part, and the only way you can do this is to substitute new fundamental categories for his own, so that you are simply pursuing a different path.

—Louis Hartz, *The Liberal Tradition in America* [1]

Louis Hartz's observation that you only demonstrate your dependence upon those whom you try to refute has proven to be even truer for Hartz than for Charles Beard and the Progressive scholars that Hartz criticized. Since its publication in 1955, *The Liberal Tradition in America* has had no rivals as the most influential book in the study of American political thought. The importance of Hartz's classic has, in turn, repeatedly led scholars to probe for its limitations and to search for ways to transcend it. But questions linger. Are we finally ready to let go of Hartz? Are we prepared to accept James Kloppenberg's recent assessment that Hartz's study "is no longer a reliable guide to the history of American public life,"[2] to treat it as a product of Cold War concerns, and to move on? If not, then how can Hartz's critics be answered? If so, then where do we turn?

149

This essay addresses these questions in the context of the study of the American Founding. I will first identify and characterize the three most explicit and important challenges lodged against Hartz's thesis as it applies to the study of the American Founding. The challenges examined include the "classical republican" interpretation of the American Founding set forth most prominently by Bernard Bailyn, Gordon Wood, and J. G. A Pocock; the "multiple traditions approach" of Rogers Smith; and the Progressive tradition of Founding scholarship.[3] I will then assess the effect and effectiveness of these challenges and provide an appraisal of what is still valuable in Hartz's interpretation.[4] My central questions, then, are, what have we learned about Hartz's thesis as applied to the American Founding since the publication of *The Liberal Tradition in America,* and what place should Hartz's classic continue to have in scholarship on the political thought of the American founders?

THE LIBERAL TRADITION AND THE AMERICAN FOUNDING

The broad outlines of Hartz's interpretation of American political thought are well known and do not require much elaboration. Hartz's most basic proposition was that American political thought was defined and explained by the "universality of the liberal idea."[5] Hartz conceived of liberalism in the "classic Lockian sense" but never set forth a crystallized definition of Lockean liberalism.[6] Instead, he associated it at various points in *The Liberal Tradition in America* with beliefs in social equality, the protection of property, limited government, natural law, commercial capitalism, "individualistic norms," "atomistic social freedom," and social mobility and the Horatio Alger story of the self-made man.[7] Hartz's diffuse definition of Lockean liberalism, then, was primarily a description not of a set of political principles but of a social order and a way of life.[8]

As Hartz presented it, the liberal tradition encompassed "wide variations" within these general beliefs, failed to supply theoretical coherence to American political thought, and was more aptly described as embedded in America's marrow than affirmed by its cerebrum.[9] Hartz also knew that not every American statesman or thinker could easily be fitted into even this capacious understanding of liberalism and that feudalism had left more than a few marks on the landscape of American political thought and development. Puritans in particular and antebellum apologists for slavery such as George Fitzhugh, Hartz conceded, were not really liberals. Nevertheless, Hartz also observed that he never meant for his liberal interpretation to be applied in an "absolute mathematical fashion," saw exceptions to his general thesis as the "liabilities of any large generalization," and believed that it was far more important to explore the many dimensions of American political psyche that the absence of feudalism and the ubiquity of liberalism illuminated than the few that they could not.[10]

When Hartz set out to explain how liberalism had become universal in American political thought, he pointed to the "mother factor of modern life": feudalism.[11] In Europe, where feudalism had been entrenched, the revolutions that had uprooted it, according to Hartz, had given rise to a trinity of ideologies: Burkean conservatism, liberalism, and socialism. In contrast, in America, the absence of feudalism had rendered Americans as "indifferent to the challenge of socialism" as it was "unfamiliar with the heritage of feudalism."[12]

The absence of feudalism and the corresponding uniformly liberal character of American political thought, Hartz further argued, yielded a "chain of insights . . . as long as the course of our national development itself."[13] Since liberalism had encountered no contests and won no victories in America that increased its subtlety or vision, American liberalism was at once "natural," "absolute and irrational," and "fixed and dogmatic."[14] It was also pervasive, constituting "America's general will." The pervasiveness of irrational Lockeanism created the "inarticulate premise of conformity" that made Americans vulnerable to the tyranny of mass opinion.[15] It also led them to worry compulsively about the consequences of an overreaching state and created a powerful set of apologetics for the middle class, but a middle class that paradoxically lacked the passionate middle-class consciousness of the European bourgeoisie.

Hartz's specific analysis of the American Founding focused almost exclusively on the character and consequences of the American Revolution and was pointed toward establishing that liberalism had "killed the socialist dream here [in America] at its very bourgeois roots."[16] Most broadly, the American Revolution became for Hartz the most vivid illustration of the effects of the absence of feudalism. The outstanding dimensions of the Revolution, according to Hartz, were the "feudal structure it did not have to destroy" and "the social goals it *did not need to achieve*."[17] The absence of feudalism, in turn, had profound implications on the kind of revolutionaries that America produced in comparison with England, France, and Russia; on the character of the American Revolution; and on the subsequent content of American political thought.

The American revolutionaries, Hartz maintained, were sober men who did not attempt to shatter the Christian concept of sin and replace it with a belief in human perfectibility and who displayed little of the "crusading intensity" and millennial enthusiasm that later characterized the "secular prophets" of the French and Russian revolutions.[18] The Americans, according to Hartz, were also thoroughly conscious that they had not been burdened by feudal institutions. This appreciation of their peculiar good fortune led the American revolutionaries to an acute understanding of the uniqueness of their own society and a fear of contamination by Europe that took the form of a "curiously Hebraic kind of separatism."[19] Unlike the prophets of the French and Russian revolutions, the American revolutionaries were not looking to act as leaders in a world revolution.

These peculiarly conservative revolutionaries "based their claims on a philosophic synthesis of Anglo-American legal history and the reason of natural law."[20] In Europe, Hartz observed, philosophers had opposed nature and tradition, reason and history, Jeremy Bentham and Edmund Burke—at least until Burke and William Blackstone had attempted to identify natural law with the evolution of the past. In America, colonial history had made such an identification seem like a simple matter of fact. Explicitly stated principles of nature and reason had been written into colonial charters and written constitutions that could be traced to the first settlements. Thus, the concept of a written constitution—"the darling of the rationalists" in Europe—had seemed like the "essence of political traditionalism" in America.[21]

If American revolutionaries were best characterized as "outraged reactionaries," the American Revolution was also not revolutionary in the sense that it had required or been accompanied by a genuine social revolution.[22] The absence of feudal structures in America, according to Hartz, meant that the revolutionaries had only been required to engage in a "mopping up campaign against feudal relics" rather than a wholesale effort to eradicate a deeply rooted set of institutions and practices.[23] Moreover, because history had already accomplished the virtual elimination of feudalism in America before the revolutionaries swept away its remaining vestiges, this campaign had further strengthened the liberal consensus and created social solidarity rather than tearing the citizenry apart as it had in Europe.

Most important, the absence of feudal structures had profound implications for Americans' relationship to state power and for the relationship of religion to revolution in America, both of which differed from those of Europe. Americans, according to Hartz, were inspired by their revolution to fear and abhor centralized state power, but because they did not have to eradicate feudal institutions, they never developed a corresponding desire to exercise centralizing power. In contrast, European liberals had been "confronted with the heritage of an ancient corporate society" and consequently were "forever devising sharp and sovereign instruments that might be used to put it down."[24] European liberals thus had a love/hate relationship with state power and interpreted Locke's teachings as providing both for the creation and the control of state power. In contrast, Americans did not grasp the implicit defense of the state that was embedded in Locke's teaching but, rather, read him entirely as the theorist of limited government.[25] For Americans, "one side of Locke became virtually the whole of him."[26] Furthermore, in Europe, "where reactionary church establishments had made the Christian concept of sin and salvation into an explicit pillar of the status quo, liberals were forced to develop a political religion—as Rousseau saw—if only to answer it." In contrast, in America, where there was considerable religious diversity and no real established church, dissenting ministers led the revolution but "did not need to make a religion out of the revolution because religion was already revolutionary."[27]

When he turned to the creation of the U.S. Constitution, Hartz discovered that in the 1780s the same Americans who had so perceptively appreciated their own uniqueness and the historical conditions that had created it had suddenly somehow become convinced that they faced social conflict from American levelers that rivaled that experienced in Europe. They thus created a constitution designed to integrate the social orders into the governmental structure and diffuse class conflict. Hartz dismissed the idea that Shays's Rebellion, the popular uprising in Massachusetts that resulted from high taxes being imposed on debt-ridden farmers during a period of recession, was on par with the great social revolutions of Europe. He also rejected the proposition that members of the Federalist Party were akin to European traditionalists. According to Hartz, the Federalists—of either 1787 or 1792—were proponents of "liberal Whiggery," not "the European *ancien regime.*"[28]

Scholars who equated the Federalists with European traditionalists were brought to this misinterpretation, Hartz further maintained, by the Hobbesian picture of social conflict in the rhetoric of the framers and by the reaction of members of the Federalist Party to the French Revolution. Nevertheless, Hartz observed, "all pessimistic views of human nature are not alike." The Hobbesian picture of social conflict presented by the Federalists during the mid-1780s suggested that man is autonomous and self-interested, but European traditionalists had accepted a "feudal bleakness about man which sees him fit only for external domination."[29] Moreover, Hartz pointed out that the Federalists did not consistently hold to the picture of America as ridden with social conflict. Instead, they made such observations when they had forgotten the broader context of Europe. When they

traveled abroad or even glanced in that direction, however, Americans re-
gained their objectivity and an appreciation of their own uniqueness.

Finally, Hartz denied that the longevity of the Constitution rested on its
utility for solving problems of social conflict. Indeed, according to Hartz,
quite the opposite was true. The Constitution failed at the time of greatest
conflict in the United States (the Civil War) and had operated smoothly for
a long time because of the consensus of national unity that undergirded it,
not the constitutional mechanics of separation of powers and checks and
balances. The famous constitutional mechanisms established in the structure of the U.S. Constitution, according to Hartz, actually depended upon
the social stability that they were said to create.

BAILYN, POCOCK, AND WOOD: THE REPUBLICAN CHALLENGE

The liberal interpretation of the American Founding and American political thought in general and even most of the specific lines of argument that
Hartz pursued were hardly novel in 1955 when *The Liberal Tradition in America* was first published. Indeed, prior to the development of the "republican
synthesis" in the 1970s, scholars were not divided between those who
stressed the importance of liberal ideas versus those who argued for the influence of other sets of ideas. Instead, they were divided over whether ideas
really matter in first place. Following the Progressive historians, many scholars concluded that the liberal ideas that had informed the Founding were
merely the projected rationalizations of underlying economic interests that
were the real motives of human behavior. Thus, even Merle Curti's 1937
essay "The Great Mr. Locke"—one of the most accomplished and influential early expositions of Locke's influence in America—defensively suggested that Lockean ideas had flourished in eighteenth- and nineteenth-
century America because they "admirably suited the needs of the more
dominant American interests."[30] Combating this view that ideas played only
an instrumental role led other scholars to plead that the American revolutionaries or founders genuinely believed what they said and to try to establish the consistency of their positions on the premise that establishing consistency would prove commitment to underlying principles. Edmund
Morgan, for example, sought to combat the Progressives' contention that
ideas mattered little to the revolutionaries and that their justifications had
shifted to protect their economic interests by establishing that the American revolutionaries' view of the extent of parliamentary sovereignty did not
fundamentally change from 1765 to 1776.[31]

Scholars also disagreed during the 1950s and 1960s about whether or not the founders' liberalism should be praised or condemned. In his remarkably popular study, *The American Political Tradition and the Men Who Made It,* Richard Hofstadter spoke of the "rudderless and demoralized state of American liberalism" and, like Hartz, sought to highlight the dangerous uniformity and limitations of American political thought.[32] Hofstadter, like Hartz, also raised the broad question of whether the founding principles of the American republic were adequate to address the realities of the twentieth century. The American founders, Hofstadter argued, believed in an unchanging human nature and thus provided no guidance for "modern humanist thinkers who seek for a means by which society may transcend eternal conflict and rigid adherence to property rights as its integrating principles."[33]

In contrast, beginning in the late 1950s, the equally influential political scientist Martin Diamond took many of the same insights that Hartz and Hofstadter had set forth and fashioned them into a defense of the founders and the American political system. A repentant socialist, Diamond characterized the American Revolution in terms that Hartz would have wholeheartedly endorsed as a "Revolution of Sober Expectations." But whereas Hartz bemoaned the narrowness of the American political tradition and its exclusion of genuinely radical alternatives, Diamond praised the founders for pursuing a revolutionary principle—the establishment of civil liberty—that could be attained rather than pursuing utopian and unattainable principles such as unlimited equality, mass fraternity, or a classless society.[34]

Scholars' reticence about challenging outright the proposition that Locke was the alpha and omega of the American Founding ended with the articulation of the "republican synthesis"—the first of several historiographical efforts to unseat Locke and Hartz. First set forth in the late 1960s and early 1970s, the republican interpretation was, as Daniel Rodgers has observed, given identity, structure, and direction in two important historiographical essays by Robert Shalhope.[35] It then gained ascendancy in the 1970s and 1980s as works by Bailyn, Wood, and Pocock became the staple interpretations of the American Founding.

"Republican revisionism" has often been characterized as an effort to repudiate the liberal interpretation of the founders' political thought by calling attention to a constellation of interpretative idioms that had been ignored by proponents of the liberal interpretation. These included most importantly "virtue" (understood as self-denying acts necessary to sustain the republic), "the public good" (with the public conceived as an organic whole), and "positive liberty" (with liberty understood here as a humanizing condition of ruling and being ruled in a political community). As Rodgers and Michael Zuckert have observed, however, there have been important variations of the republican interpretation emanating from different understandings of republicanism that scholars have set forth.[36] Most important for our purposes, each of these variations bears differently on Hartz's liberal interpretation.

For his part, Bernard Bailyn argues that the American Revolution was heavily influenced by the political and social thought of a group of seventeenth- and eighteenth-century "coffee house radicals and opposition politicians."[37] The political thought of these radicals, Bailyn maintains, centered upon the belief that power (understood as "the dominion of some men over others") was aggressive, ever expanding, and inherently antagonistic to liberty.[38] They also repeatedly emphasized the uniqueness of England's mixed constitution as a means for preserving liberty and the tendency of ministers and governments in general to "corruption" (the pursuit of private gain at public expense). Most important, according to Bailyn, this "Country Party" ideology of English radicals could be seen as the center of the "ideological origins of the American Revolution" because it served as the framework in which other strains of political thought, such as Enlightenment rationalism, common law traditions, and covenant theology, were fused into a structured universe of thought. With their thought conditioned and limited by this Whig variation of classical republicanism, colonists could not help but look upon the series of events that took place during the 1760s and 1770s—from the Stamp Act to the Boston Port Act—as evidence that a conspiracy had been launched against their liberties and that the British Constitution and government were unbalanced and corrupted.

Bailyn's novel interpretation springs from his deep immersion in the revolutionary pamphlets that accompanied the American Revolution and is joined with a novel understanding of the role of ideas drawn from the cultural anthropologist Clifford Geertz. In particular, Bailyn uses Geertz's conception of ideology to establish the social force of the radical Whig ideas that he had come to believe were central to the revolutionaries' thinking and thus to lead historians out of seesawing exchanges between proponents of the Neo-Whig and Neo-Progressive interpretations of the American Revolution. Neo-Whig historians had attempted to establish the veracity of the constitutional principles that the American revolutionaries evoked and the sincerity and rectitude of their motives; in stark contrast, Progressive historians treated the revolutionaries' ideas as propaganda that masked their economic motives, charged the revolutionaries with shifting and inconsistent positions designed only to protect their interests, and at times dismissed altogether any role for ideas in the American Revolution. Drawing upon Clifford Geertz's concept of ideology as a public matrix of ideas that are not epiphenomenal and thus could not easily be manipulated by historical actors, Bailyn argues that it is no longer necessary to prove the veracity of the revolutionaries' motives in order to establish the central—social—role of ideas in the Revolution. Saturated in English opposition ideology, the American revolutionaries could not help but see conspiratorial designs in the imperial policies passed after 1763. The frenzied, conspiratorial rhetoric of American revolutionaries was thus not simply a set of surface justifications for underlying economic interests. It was at once cause and consequence of the American Revolution.

To be sure, Bailyn differentiates Locke from the English opposition ideologists—Andrew Marvell, Andrew Fletcher, Henry Neville, John Trenchard, Thomas Gordon, Benjamin Hoadly, Algernon Sidney, and Henry St. John Viscount Bolingbroke—who he believes were "devoured by the colonists" during the American Revolution.[39] Unlike subsequent proponents of this interpretation, however, Bailyn does not initially seem to have had the goal of refuting the liberal interpretation, including Hartz's variation of it. Indeed, Hartz is not mentioned in *The Ideological Origins of the American Revolution*. Furthermore, the importance of the concept of "virtue," which was so important to subsequent anti-Lockean and anti-Hartzian variations of the republican interpretation, is not listed as one of the attributes of English opposition ideology.[40]

Instead, Bailyn characterized the Whig ideology in which Americans had immersed themselves as "a peculiar strain of anti-authoritarianism" "based on extreme solicitude for the individual and equal hostility to government" and suggested that it carried into modernity "the traditional anti-statist convictions of seventeenth-century liberalism."[41] The "key concepts" of opposition ideology, he further suggested, included natural rights and the contractual basis of government.[42] Bailyn thus did not contrast Anglo-American republicanism with the social contract–natural rights tradition of liberalism or charge it with many of the anti-Hartzian connotations that it would later be given.[43] Indeed, the variation of the Whig ideology that Bailyn contended influenced the American revolutionaries can readily be integrated into a liberal interpretation, and Bailyn, like Hartz, found the sources of Americans' fear of centralized state power in the ideas that informed the American Revolution.

The republican interpretation became rephrased as an alternative to Hartz's liberal tradition primarily through the works of Gordon Wood and, even more, J. G. A. Pocock. Wood begins his important work *The Creation of the American Republic* with an account of the ideology of the American Revolution that at once follows Bailyn's lead and stresses the importance of English opposition ideology to the Americans, but also characterizes this ideology, as Bailyn initially at least did not, as a form of *classical* republicanism. Like Bailyn, Wood argues that the American revolutionaries' fear of corruption had led them to see a conspiracy against liberty in English policies after 1769 and thus to take up arms. Wood, however, further argues that the American revolutionaries conceived of the public along classical lines as an organic whole with a unitary interest and believed the promotion of the common good (understood as the welfare of the whole corporate society, not as a mere aggregation of interests) "would be the only objective of the government."[44] He also contends that the American revolutionaries believed in the fragility of republics and the need for the exercise of virtue by the citizenry to preserve them.

Indeed, Wood's broadest concern in *The Creation of the American Republic* is with tracing the path of Americans' understanding of the importance of virtue from the Revolution to the formation of the Constitution. In this dimension of his project, Wood argues that political leaders began to reconsider the viability of their classical conception of virtue under the pressure of a crisis of republican government that took place in the states during the mid-1780s. The passage of populist legislation in the state governments and the growing influence in the states of "new men" without the social status or refinement of the elite, according to Wood, led many of the gentlemen leaders of the early republic to the conclusion that virtue had been lost in the young nation. Eventually, the men who later became the framers of the Constitution abandoned both the belief that republican government had to be established in a small territory and the belief that the fate of republicanism in America depended upon the virtue of the citizenry. Instead, the framers developed a distinctly American and modern political theory based on the belief that the public good would somehow emerge if individuals would simply pursue their own interests.[45]

Ultimately, as Wood describes it in the penultimate sections of his most important and influential study, the novel political theory of the framers was filled with perplexing ambiguities. On the one hand, according to Wood, the ratification of the Constitution marked "the end of classical politics" and the formation of a political system designed to integrate and harmonize the many diverse interests of the nation. On the other hand, however, Wood also argues that the framers continued to show concern for virtue by constructing an electoral scheme that was designed to blunt the rising tide of democracy, filter members of the disinterested gentry into national office, and thereby help ensure continuing control of the national government by virtuous members of the gentleman elite.[46]

Most important for our purposes, Wood's prodigious effort to trace the path of virtue from the revolutionaries' acceptance of the classical idea to the formation of a Constitution that relied on governmental mechanisms that checked interest with interest leads him squarely—but ambiguously—back to Hartz. In one of the most frequently cited passages from *The Creation of the American Republic*, Wood wrote,

> Considering the Federalist desire for a high-toned government filled with better sorts of people, there is something decidedly disingenuous about the democratic radicalism of their arguments, their continual emphasis on the popular character of the Constitution, their manipulation of Whig maxims, their stressing of the representational nature of all parts of the government, including the greatly strengthened executive and Senate. In effect they appropriated and exploited the language that more rightfully belonged to their opponents. *The result was the beginning of a hiatus in American politics between ideology and motives that was never again closed. By using the most popular and democratic rhetoric available to explain and justify their aristocratic system, the Federalists helped to foreclose the development of an American intellectual tradition in which differing ideas of politics would be ultimately and genuinely related to differing social interests. In other words, the Federalists in 1787 hastened the destruction of whatever chance there was in America for the growth of an avowedly aristocratic conception of politics and thereby contributed to the creation of the encompassing liberal tradition which mitigated and often obscured the real social antagonisms of American politics. By attempting to confront and retard the thrust of the Revolution with the rhetoric of the Revolution, the Federalists fixed the terms for the future discussion of American politics. They thus brought the ideology of the Revolution to consummation and created a distinctly American political theory but only at the cost of eventually impoverishing later American political thought.*[47]

For Wood, then, Hartz is not wrong to suggest that liberalism had become dominant. He is wrong only to suggest that it had been dominant from the beginning. Republicanism, in other words, is characterized in Wood's scholarship—especially his most mature formulations of this thesis in *The Radicalism of the American Revolution*—as the ideology behind an antimonarchical moment in American history. Furthermore, Wood disagrees with Hartz about the Federalists. They were, he suggests in the quotation above, at least in some sense potentially the genuine European-style conservatives who, according to Hartz, had never appeared in America and thus could not come back on the scene. Nevertheless, the Federalists' unwillingness to link their interests and ideas, Wood argues, impoverished later American political thought in precisely the ways that Hartz had suggested. Most important, Wood interprets the constitutional settlement of 1787 as the establishment of the hegemony of the absolute liberalism that, he and Hartz contend, has subsequently enveloped American political thought.

It remained for J. G. A. Pocock to give the republican interpretation its most explicitly anti-Hartzian formulation. Pocock's contribution to the republican interpretation—or, to his critics, his exaggeration of it—is to integrate the scholarship of Bailyn and Wood into a global narrative of the "Atlantic Republican Tradition." This narrative traces the history of the language of civic humanism from its roots in antiquity through three phases: fifteenth- and sixteenth-century Florence, mid-seventeenth-century England, and eighteenth- and nineteenth-century America.[48] Like Wood, Pocock spoke of the importance of virtue within this political language, but he emphasizes to a degree that Wood (and certainly Bailyn) had not the importance of "positive" liberty to engage in self-defining forms of political participation as the defining element of civic humanist tradition. Pocock insists that his narrative tracing the continuity of the discourse of "civic" or participatory liberty and the various dialectics and ambiguities between virtue and commerce and virtue and fortune that characterized it is a "tunnel history"—a history that traces the path of a single language over time, documents its emergence in "the daylight of a new country," but simultaneously presupposes the presence of other languages with both parallel and intersecting histories. He thus—now at least—suggests that liberalism and republicanism were both present in the American Founding and denies that the republican interpretation is itself an effort to erect a new consensus interpretation.[49]

Most important, Bailyn's formulation of Whig opposition ideology as a form of antistatism that included natural rights philosophy and the social contract tradition is at least compatible with Hartz's understanding of the founders' political thought, and Wood, like Hartz, found an encompassing liberalism emerging from the Founding. In contrast, Pocock intended the republican interpretation "as an attack on the paramountcy given to Locke by Hartz," especially "the assumption that Locke was so universal, ubiquitous, and authoritative a figure that all thinking was obliged to descend from him."[50] Pocock also suggests that, if a Lockean ethos had ever established hegemony over American political thought, it had had to do so against "travail and trauma, from an intense and occasionally tragic struggle between opposing ideals and against a sense of history's march," that the tensions resulting from the struggle out of which it emerged remain ingrained in the American value system, and that republicanism "survived to furnish liberalism with one of its modes of self-criticism and self-doubt."[51]

Two strategies are central to Pocock's goal of "deconstructing the Lockean monolith posited by Hartz."[52] First, Pocock has sought to establish new fundamental categories of historical analysis by suggesting that scholars should not be particularly concerned (as Hartz was) with the displacement of feudalism by Lockean liberalism but, rather, should examine the problems around which, according to Pocock, eighteenth-century political debates were principally organized. The eighteenth-century debate including the American Founding, Pocock argues, was organized principally around a debate about the merits and problems of ongoing historical change. That debate pitted "Country Party" radicals, who resisted historical change or at least held reservations about its effects and thus expressed sympathy for the classical republican concerns for political participation, virtue, and independence, against "Court" advocates, who supported a constellation of proposals—including the growth of banks and paper credit, the professionalization of armies, and the expansion of bureaucracies—and who asserted the irrelevance of virtue, sought to establish new forms of dependence, and in general embraced finance capitalism and historical change. Locke, according to Pocock, simply was not a central figure in these eighteenth-century debates because his political thought was organized not around these historical concepts but, rather, around questions about when a ruler might be resisted. "From 1688 to 1776 (and after)," Pocock has written, "the central question in Anglophone political theory was not whether a ruler might be resisted for misconduct, but whether a regime founded on patronage, public debt, and professionalization of the armed forces did not corrupt both governors and governed; and corruption was a problem in virtue, not in right, which could never be solved by asserting a right to resistance."[53]

Second, in addition to telling the story of eighteenth-century political thought without reference to Locke until Locke's importance can be accurately reassessed, Pocock has sought to explain the ideology and politics behind the vehemence with which scholars have rejected the republican interpretation and simultaneously to discredit Hartz's thesis by exposing its function in American historiography, particularly its role as an exegesis in the American civil religion and its importance to the doctrine of American exceptionalism. With these goals in mind, Pocock observes that the liberal interpretation is sacred not only to defenders of liberalism but also to its critics, who "maximize its role in order to provide themselves with an antithesis."[54] He also points out that many conventional American historians are governed by two imperatives. They must recognize the necessity of a foundational myth and affirm "the premise of inescapable liberalism."[55] The foundational myth of American history, according to Pocock, is that there was an original covenant made to certain principles. The historians' task is then to ascertain what those principles are and to consider whether or not the covenant has been upheld or allowed to lapse. Analyses of how the covenant has been allowed to lapse take the form of jeremiads—extended, guilt-inducing lamentations. The premise of inescapable liberalism is the belief that "American political thought was and always had been Lockean without the possibility of an alternative—it was literally impossible for Americans to think any other way."[56]

Hartz is, according to Pocock, one of the central conveyers of the foundational myth, a proponent (if an unlikely and peculiar one) of the jeremiad, and the scholar who has given "the premise of inescapable liberalism" its "decisive formulation."[57] Pocock writes:

> The Hartzian thesis has become part of the American jeremiad. From perspectives not necessarily Marxist, though now and then touched by Marxist presuppositions, it represents America as a society isolated from mankind by the exceptionality of its liberalism and condemned to proclaim as universal socio-political beliefs elsewhere regarded as obsolete. The heirs of Hartz can be as critical of liberal values as he was himself; since it became the function of the intelligentsia to express alienation, the liberal intellectuals have been liberalism's most effective critics. They are, however, wholly committed to maintaining the primacy of that which they would criticize—much as Marxist historians must affirm the triumph of the bourgeoisie, since without it Marxism would lose its *raison d'être*. To attack liberalism is one thing; to challenge its historical reality is unforgiveable. Writing in conventional modes of American historiography, they have made the commitment to maintain liberalism the definition of the national identity (or "American experiment"). To doubt it is to doubt the reality of the experiment, and of the identity.[58]

Pocock's goals, then, have been to get scholars to consider the possibility that there was no initial covenant, no foundational set of liberal principles, and thus that American history is not exceptional. Within this context, suggesting that liberalism was not particularly relevant to eighteenth-century problems is the unkindest cut of all because it suggests to exponents of the jeremiad—whether liberal, Marxist, or Calvinist—that their "giant is only a windmill."[59] American history, Pocock further suggests with his story of the multiple transmissions of the Atlantic republican tradition, was not born wholly liberal but, rather, shared a history with other (European) cultures. Such an interpretation, Pocock contends, was "sure to be repudiated both by Americans refusing to continue the history of Europe and by Europeans refusing to have it continued by Americans."[60]

ROGERS SMITH: INEGALITARIAN IDEOLOGIES AND ASCRIPTIVE HIERARCHY

A second major effort to challenge Hartz's liberal interpretation that has important implications on scholarship on the American Founding has been set forth most forcefully by University of Pennsylvania scholar Rogers Smith.[61] Smith's challenge to Hartz's claims about the ubiquity and hegemony of the liberal tradition is built around his call for acknowledging the strength and persistence of fundamentally illiberal ideas, or what Smith calls "inegalitarian ascriptive traditions," in American political thought.[62] Inegalitarian ascriptive traditions include: (1) various forms of nativism; (2) biblical, scientific, and racial justifications for slavery and the displacement of Native Americans; (3) justifications for the subordination and depoliticization of women, such as "republican motherhood," "coverture," and "domestic sphere ideology"; and (4) claims about the natural superiority of Anglo-Saxons and contentions that they are a "chosen people." Unlike "liberal and democratic republican views describing citizenship as a human creation that ought to rest on the consent of all involved," inegalitarian ascriptive ideologies assign political identities—"including full citizenship with eligibility for voting rights and the highest political offices—on the basis of such ascribed characteristics as race, gender, and the usually unaltered nationality and religion into which people were born."[63] In short, these ideologies suggest that some individuals are naturally more fit than others to participate in politics and that they have a natural right to privileges denied to others.

For Smith, the problem with the analyses set forth by scholars relying on Tocquevillian frameworks, including not only Hartz's but also those of Gunnar Myrdal, Samuel Huntington, and Ira Katznelson, is *not* their conclusions that there was initially no hereditary monarchy or nobility in America, that feudalism was effectively absent, and that political and material conditions reinforced equality among white males. These are, according to Smith, the "real if partial truths" that Hartz and others identified.[64] The broadest problem with the accounts of Hartz and other proponents of the liberal interpretation is that they parrot the narrow framework adopted by Alexis de Tocqueville. Writing in the nineteenth century from the perspective of an aristocratic European man, Tocqueville understandably examined American society largely through the lens of the relationships among white men, especially those of northern European ancestry. This perspective led Tocqueville—and later Hartz—to conclude that the most striking fact about America was the absence of a monarch, an aristocracy, and feudal institutions and conversely the relative equality of condition among these men and the pervasiveness of liberalism.

Nevertheless, the absence of one form of ascriptive hierarchy (hereditary monarchy and nobility), Smith argues, does not establish the absence of all forms of ascriptive hierarchy or the hegemony of liberalism. According to Smith, "the comparative moral, material, and political egalitarianism that prevailed at the founding among moderately propertied white men was surrounded by an array of other fixed, ascriptive systems of unequal status."[65] What Hartz and others have not recognized is that these systems and the sets of illiberal ideas that supported them have been as "deeply constitutive of American national identity" as liberalism.[66] Indeed, far from being exceptions to a dominant egalitarian ethos or ephemeral prejudices accepted only in culturally backward enclaves, many of these ascriptive ideologies have been elaborate, structured, "genuine," and even at times "prestigious intellectual traditions" that "have had recurring power in American life."[67] They have enforced white male dominance and even, at times, provided identity to persons oppressed by them.

Because he parroted the European categories of analysis of Tocqueville, Smith further argues, Hartz altogether ignores the condition of women, generally dismisses the treatment of Native Americans, and provides an inadequate discussion of race and racism. Hartz also does not grasp, according to Smith, the full range of conflict and oppression that took place in America. Unlike some of the proponents of "consensus history" and celebratory versions of the liberal tradition, Hartz never suggests that ideological homogeneity had established an absence of conflict in America. Instead, he suggests that conflict would arise when irrational Lockeanism resulted in oppression and violence against "un-American" challengers to liberal values. Hartz also focuses on the classic conflicts in American history between majority rule and the protection of individual rights, especially property rights. For Smith, however, this understanding of the boundaries of conflict in America ignores the persistent patterns of repression justified by ascriptive ideologies and recurring conflicts faced by those who have sought to have liberalism live up to its ideals. Finally, Hartz, according to Smith, largely ignores ascriptive ideologies, but when forced to acknowledge their presence, treats them as alien to the prevailing liberal ethos or engages in "tortured" efforts to somehow establish that they are simply varieties of liberalism.[68]

These differences are vividly displayed in the strikingly different accounts that Hartz and Smith give of colonial America and the American Founding.[69] Whereas Hartz emphasizes the cultural and ethnic homogeneity of colonial America, the relative equality of the colonists, the absence of a real aristocracy or the institutions of feudalism, and (implies, at least) the serenity of the New World, Smith emphasizes the variations of red, white, and black peoples—male and female—present in colonial society, the patterns of hierarchy and subordination among these peoples, and the laws and customs that created political exclusions. Most broadly, Smith describes colonial America as a "contested wilderness" involving colonists in "endlessly impending and active warfare with rival European powers and diverse tribes, and disputes between the colonists and the home government, as well as a tale of European expansion and colonial growth."[70] Although Smith is never this blunt, his essential point against Hartz is that the "storybook truth" that America had been spared the institutions of feudalism and with them the oppressions that they created hardly mattered for women, slaves, and Native Americans, who faced an equally fierce set of oppressions justified by inegalitarian ideologies.[71]

Smith also challenges Hartz's contention about the grip of liberalism on the minds of the founders by focusing upon the manner in which paternal, elitist, and racist ideologies and the institutions of ascriptive hierarchy that they sought to justify were blended—often in a volatile and logically incoherent mix—with liberalism in the early republic in laws and the writings of leading founders. Hartz provided no real detailed analysis of the foundational texts of the American Founding and only cursory remarks about particular individual thinkers. These remarks are almost always efforts to establish that individual American statesmen or intellectuals—even those normally characterized as European-style traditionalists—are properly characterized as proponents of Lockean liberalism.

In contrast, although Smith finds few traditionalists in America, he documents how inegalitarian and ascriptive ideologies were espoused by leading intellectuals and mixed alongside the principles of classical liberalism even in the documents that Americans have read as the quintessential expressions of American liberalism. Smith, for example, points out that Thomas Jefferson's *Notes on the State of Virginia* contains not only important statements of Jefferson's opposition to slavery, rooted in his commitment to liberalism, but also the "most intellectually prestigious statement of inherent black inferiority" in American political thought.[72] Similarly, Smith observes that Thomas Paine's revolutionary pamphlet *Common Sense,* often viewed as a classic statement of Lockean liberalism and thus the universal rights of man, also contains "the more parochial claim that Americans were an essentially Anglo-Saxon people, specially chosen by the Protestant God to carry forth the torch of freedom that was the emblem of their race."[73]

Finally, Hartz's animus was to show that European categories of socialist, bourgeois, and aristocrat were not replicated in the United States and thus that members of the Federalist Party were best thought of as aristocratic Whigs, not Burkean conservatives. In contrast, Smith analyzes the Federalist and Jeffersonian parties as contrasting blends of liberalism, republicanism, and ascriptive notions of American identity. The Federalists, he observes, advanced classical liberal policies that favored financial and commercial elites. Initially at least, they sponsored relatively passive policies toward unconquered western tribes and were opponents of slavery. Nevertheless, "a predilection toward nativism" and the continued subordination of women were also deeply embedded in the political thought of the Federalist Party.[74] The Jeffersonians, in contrast, were the party of westward expansion, state power, and agrarian republicanism but also, "in a bitter irony, the defenders both of citizenship based on mutual consent [for white males] and of aggressive civic racism."[75]

THE PROGRESSIVE CRITIQUE OF HARTZ

The final challenge to Hartz's interpretation of the liberal tradition in America and his particular understanding of the American Founding examined in this essay is also the oldest and most enduring. First formulated by James Allen Smith and Charles Beard in the early twentieth century, the original formative statements of the Progressive interpretation were published four decades before *The Liberal Tradition in America.* Thus, while we can only speculate about how Hartz might have responded to the articulation of the republican interpretation and Smith's multiple traditions approach, we have Hartz's direct response to the initial versions of the Progressive interpretation.

At this point in the study of the American Founding, the Progressive interpretation itself has a considerable history, with contributions from at least three generations of scholars from Smith and Beard, to Merrill Jensen and Jackson Turner Main, to Staughton Lynd and Woody Holton.[76] A massive body of scholarship done by social historians on the American founders examining the subordination of women, Native Americans, slaves, and the poor in the early republic is also Progressive in spirit, if not strictly based on the economic analyses of the original Progressives.[77]

Briefly put, Progressivism stands as an enduring critique of Hartz's liberal interpretation in both methodology and substance. As pointed out earlier, Hartz did not believe that most Americans accepted Lockean liberalism at more than a subconscious level. Obviously, however, he treats ideas as they become pervasive and form the ethos of a nation as vital subjects of analysis. A consistent theme of Progressive analysis (especially strong among the early Progressives), however, is extreme skepticism about the importance of ideas as motives for behavior and a corresponding belief that economic interests are the "primordial or fundamental."[78]

Many of the early Progressives also believed—following a loose-jointed conception of economic determinism—that history is best understood as a series of struggles between those with and those without property, or at least between holders of different forms of property.[79] Initially at least, the Progressives' belief in the primacy of economic interests and their conflict model of American history committed them to empirical studies to support their contentions about the stratification of American society and the economic character of recurring conflicts. As Daniel Rodgers has succinctly put it, "The Beardian paradigm organized American history around a restless sea of conflicting material interests."[80]

The Progressives' methodological commitments and inclinations have been crystallized into a series of interpretations that together present a formidable and enduring view of the American Founding—several dimensions of which are parroted even by scholars with radically different approaches. First, in polar contrast to Hartz, the Progressives portrayed colonial America as an aristocratic vestige of European society with entrenched feudalistic institutions that concentrated wealth and with considerable social stratification. Nevertheless, the American Revolution, according to the Progressives, accelerated a revolution within America that, in Carl Becker's famous formulation, meant that the battle with Great Britain over "home rule" was accompanied by an equally intense struggle over "who should rule at home."[81] Progressives then argued that the social conflict that attended the American Revolution broke out again during the mid-1780s in a series of economic conflicts within the states over debtor relief legislation such as stay laws delaying the collection of debts, acts calling for the printing of paper money, and laws abrogating contracts. Elite concerns for the security of their property interests were most vividly illustrated, however, in the reaction that the men who later wrote and ratified the Constitution had to Shays's Rebellion—the popular uprising in Massachusetts that resulted from high taxes being imposed on debt-ridden farmers during a period of recession. The efforts of Daniel Shays and his rebels to close down the Massachusetts state courts and the series of laws in the states that endangered the property of creditors, Progressives have persistently argued, were the primary source of the framers' desire to create a strong national government, which would protect their economic interests where the states had failed.

The delegates who attended the Constitutional Convention, the Progressive interpretation continues, were an economic elite, unrepresentative of the American population, and "were immediately, directly, and personally interested in the outcome of their labors at Philadelphia, and were to a greater or less extent economic beneficiaries from the adoption of the Constitution."[82] This resulted in the creation of a constitution that was both antidemocratic and tilted in favor of the economic interests that created it. It was antidemocratic in the sense that it sought—through extent of territory, inadequate representation, and the system of separation of powers—to stifle the rule of popular majorities that might threaten the property of the framers. It was biased toward business and mercantile interests because it contained positive powers, such as the power to regulate interstate and foreign commerce, that could be used to further the interests of these groups. Most Progressives also suggest that the Federalists and Anti-Federalists represented distinct economic interests and that the conflict that had led to the calling of the Constitutional Convention continued during the ratification struggle over the Constitution. Finally, Progressives have argued that the first political parties—the Jeffersonian Republicans and the Federalists—were composed of distinct economic groups and that the battles between agrarian and mercantile interests continued into the 1790s.

Hartz responded only to the earliest wave of Progressive scholarship, only to a limited number of these points of this interpretation, and then only in the broadest of terms. He conceded that the Progressives had "uncovered beneath our struggle for national independence a whole series of domestic conflicts."[83] Nevertheless, he never provided anything like a formal defense of the study of ideas against the Progressives' claim that ideas were merely rationalizations of underlying interests. He also did not sift through the empirical debates over the social and economic characteristics of the delegates to the Constitutional Convention or over differences in the social and economic characteristics of the Anti-Federalists and the Federalists, provide an alternative account of the motives of the framers of the Constitution, or set forth an alternative to the Progressives' interpretation of the Constitution.

Instead of dirtying his hands in such details, Hartz presented a series of observations about the exceptional quality of American society and the sources and limitations of Progressive analysis. Hartz's response to the picture of social stratification in America suggested by the Progressives was to argue that America had only a "frustrated" aristocracy that felt guilty for "trying to break out of the egalitarian confines of the middle class," that the few individuals considered aristocrats in America had inspired neither love nor hatred, and that, unlike European aristocrats, the top strata of American society had never been a leisured class but, rather, had always been required to engage in capitalistic ventures to sustain their wealth.[84] Similarly, his response to the Progressives' evidence of social conflict during the American Revolution and leading up to the formation of the Constitution and their account of the importance Shays's Rebellion was to suggest that these conflicts in America dimmed in comparison with the great revolutions of Europe.[85] Hartz's specific response to the Progressives' account of Shays's Rebellion was to maintain that a "bourgeois ethic" was present even at the "outermost limit of American radicalism."[86] Thus, Hartz argued that Daniel Shays lacked the ideological resources to produce a genuinely radical political thought and was really only an "extension himself of populist liberalism." Shays's rebels, like the Progressives themselves, "were inside, rather than outside, the liberal process of American politics."[87]

Even more broadly, Hartz argued that the choice between conflict and consensus was a false one and that social conflict in the United States took place within the context of a broader consensus that limited and defined it. The universality of liberalism, in other words, set both the character and meaning of the conflict that took place.[88] Finally, in a critique that was at least partly ad hominem and must have inflamed them, Hartz suggested that the Progressive historians were themselves a product of irrational Lockeanism, had no comparative perspective that might have allowed them to transcend subjective history, and were therefore as deserving of the title of American innocents as any other group of American scholars.[89]

> Where then lay the nativism of Beard and J. Allen Smith? It is not simply in the fact that they did not attempt the European correlations. This hid something deeper: their theory was a projection of the Progressive social orientation, which was compact of America's irrational liberalism.

The agitation of Brandeis and Wilson was the agitation of Western
Liberal Reform altered by the fact that, fighting only Whiggery, rather
than Toryism and socialism too, it was able no more than Whiggery to
perceive the nature of its liberalism. It was as if Lloyd George were
fighting only the reactionary members of the Liberal party who, in any
case, had no Tory party to enter if they were dissatisfied with him.
Hence, with the whole scheme of liberal unity blacked out, Whiggery
became for the Progressives a frightful "conservatism," whereas it itself
became "progressive" or "radical," a set of terms which meant nothing
insofar as Western history of Western political alignments as a whole
went. Armed with these tools, and as blind as the Progressives
themselves to the natural liberalism of the nation, Beard and Smith
went back to the origins of American history, splitting it up into two
warring camps, discovering a "social revolution" in the eighteenth
century, and in general making it impossible to understand the
American liberal community. Their treatment of the Constitution may
have lacked the piety of the "patriotic" historians, but it was as
"American" as anything those historians developed.[90]

In Progressive scholarship, Hartz continued, a Jeffersonian democratic
hero always emerges to conquer the Hamiltonian capitalist villain, and no
problems are presented that cannot be solved by an insurgence of part of
the community. In contrast to the "many comforts" of the Progressive interpretation and the "continuous and almost complacent note of reassurance
that it offered," the liberal society analyst could offer no such optimism
about the future, especially about the ability of the United States to find its
way in the world with its limited intellectual perspective.[91]

ASSESSING HARTZ'S CRITICS AND HIS LEGACY

Where does all of this leave Hartz and his classic? Which dimensions of
Hartz's thesis are enduring and which have subsequently been refuted?
How does Hartz fare against his challengers? Has anyone broken free of his
fundamental categories of analysis? In seeking to establish what is enduring
in *The Liberal Tradition in America,* a common and understandable strategy—
given its dated quality, its status as a classic, the sweeping character of the
generalizations that Hartz made, and the avalanche of specific criticisms
lodged against his arguments—is to point to the big picture. As John Gunnell has recently observed, even Hartz's critics concede that he "elicited
some deep insight into the character of American culture and politics" and

"provided a basic window into American political life."[92] Among the broadest insights about American political thought and the course of American political development that Hartz's liberal interpretation illuminates are the conservative character of the American Revolution, the virtual absence of both European socialism and Burkean or traditionalist conceptions of political thought in the United States, the pervasiveness and continuity of fears of governmental power, and the remarkable stability (with the exception of the Civil War) of American politics and society.

Of these, the most important for Founding scholarship has been Hartz's insight into the exceptional character of the American Revolution. The American Revolution, as Hartz keenly recognized and students of the American Founding both before and after his work have continuously affirmed, lacked the fanaticism and violence associated with the French and Russian revolutions. It also called forth a different kind of revolutionary—a conservative revolutionary inoculated by a century of the practice of self-government against the enthusiasms that would later infect his French and Russian counterparts.

In addition to this foundational point, *The Liberal Tradition in America* is now important in scholarship on the American Founding primarily for the academic debates that it catalyzed and shaped. The academic debate in the study of the American Founding that Hartz's work most profoundly shaped was the republicanism versus liberalism debate, which, as Gunnell also observed, would probably not have taken place had it not been for Hartz's study.[93] It has been fashionable for at least a decade to observe that this debate is now exhausted and was conducted on the basis of dubious terms. As numerous scholars have pointed out, "liberalism" and "republicanism" are scholarly constructs that would not have been readily identifiable to the historical actors as competing sets of ideas. Instead, as most commentators in this debate quickly realized, these sets of intellectual idioms were intertwined in the political thought of the founders in the ways that an either-republicanism-or-liberalism formulation cannot capture.[94]

Nevertheless, two contributions of the republicanism versus liberalism debate are relevant to discussions of the legacy of Louis Hartz. First, *The Liberal Tradition in America* and the republicanism versus liberalism debate inadvertently catalyzed the development of a much more sophisticated understanding of the historic John Locke and his role in the American Founding than had previously been established. By the 1970s, Hartz's classic, C. B. MacPherson's *The Theory of Possessive Individualism,* the work of Daniel Boorstin, and various studies in American exceptionalism were often grouped together and characterized as ahistorical products of the

Cold War.[95] Such grand synthetic interpretations, many scholars concluded, said more about contemporary American political culture and the American character than about eighteenth-century political thought and the intellectual origins of the American republic.[96] Reacting at once against the republican interpretation, the view of Locke and liberalism presented in consensus history, and Marxist interpretations of the origins of liberalism and capitalism, historians such as Joyce Appleby and Isaac Kramnick constructed a new liberal interpretation and searched for and found a historical Locke who, they established, had been quite influential in the American Founding. Liberal ideas, Appleby in particular has suggested, were initially set forth as *egalitarian* defenses of market economies against the privileges created by monarchy and mercantilism. Instead of suggesting that the United States was born liberal, both Kramnick and Appleby stressed the persistence of republican ideas of virtue, corruption, and the public good even as they also emphasized the novelty and liberating potential of liberalism as it emerged in the seventeenth and eighteenth centuries. As commerce expanded, Appleby argues, men began to search for and found a language for justifying the market economies that were already operating. Eventually, the rights-bearing, industrious individual celebrated in Locke's treatises emerged to challenge the republican citizen as the way that statesmen and philosophers conceived of man.[97]

Second, the recognition of the presence of a multiplicity of traditions of political thought in the American Founding moved the debate about the relative influences of republicanism versus liberalism into a debate about the terms upon which a multiplicity of diverse political languages, traditions, or idioms influenced the Founding. The movement of the republicanism versus liberalism debate from an "either/or" to a "both/and" stage, in turn, has led to a much richer understanding of the intellectual traditions that informed the American Founding, the various functions that they performed, and the ways in which they were intertwined and interacted than we previously had. Since the late 1980s, scholars have argued over what kind of multiple traditions approach provides the best framework for interpreting the American Founding and whether the synthesis achieved was coherent or not. Even as Hartz's claim about the universality of liberalism has been rejected, the importance of the liberal tradition has been reaffirmed by some scholars who have suggested that liberalism provided the organizing logic upon which other sets of ideas were integrated into an American amalgam.[98]

If we move from a consideration of the debates that Hartz helped catalyze and shape to a consideration of whether or not he has been displaced by the three challenges examined in this essay, then we can gain a still better sense of the strengths and limitations of *The Liberal Tradition in America.* Even by the admission of its most vocal advocates, republicanism has not proven to be an alternative to the liberal interpretation of the American Founding. As indicated above, the establishment of the "republican synthesis" led to a vigorous counterrevolution by advocates of the liberal interpretation. The defenders of republicanism responded to this counterrevolution by saying that they had never meant to suggest that republicanism was the exclusive language of American political thought. Most also readily conceded that liberalism had become dominant at some point in American history. Once they had conceded the mixed character of early American political thought and the eventual hegemony of liberalism, however, the strong claim that republicanism could serve as a new fundamental category of analysis or even an alternative voice or a language of self-criticism and self-doubt for liberalism was substantially diminished. If liberalism and republicanism were not incompatible and the historical participants themselves blended them, then how could republicanism serve as a meaningful alternative to liberalism?

The Progressive interpretation represents a more enduring challenge to Hartz's thesis, particularly his view of the social structure of the early American republic and his interpretation of the intensity and character of social conflict in the American Founding. In assessing the debate between Hartz and the Progressives about social stratification in colonial and revolutionary America and whether social conflict was extensive or relatively unimportant, we must first realize that our judgment depends upon what standards we use to measure social stratification and meaningful social conflict. Obviously, Hartz strategically set a very high standard—a European standard—for what constitutes meaningful social stratification and social conflict. Imposing this standard had both the intention and effect of deflecting the Progressives' claims without really challenging the validity of their empirical points. As Daniel Rodgers has said, Hartz and many of the consensus historians with whom he was loosely allied did not so much confront the "accumulated Beardian evidence of endemic social conflict" as raise "the stakes of what counted as *meaningful* conflict, until every conceivable demonstration of conflict short of Jacobin or Bolshevist revolution vanished in the all-pervasive liberal consensus."[99]

Over the century since Charles Beard published *An Economic Interpretation of the Constitution,* however, the Progressive interpretation has established a continuity of evidence that challenges Hartz's portrait of a relative absence of social conflict in the early republic and of a truncated, frustrated aristocracy. At minimum, the Progressives and those sympathetic to their interpretations have established that there is extensive evidence in the writings and speeches from the 1780s suggesting that both ordinary Americans and the elite founders saw their society as splintered into competing groups. The writings and speeches of the elite founders also establish that many of them viewed their role as containing the democratic impulses unleashed by the American Revolution.[100] As Woody Holton has recently shown, the claim that the framers sought to contain democracy is strengthened by a consideration of the positions of opponents and supporters of constitutional reform on the desirability of large polities, large electoral districts, and constitutional reform. Proponents of these measures, Holton has established, were most likely to be opponents of debtor relief legislation and in favor of increased taxation; in contrast, Americans who wished to keep the sphere and role of the national government modest were most likely to be in favor of debtor relief and tax relief.[101] Finally, although most Founding scholars seem to believe that Forrest McDonald refuted any economic interpretation of the formation of the Constitution, economic analysis has consistently supported the proposition that the delegates to the Constitutional Convention were disproportionately wealthy, urban, and commercial in their interests and that in the ratification process delegates who represented commercial coastal regions were much more likely than ones representing the interior to support the Constitution.[102]

If the Progressive interpretation of the American Founding stands as an enduring alternative to Hartz's liberal interpretation, Rogers Smith's multiple traditions interpretation represents the most foundational challenge to Hartz's fundamental categories of analysis. Put bluntly, Hartz did not give sufficient attention to issues of race and gender in American politics and missed the broad and important role played by inegalitarian, ascriptive ideologies. In contrast, Smith establishes that inegalitarian ideologies were popular and long-lived, had important effects on public policy, were defended by leading intellectuals, and were important in the construction of political identities—including even among the groups whose subordination was justified by them. These attributes establish that inegalitarian ideologies are as worthy to be called a "tradition" as is liberalism. Indeed, whereas "liberalism" is properly thought of as an "implicit" tradition because it is best characterized as a heuristic construct created by scholars to aid the analysis of a problem, inegalitarian ascriptive ideologies constitute "explicit" traditions of political thought, Smith persuasively argues, because they existed as social phenomena and were espoused explicitly by the historical actors.[103] Most important, once the potency and persistence of these traditions are established, then, Hartz's claims about the stranglehold of liberalism on American political thought evaporate—though American political thought becomes even more sinister, complex, and compromised than Hartz suggested.

Most important for purposes of this essay, proponents of the republican, Progressive, and multiple traditions interpretations set forth an avalanche of studies that leave few of Hartz's specific insights intact and cut to the core of his deepest assumptions. Scholars of the American Founding can still appreciate Hartz's eloquent statement of the conservative character of the American Revolution and the American revolutionaries. Hartz also provided the framework for understanding America's moralistic attitude in foreign policy and the characteristically American tendency to oscillate between isolationalism and the desire to reform the world in its own image. Yet another way that we can continue to benefit from Hartz is by following his plea for the comparative analysis of American political thought and by teasing meaning from his cryptic and puzzling comparisons. Finally, *The Liberal Tradition in America* will also need to be read to understand the debates and insights that it has fueled. Nevertheless, to use an analogy from theater, Hartz's classic had a remarkable run, but it is time for a different production.

NOTES

1. Louis Hartz, *The Liberal Tradition in America: An Interpretation of American Political Thought since the Revolution* (San Diego: Harcourt Brace Jovanovich, 1955), 28.

2. James Kloppenberg, "In Retrospect: Louis Hartz's "The Liberal Tradition in America," *Reviews in American History* 29 (September 2001): 465.

3. There are at least three other major lines of criticism that seek to displace or challenge Hartz. Several scholars have argued that Hartz paid insufficient attention to the importance of religion in American political thought. See, for example, Barry Shain, *The Myth of American Individualism: The Protestant Origins of American Political Thought* (Princeton, N.J.: Princeton University Press, 1994), where Shain emphasizes against Hartz the importance of Protestant communitarianism. Other scholars—including most famously Garry Wills—have argued that the ideas of the Scottish Enlightenment provide a modern, but communitarian, alternative to liberalism that was central to the American Founding. Wills, *Inventing America: Jefferson's Declaration of Independence* (Garden City, N.Y.: Doubleday, 1978); Wills, *Explaining America: The Federalist* (Garden City, N.Y.: Doubleday, 1981). Still other scholars have argued that efforts to eradicate feudalism during the American Founding were at best incomplete and that feudal institutions persisted in America into the twentieth century. See Karen Orren, *Belated Feudalism: Labor, the Law, and Liberal Development in the United States* (New York: Cambridge University Press, 1991).

4. This essay has the specific goal of evaluating Hartz's interpretation with regard to Founding scholarship. For more general appraisals of Hartz's thesis, see the essays in this volume and Phillip Abbott, "Still Louis Hartz after All These Years: A Defense of the Liberal Society Thesis," *Perspectives on Politics* 3 (March 2005): 93–120; Benjamin Barber, "Louis Hartz," *Political Theory* 14 (August 1986): 355–358; John Patrick Diggins, "Knowledge and Sorrow: Louis Hartz's Quarrel with American History," *Political Theory* 16 (August 1988): 355–376; Brian Glenn, "Louis Hartz's *Liberal Tradition in America* as Method," *Studies in American Political Development* 19 (Fall 2005): 234–239; John Gunnell, "Louis Hartz and the Liberal Metaphor: A Half Century Later," *Studies in American Political Development* 19 (Fall 2005): 196–205; Catherine Holland, "Hartz and Minds: The Liberal Tradition after the Cold War," *Studies in American Political Development* 19 (Fall 2005): 227–233; Richard Iton, "The Sound of Silence: Comments on 'Still Louis Hartz after All These Years,'" *Perspectives on Politics* 3 (March 2005): 111–120; Kloppenberg, "In Retrospect," 460–476; Leonard Krieger, "A View of the Farther Shore," *Comparative Studies in History and Society* 5 (April 1963): 269–273; Kenneth McNaught, "Comment" in *Failure of a Dream? Essays in the History of American Socialism*, ed. John H. M. Laslett and Seymour Martin Lipset (Garden City, N.Y.: Doubleday/Anchor, 1974), 409–418; Marvin Meyers, "Louis Hartz, *The Liberal Tradition in America*: An Appraisal," *Comparative Studies in Society and History* 5 (April 1963): 261–268; James A. Morone, "Storybook Truths about America," *Studies in American Political Development* 19 (Fall 2005): 216–226; Carol Nackenoff, "Locke, Alger, and Atomistic Individualism Fifty Years Later: Revisiting Louis Hartz's *Liberal Tradition in America*," *Studies in American Political Development* 19 (Fall 2005): 206–215; Marc Stears, "The Liberal Tradition and the Politics of Exclusion," *Annual Review of Political Science* 10 (2007): 85–101; Sean Wilentz, "Uses of *The Liberal Tradition*: Comments on 'Still Louis Hartz after All These Years,'" *Perspectives on Politics* 3 (March 2005): 117–120; Alan Wolfe, "Nobody Here but Us Liberals," *New York Times*, July 3, 2005, http://www.nytimes.com/2005/07/03/books/review/03WOLFEL.html?_r=1&oref=slogin.

5. Hartz, *The Liberal Tradition in America*, 6.

6. Ibid., 4.

7. Ibid., 5, 11, 16, 18, 23, 53, 54, 60, 62, 72. Quotations are on 60, 62.

8. Ultimately, for Hartz, as Marvin Meyers observed, Locke "connotes the ethos of a nation born equal." See Meyers, "Louis Hartz, *The Liberal Tradition in America*," 263. Similarly, Daniel T. Rodgers has written, "in the Hartzian paradigm, Locke had been shorthand for a general state of mind" and "except as a tag for an arrangement of society and culture, Locke hardly mattered to the Hartzians." Rodgers, "Republicanism: The Career of a Concept," *Journal of American History* 79 (June 1992): 17, 13. Hartz's "liberal tradition," then, blurs the distinction—recently drawn by James Ceasar—between a "public philosophy" and a "tradition." Liberalism was "in the air" and was thus a popular creed or "public philosophy" (admittedly for an unphilosophic people), but it was also a "tradition," when traditions are understood as "prefabricated essences" that "analysts have imported from the outside in order to

organize and make sense of the disparate ideas of American political life." For Ceasar's distinction between "traditions" and a "public philosophy," see James W. Ceaser, *Nature and History in American Political Development: A Debate* (Cambridge, Mass.: Harvard University Press, 2006), 11–16. And indeed, few, if any, of the historical actors that Hartz analyzed used the term "liberalism" in the way that he did or described themselves as proponents of a "liberal tradition."

9. See Hartz, *The Liberal Tradition in America*, 26. See also 11, 62, and 140, where Hartz famously describes American political thought as "a veritable jigsaw puzzle of theoretical confusion," suggests Lockean ideas are so deeply embedded in the American mind by their peculiar historical experience and material conditions that they are best thought of as "instinctive," producing a way of life that "usually does not know that Locke himself is involved."

10. Ibid. Quotations are on 8 and 4. See also the discussion on 21.

11. Ibid., 24.

12. Ibid., 6.

13. Ibid., 22.

14. Ibid., 5, 6, 9.

15. Ibid., 59, 57.

16. Ibid., 78.

17. Ibid., 35, 50 (emphasis in the original).

18. Ibid., 36, 39.

19. Ibid., 37.

20. Ibid., 47.

21. Ibid., 49.

22. Ibid., 48.

23. Ibid., 69.

24. Ibid., 43–45, 59–63. Quotation is on 44.

25. Hartz's most elaborate version of this argument was that Locke was the theorist who had released men from the associations of class, church, guild, and place and thus made the state the only association that might legitimately coerce individuals. His teaching could therefore be understood to require first the fortification and defense of state power. Indeed, eighteenth-century liberals in France had believed the concept of state absolutism was consistent with Locke's teachings. In America, in contrast, men were never encumbered by feudal associations. Thus, when Americans moved from the idea of the state of nature to the contractual idea of organizing the state, they were only concerned with limiting state power. See Ibid., 59–60.

26. Ibid., 60.

27. Ibid., 40–43. Quotations are on 40 and 41, respectively.

28. Ibid., 80. Hartz's discussion of "the Federalists" is confusing because he does not clearly and explicitly state when he is talking about the framers of the Constitution and when he is talking about members of the Federalist Party of the early 1790s. These groups were not, of course, identical.

29. Ibid.

30. Merle Curti, "'The Great Mr. Locke': America's Philosopher, 1783–1861," *Huntington Library Bulletin* 11 (1937): 109–110, 151. Quotation is on 151.

31. Edmund S. Morgan and Helen Morgan, *The Stamp Act Crisis: Prologue to Revolution* (Chapel Hill: University of North Carolina Press, 1953). For the disagreements between the Progressives and "Neo-Whig" historians on the motives of the American revolutionaries, see Gordon Wood, "Rhetoric and Reality in the American Revolution," *William and Mary Quarterly* 23 (January 1966): 3–32.

32. Richard Hofstadter, *The American Political Tradition and the Men Who Made It* (1948; reprint, New York: Vintage Books, 1974), xxxvi.

33. Ibid., 21.

34. Martin Diamond, "The Revolution of Sober Expectations," in *The American Revolution: Three Views,* by Martin Diamond, Irving Kristol, and Warren G. Nutter (New York: American Brands, 1975), 57–85.

35. Rodgers, "Republicanism," 11; Robert E. Shalhope, "Toward a Republican Synthesis: The Emergence of an Understanding of Republicanism in American Historiography," *William and Mary Quarterly* 29 (1972): 49–80; Shalhope, "Republicanism and Early American Historiography," *William and Mary Quarterly* 39 (1982): 334–356.

36. See Michael Zuckert, *Natural Rights and the New Republicanism* (Princeton, N.J.: Princeton University Press, 1994), 150–164. Rodgers has observed differences between the St. Louis school of republicanism that includes Pocock, Lance Banning, and John Murrin and the Harvard school led by Wood. Whereas proponents of the St. Louis strain speak of a tradition of republicanism rooted in civic humanism and trace the continuity of republicanism in the United States into the nineteenth century and indeed throughout American history, proponents of the Harvard school understand republicanism as a form of "Country Party ideology" and argue that it was eclipsed by liberalism in the late eighteenth and early nineteenth centuries. See Rodgers, "Republicanism," 18–20.

37. Bernard Bailyn, *The Ideological Origins of the American Revolution* (1967; enlarged ed., Cambridge, Mass.: Harvard University Press/Belknap Press, 1992), 35.

38. Ibid., 56.

39. Ibid., 43.

40. Remarkably, the concept of "virtue" is indexed only in the 1992 edition of *The Ideological Origins of the American Revolution* (not the 1967 edition), and that index points to passages included in the essay that Bailyn appended to the later edition.

41. Ibid., xii, 48; Bernard Bailyn, "The Central Themes of the American Revolution: An Interpretation," in *Essays on the American Revolution,* ed. Stephen G. Kurtz and James H. Hutson (Chapel Hill: University of North Carolina Press, 1973), 9.

42. Bailyn, *The Ideological Origins of the American Revolution,* 45. Bailyn also did not suggest that opposition thinkers were vastly more important than Locke to the

American revolutionaries. He wrote, "The writings of Trenchard and Gordon ranked with the treatises of Locke as the most authoritative statement of the nature of political liberty and above Locke as an exposition of the social sources of the threats it faced." Ibid., 36.

43. See Zuckert, *Natural Rights and the New Republicanism*, 150–164.

44. Gordon Wood, *The Creation of the American Republic, 1776–1787* (1969; reprint, Chapel Hill: University of North Carolina Press, 1998), 53–70. Quotation is on 54.

45. Wood's interpretation of the path of virtue has been challenged in a thoughtful essay by Lance Banning, "Some Second Thoughts on Virtue and the Course of Revolutionary Thinking," in *Conceptual Change and the Constitution*, ed. Terrence Ball and J. G. A. Pocock (Lawrence: University Press of Kansas, 1988), 194–212.

46. Wood, *The Creation of the American Republic*, 469–564, 593–615. Quotation is on 606.

47. Ibid., 562 (emphasis added).

48. This narrative is provided in its most complete form in J. G. A. Pocock, *The Machiavellian Moment—Florentine Political Thought and the Atlantic Republic Tradition* (Princeton, N.J.: Princeton University Press, 1975). See also several other of Pocock's works: "Civic Humanism and Its Role in Anglo-American Thought," in *Politics, Language, and Time: Essays on Political Thought and History* (New York: Atheneum Press, 1971), 80–103, "Machiavelli, Harrington, and English Political Ideologies in the Eighteenth Century," *William and Mary Quarterly* 22 (October 1965): 549–583; "Virtue and Commerce in the Eighteenth Century," *Journal of Interdisciplinary History* 3 (Summer 1972): 119–134, "Between Gog and Magog: The Republican Thesis and the Ideologica Americana," *Journal of the History of Ideas* 48 (April–June 1987): 325–346, "*The Machiavellian Moment* Revisited: A Study in History and Ideology," *Journal of Modern History* 53 (March 1981): 49–72, "The Myth of John Locke and the Obsession with Liberalism," in *John Locke*, ed. J. G. A. Pocock and Richard Ashcraft (Los Angeles: William Andrews Clark Memorial Library, 1980), 1–24, "Cambridge Paradigms and Scotch Philosophers: A Study of the Relations between the Civic Humanist and the Civil Jurisprudential Interpretation of Eighteenth-Century Social Thought," in *Wealth and Virtue: The Shaping of Political Economy in the Scottish Enlightenment*, ed. Istvan Hont and Michael Ignatieff (Cambridge: Cambridge University Press, 1983), 235–252, and "Virtues, Rights, and Manners," *Political Theory* 9 (August 1981): 353–368.

49. See Pocock, "Cambridge Paradigms and Scotch Philosophers," 246–247. In *The Machiavellian Moment*, however, Pocock argued that "not all Americans were schooled in this [the neoclassical] tradition, but there was (it would almost appear) no alternative tradition in which to be schooled." Pocock was thus initially at least ambiguous about whether Lockean liberalism was even present at the Founding. Pocock, *The Machiavellian Moment*, 507.

50. Pocock, "Between Gog and Magog," 339.

51. Pocock, "Virtue and Commerce in the Eighteenth Century," 132; Pocock, "Between Gog and Magog," 341.

52. Pocock, "Between Gog and Magog," 341.

53. Quotation is from Pocock, "Virtues, Rights, and Manners," 364. For Pocock's interpretation of the irrelevance of Locke, see Pocock, "Virtue and Commerce in the Eighteenth Century," 127–130; Pocock, "The Myth of John Locke and the Obsession with Liberalism," 3–24.

54. Pocock, "*The Machiavellian Moment* Revisited," 70.

55. Pocock, "Between Gog and Magog," 338.

56. Ibid.

57. Ibid.

58. Ibid., 338–339.

59. Ibid., 337.

60. Ibid., 342.

61. Rogers M. Smith, *Civic Ideals: Conflicting Visions of Citizenship in U.S. History* (New Haven, Conn.: Yale University Press, 1997). See also Smith's preliminary essays for which *Civic Ideals* is the culmination: "The 'American Creed' and American Identity: The Limits of Liberal Citizenship in the United States," *Western Political Quarterly* 41 (1988): 225–251; "'One United People': Second-Class Female Citizenship and the American Quest for Community," *Yale Journal of Law and Humanities* 1 (1989): 229–293; "Beyond Tocqueville, Myrdal, and Hartz: The Multiple Traditions in America," *American Political Science Review* 87 (1993): 549–566; "Unfinished Liberalism," *Social Research* 61 (Fall 1994): 631–670. See also the exchanges between Smith and his critics: Jacqueline Stevens, "Beyond Tocqueville, Please!" and Smith, "Response to Jacqueline Stevens," both in *American Political Science Review* 89 (December 1995): 987–990, 990–995; Karen Orren, "Structure, Sequence, and Subordination in American Political Culture: What's Traditions Got to Do with It?" and Smith, "Response to Karen Orren," *Journal of Policy History* 8 (1996): 470–478, 478–490. For two other similar accounts that emphasized cultural dissensus and ideological confrontation in American political thought, see Richard J. Ellis, *American Political Cultures* (New York: Oxford University Press, 1993); and James A. Morone, "The Struggle for American Culture," *PS: Political Science and Politics* 29 (September 1996): 425–430.

62. Smith, *Civic Ideals*, 3.

63. Ibid.

64. Smith, "Beyond Tocqueville," 555.

65. Ibid., 549.

66. Smith, "Response to Jacqueline Stevens," 991.

67. Smith "'One United People,'" 233; Smith, "Beyond Tocqueville," 554.

68. Smith, *Civic Ideals*, 24–26. Quotation is on 24.

69. Smith's emphasis on the diversity of peoples in colonial America, the complex interactions among them, and the varied and intense conflicts that they faced is reinforced by much recent work in colonial history. See for example Alan Taylor's

critique of the traditional and "fundamentally happy" story of colonial history as a tale of the American people becoming an exceptional people. Taylor, *American Colonies* (New York: Penguin, 2001), esp. x–xvii. Quotation is on x.

70. Smith, *Civic Ideals*, 54.

71. Hartz, *The Liberal Tradition in America*, 3.

72. Smith also calls Jefferson's comments about black inferiority "the cornerstone statement of American scientific racism." Smith, *Civic Ideals*, 104–105.

73. Ibid., 75.

74. Ibid., 140.

75. Ibid., 138.

76. See, for example, James Allen Smith, *The Spirit of American Government: A Study of the Constitution; Its Origin, Influence, and Relation to Democracy* (1907; photostatic reprint, Cambridge, Mass.: Harvard University Press, 1965); Charles Beard, *An Economic Interpretation of the Constitution of the United States* (1913; reprint with new introduction, New York: Free Press, 1986); Merrill Jensen, *The Articles of Confederation: An Interpretation of the Social-constitutional History of the American Revolution, 1774–1781* (Madison: University of Wisconsin Press, 1940); Jackson Turner Main, "Government by the People: The American Revolution and Democratization of the Legislatures," *William and Mary Quarterly* 33 (July 1966): 391–407; Staughton Lynd, *Anti-federalism in Dutchess County, New York: A Study of Democracy and Class Conflict in the Revolutionary Era* (Chicago: Loyola University Press, 1962); Gary Nash, *The Unknown American Revolution: The Unruly Birth of Democracy and the Struggle to Create America* (New York: Viking Press, 2005); Woody Holton, *Unruly Americans and the Origins of the Constitution* (New York: Hill & Wang, 2007). See also Robert McGuire, *To Form a More Perfect Union: A New Economic Interpretation of the United States Constitution* (New York: Oxford University Press, 2003); and Robert McGuire and Robert Ohsfeldt, "Economic Interests and the American Constitution: A Quantitative Rehabilitation of Charles A. Beard," *Journal of Economic History* 44 (June 1984): 509–519, for a new economic interpretation of the Constitution that has considerable sympathies for Beard's original version.

77. See my discussion of the multicultural approach to the study of the Founding in Alan Gibson, *Interpreting the Founding: Guide to the Enduring Debates over the Origins and Foundations of the American Republic* (Lawrence: University Press of Kansas, 2006), 64–85.

78. Charles Beard, "Introduction to the 1935 Edition," in *An Economic Interpretation of the Constitution of the United States*, xlviii. Few Progressives—including Beard— ever consistently held to the proposition that ideas were merely the surface rationalization of underlying economic interests. Instead, even most early Progressives treated speeches and writings as sincere reflections of motives, if, that is, they conveyed ideas that supported their interpretations. Few contemporary Progressives treat rhetoric as purely instrumental; instead, they study the speeches and writings of the dispossessed to support their interpretations.

79. Beard most commonly and explicitly suggested that the lines of conflict in American society were between holders of "personalty" (fluid capital most often

held by merchants, money lenders, and security holders) and "realty" (most prominently land held by middling or poor farmers, who were also likely to be debtors).
Nevertheless, other Progressives and even Beard at times also suggested that the primary sources of division and conflict were between rich and poor, commercial and
noncommercial interests, or interior and coastal regions. See Alan Gibson, *Understanding the Founding: The Crucial Questions* (Lawrence: University Press of Kansas,
2007), 22.

80. Rodgers, "Republicanism," 12.

81. Carl Becker, *The History of Political Parties in the Province of New York,
1760–1776* (Madison: University of Wisconsin Press, 1960), 22.

82. Beard, *An Economic Interpretation of the Constitution of the United States*, 149.

83. Hartz, *The Liberal Tradition in America*, 67.

84. Ibid., 8, 52. Quotation is on 8.

85. Ibid., 67–69.

86. Ibid., 68.

87. Ibid., 70, 78.

88. Ibid., 20.

89. Ibid., 28–30. See also Louis Hartz, *The Founding of New Societies: Studies in the
History of the United States, Latin America, South Africa, Canada, and Australia* (New
York: Harcourt, Brace & World, 1964), 69–70, and the footnote accompanying these
pages.

90. Hartz, *The Liberal Tradition in America*, 29.

91. Ibid., 31–32.

92. Gunnell, "Louis Hartz and the Liberal Metaphor," 204.

93. Ibid.

94. Gibson, *Understanding the Founding*, 131.

95. C. B. MacPherson's classic study *The Political Theory of Possessive Individualism:
Hobbes to Locke* (Oxford: Oxford University Press, 1962); Daniel Boorstin, *The Genius
of American Politics* (Chicago: University of Chicago Press, 1953). See also, for example, Seymour Martin Lipset, *The First New Nation: The United States in Historical and
Comparative Perspective* (New York: Basic Books, 1963); David Potter, *People of Plenty:
Economic Abundance and the American Character* (Chicago: University of Chicago Press,
1954); David Reisman, *The Lonely Crowd: A Study of the Changing American Character*
(1950; reprint, New Haven, Conn.: Yale University Press, 1969).

96. Joyce Appleby expressed this view of the critics of the Lockean interpretations of American society and the American character written during the 1950s and
1960s when she wrote that proponents of the republican interpretation can be credited with showing that "liberalism did not sprawl unimpeded across the flat intellectual landscape of American abundance." See Joyce Appleby, "Republicanism in Old
and New Contexts," *William and Mary Quarterly* 42 (January 1986): 26.

97. Joyce Appleby, *Capitalism and the New Social Order: The Republican Vision of the
1790s* (New York: New York University Press, 1984); Appleby, "Republicanism in
Old and New Contexts," 26–32; Appleby, "Republicanism and Ideology," *American*

Quarterly 37 (Fall 1985): 461–473; Isaac Kramnick, "Republican Revisionism Revisited," *American Historical Review* 87 (June 1982): 629–664; Kramnick, *Republicanism and Bourgeois Radicalism: Political Ideology in Late Eighteenth-Century England and America* (Ithaca, N.Y.: Cornell University Press, 1990).

98. See Gibson, *Understanding the Founding*, 130–164, for a retrospective analysis of the contributions of the republicanism-liberalism debate and the various strategies that scholars have used for establishing the patterns of interaction between multiple traditions of political thought that informed the American Founding.

99. Rodgers, "Republicanism," 14.

100. See in particular Holton, *Unruly Americans and the Origins of the Constitution.*

101. Woody Holton, "Divide et Impera": Federalist 10 in a Wider Sphere," *William and Mary Quarterly* 62 (April 2005): 175–212.

102. Gibson, *Understanding the Founding*, 15–45, esp. 38–45.

103. Rogers Smith, "Liberalism and Racism: The Problem of Analyzing Traditions," in *The Liberal Tradition in American Politics: Reassessing the Legacy of American Liberalism*, ed. David Ericson and Louisa Bertch Green (New York: Routledge, 1999), 11–14.

CHAPTER 6

Change We Already Believe In? The Liberal Tradition and the American Left

Marc Stears

Louis Hartz was famously dismissive of the prospects of the American Left. Radical intellectuals and activists in America, he argued, were constrained not only by the broader American public's unwillingness to contemplate their political programs but by their own inability to break free of the Lockean tradition that shaped all political thinking in the United States. Across the course of American history, Hartz insisted, radicals exhibited a "pathetic clinging" to all of the key elements of that Lockean tradition, including its doctrine of individualist ethics, general hostility to the power of the state, and intense antielitism.[1] Radical intellectuals were thus constantly to be found attempting to advance their political programs in language that ill-served their underlying purpose. They valorized individual liberty while arguing for a larger state; they celebrated private property while insisting on the need for greater taxation; and they retold Horatio Alger myths of personal achievement while demanding collective bargaining rights for organized labor. It was, Hartz concluded, a disastrous intellectual approach. It ensured that the Left was all but redundant in American politics, its goals unrealized, its arguments rendered "practically unintelligible."[2]

This was not just a claim about ill-chosen political discourse, though. For Hartz, it was also an argument about the American Left's relationship to its nation's political identity and political past. The American Left's inability to think and argue beyond the conceptual confines of the Lockean tradition, Hartz argued, was not only the result of an intellectual limitation. It was also the product of an unwillingness to contemplate the need for a political future for the United States that was markedly different from the political past. Unlike European lefts, which regularly insisted on the desirability of dramatic, epochal, breaks from their own histories, radicals in the United States enveloped their visions in a language of nostalgic longing. They talked not of overcoming current limitations but of "recapturing" lost glories. The liberal tradition of America was not to be transcended but to be somehow "restored," its values of freedom, independence, and social equality to be saved from emergent enemies rather than replaced by alternative visions.

As with almost every aspect of Hartz's scholarship, this argument has become hugely controversial of late. A new generation of historians and philosophers has contended that far from being an inevitable constraint on radicalism, the American liberal tradition has often provided radicals with great resources. An argument exemplified by Richard Rorty's *Achieving Our Country,* and made at other times by Eric Foner, Gary Gerstle, Carol Horton, Desmond King, James Kloppenberg, and Rogers Smith, thus contends that throughout the course of the Republic's history American radicals' use of the American liberal tradition has been far more creative and far more successful than Hartz ever recognized.[3] Indeed, these scholars often insist that the liberal elements of American political identity and the American political past represent the best means of forwarding a radical political agenda. This is a contention that has been further enhanced of late, of course, by Barack Obama, whose eloquent and widely celebrated campaign speeches frequently combined the promise of a radical new beginning for the United States with the very nostalgia for the American liberal past so roundly criticized by Hartz over fifty years ago.[4]

The questions this disagreement raises are of great importance, then, for Hartz scholarship and, especially, for Hartz's reputation as an analyst of the American Left. They are also consequential, though, for our understanding of American radicalism more generally. Many commentators outside the United States, after all, were deeply puzzled as to how candidate Obama was able to couple an ambitious message of "change" with a staunchly patriotic invocation of "American values" and the "American liberal heritage." A return to Louis Hartz's analysis of this kind of combination should, therefore, still provide the basis for insights today.

THE CHALLENGE TO HARTZ

Louis Hartz's preferred explanation for the American Left's failure to break from the liberal tradition concerned America's and Europe's contrasting historical experiences with revolutionary change. The United States had been "born liberal" and had thus never experienced the revolutionary break from feudalism that shaped the ideological memories of Europe. The result was a nation that was locked in reverence to the past. Radicalism in America was thus destined always to fail because it looked *backward* to a mythic period of liberal idealism rather than *forward* to a new polity grounded in contrasting political ideals. American radicalism was doomed because it failed to recognize that "as for a child who is leaving adolescence, there is no going home again for America."[5] Such reverence for the past, combined with the power of the liberal tradition itself, locked American radicals into a language that was desperately ill-suited to their ends.

All of these elements of the argument have been contested by more recent scholars. Far from constraining radicalism, they argue, American liberalism and the historic story of American politics have provided an invaluable resource for radical political argument in the United States. Serious, intelligent, and occasionally successful radical campaigns have thus been led in the name of core liberal values, including those of personal liberty and social equality, and the invocation of historic examples has often provided those campaigns with an experiential solidity and an emotional appeal that they would otherwise have lacked.[6] These scholars insist that there are two reasons why Hartz was wrong to believe that there was a contradiction between an endorsement of U.S. liberal political history, on the one hand, and a call for dramatic political change, on the other hand.

First, it is argued that liberal political ideals are far more plastic than Hartz appeared to comprehend. Seen as such, liberal concepts and terminology are more than capable of being used to justify far-reaching political change as well as to demand conservation of a prevailing order. The idea of "liberty," for example, can be defined in such a way as to demand an opening up of opportunities for all, just as it can also be used as a reason to restrict state activity. The notion of "social equality," similarly, can be understood to demand far-reaching state intervention in the name of an egalitarian order, as well as to justify the hostility of elite governance that might argue against the self-same interventions.[7] The contest *over* liberal meanings and liberal languages thus matters just as much as the contest *between* liberalism and rival political ideologies.[8]

Second, it is contended that just as the languages of liberalism might be open to radical, as well as conservative, interpretations, then so too might patriotism and the celebration of the American past be open to rival roles. On such a view, even the most radical political movements might be able to draw on the emotions of patriotism in the search for popular resonance. Radicals as well as conservatives thus need, in Richard Rorty's terms, to be able to tell "inspiring stories about episodes and figures in the nation's past—episodes and figures to which the nation should remain true."[9] National pride in the United States and its historical story, on such a view, far from being an inevitable limitation on American radicalism, has in fact been an invaluable part of its appeal.

The American Left's relationship to the liberal tradition and the American past has thus become another central battleground on which the reputation of Louis Hartz depends. If Hartz was right, then American radicals were thwarted both intellectually and politically by their constant need to cast their arguments in liberal terms and by their unwillingness to countenance dramatic breaks from the American past. If, on the other hand, his more recent critics have the upper hand, then both the liberal tradition and the celebration of American history will be seen to have been of great service to the American Left.

As explained in the introduction, the importance of this debate also transcends the historic and the interpretive, extending right into the heart of contemporary American politics. For if the present-day Left believes Hartz, then it should seek ways of breaking the hold of liberalism on its own psyche and begin to contemplate more dramatic shifts for the political future. But if the critics prevail, then all efforts to argue for far-reaching change should both be couched in terms inherited from Locke and be cast as parts of a long and noble history that stretches back to the Founding. There would still, of course, be "change" in that radical vision, but it would, to coin a phrase, be change that we already believe in.

THE PROGRESSIVE ERA: AMERICANISM RECONCEIVED

Of all the moments of the twentieth century in which radical politics appeared to flourish in the United States, it is the Progressive era, which stretched from the century's opening to the outbreak of World War I, that is probably celebrated most. These were years that witnessed Theodore Roosevelt's Bull Moose campaign for the presidency as leader of the short-lived Progressive Party, in which numerous states embarked on social welfare reform, and when even the federal government itself appeared ripe for far-reaching change. In *The Liberal Tradition*, however, Louis Hartz was as dismissive of the radicalism of the period as he was of that of any other moment. "What sort of program did the American progressives advance even during the vivid days of the New Freedom and the Bull Moose?" he asked. "The answer in general," he continued, "is obvious enough." Progressives offered a version of the national liberal tradition, emphasizing the need to restore lost

American freedoms, to wind back the powers of growing industrial trusts and corporations, to overcome the anxieties fostered by industrial capitalism, and to allow each individual American citizen the chance to find his or her own happiness independently of the powers of an expanding state machine. Although they were often dressed up as radical suggestions, all of these aspirations, Hartz insisted, demonstrated just the kind of "pathetic clinging to Americanism" that he derided.[10] Progressives, for all their bluster, were incapable of conceiving of an American future radically different from the American past and made no significant case for grounding American politics on a distinctly new set of values and ideals.

It is easy to see how Hartz came to this view. The Progressive era was rich with nostalgia and regret. In their scholarly and political writings, Progressive intellectuals and activists regularly bemoaned the loss of the open frontier, the relative decline of the agricultural sector, the squalor and social tensions inherent in urban life, and the rapid expansion in economic inequality that coincided with the rise of industrial capitalism.[11] Such social transformations, they argued, undermined the political ideals that Americans had espoused since the Founding. It was hard for American citizens any longer to be "free" in the face of ever-expanding corporate power, Progressives argued, nor could such citizens easily assert their social equality amid the new hierarchies and exclusions of the urban centers. Political action was thus demanded precisely in order to prevent the new industrial order from transforming American citizens from free and equal men into "a nation of slaves."[12]

Moreover, Progressive hopes for the success of such action also appeared to be grounded in the expectation that it would be citizens' sense of pride in the American past that would rally them to the Progressive political cause. "The average American is nothing if not patriotic," Herbert Croly noted in his Progressive era masterpiece *The Promise of American Life,* and that patriotism was said to play an essential role in mobilizing citizens in response to the challenges of the early twentieth century. "The faith of Americans in their own country pervades the air we breathe," Croly continued, and it was reasonable to suppose therefore that it would provide the emotional motive force for any effort at political change.[13]

On closer examination, however, the Progressives' relationship to both the American liberal tradition and the American political past was far less clear-cut than Hartz suggested. Indeed, even a further reading of Croly's own work confuses the picture. For although Croly did argue that American liberal ideals were being undermined by developments in the social and industrial realm, he did not insist that political action was required in order for those ideals to be saved. Indeed, quite to the contrary: he openly derided those who believed that what Americans needed to do was "to continue resolutely and cheerfully along the appointed path."[14] "The reader who expects this book to contain [such an argument] will be disappointed." Instead, Croly insisted that the social and economic transformations that the United States had undergone required a *new* approach to politics rather than a continuation of the old. The job of the Progressive, he argued, was to "emancipate [American citizens] from their past," not to attempt to restore it.[15] Croly continually called for change, not continuity: change in political values and in the mechanisms required to realize those values in practice. The "cherished principle[s]" of the American past, Croly concluded, are "dangerous and fallacious a chart" to political progress in the present. The changed social situation demands "a criticism of traditional American ideas" and their replacement with something new, something better suited to the actual demands of the modern era.[16]

This emphasis on newness—on crafting a different political order in response to the newly emerging social and industrial order—extended far beyond Croly. Although some of the Progressives who endorsed Woodrow Wilson's New Freedom platform did respond rather more nostalgically to the challenges of the age, many others joined with Croly in calling for a radical new beginning for American politics, including fellow editors of the *New Republic* Walter Lippmann and Walter Weyl, noted sociologists Charles Cooley and Simon Nelson Patten, and social campaigners Jane Addams and Paul Kellogg. Indeed, many of these made the argument for innovation even more clearly than Croly did. For Walter Lippmann, for example, it was fundamental to any Progressive vision that it be seen not as a task of "restoration" but as one of "transformation." Progressive reform, Lippmann argued, must be "an effort for which there is no precedent," an effort that by definition could not be grounded in the past.[17] It was a view, and a rhetoric, that was widely shared.[18]

When they turned to give substance to their call for a dramatic shift, these Progressives usually began at the level of core political ideals. The American past, they argued, had been shaped by a set of political ideas that emphasized an atomistic individualism and a limitation on state power, but while such ideas might have been well suited to a primarily rural society, they were ill-designed to the needs of an urban and industrial age. Shaped by liberalism, Americans shared astonishingly little sense of the larger social unit to which they belonged; they had, in the British commentator H. G. Wells's terms, "no sense of state."[19] But the new age, these Progressives continued, would require a new emphasis, with attention switched from the independent individual to the possibility of national solidarity, social justice, and the common good. An industrial society of squalor, inequality, and potential social conflict, Charles Cooley explained, needed to be placed "under the sway of common principles of kindness and justice."[20] With a "new and growing industrial population," Paul Kellogg continued, "unless it shall suffer for the ordinary needs of life, [the nation] must think in terms of the whole community, must make a long plan for the future, must supply public interest and motive to keep its scheme going."[21]

The call to change did not only lie in the ideational realm. These Progressives were also insistent on the need for transformation in the formal political institutions of the United States. America, they argued, was stuck with "a political system" designed for a "totally different civilization."[22] The U.S. Constitution had been drawn up to govern a rural society by framers who were skeptical about democratic input into political decision making and who were primarily concerned with preventing abuse of power.[23] It was, therefore, entirely unsuited to the possibilities of politics in an industrial age: the federal system excessively limited the authority of the national government; the separation of powers between legislature and executive made coordination between the branches cumbersome at best, impossible at worst; and the doctrine of judicial review allowed just nine conservative Supreme Court justices to strike down any intelligent responses to industrial life that did manage to make it through the legislature.

Moreover, Progressives continued, the behaviors encouraged by such an institutional structure only went to reinforce the worst elements of public opinion. The vast majority of Americans, they insisted, were already individualists by inclination, with a tendency to focus excessively on their own self-interest and an inability to recognize the essential interconnections of industrial society, yet the prevailing political order only encouraged these tendencies still further. The rights-obsessed negativity of a political order shaped by an emphasis on individual protections rather than on collective possibilities could do nothing to overcome the problems America faced in an industrial age.[24]

What was required, Progressives therefore urged, was a radical reconstruction of the institutional order of American politics in the hope—and belief—that such a reconstruction would in turn reshape the values and opinions of the American citizenry at large.[25] A whole host of suggestions appeared to fit the bill. Many Progressives called for a radical expansion of mechanisms of "direct democracy." Citizens should be empowered, they argued, to bring their own issues to the legislative agenda by means of "initiatives"; they should be allowed to veto other pieces of legislation by means of referenda; they should be able to control electoral candidates by means of direct primaries, "mandates," and recall elections; and they should be able to overturn judicial review in cases where conservative judges stood out against popular opinion. Such mechanisms, it was contended, would allow the American people to speak directly for themselves and, more importantly, would enable a new spirit of national loyalty, unity, and responsibility to be fostered as they did so.[26]

Other Progressives had a different institutional emphasis, even though their underlying purpose was the same. Herbert Croly, Walter Lippmann, and Walter Weyl, for example, argued that what was needed was not greater democratic input but more powerful executive leadership. On this view, it was presidents, governors, and mayors who were to be charged with overcoming the limitations on American government and of instilling a sense of togetherness, often through the simple force of their personality. Theodore Roosevelt was most often the model here: he was "a man of will in whom millions of people have felt the embodiment of their own will."[27] But less-well-known figures mattered too. The Progressive activists of Cleveland, Ohio, for example, used poetry to celebrate Mayor Tom Johnson for moving them beyond the despair of individualism and into the possibilities of collective action: "He found us striving each his selfish part," they memorialized. "He left a civilization with a civic heart."[28]

What the Progressive era witnessed in radical politics, therefore, was far from the simple reinforcement of traditional liberal values or the celebration of the liberal past that Hartz suggested. It is true that there was patriotism in Progressive politics, but there was also an insistence on the need for far-reaching change. Indeed, when the American past was mentioned, it was usually to insist further on this necessity. "From the beginning," Croly outlined, the United States "has been figured as the land of *promise*" rather than the land of attainment. True loyalty to "the national tradition," true patriotism, "rather affirms than denies the imaginative projection of a better future."[29] If that meant abandoning once deeply held aspirations and radically altering a political structure that had previously been held in considerable esteem, then so be it. Indeed, as far as those values and that structure were concerned, the more far-reaching the change the better. "The best that can be said on behalf of the traditional American system of political ideas," Croly thus concluded, "is that it contained the germ of better things."[30] Nationalistic though Progressivism undeniably was, it was not a movement that embraced the American past or held fast to its liberal tradition.

THE DEPRESSION YEARS: AMERICANISM RADICALIZED

These Progressives' hope for widespread change in values and in political structures did, however, not survive World War I. Progressivism of this sort faced two extremely difficult challenges in the late teens and early twenties. The first was a straightforwardly political challenge. The Progressive Party itself failed to survive the presidential election of 1912, leaving the movement without a stable home at exactly the moment when more conservative forces in American politics, including increasingly powerful business interests, began to rally successfully around the Republican Party. The political prospects for Progressivism thus declined sharply in the early 1920s, leaving Robert La Follette's unsuccessful campaign for the presidency in 1924 the last real hurrah of Progressivism as an organized force.[31]

The second, and more deeply troubling, challenge, however, came less from partisan politics and more from the world of ideas. It was posed by the extraordinarily widespread and hostile assertion that any form of radicalism was essentially incompatible with American national identity. The war years had witnessed the first U.S. Red Scare, a moment that gave birth to a host of arguments that radical politics of all sorts was the invention of alien forces, especially of undesirable immigrant communities. Wartime citizens flocked to exclusionary and conservative causes, all of which made the same essential argument. Organized groups going by such names as the Better American Federation, the National Association for Constitutional Government, and the National Security League thus rejected all leftists as "un-American," even classifying them as unworthy of membership in the Republic itself.[32]

In the face of this kind of assault, the Progressives' rejection of prevailing American values became very difficult to sustain. Calls for change, either to values or to institutional orders, ceased to appear patriotic, and demands for continuity now appeared to chime better with the American mood. It was in this context that a new generation of radically inclined intellectuals, commentators, and activists began to return to the liberal ideals and liberal histories that had previously been the subject of such disdain. Writers such as Arthur Bingham, Stuart Chase, John Dewey, Robert Morss Lovett, George Soule, and Ordway Tead thus began to reconsider ways in which radical politics could be rendered compatible with the American liberal tradition. The Progressive vision of a new political order would have to be substantially moderated if it was to flourish in such conservative times, they all insisted. If "radicalism" was to succeed in the postwar United States, Arthur Bingham provocatively suggested, it would have to be "Americanized."[33]

This theme stretched throughout the Left's—or at least the noncommunist Left's—writings and arguments in the interwar years, but no one was better at making that case than John Dewey. Dewey had already emerged as a political philosopher and commentator of note in the Progressive era, but it was in the interwar years that he made his particular mark, and the major subject of his work throughout this period was ways in which the American liberal tradition, with its values of individualism, its skepticism of the state, and its concern for social equality, could be rendered compatible with a radical political agenda. He began that argument by insisting that although the future orientation of Progressivism was not entirely misconceived, the movement's willingness to abandon the past was. "The passage or transition" from the present to the future, he argued, always had to draw on "something" that was already there, lurking in the prevailing order even if generally overlooked; the future could not be made out of new cloth. The task of even the most ambitious radical, Dewey thus suggested, had to begin with "the process of viewing and examining the present to discover what possibilities are resident in it."[34]

On this account, therefore, the role of the radical was to reflect on the values that Americans already appeared to share and understand better how those values could be more fully realized in a future political order through the means of radical politics. "The idea that liberalism cannot maintain its ends and at the same time reverse its conception of the means by which they are attained is folly," Dewey insisted.[35] Radicalism should not be about the rejection of the liberal tradition and the American past; rather, it should be about explaining how the "enduring values for which earlier liberalism stood" now required a different kind of practical politics.[36]

This interwar effort to explain how traditional liberal ideas could be employed to justify radical political programs often concentrated on the value of individual liberty, as scholars like Eric Foner and Gary Gerstle have pointed out.[37] Earlier generations of Americans, Dewey and colleagues argued, had been absolutely right in their assertion that "every individual should have the utmost opportunity for growth, for development of character and personality," and that it should be the task of political action to ensure that no efforts to "restrict, distort or prevent the development of [such] individuality" should ever be permitted.[38] These generations had been wrong though, Dewey and his supporters continued, in thinking that all that was necessary in order to avoid such restrictions was a limitation on the power of government. Instead, as times and social conditions changed, so did the threats to individual liberty and development. Whereas governing authority might therefore have provided the greatest danger in the rural society of the eighteenth century, the primary perils in the twentieth were those offered by the behavior of large industrial corporations and the economic inequalities that they engendered.

"What are the valid and enduring elements of the original liberal creed?" George Soule thus asked. "They center, of course about the fulfilment of the individual . . . [who] needs room to grow, power to exercise his faculties, the capacity to lead as rich and purposeful a life as possible."[39] But what that entailed in interwar America was not the absence of government action; it was the development of a regulated, coordinated, welfare-oriented economic plan that went far beyond the halfhearted experiments of the New Deal: "The creation of an order in which industry and finance are socially directed in behalf of institutions that provide the material basis for cultural liberation and growth of individuals," Dewey concluded the argument, "is now the sole method of social action by which liberalism can realize its professed aims."[40]

This position found a ready audience among radicals of all stripes in the interwar years. The idea that radical ideals were somehow already implicit in values that had a long national heritage and an apparently unquestionable place in American political identity seemed, after all, extraordinarily attractive to those who often felt that American politics was leaving them behind. In reviewing Dewey's masterpiece *Liberalism and Social Action,* the radical periodical *Common Sense* could thus suggest that it offered "the synthesis between liberalism and radicalism which many . . . have been craving."[41] Nor was this approval confined to the more moderate elements that might have already been sympathetic to the liberal past. In fact, the approach was frequently invoked in defense of some of the more dramatic means of political engagement that characterized the late interwar years.

This was a period of exceptionally bitter conflict in American politics and society, characterized by riots in industrial centers and a vast new array of forms of industrial action, including the strikes and sit-downs masterminded with particular expertise by John L. Lewis's Congress of Industrial Organizations, and, surprising though it might seem, participants in and advocates of these actions often made recourse to the argument that Dewey and colleagues had laid out.[42] John Lewis himself was thus frequently to be found insisting that it was the ideals of the American liberal past that provided the motivation for the dramatic strategies of the present. "I think the organization of the workers in the mass production industries," he explained, is required to make the "greatest contribution" towards the "preservation" of American political values. Only radical trade unionism, he continued, could prevent big businesses from threatening the "freedom" and "democracy" due to each and every American citizen.[43]

In so claiming, Lewis was not pushing the argument of the radical intellectual contemporaries any further than they themselves were willing to go. Indeed, many radical intellectuals even went one step further in linking their reinterpretation of traditional liberal values with the advocacy of dramatic forms of political action. In his 1936 *Future of Liberty,* George Soule outlined a theory that accepted the "legitimacy of revolution" in the service of liberal ideals. "Not merely the revolution that my forefathers helped to make in the eighteenth century, but any new revolution that may be justified in the interest and reason of the common man."[44] John Dewey agreed. Calling on the "tradition of Jefferson and Lincoln," he insisted that interwar radicals should never "weaken and give up" in the face of opposition to reform but should always instead make a "whole-hearted effort" to make their oft-articulated ideals and values into "a living reality," even if that meant employing political means that seemed on the surface remarkably illiberal.[45] "What can I do?" the editor of the radical monthly *Common Sense* asked. "Organize and learn," was the answer. American citizens "must prepare for the big battle ahead, when we the people will rise against the stupid and selfish who now sit in the seats of power." Only then, after a period of intense struggle at the ballot box and on the streets, might core liberal values be realized in the industrial age. Only then would "Americans be able to hold their heads up again."[46]

By the outbreak of World War II, therefore, a distinctive mode of radical argumentation had emerged in the United States. It took political ideals long associated with American political identity and gave them a new, more radical, twist. This enabled American radicals to interweave a "backward-looking nationalist perspective," which they could expect to have great emotional appeal, with a more "progressive dimension" that emphasized the importance of dramatic shifts in social and economic policy and endorsed a whole host of dramatic forms of political engagement as well.[47] A few hard-nosed skeptics still rejected this vision as naively conservative in its patriotism. Samuel Schmalhausen, for example, thought that even if Dewey "feels at home in [his] own country," that was "too bad," because, in fact, "America is urgently in need of philosophers possessed not only of intellectual clarity but more particularly of spiritual courage."[48] But these voices were extremely few and far between. Most American radicals were too excited about the prospects of drawing on a distinctively American political heritage in order to construct a better future to worry about prewar concerns with the desirability of those values themselves. The task of radicals was not to reject either the liberal tradition or the American past, as it had been in the Progressive era, but to demonstrate that the "history of the republic" is as yet an "inadequate embodiment of the aspirations with which it began" and to rebuild its politics accordingly.[49]

THE POSTWAR YEARS: AMERICANISM RESTORED

It is these sorts of arguments that have been extensively celebrated recently by a wide and varied group of scholars. Otherwise dissimilar thinkers such as Eric Foner, Gary Gerstle, Richard Rorty, and Cornel West have all suggested that this interwar account provided, and could still provide, invaluable resources for radical political action in America. Contrary to Hartz's pessimistic view, they suggest, this interwar approach demonstrates that it was possible for American radicals both to assert that the United States was a "great, noble [and one might add *liberal*] country" and at the same time to strive for far-reaching political reform.[50]

Despite its attractions, however, this rendering of radicalism's relationship to the liberal tradition and to the American political past did have its historical limitations. Most importantly, it did not last for long as the Left's primary argument about the role of the American liberal tradition in radical politics. For another crucial shift in America's radicals' attitudes to the liberal tradition occurred in the aftermath of World War II, a shift that once again dramatically reoriented the American Left's relationship to its nation's past and that casts the confidence of these recent scholars more into doubt.

That shift began in the immediate aftermath of World War II with a significant loss of faith in two key elements of the radical position in the interwar years: first, the belief in the acceptability of dramatic and direct forms of political action, and second, the belief in the necessity of far-reaching, transformative change in the social and economic structure of the United States. Rocked by the experience of the war, and especially by a growing sense of the dangers of totalitarian communism, many in the American Left in the post–World War II years grew increasingly suspicious of what they saw as dangerous utopian theorizing that came close to accepting the legitimacy of a fully insurrectionary politics. "Disillusionment with the idea of revolution is one of the most interesting features of American intellectual life today," the young Michael Walzer explained. "After seeing the terror and the purge and all that goes with the revolutionary transformation of society, the brutal manipulation of human beings, the corruption of culture—after seeing all this we are none of us, I suppose, revolutionaries." "We have denounced Bolshevik realism," Walzer concluded, and instead pursued an agenda of reform that was always grounded in persuading fellow citizens rather than in winning a battle "of organizational pressures."[51]

The emphasis in the post–World War II years still had to be on using liberal ideals to justify programs of political reform, then, but it could no longer be on employing those ideals to defend dramatic political action in order to secure far-reaching reforms of which most citizens might be highly skeptical: that was a dangerous form of politics, a form of politics as manipulation that had led to the decline of democracies in western Europe and the rise of communism in the east. Instead, when radicals spoke about American liberalism, they spoke more in terms of an already secured achievement, one that needed to be protected against the dangerously utopian aspirations that had seized control of the mind of Europe and that continued to threaten the shores of the United States.[52]

This view took a remarkable hold on the radical imagination in the immediate postwar United States. It is demonstrated most clearly by the remarkable popularity accorded to Gunnar Myrdal's 1944 study *An American Dilemma: The Negro Problem and Democracy.* Myrdal's book concentrated on probably the single most contentious subject in the politics of the United States—the "scar of race" and the deep injustices to which African Americans were subject—and on the surface at least Myrdal's position was very close to that presented by Dewey and colleagues in the interwar years. The clearest and most persuasive means of arguing against racial injustice in the United States, Myrdal insisted, lay in the invocation of long-established liberal ideals. Racial injustice such as the disenfranchisement of African Americans in the South and their exclusion from a whole host of social, economic, and political opportunities across the nation, he explained, clearly violated core ideals of freedom and of equality that had been central to the American political tradition since the Declaration of Independence. The "subordinate position of Negroes is perhaps the most glaring conflict in the American conscience and the greatest unsolved task for American democracy," Myrdal argued, even citing Dewey as a source for the claim.

But despite the surface similarity between their positions, something crucial had changed. Myrdal's view was far more conservative than Dewey's was ever intended to be in two crucial ways. First, Myrdal did not believe that racial injustice should be fought in any way other than by an appeal to *conscience*; the disjuncture between America's professed liberal ideals and its actual racial practices, he insisted, should be overcome not by the dramatic, direct-action politics associated with the struggles of the Depression era but, rather, by a sustained, peaceable, essentially "moral" appeal to "the hearts of Americans."[53] "The status accorded to the Negro in America represents *nothing more*... than a century-long lag of public morals," Myrdal asserted, and therefore required solely a moral response.[54]

Second, he also therefore believed that most Americans were ready and willing to admit that the incompatibility between liberal ideas and racial practices existed and that no significant ideological work was required to get them to appreciate that disjuncture. The task of the radical was, therefore, no longer to *reinterpret* liberal ideas, to rework them so that they served new ends, as it had always been to the interwar generation. Instead, it was seen to be a question simply of drawing out already existing understandings—of activating moral concerns that were already there—in order to serve the noble purposes that almost all Americans were, at some level, already willing to accept. Radicalism was now about maintaining and restoring the American liberal tradition.

This was an extraordinarily important turnaround from the position outlined prior to the war. This, then, was a time when the vaulting ambitions of the past appeared consigned to history, dismissed as dangerous illusions and precursors of totalitarianism, and the role of the radical became instead the maintenance of prevailing liberal ideals and their gradual expansion into areas of life where they had previously been excluded. It was a change that became deeply entrenched in an era shaped both by an intensifying Cold War with the Soviet Union and by a sense that New Deal liberalism had resolved most of the pressing problems of the industrial age. It gave birth to the "consensus" theory in sociology and American political history and allowed commentators like Daniel Bell and Judith Shklar to describe the United States as both "beyond ideology" and "after utopia."[55]

For a while, indeed, it appeared that almost every serious commentator on American politics agreed that the United States stood apart from the rest of the world because it was characterized by a widespread consensus on core liberal ideals and that this consensus provided the crucial emotional and political glue that kept a diverse nation together and prevented it from drifting toward extremism. Even many of those who had been responsible for the bolder prewar positions accepted this new position in the 1940s and 1950s, including John Dewey himself, who argued throughout the 1940s that he and his colleagues had underemphasized the threats of totalitarianism in the 1930s and had underestimated the strengths of American liberalism as already established.[56]

What all of this meant was that the last vestiges of the transformative agenda of the Progressive era dropped away. The relationship between radicals and the American liberal tradition ceased to be largely critical and became instead conceptualized as one of mutual support. Indeed it often appeared that liberalism, radicalism, and Americanism collapsed into one at that moment.

THE CHALLENGE TO LIBERALISM: AMERICANISM REJECTED

It was in this environment, of course, that Louis Hartz wrote *The Liberal Tradition in America*.[57] Looking around at his colleagues, he saw scholars and aspirant radical politicians displaying a deeply dismaying sense of "caution," an "unwillingness to play with [supposedly] dangerous ideas" that threatened to become "a paralysis of mind" that would put paid to any kind of political and social innovation of the sort that previous generations had desired to pursue.[58] It is easy to see how, in such a context, he came to believe that American radicals had always been unable to free themselves of the hold of liberal tradition and its past. In short, Hartz was simply reading back into history the limitations of his own age, a frequent mistake of historians of political thought, even if not a particularly edifying one.

Even if Hartz could be criticized for that, though, what he could not be blamed for was failing to think through the consequences of the position to which he bore witness. For the position adopted by the putative radicals of the early postwar years was not a stable one. Just as Hartz predicted, that position made it extremely difficult to criticize the prevailing order and too frequently left radicals identifying with their natural ideological opponents as they sought to distinguish themselves from their communist alternative. When a new generation of leftists emerged in the later 1950s, they found their attempts to criticize the prevailing social, economic, and political order continually obstructed by the widespread assumption that American liberal ideals were beyond question. "The end of ideology perspective," C. Wright Mills complained in 1959, is "itself an ideology, [just] one supportive of American institutions" as they currently exist.[59]

As pressures for more far-reaching change picked up in the later 1950s and early 1960s, therefore, it was unsurprising that the American liberal tradition no longer appeared to be an ally to reform but an obstacle. The constant attention given to the American liberal tradition as a precious achievement to be nurtured and maintained left the new radicals feeling merely "powerless, distracted, and confused."[60] When the so-called New Left intellectuals and activists thus began to outline an alternative ideological vision for the postwar era, they found themselves doing so in a language that was almost entirely hostile to both American liberalism and the American past because, as they saw it, both had been colonized by the defenders of the status quo and the maintainers of consensus.

New Left writers such as Paul Booth, Tom Hayden, Todd Gitlin, and Carl Oglesby might have been more sympathetic to elements of the liberal tradition in different circumstances. They almost certainly would have rallied to

Dewey's cause in the interwar years. But by the time they emerged on the American scene, liberalism was almost entirely associated with a postwar sellout to the established order; it was associated with what was called the "corporate liberalism" of the military-industrial complex, a liberalism that failed to interrogate the "true" meaning of ideals such as freedom and social equality but chose instead to imply that those ideals were well served by the prevailing political order.[61]

It was for this reason that the New Left explicitly decried the language of liberalism; it almost always described the label "radical" as an alternative rather than as a complement to the label "liberal." The radicals of the New Left were not the "resurrectors" of the best of liberalism, Tom Good explained in the monthly *New Left Notes* in 1966; rather, they stood against "even the best" that "liberal philosophy" had to offer.[62] That "might sound mighty anti-American," Carl Oglesby continued in the same periodical, but "I say: Don't blame me for that!" The blame instead lay with those who after World War II "mouthed . . . liberal values" but did so too often in defense of the prevailing order and in so doing "broke my American heart."[63]

CONCLUSION

By the end of the 1960s, then, the story of American radicals' attitude to the liberal tradition and the American past had almost come full circle. The century had opened with a Progressive movement that, on the whole, sought to transcend American liberalism, turning its back on that liberalism's perceived atomistic individualism in search of a new value order capable both of celebrating communality and of pursuing common goods through a highly organized and dramatically empowered political machine. That attempt to break with the past had proven short-lived and was replaced, for a while at least, with a wily attempt to employ traditional liberal languages for far more radical ends. In the interwar years, therefore, and especially in the depths of the Depression, radical intellectuals and activists followed John Dewey's lead in making liberal idealism work for the cause of dramatic change. In rehabilitating the liberal tradition, however, Dewey and his colleagues set in train a far deeper transformation in radical attitudes, one that led to the emergence of so-called consensus theory in the period after World War II, when radicals appeared to lose much sense of detachment from liberalism, the American past, and the American present. It was not surprising when that position too was superseded by a thoroughgoing rejection that once again saw the liberal tradition fall into disfavor.

Tracing this roller-coaster journey through the course of the twentieth century does not, of course, tell us where things should end. Historians will be divided over which of the approaches sketched here was the more intellectually coherent and which was the more politically successful. Each period will no doubt have its champions desperately seeking to restore that approach to radical politics in the present day. As mentioned at the outset, it is not the purpose of this chapter to resolve that argument. Instead, I have presented an account of the diversity of available positions demonstrating both that Louis Hartz was wrong to think that American radicals have always been locked into a Lockean liberal frame and that his latter-day critics are also misguided when they suggest that the liberal tradition has always been easily manipulated by radical intellectuals and activists. The truth is rather that although liberalism has sometimes come to the aid of American radicals, it has also on occasion provided an obstacle. All that can be said for certain, therefore, is, in the words of George Soule, that the minds of American radicals have continually been "deeply troubled by a conflict of ideas—the conflict between the necessity for change and loyalty to American tradition."[64] They are likely to continue to be so well into the future.

NOTES

1. Louis Hartz, *The Liberal Tradition in America* (San Diego: Harcourt, Brace, 1991), 232.

2. Ibid., 233.

3. See Richard Rorty, *Achieving Our Country: Leftist Thought in Twentieth Century America* (Cambridge, Mass.: Harvard University Press, 1998). See also Eric Foner, *The Story of American Freedom* (New York: Norton, 1998); Gary Gerstle, "The Protean Character of American Liberalism," *American Historical Review* 99 (1994): 1043–1073; Carol Horton, *Race and the Making of American Liberalism* (Oxford: Oxford University Press, 2005); Desmond King, *In the Name of Liberalism: Illiberal Social Policy in the USA and Britain* (Oxford: Oxford University Press, 1999); James Kloppenberg, *Uncertain Victory: Social Democracy and Progressivism in European and American Thought, 1879–1920* (New York: Oxford University Press, 1986); Rogers Smith, *Stories of Peoplehood: The Politics and Morals of Political Membership* (Cambridge: Cambridge University Press, 2003). For an overview and introduction, see Marc Stears, "The Liberal Tradition and the Politics of Exclusion," *Annual Review of Political Science* 10 (2007): 85–101.

4. See editorial, "Obama Jumps into Presidential Fray," *Washington Post,* January 17, 2007. See, too, Barack Obama, *The Audacity of Hope: Thoughts on Reclaiming the American Dream* (New York: Crown, 2006).

5. Hartz, *The Liberal Tradition in America*, 32.

6. David J. Lorenzo, "Attaining Rogers Smith's Civic Ideals," *Political Theory* 30 (2002): 357.

7. See Foner, *The Story of American Freedom*, xii–xxii.

8. See Michael Freeden, *Liberal Languages: Ideological Imaginations and Twentieth Century Progressive Thought* (Princeton, N.J.: Princeton University Press, 2005).

9. Rorty, *Achieving Our Country*, 3–4.

10. Hartz, *The Liberal Tradition in America*, 229, 233.

11. For introductions to this theme in Progressive writing, see Alan Dawley, *Struggles for Justice: Social Responsibility and the Liberal State* (Cambridge, Mass.: Belknap Press, 1991); Charles Forcey, *The Crossroads of Liberalism: Croly, Weyl, Lippmann, and the Progressive Era, 1900–1925* (New York: Oxford University Press, 1967); David E. Price, "Community and Control: Critical Democratic Theory in the Progressive Period," *American Political Science Review* 68 (1974): 1663–1678.

12. Louis Brandeis, "On Industrial Relations," in *The Curse of Bigness* (New York: Kennikat Press, 1962), 81.

13. Herbert Croly, *The Promise of American Life* (1909; reprint, Boston: Northeastern University Press, 1989), 3.

14. Ibid., 5.

15. Ibid.

16. Ibid., 153.

17. Walter Lippmann, *Drift and Mastery: An Attempt to Diagnose the Current Unrest* (New York: Kennerley, 1914), 87.

18. See, for paradigmatic examples, Simon Nelson Patten, *The New Basis of Civilization* (New York: Macmillan, 1907); and W. A. White, *The Old Order Changeth: A View of American Democracy* (New York: Macmillan, 1910).

19. H. G. Wells, *The Future in America: A Search after Realities* (New York: Harpers, 1906), 153.

20. Charles Cooley, *Social Organization* (New York: C. Scribner's Sons, 1902), 83, 89.

21. Paul Kellogg, untitled manuscript in the Paul Kellogg Papers, Social Welfare History Archive, University of Minnesota, Minneapolis, 3/28/12. For more on this theme, see Mark Hulliung, *The Social Contract in America: From the Revolution to the Present Age* (Lawrence: University Press of Kansas, 2007), 188–191.

22. Walter Lippmann, *Preface to Politics* (New York: Kennerley, 1913), 286.

23. See Herbert Croly, *Progressive Democracy* (New York: Macmillan, 1914), 43; and Walter Weyl, *The New Democracy: An Essay on Certain Political and Economic Tendencies in the United States* (New York: Macmillan, 1912), 15–16.

24. See Weyl, *The New Democracy*, 36.

25. For more on this argument, see Marc Stears, "The Political Conditions of Social Justice," in *Forms of Justice: Critical Perspectives on David Miller's Political Philosophy*, ed. Daniel Bell and Avner de Shalit (Lanham, Md.: Rowman & Littlefield, 2003).

26. Jane Addams, "The Progressive's Dilemma," typescript, in the Paul Kellogg Papers, 35/331.

27. Lippmann, *Preface to Politics*, 220.

28. See David J. Goldberg, *Discontented America: The United States in the 1920s* (Baltimore: Johns Hopkins University Press, 1999), 3.

29. Croly, *The Promise of American Life*, 3 (emphasis added).

30. Ibid., 51.

31. See Amos Pinchot, *History of the Progressive Party, 1912–1916* (New York: New York University Press, 1958); and Eugene Tobin, *Organize or Perish: America's Independent Progressives, 1913–1933* (New York: Greenwood Press, 1986).

32. See the files in the League for Industrial Democracy Records, Tamiment Institute, New York University, New York, 49/3/1. See too Oscar A. Hilton, "Public Opinion and Civil Liberties in Wartime, 1917–1919," *South Western Social Science Quarterly* 28 (1947): 201–224; and Harold Stearns, *Liberalism in America: Its Origin, Its Temporary Collapse, Its Future* (New York: Boni & Liverlight, 1919).

33. Arthur Bingham, "What Does American Mean?" *Common Sense* 4 (1935): 24.

34. John Dewey, "Social Change and Its Human Direction," *Modern Quarterly* 5 (1930): 423.

35. John Dewey, *Liberalism and Social Action* (1935; reprint, Amherst, Mass.: Prometheus Books, 2000), 60.

36. Ibid., 41.

37. See the superb discussions in Foner, *The Story of American Freedom*, 195–219; and Gary Gerstle, *Working-Class Americanism: The Politics of Labor in a Textile City, 1914–1960* (New York: Cambridge University Press, 1989).

38. Editorial, "Liberalism Twenty Years After," *New Republic*, January 23, 1935, 290; John Dewey, "The Future of Liberalism," *Journal of Philosophy* 22 (1935): 231.

39. George Soule, *A Planned Society* (New York: Macmillan, 1932), 86.

40. Dewey, *Liberalism and Social Action*, 60.

41. Arthur Bingham, "Liberalism and Social Action," *Common Sense* 4 (1935): 28.

42. For introductions to the period, see Irving Bernstein, *Turbulent Years: A History of the American Worker, 1933–1941* (Boston: Houghton, 1970); and Robert H. Zieger, *The CIO, 1935–1955* (Chapel Hill: University of North Carolina Press, 1995).

43. John L. Lewis, "The Struggle for Industrial Democracy," *Common Sense* 6 (1937): 8–11.

44. George Soule, *The Future of Liberty* (New York: Macmillan, 1936), 7.

45. Dewey, *Liberalism and Social Action*, 91–92.

46. Editorial, "What Can I Do?" *Common Sense* 1 (1933): 2.

47. Gerstle, *Working-Class Americanism*, 174–175.

48. Samuel Schmalhausen, "The Logic of Leninism," *Modern Quarterly* 5 (1930): 460.

49. Soule, *A Planned Society*, 11.

50. Rorty, *Achieving Our Country*, 59.

51. Michael Walzer, "The Idea of Resistance," *Dissent* 7 (1960): 370.

52. See Ira Katznelson, *Desolation and Enlightenment: Political Knowledge after Total War, Totalitarianism, and the Holocaust* (New York: Columbia University Press, 2003).

53. As described by John Dryzek, *Deliberative Democracy and Beyond: Liberals, Critics, Contestations* (Oxford: Oxford University Press, 2000), 51–52.

54. Gunnar Myrdal, with Richard Sterner and Arnold Rose, *An American Dilemma: The Negro Problem and Modern Democracy* (New York: Harper & Brothers, 1944), 21, 24 (emphasis added).

55. See Daniel Bell, *The End of Ideology: On the Exhaustion of Political Ideas in the Fifties* (Cambridge, Mass.: Harvard University Press, 1960); Robert A. Dahl, *Who Governs? Democracy and Power in an American City* (New Haven, Conn.: Yale University Press, 1961); Richard Hofstadter, *The American Tradition and the Men Who Made It* (New York: Vintage, 1974); Judith Shklar, *After Utopia: The Decline of Political Faith* (Princeton, N.J.: Princeton University Press, 1957). For an excellent overview of the period, see Robert Booth Fowler, *Believing Skeptics: American Political Intellectuals, 1945–1964* (Westport, Conn.: Greenwood Press, 1978).

56. For a fascinating account of Dewey's conversion, see Robert Westbrook, *John Dewey and American Democracy* (Ithaca, N.Y.: Cornell University Press, 1991).

57. I develop this point further in my chapter with Desmond King in this volume.

58. Louis Hartz, "Goals for Political Science: A Discussion," *American Political Science Review* 45 (1951): 1005.

59. C. Wright Mills, *The Sociological Imagination* (Oxford: Oxford University Press, 1959), 188.

60. Tom Hayden, *Radical Nomad: C. Wright Mills and His Times* (Boulder, Colo.: Paradigm, 2006), 177 (first written in 1959).

61. See Staughton Lynd, "The New Left," *Annals of the American Academy of Political and Social Sciences* 382 (1969): 64–72.

62. Tom Good, "Ideology and the SDS," *New Left Notes* 1 (1966): 5.

63. Carl Oglesby, "Liberalism and the Corporate State," *New Left Notes* 1 (1966): 2.

64. Soule, *The Future of Liberty*, 1.

PART FOUR

From Yesterday to Today

CHAPTER 7

The Liberal Tradition in an Age of Conservative Power and Partisan Polarization

Richard J. Ellis

Louis Hartz's *Liberal Tradition in America* was written against the backdrop of nearly twenty years of Democratic control of the presidency and Congress. By the time the book was published in 1955, Dwight Eisenhower had become president, but he got there less by embracing conservatism than by reconciling himself and his party to the liberal welfare state. Conservatism as an ideology and a political movement seemed marginal to American politics. Conservatives were the polity's extremists and cranks—loud and colorful but largely ineffectual and powerless. On the left there appeared to be no frontal challenge to capitalism; capitalism was to be regulated and shored up, not overthrown or subverted. There were still plenty of policy differences between Eisenhower's Republicans and Adlai Stevenson's Democrats, but there seemed to be no fundamental cleavages over first principles. What differences there were could be negotiated through bargaining and compromise. In short, Hartz penned his classic treatise in an age of liberal power and partisan consensus.

How well does Hartz's thesis of a hegemonic liberal tradition measure up against the politics of the past fifty years, particularly the last three decades, which have been marked by conservative power and partisan polarization? Hartz, of course, never claimed that liberals would triumph over conservatives; rather, his claim was that both liberals and conservatives were really liberals underneath. Nor did Hartz claim that there were no significant political differences between the Left and Right in the United States; rather, his claim was that those differences were bounded by a shared commitment to Lockean liberal principles. On the left, that commitment manifested itself in support for market capitalism, and on the right, in a preoccupation with limiting the state. Absent on the left was a vibrant socialist movement, and missing on the right was a paternal ethos of noblesse oblige. Lacking leveling egalitarianism on the left and complex hierarchy on the right, all that remained in the United States was competitive individualism.

On one view, then, the politics of the last half century are perfectly compatible with Hartz's thesis. On the left, the Great Society was no more socialist than was the New Deal. Both sought to reform capitalism rather than replace it. Both Lyndon Johnson and Franklin Delano Roosevelt largely justified government programs in the language of equality of opportunity rather than equality of results.[1] On the right, Reagan Republicanism came to power by invoking the old laissez-faire ethos. Government, Ronald Reagan declared in his first inaugural address, was the problem, not the solution.

The presidency of Bill Clinton in the 1990s seemed to reaffirm Hartz's thesis with a vengeance. In his 1993 inaugural address, Clinton declared the problem of ideology to be over. The "great debate over the role of government," Clinton insisted, had been "resolved for our time." Government, he said, was neither the problem nor the solution. Instead, the American people themselves were the solution. Sounding more like a Reagan Republican than a New Deal or Great Society Democrat, Clinton called for a "humble" government that did "not to try to solve all our problems for us," a leaner government that "live[d] within its means" and "did more with less." Just as Eisenhower had accepted the basic structure of the welfare state created by Roosevelt's New Deal, so Clinton seemed to be prepared to assent to the fundamental assumptions of the Reagan Revolution.

Far from disproving the Hartzian thesis, then, the politics of the last thirty years have arguably witnessed a powerful reassertion of Lockean liberalism in its purest, antistatist form. Income inequality has gotten larger, not smaller, yet there has been no sustained political movement to reverse that trend. Tax cuts have become a pervasive, inescapable feature of the American political landscape, despite the fact that the tax burden in the United States is low relative to that of most other advanced industrial societies.[2] The American welfare state remains a laggard, judged by any number of indicators, including child care, vacation time,[3] sick leave, job training, and a host of social services. Among the thirteen most advanced industrial societies, the United States ranks dead last in infant mortality.[4]

The question, "Why no national health insurance in the United States?" seems like the twenty-first-century version of Hartz's framing question, "Why no socialism in the United States?"

THE RISE OF CONSERVATIVE POWER

Yet the Hartzian lens obscures at least as much as it reveals about contemporary American politics, particularly about conservative political power. For argument's sake, let us concede Hartz's point about the left wing in the United States. Granted there was much in the New Left in the 1960s that was fundamentally at odds with the liberal tradition,[5] but the New Left, contra Rush Limbaugh and Newt Gingrich, did not come to power. The same cannot be said, however, of the conservative movement of the 1960s. True, the conservative's banner bearer Barry Goldwater was thrashed in 1964, swept away in the high tide of liberalism. Lyndon Johnson's victory seemed at the time to represent an emphatic triumph of the liberal center over the conservative fringe. But from the perspective of the early twenty-first century, 1964 looks more like the birth of a conservative grassroots movement that would come to power with the election of Reagan in 1980.

Of course, there is much about this conservative movement that is thoroughly liberal in the Lockean sense. Antipathy to governmental power and the tax revolt that fueled the Right's rise to power fall comfortably within the confines of the liberal tradition. There is little in Goldwater or Reagan or George W. Bush that is comparable to the Tory ethos of noblesse oblige. If class is the only category that matters, then Hartz's thesis would appear to be every bit as valid in 2008 as it was in 1928. Reagan's faith in the unregulated marketplace was just as extravagant as Herbert Hoover's. But an economic analysis is an inadequate guidepost to understanding the rise of contemporary conservatism, for if class and economics were all that mattered, the Republicans would not have become the dominant political force in American politics.

To reduce the Republican Party to its antitax, antistate rhetoric and policies is to miss the authentically nonliberal and antiliberal elements in the party's creed. Moreover, these nonliberal elements are not just the province of a few cranks at the margins of the party; instead, they constitute defining features of party ideology that help explain the rise to power of the Republican Party. Hartz is correct that American conservatism bears scant resemblance to Tory conservatism in Great Britain, but it does not follow that conservatism in the United States is simply a manifestation of the liberal tradition. Once we discard the blinkers that limited Hartz's field of vision to the category of class, we can begin to appreciate the power of distinctively conservative ideas, organizations, and movements in the United States. In particular, understanding modern American conservatism requires taking into fuller account the roles of religion, gender and the family, and race.

The conservative movement that took root in the 1960s combined two distinct philosophical strands: one was libertarian, the other social conservative. The former fit snugly within the Hartzian consensus, but the latter was neither derived from nor bounded by liberal assumptions. Libertarianism, like liberalism, placed concern for individual liberty at its center. The libertarian critique of liberals was that they had abandoned liberalism in their desire to use government to redress inequalities. Social conservatives, however, mounted a quite different critique. Liberals, according to social conservatives, had allowed individual rights to erode community standards, to break down discipline and authority in the family, and to undermine religious faith and moral absolutes. As Rebecca Klatch summarizes the difference, the laissez-faire or libertarian conservative defined the problem with America in terms of the loss of individual liberty, whereas the social conservative envisioned an America plagued by "moral decay." While libertarianism was "rooted in the classical liberalism of the nineteenth century," social conservatism was "rooted in religious belief," specifically Christianity.[6]

If, as Klatch finds, Christianity is "the central lens" through which social conservatives view the world, then no understanding of modern conservatism will take us far that does not place religion at its center. For social conservatives, the United States is fundamentally a Christian nation. American national identity, in their view, is inseparable from a belief in God. The nation's ills are, at bottom, moral failings that have resulted from a turning away from God. Redeeming the nation requires Americans to reject secular humanism and to walk once again along the path of righteousness.[7] Like Karl Marx, who famously dismissed religious faith as the opiate of the masses, Hartz leaves us ill equipped to take this religious rhetoric seriously.

Of course, social conservatives have learned to employ the language of liberal rights. The defense of prayer in schools is often couched in terms of the free exercise of religious belief. Criticisms of sex education in the schools are framed as a defense of the rights of parents to shape the education of their children. And, most notably, the attack on abortion is made in terms of defending the right to life.[8] However, social conservatives do not only or even mostly speak in the liberal language of rights. They also rely heavily on nonliberal languages that are steeped in religious commitment. The curriculum of public schools, for instance, is frequently assailed by activists for promoting homosexual or promiscuous lifestyles and for teaching cultural relativism rather than morality. Opposition to abortion is framed as part of a wider defense of what Pope John Paul II identified in the early 1990s as a "culture of life," a culture that required "protection of God's work of creation." Far from hiding such language in public, social conservatives succeeded in writing the commitment to a "culture of life" into the platform of the Republican Party in 2004. Significantly, President George W. Bush spoke of a "culture of life" far more often than he did the "right to life."

In the social conservative vision, as Klatch points out, "the family stands at the center." To the social conservative, "the family is the basis of everything." If it crumbles, then "everything else goes."[9] Liberalism's relentless championing of individual rights is seen as undermining both the autonomy of the family and the authority relations and gendered divisions within the family. The social conservative concern is not only that granting rights to children provides the state with a warrant to invade the sacred domain of the family—an eminently liberal concern since it involves the boundary between public and private—but that endowing children with rights subverts the authority of parents and upsets the natural ordering of human relations.

For social conservatives, feminism is among the most subversive and dangerous of doctrines. Most social conservatives do not believe that women should remain in the kitchen, barefoot and pregnant; only 20 percent of white "core evangelicals"—those who regularly attend evangelical churches, believe the Bible is the word of God, and say religion is very important to them—agree that a woman's place is in the home. However, most social conservatives do believe that feminism devalues the roles of mother and homemaker and that the social order is better off if women tend to the home.[10] The feminist preoccupation with women's self-fulfillment, social conservatives believe, pulls apart families that are properly based on loyalty and devotion. Even when divorce is not the result of women's liberation, children are cut adrift from their moral moorings as the mother places her personal satisfaction over the needs of her children.

From a Hartzian perspective, the fierce battle over the equal rights amendment (ERA) in the 1970s must remain something of a mystery. Who would have predicted that the most liberal of societies would balk at the notion that equal rights for women should be inscribed in the Constitution? To be sure, some of the arguments against the ERA employed rhetoric that did not challenge fundamental liberal precepts. Some argued, for instance, that the amendment was not so much subversive as unnecessary, since the Constitution already protected the rights of women. But this was not the rhetoric that activated the thousands and thousands of women who mobilized in opposition to the ERA. They rallied against the ERA because they saw it as part of a concerted feminist assault on God-given differences between men and women. The ERA, social conservatives believed, would subvert the ordered differences that for all of recorded history had provided the foundation for healthy families and societies.

Also puzzling from the Hartzian perspective is the ferocity of the conservative attack on gay marriage and gay rights. Perhaps one might try to reduce these attacks to a matter of unprincipled prejudice against lesbians and gays, but that would be to wear the very liberal blinders that Hartz urges us to cast aside. The social conservative argument against gay marriage is principled, but its principles are derived not from a liberal tradition but from religious beliefs that posit innate differences between men and women. Like feminism, gay rights pose a fundamental threat to the social conservative worldview.

Nor is it possible to save the Hartzian thesis by portraying the antipathy to homosexuals as peripheral to the mainstream of American politics. About four in ten Americans consistently reject the fundamental liberal notion that homosexual relations between consenting adults should be legal.[11] Moreover, in the opening decade of the twenty-first century, same-sex marriage has been one of the Republicans' most favored wedge issues. In 2004, conservative activists placed same-sex marriage bans on the ballot in thirteen states, including the pivotal state of Ohio. An average of over seven in ten voters approved the bans. Republicans hoped the ballot measures would boost Bush's support among the evangelical community, and the best available evidence suggests that the ballot measures did exactly that. Gay marriage may not have tipped the election to Bush, but it was one of a number of factors that helped the president improve on his 2000 showing.[12]

In short, the Hartzian class-based lens misses the hierarchical heart of contemporary social conservatism. Social conservatives draw on the Bible to defend the hierarchical relations of the family: the parents' authority over children as well as the husband's over the wife. The husband is supposed to be "the head of the family." As the Southern Baptist Convention put it in 1998, God intended the husband to "provide for, protect and lead his family," while the wife is to "submit graciously."[13] In the view of social conservatives, family roles and obligations differ by sex because men are innately different from women. Only when those differences are respected can the family and society function effectively. Both feminism and gay rights thus subvert the hierarchical ordering of "the traditional family."

Hartz leaves out something else that is central to an understanding of the rise of Republican power over the last three decades: race and the South. It is not that Hartz failed to notice the South or the conflict between blacks and whites. Two chapters of *The Liberal Tradition* are devoted to "the feudal dream of the South," but Hartz ultimately dismissed southern political thought as "a simple fraud" and a philosophical "madhouse." Bound by liberal chains, Hartz explains, proslavery apologists writhed in "philosophic pain" as they tried in vain to construct a coherent defense of organic hierarchical social relationships in a fundamentally liberal world. Despite the best efforts of theorists such as George Fitzhugh, this "great conservative reaction" perished after the Civil War without leaving any significant imprint on the mind of the nation.[14]

Hartz is correct that Fitzhugh's pseudofeudal critique of capitalism has had little resonance in the United States, but he is far too quick to conclude that Fitzhugh's oblivion demonstrates the "utter dominion" of the liberal ideal in America. Hartz is not unaware of the illiberal features of the South. Locke, he notes, "had been imperfect there to begin with," and "the brute emancipation of the slaves was hardly enough to make him perfect."[15] Hartz, however, quickly forgets even this modest caveat in his rush to affirm the hegemony of liberal capitalism. But if Hartz is right that the key to the nation's liberal identity is that Americans are "born equal, instead of becoming so," then surely the starting point for understanding the South is its illiberalism. Blacks and whites were not born equal, and few whites regarded blacks as their equals. This is not just a matter of Locke being a little imperfect.

Rogers Smith is right that the history of race in the United States cannot be told simply as a story of liberal ideals versus illiberal practices. Indeed, Hartz's own methodology warns against telling the story in these terms. For Hartz, ideas are not disembodied, floating above social relations. Liberal ideas are grounded in liberal social relations. But if Hartz is right to devote attention not only to ideas but also to social practices, then surely he is wrong to give so little credence to the hierarchical character of southern race relations and the ideas that sustained those relations.

To be sure, the South lacked the finely graded hierarchical categories of a society such as Brazil, which recognized in law those who were neither black nor white.[16] In the United States, in contrast, the law acknowledged only two categories of people: black and white. And Hartz is also helpful in understanding the liberal logic that spurred white supremacists to insist that blacks were animals or property rather than human beings. If all men were equal, then there was a powerful rhetorical logic driving whites to deny that blacks were human.[17] But while Hartz's thesis can illuminate aspects of race relations in the United States, it obscures far too much about actual patterns of southern social relations and ideology.

Segregationist rhetoric largely did not deny the humanity of black people.[18] Instead, it rested centrally on the notion that blacks and whites had different aptitudes and abilities and that the functioning of the social order depended on everybody knowing his or her proper place. "Keep[ing] Mister Nigger in his place" expressed not simply white racism but a hierarchical worldview of superiority and subordination. So long as those hierarchical relations were observed, blacks and whites could live together peacefully and productively. Black people, after all, were "born and made to serve," and white people, to rule. In the minds of segregationists, this social order suited blacks as well as whites. The South's problems stemmed from outside agitators who threatened to upset age-old patterns of deference and obedience by making blacks "uppity," leading them to forget their place. Segregationists did not have to read Fitzhugh to construct a hierarchical defense of a social order based on ascriptive inequality.[19]

But what does this segregationist ideology have to do with the rise of modern conservatism? On one reading, not much. So long as the ideology was about keeping blacks in their place, some argue, conservatives were consigned to the national sidelines. Only when conservatives abandoned the traditional language of white supremacism in favor of the liberal language of nondiscrimination were they able to use race to forge a governing coalition. According to this view, conservatives triumphed by successfully arguing that liberals favored policies that were fundamentally illiberal. Quotas, busing, and other species of affirmative action treated individuals as members of an ascriptive group rather than as individuals. Reverse discrimination was as unconscionable as traditional discrimination.[20]

It is true that much of the national discourse on race today takes place within the confines of a broadly defined liberal tradition, though conservatives are correct that the Left's rhetoric of diversity at times disguises significant departures from that liberal tradition. However, to reduce the Republican strategy on race to a reassertion of Lockean liberal principles is to obscure how the Republicans actually displaced the Democrats as the dominant party in the South. Nixon's southern strategy in 1968 was not to highlight reverse discrimination but to champion "law and order," and for many Americans the law was white and disorder black. Southerners who deserted the Democratic Party generally did so not because they perceived the Republican Party to embody liberal principles of nondiscrimination but, rather, because they perceived the Republican Party to be more sympathetic to their way of life and more committed to helping them preserve their traditional communities, schools, families, and churches.

In the 1950s southern whites had vowed "massive resistance" to court-ordered integration, but the more enduringly important resistance took the form of white flight. If whites could no longer keep blacks in their place, then whites would leave the cities to the blacks and re-create all-white communities in suburbia. If whites could not exclude blacks from their public schools, then they would establish private schools instead, preferably religious ones that could escape the meddlesome hand of the federal government. If whites could not exclude blacks from public facilities such as swimming pools, then whites would stop paying taxes. Low taxes, school vouchers, and privatization of public services have all become familiar themes of modern conservatism, and on the surface, as historian Kevin Kruse notes, they seem to have "little or nothing to do with race." But in the South even the most Lockean rhetoric is steeped in racial hierarchy. And not only in the South: Republican attacks on the welfare state have been so successful because large chunks of white America believe the government is "funneling their tax dollars to 'inner-city substance-abusing blacks.'" In short, opposition to social welfare policies in the United States attests not simply to the power of Locke but to the power of race.[21]

PARTISAN POLARIZATION

One of the most striking features of contemporary American politics is its increasingly partisan polarization. Democrats almost universally disliked and distrusted George W. Bush. In 2006, fewer than 10 percent of Democrats expressed approval of Bush's job performance. Republicans, on the other hand, consistently viewed Bush's performance positively. In 2006, over 82 percent of Republicans approved of the job Bush was doing. This yawning gap between Democratic and Republican evaluations of presidential performance is unprecedented in modern American history. Between the presidencies of Dwight Eisenhower and Jimmy Carter, the average partisan gap in approval ratings was 34 percentage points. The Reagan presidency witnessed a significant jump in polarization, with Republican approval ratings 52 percentage points higher on average than Democratic approval ratings. Bill Clinton's presidency was even more polarized, with an average difference between Republicans and Democrats of 55 points. The terrorist attacks of September 11, 2001, briefly disrupted this polarized pattern, as Democrats rallied around Bush, but within a year the intense polarization returned. Even during Bush's final year in office, when his popularity plummeted to unprecedented lows, the gap between Democratic and Republican evaluations still averaged about 60 points.[22]

Does this partisan polarization matter for Hartz's thesis? Granted that
Hartz penned *The Liberal Tradition* at a time of relatively low partisan polarization—lots of Democrats liked Ike, especially in his first term—but do
high levels of party polarization invalidate the Hartzian thesis? Not necessarily. A highly partisan political environment may be compatible with the
consensus thesis if the conflict takes place within the parameters of agreed-
upon fundamentals. After all, Hartz was not unaware of the highly partisan
character of late-nineteenth-century political conflict,[23] but he regarded
these political battles as much ado about very little. The key question for
Hartz is not how much fighting there is or how fervent the fighting is, but
what is being fought over. Hartz's view of American politics mirrors that
well-worn wisecrack about academia: its fights are so vicious because the
stakes are so low.

But are the stakes in contemporary American politics really as low as
Hartz would lead us to believe? Or, alternatively, is modern American political life best characterized by what James Hunter has labeled a "culture
war"?[24] Certainly many conservatives believe that the contemporary political struggle does involve a fundamental contest over first principles. As Pat
Buchanan expressed it in his notorious speech at the 1992 Republican Convention, the battle between Bill Clinton and George Herbert Walker Bush
was part of "a cultural war" and "a religious war . . . for the soul of America."[25] Is Buchanan's rhetoric just another example of what Hartz derides as
"the shadow conflict" that characteristically conceals rather than illuminates the contours of American political culture?[26] Or has Buchanan, for all
his rhetorical excesses, grasped a fundamental truth, that contemporary
American politics is characterized by a contest between fundamentally opposed worldviews?

The leading scholarly skeptic of the culture war thesis is Morris Fiorina,
but even he does not dispute that something like a culture war animates
political elites. Indeed, "the central puzzle of modern American politics,"
according to Fiorina, is the disconnect between an increasingly polarized
political class and an electorate that is only minimally polarized. Fiorina's
tentative answer is that primary elections are the probable culprits, since
turnout in primary elections is often low and dominated by the politically
active.[27] However, Fiorina's explanation for American politics' "central
puzzle" undermines the strict dichotomy he erects between "the political
class" and the mass public and suggests instead that we need to differen-
tiate more carefully between different strata of the general public. There is
no questioning that a large swath of the public does not think in ideological terms or pay close attention to politics. These people vote infrequently,

know little about politics, and are only dimly aware of the issues and rhetoric that divide political elites. If there is a culture war, these people are blissfully innocent of it. However, if we look at more politically active citizens, there is strong evidence of increased polarization. And the more active the citizens, as Alan Abramowitz has shown, the more polarized and ideological are their views.[28]

Fiorina is right to be skeptical of extravagant claims like the one made by Bush strategist Matthew Dowd, who told a journalist in 2003 that "80 to 90 percent of the country . . . looks at each other like they are on separate planets."[29] But Abramowitz and others are right that polarization is not limited to a narrowly defined political class. Substantial segments of the American public are sharply divided by party on a range of public policy issues. Yes, the political class is more polarized and ideologically consistent than the American public. But that elite polarization is both cause and effect of polarization among the politically attentive stratum of the general public. Elite polarization shapes the way citizens view politics, which in turn shapes the incentives elites face in crafting their electoral appeals.

Even if one accepts that political attitudes are significantly more polarized by party than they were in the 1950s, that still does not necessarily mean that we are in the midst of a culture war. As Fiorina points out, party polarization can occur without any change in the distribution of opinions between liberals and conservatives. Imagine a society in which there are 100 liberals, half of whom are Democrats and half of whom are Republicans, 100 moderates, all Independents, and 100 conservatives, half of whom are Democrats and half of whom are Republicans. Although there is nothing approaching a consensus on ideology or issue positions in such a society, nor is there any partisan polarization. Now imagine another society, one in which the 100 liberals are all Democrats, the 100 moderates are all Independents, and the 100 conservatives are all Republicans. In the latter society, where parties are extraordinarily polarized, politics will be more bitter and compromise more difficult, but there has been no change in the aggregate distribution of opinions. There are as many people in the center of the political spectrum as there were in the society that was free of polarization.[30]

However, at least at the elite level, the empirical record suggests there has been a hollowing out of the center. Among members of Congress, for instance, increasing party polarization has coincided with a decreasing number of moderates in each party. Politics matters. In the South, conservative Democrats have given way to even more conservative Republicans. And in the Northeast, liberal-to-moderate Republicans have given way to even more liberal Democrats. Although logically they need not be connected, partisan polarization has in fact made for a more ideological politics.[31]

Does this more ideological politics qualify as a "culture war"? The hyperbolic language of "war," while certainly evocative and attention-grabbing, is unfortunate.[32] Republicans and Democrats may be fiercely contesting fundamental principles, but they can hardly be said to be at war. The important question is not whether the conflict is best described as a war but whether the conflict is best conceived as a contest between rival ways of life and worldviews or whether the conflicts, however fiercely contested, are confined within a broader agreement on political fundamentals.

At one level, of course, political conflict in the United States does take place within a fundamental consensus about the value of constitutional democracy. Outside of a few left-wing intellectuals, nobody criticizes the idea of a written constitution, though many right-wing activists determinedly seek to amend it. Virtually everybody agrees that elections are the way the nation should sort out political disagreements. Even when an election is perceived by many to have been stolen, Americans seem willing to accept the outcome as legitimate. There is a widespread consensus that political differences are not to be settled by war or violence. Those who "take the law into their own hands," as some antiabortion activists have done, are generally shunned rather than glorified. This is not an unimportant achievement, but it does not really set the United States apart from other Western industrial democracies. The politics of all Western industrial democracies are sustained by a rough consensus on the rules of the political game. There is nothing particularly exceptional about the United States in this regard.

Too often the Hartzian thesis is affirmed without systematically comparing the ideological distance between parties in the United States with the ideological distance between parties in European nations. European parties are simply assumed to be more ideologically cohesive than the catchall parties of the United States. The authority of Alexis de Tocqueville is frequently trotted out as proof. Parties in the United States, Tocqueville wrote, were "based not on principles but on material interests," whereas in Europe "great political parties" battled over fundamentals. For a European observer, Tocqueville wrote, the party quarrels in the United States seemed "either incomprehensible or puerile," and he was hard-pressed to say whether "one ought to pity a people that takes such wretched trifles seriously or envy the good fortune that permits it to do so." Perhaps Tocqueville was right about the parties of his day, but is his judgment a sound guide to contemporary party politics?[33]

The evidence of a categorical difference between American and European parties is surprisingly weak. In a 1994 study, for instance, Hans-Dieter Klingemann and his colleagues found that Democrats and Republicans were "reasonably cohesive internally, when compared with political parties in other systems" and that "their platforms are quite clearly differentiated from each other in an ideologically consistent fashion." When comparing U.S. parties to British or even to "the presumably more sharply delineated German parties," they found "no less difference or distinctiveness in the United States than elsewhere."[34]

The difference between European nations and the United States, as John Gerring has pointed out, may be less the extent of ideological consensus or dissensus and more the content of the consensus. Gerring offers the telling example of Sweden, a society in which democratic socialism is perhaps more ensconced in public policy than anywhere else in Europe. Even the most conservative parties in Sweden have generally been willing to accept the legitimacy of the nation's welfare state. "The world's most socialist democracy," Gerring concludes, "may also be one of the world's most consensual democracies." By the same token, the world's most capitalistic democracy, the United States, is perhaps one of the world's least consensual democracies. Although the welfare state is less well developed in the United States than elsewhere, its legitimacy is continually under attack. Even if the Democratic Party is further to the right than most of the left parties of Europe, that is more than compensated for by the Republican Party, which, as Gerring points out, "has been to the right of its ideological cousins [in other countries] on most redistributive questions since the 1920s." As a result, "party conflict on redistributive matters in the United States has taken place further to the right on the ideological spectrum but with at least as much space separating the major parties as in most other party systems."[35]

Of course, there is more to political conflict than economics and redistribution. Those who posit a culture war in contemporary America point in particular to the religious dimension of partisan conflict. The religious conflict is not between Protestants and Catholics or between Christians and Jews; rather, the fissure runs between those for whom religion matters a great deal and those for whom religion matters little or not at all.

A study of 2004 national convention delegates found marked differences between the religiosity of Democratic and Republican delegates. A majority of the Republican delegates reported that they attended church at least once a week, whereas only about one-quarter of Democratic delegates said the same. Six in ten Democratic delegates did not attend church more than a couple times a year, whereas only 30 percent of Republican delegates reported similarly low levels of religious attendance. Thirty-six percent of Democratic delegates reported that they seldom or never attended religious worship, while fewer than 15 percent of Republican delegates made that same concession[36]

The more religious and the more evangelical the delegates, the more conservative their political ideology, particularly on the Republican side. Among Republican delegates who were white evangelical Protestants and attended church at least once a week (about one-quarter of Republicans fit this description), half described themselves as "very conservative." In contrast, only about one-quarter of white evangelical Protestant delegates who attended church less than once a week described themselves as "very conservative." A mere 6 percent of Republican delegates who were mainline Protestants and attended church less than once a week (about one in five Republican delegates fit this description) characterized themselves as very conservative, and 41 percent described themselves as politically moderate. In contrast, fewer than one in ten Republican evangelicals who attended church at least once a week described themselves as politically moderate. On the Democratic side, the groups most likely to describe themselves as "very liberal" were the religiously unaffiliated and those who identified with a religion other than Christianity.[37]

These religious divisions are evident not only among party activists but among the electorate as well. Exit polls in the 2004 election found that almost two-thirds of those who attended religious services more than once a week voted for George W. Bush, while only about one-third voted for Democrat John Kerry. In contrast, among those who never go to religious services, the numbers were almost exactly reversed, with 62 percent voting for Kerry and only 36 percent voting for Bush. If one looks only at whites, the relationship between religiosity and the vote is stronger still, since African Americans are the most loyal and religious Democratic constituency. Fewer than three in ten whites who attended church at least weekly voted for Kerry, whereas better than seven in ten voted for Bush. It might be thought that the relationship between religion and the vote is simply an artifact of the fact that Bush polled best in the South, which is the most religious region of the nation, but the robust relationship between church attendance and the 2004 vote held in every region of the country.[38]

The relationship between politics and religion is tighter still if one factors in religious beliefs. Using a battery of questions that measured religious belief (such as belief in God and belief in evolution) as well as behavior (e.g., church attendance and private prayer), John Green found even more compelling evidence of the connection between religion and voter choice.

In 2004, religious traditionalists—that is, those who were not only highly religious but fundamentalist or orthodox in their beliefs—voted overwhelmingly for Bush. Nearly nine in ten of white traditionalist evangelicals voted for Bush. Among mainline Protestants, white traditionalists preferred Bush over Kerry by about a two-to-one margin. Seventy-two percent of white Catholic traditionalists backed Bush and only 28 percent voted for Kerry. Seven in ten traditionalists identified themselves as Republicans, while only 20 percent identified themselves as Democrats. Put the other way around, religious traditionalists made up nearly 45 percent of the Republican coalition and only a small fraction of the Democratic coalition. If traditionalists were Bush's biggest backers, Kerry's support was greatest among those who claimed no religious affiliation. Seventy-two percent of these people (constituting about 16 percent of the population) voted for Kerry and only 28 percent for Bush. Among the small band of avowed atheists or agnostics (representing only a little over 3 percent of the population), only 18 percent voted for Bush, and 82 percent voted for Kerry.[39]

The divide between religious traditionalists and those whom Green describes as religious modernists (those who reject religious orthodoxy and have lower levels of religious engagement) as well as the religiously unaffiliated is reflected not only in partisan identification and voter choice but in issue positions as well, particularly on social issues such as abortion and stem-cell research. Among evangelical Protestants, for instance, 84 percent of traditionalists opt for the prolife position, that abortion should always be illegal or legal in only a few, limited circumstances, whereas nearly two-thirds of modernist evangelicals take the prochoice side, that abortion should be legal in all or at least many circumstances. Among Catholics, there is the same sharp division between traditionalists and modernists. Seventy-seven percent of traditionalist Catholics adopt the prolife stance, while nearly 80 percent of modernist Catholics are prochoice. Roughly three-quarters of those who are not affiliated with any religion take the prochoice position, as do 84 percent of those whose faith is other than Christian. Over 90 percent of atheists and agnostics take the prochoice position, and none at all take the extreme position that abortion should always be illegal.[40]

Opinions on stem-cell research divide along similar religious fault lines. In August 2004, the Pew Research Center asked people whether they thought it was more important to conduct "stem cell research that might result in new medical cures" or whether it was more important not to destroy "the potential life of human embryos involved in this research." About eight in ten of those who attended church seldom or never supported stem-cell research, whereas seven in ten of those who attended church more than once a week opposed such research. Those Protestants who described themselves as "born-again" were much more likely to oppose stem-cell research than any other religious group. Jews and those who identified with no religion were twice as likely to support stem-cell research as born-again Protestants, and three times as likely as born-again Protestants who went to church at least once a week.[41]

The story is similar for same-sex marriage. Offered a choice between traditional marriage defined as a union between one man and one woman, civil unions for gay couples, or same-sex marriage, traditionalist evangelicals opt overwhelmingly for traditional marriage. Nine in ten rejected the idea of either civil unions or same-sex marriage. In contrast, almost six in ten modernist evangelicals preferred to see the law recognize either civil unions or same-sex marriage. The same stark divisions were evident among mainline Protestants and Catholics. Half of modernist Catholics, for instance, favored same-sex marriage and another 30 percent preferred civil unions. In contrast, only 11 percent of traditionalist Catholics were willing to allow gay marriage, and another 18 percent would sanction civil unions. The group that was, by far, the most supportive of same-sex marriage were atheists and agnostics, 72 percent of whom favored recognizing same-sex marriage. Another 21 percent of atheists and agnostics wished to see same-sex unions recognized, and only 7 percent insisted on the traditional definition of marriage.[42]

One should be careful, of course, not to exaggerate these differences. Even on divisive questions such as abortion, many Americans occupy positions that are far more open to compromise than the zealous rhetoric of the activists would lead us to think. Even among traditionalist evangelicals, for instance, only 32 percent say abortion should be illegal in all circumstances. Most traditionalist evangelicals, like most Americans, opt for a position on this contentious issue that lies between the extremes staked out by the activists.

Nonetheless, the ideological divisions that bolster partisan polarization and the increasing political salience of religious commitments cannot be ignored. The divisions between the parties cannot be passed over as trivial or puerile, and only a doctrinaire Marxist could dismiss religious divisions as unimportant. Certainly no self-respecting liberal can pass off as trivial the fact that 44 percent of the population of the United States believes that evolution is false, and that two-thirds of these skeptics think it is "definitely false." A division over scientific facts might not matter much if it did not manifest itself politically, but, as we have seen, these religious beliefs correspond closely with fundamental political and partisan differences. The Republican Party has become the ideological home of religious traditionalists, and this has helped drive the party's positions on social issues far from the positions taken not only by the more secularly oriented Democratic Party but also from the positions taken by governments in most advanced industrial societies.

AMERICAN EXCEPTIONALISM

When we cast our eyes abroad, we see that there is much about American public policy that fits the Hartzian thesis well. Consider, for instance, the fact that the United States continues to be the only advanced industrial society without universal national health care. In 1993, the Clinton administration unsuccessfully pushed health care reform, an episode that dramatically highlighted the Lockean limitations on American political discourse. Afraid that a single-payer system would be shot down, the administration pressed for a complex scheme that would have required employers to provide health insurance to their employees. Although Clinton's plan limited the federal government's direct involvement in providing health insurance, opting instead for competition between health maintenance organizations (HMOs), conservatives and insurance companies immediately battered the plan as big government run amok. By raising the familiar specter of socialized medicine, the plan's opponents were able to scare the public into abandoning their initial support for the plan. Not for the first time in the twentieth century, the Lockean ethos helped keep U.S. health policy exceptional.

But while a comparative lens, as Hartz stressed, is essential to bring into focus what is distinctive about the United States, much of that distinctiveness is not consistent with the Lockean thesis. Hartz leads us to expect a weaker or smaller state in the United States, and yet in a number of notable respects the American state is more intrusive, more coercive, and larger than European states. In at least two policy domains a comparative perspective yields results that are inconsistent with the Lockean thesis: (1) incarceration and capital punishment, and (2) gay marriage and gay rights. In neither of these areas does U.S. public policy reflect Lockean liberal commitments. Instead, compared to other advanced industrial nations, American public policy in these areas is more interventionist and less liberal in the classical Lockean sense of the term.

Prisons and Capital Punishment

No advanced industrial society imprisons more of its citizens than does the United States. In Japan, fewer than 6 out of every 10,000 people are in prison. In the Scandinavian countries, about 7 of every 10,000 people are behind bars. In Italy, France, and Germany, the incarceration rate is about 10 for every 10,000 people. England and Spain imprison more of their people, but still the rate is only about 14 per 10,000. Russia, a notoriously dangerous society, imprisons people at a much higher rate; almost 55 of every 10,000 people in Russia are in prison. But even that famously dysfunctional society lags behind the United States, where over 70 out of every 10,000 people are in prison. One-quarter of the world's prisoners are in the United States.[43]

Moreover, the reach of "the penal state" in the United States is not limited to those in prison. As Marie Gottschalk points out, "on any given day, nearly seven million people are under the supervision of the correctional system, including jail, prison, parole, probation, and other community supervision sanctions." That means that one out of every thirty-two adults is being directly supervised by the state. And, of course, millions more are employed by what Gottschalk calls the carceral state.[44]

These aggregate numbers, moreover, disguise massive differences among subpopulations in the United States. According to data from 1995, almost 700 of every 10,000 African American males are in prison, ten times the already very high national average and about seven times the rate for white males in the United States. An African American male in the United States is well over a hundred times more likely to be in jail than a person living in Japan or Norway, seventy times more likely than a resident of Italy or Germany, fifty times more likely than a person in England or Wales, and ninety times more likely than a white woman in the United States.[45]

It was not always this way. When *The Liberal Tradition* was published in 1955, the incarceration rate in the United States was roughly the same as the rates in western Europe today. Beginning in the 1970s, however, the prison population and prison construction in the United States began to skyrocket. In three decades, between 1973 and 2001, the U.S. prison population increased fivefold.[46]

Not only do Americans show a far greater willingness to allow the state to incarcerate their fellow citizens, but they also show a greater willingness to allow the state to execute offenders. In western Europe, where capital punishment is viewed in classically liberal terms as an issue of human rights, no individual has been executed by the state since the late 1970s. In virtually every European nation, capital punishment is forbidden by law. In contrast, in the United States capital punishment is legal in thirty-eight states as well as at the federal level. Between 1995 and 2008, nearly 900 people were executed in the United States, and thousands more were under sentence of death.[47]

Once again, at the time Hartz was writing *The Liberal Tradition*, the United States did not look all that exceptional. Capital punishment in the United States had declined markedly since the 1930s, as it had across the Western world. In 1935, there were about 200 executions in the United States, and by 1955 that number had dropped to 76. A decade later, in 1965, only 7 people were executed, and between 1968 and 1976 there were no executions at all in the United States. Although capital punishment had not been formally abolished, the postwar American polity seemed to be following much the same abolitionist trend as western Europe and Canada.[48]

Capital punishment, like incarceration rates, is not randomly distributed across the United States. Instead, it is concentrated overwhelmingly in those states that have voted Republican in the last several presidential elections, particularly the South. Ninety-five percent of the 1,057 executions that occurred between 1977 and 2006 took place in the thirty states that voted for George W. Bush in both 2000 and 2004. Most of the states that went Democratic in 2000 or 2004 had no executions at all during this period, whereas only a handful of Bush states (Kansas, North Dakota, South Dakota, Alaska, and West Virginia) could make the same claim. Roughly 80 percent of the nation's executions were in southern states, and the leader by far was the president's home state of Texas, which accounted for about 35 percent of the nation's executions. In 2006, 45 percent of the nation's executions occurred in Texas, and only one execution occurred in a blue state.[49]

Here then is a glaring anomaly in which the public policies of the United States run directly counter to the Hartzian thesis. Far from endorsing an antistatist position, Americans are at the extreme prostate pole. What Hartz's class-based lens obscures is the little matter of race. The face of crime and punishment in America is black. Blacks make up a little under 13 percent of the population, yet 40 percent of the people executed in 2007 were black, and 42 percent of the 3,200 people on death row in 2005 were black.[50] Public opinion polls consistently show a great divide between the views on capital punishment held by blacks and whites. A poll conducted in 2000, for instance, found that only 38 percent of blacks supported capital punishment, whereas nearly 70 percent of whites expressed support for capital punishment.[51] It is difficult to escape the conclusion that white Americans are more supportive of capital punishment and incarceration than people in other western nations in part because white Americans see the punishment being inflicted on people who do not look like them.[52]

Same-Sex Marriage and Sodomy

If the neglect of race leaves Hartz ill-prepared to deal with the distinctive U.S. penal policy, the neglect of religion leaves him ill-equipped to explain the distinctiveness of the nation's policies regarding homosexuality and re-production. Consider, for instance, same-sex marriage. Over the last decade or more, there has been an unmistakable move among most ad-vanced industrial nations toward the legal recognition of gay and lesbian re-lationships. Among the nations that have moved in this liberal direction are Sweden, Norway, Denmark, the Netherlands, Belgium, France, Germany, Austria, Switzerland, Spain, Portugal, the Czech Republic, Hungary, the United Kingdom, Canada, and New Zealand. In the United States, in con-trast, the federal government has passed the Defense of Marriage Act, and an overwhelming majority of states have passed similar measures that up-hold marriage as a union between a man and a woman.[53]

The United States has also been much slower to decriminalize consen-sual acts between gay people. At the time of the 2003 *Lawrence v. Texas* rul-ing that struck down sodomy laws, thirteen states still had sodomy statutes in effect, and these states were overwhelmingly concentrated in the South. In contrast, much of Europe had decriminalized homosexual rela-tions in the nineteenth century, and the laggard nations did so in the 1960s and 1970s.[54]

The United States has also been comparatively slow to pass laws banning discrimination based on sexual orientation. As of 2007, twenty states had banned discrimination based on sexual orientation. Only three of these (Nevada, Colorado, and Maryland) were states that voted for Bush in 2000 and 2004, and only three states (Delaware, Pennsylvania, and Michigan) that Kerry carried are not among the tolerant twenty. In contrast, in 2000 the European Union adopted the Charter of Fundamental Rights, which outlaws "discrimination on the grounds of sexual orientation and also guar-antees a right to marry and form a family."[55]

These policy differences between the United States and other advanced industrial societies are not simply a function of European elites' pursuing policies that are at odds with the views of their citizenries. Rather, the policy differences reflect the fact that Europeans seem less inclined to have the state regulate sexual behavior or discriminate against homosexuals. A 2004 Gallup poll, for instance, found that two-thirds of those in Great Britain and nearly the same number in Canada said they favored a law allowing homo-sexual couples to legally form civil unions that would provide some of the legal rights of married couples. In contrast, in the United States, under half supported the idea. Opinion in the United States was both more polarized and less liberal than opinion in Canada and the United Kingdom.[56]

Why does a liberal nation adopt and support policies relating to homosexuality and sexuality that are more illiberal than the policies adopted by most other advanced industrial nations? The short answer seems to reside with America's exceptionally high levels of religiosity. Religion is far more important to most Americans than it is to citizens in most other industrial nations. In 2003, for instance, Gallup found that 60 percent of Americans agreed that religion was "very important" in their lives, a response given by only 28 percent of Canadians and 17 percent of Brits. In Great Britain, 50 percent allowed that religion was not very important in their lives, whereas in the United States only 17 percent made the same admission. Americans did not just *say* religion was more important to them, they also went to church more. Forty-three percent of respondents said they had attended religious services in the past week, whereas only 17 percent of those in Great Britain reported having done the same.[57]

Of course, many Americans are just like their European counterparts. About 37 percent of Americans say that religion is not important in their political thinking. In particular, the religiosity of Democrats—African Americans excepted—looks quite a lot like the religiosity of most Europeans. What sets the United States apart is not liberal Democrats, most of whom are not any more religious than the average European, but conservative Republicans, for whom religion is politically important in a way that is unimaginable in most European nations. Those whom John Green describes as religious traditionalists are much more prone than religious modernists to report that their religious beliefs shape their political views. Eight in ten traditionalist evangelicals—a group that is overwhelmingly Republican—say religion is important in shaping their political thinking. In contrast, only 12 percent of modernist Catholics and 15 percent of modernist mainline Protestants say the same thing.[58]

Opposition to gay rights and same-sex marriage is, of course, not limited to the most religious and most fundamentalist Americans. But survey research emphatically demonstrates that opposition to gay marriage and gay rights is strongest among Green's religious traditionalists, and that the relationship holds whether one is looking at evangelical Protestants, mainline Protestants, or Catholics. The more religious and the more literalist or fundamentalist a person's religious views, the more likely that person will be to oppose same-sex marriage and the extension of legal protections for gay people. The language of liberalism and individual rights is undeniably a powerful discourse in the United States, but at least as potent are the justifications rooted in religious traditions, particularly those that rely on biblical literalism to guide thought and action.[59] Even when religious justifications are absent, the conservative language of "family values" is available for use, and it has proven itself more than a match for the liberal tradition in the United States.

CONCLUSION

From the vantage point of the early twenty-first century, then, five aspects of Hartz's thesis appear to be most in need of a corrective.

First, compared to Europe, the United States is not as uniformly antistatist as Hartz suggested. Indeed, in some areas the United States has built up a far more coercive and powerful state than exists in Europe. This is notably true in the area of crime and punishment. The United States has far more prisons, prisoners, and executions than anything one finds in Europe. The U.S. military-industrial complex is also far more powerful and more richly developed than is true of the defense establishments of other advanced industrial societies. As a percentage of GDP, the United States spends about four times what Canada, Ireland, Spain, and New Zealand spend on defense, and nearly twice what the United Kingdom, Australia, and France spend. Also on issues of sexuality and homosexuality, the United States has often sanctioned greater government involvement in the regulation of private lives than is tolerated in European nations.

Second, even those aspects of American public policy that are congruent with the Hartzian portrait appear to be driven at least as much by race as by class. The laggard welfare state, the absence of national health care, the hostility to taxes, and the support for private schools and privatized public services are all inextricably linked to race. Feudalism's absence may have been important in shaping America's distinctive public policy patterns, but so too is the presence of racial subordination and heterogeneity.

Third, American exceptionalism over the last quarter century seems to be driven less by a Lockean liberal consensus than by conservative Republicanism. Conservative Republicans push policy so far to the right that America does indeed often look decidedly different from its European cousins. If the United States pursued the policy agenda of the Democratic Party, however, on many issues the policies of Europe and America would converge. That convergence would be a result not so much of the leftward tilt of the Democratic Party but of the dimming in Europe of the socialist enthusiasms of the twentieth century. It is the Right and not the Left in the United States that makes the United States seem so unfamiliar and even unintelligible to so many Europeans.

Fourth, religion is far more important as a source of political ideology and public policies in contemporary America than Hartz allowed. This is not a matter of disembodied Puritan ghosts rattling around in the attic of the American mind. Rather, it is a recognition that today's social conservatives derive many of their political positions from deeply held religious beliefs and that a dense network of religiously steeped organizations, including the Moral Majority, Family Research Council, Focus on the Family, and Concerned Women for America, has succeeded in mobilizing religiously conservative Americans. Their biblically derived "Thou shalt nots" have, moreover, as James Morone points out, "pushed public power into private lives," thereby transgressing the Lockean liberal boundary separating public and private spheres.[60]

Fifth, understanding American exceptionalism requires placing the South at the very center of the analysis. Hartz's dismissal of the South as the freaky fun house of American political thought is among his most serious failings. The contemporary South is both less philosophically tortured and less liberal than Hartz was willing to allow. Remove the South, moreover, and the United States starts to look a lot more like Europe.[61] Without the South, for instance, capital punishment would probably have been abolished decades ago, or at least its incidence would be so infrequent as to constitute a de facto abolition. Absent the South, the religiosity of Americans no longer looks quite so exceptional, and certainly it looks a lot less fundamentalist. The South is no bizarre sideshow; instead, over the last several decades it has been the engine that has driven the nation's political culture rightward and sustained its exceptionalism.

NOTES

1. A partial exception is LBJ's memorable 1965 speech to Howard University, in which he declared that the administration sought "not just equality as a right and a theory but equality as a fact and equality as a result." Although Johnson insisted that "opportunity is essential, but not enough," he also explained his position in terms of the familiar American metaphor of guaranteeing an equal chance in the race of life. Freedom, Johnson explained, was insufficient because one cannot "take a person who, for years, has been hobbled by chains and liberate him, bring him up to the starting line of a race and then say, 'you are free to compete with all the others.'" Such a race was inherently unfair, the result predetermined by the start. Affirmative steps, the president intimated, were needed to ensure that "Negro Americans" had a fair chance to compete in the competitive race of American economic life. Although certainly a bold defense of governmental action, the speech was also clearly cast so as to underscore that such programs were consistent with the nation's long-standing liberal

ideals. President Lyndon B. Johnson's Commencement Address at Howard University: "To Fulfill These Rights," June 4, 1965, http://www.lbjlib.utexas.edu/johnson/archives.hom/speeches.hom/650604.asp.

2. According to a 2006 study, taxes in the United States, at all levels of government, equaled 25.6 percent of the gross domestic product (GDP). The tax burden in the other twenty-nine Organization for Economic Cooperation and Development (OECD) nations was around 34 percent, with Sweden the leader at 50.6 percent and Mexico the laggard at 19 percent. See Sonya Hoo and Eric Toder, "The U.S. Tax Burden Is Low Relative to Other OECD Countries," *Tax Notes*, May 8, 2006, 695, http://www.urban.org/url.cfm?ID=1000976 (accessed August 13, 2007). Although taxes are relatively low in the United States, Americans are more likely to complain that taxes are too high. See Graham K. Wilson, *Only in America? The Politics of the United States in Comparative Perspective* (Chatham, N.J.: Chatham House, 1998), 29.

3. The World Tourism Organization estimates that Americans take an average of thirteen days of vacation annually, which is well under half of what Europeans typically enjoy. Italians, for instance, average forty-two vacation days per year, and the French thirty-seven days. A recent survey of twenty-one advanced industrial nations found that the United States was the only country in which the government "does not require employers to provide paid leave." The European Union directs all member nations to provide at least four weeks of paid leave, and many European nations require more than that minimum. See TNR, "Getaway," *New Republic*, August 6, 2007, 3–4. The twenty-one-nation study is reported in Rebecca Ray and John Schmitt, "No-Vacation Nation," May 2007, Center for Economic and Policy Research, http://www.cepr.net/documents/publications/working_time_2007_05.pdf (accessed August 6, 2007).

4. Ichiro Kawachi, "Why the United States Is Not Number One in Health," in *Healthy, Wealthy, and Fair: Health Care and the Good Society*, ed. James A. Morone and Lawrence R. Jacobs (New York: Oxford University Press, 2005), 20.

5. See Richard J. Ellis, *American Political Cultures* (New York: Oxford University Press, 1993), 56–57; also see Ellis, *The Dark Side of the Left: Illiberal Egalitarianism in America* (Lawrence: University Press of Kansas, 1999).

6. Rebecca Klatch, *Women of the New Right* (Philadelphia: Temple University Press, 1987), 4–5. Also see Lisa McGirr, *Suburban Warriors: The Origins of the New American Right* (Princeton, N.J.: Princeton University Press, 2001); and Donald T. Critchlow, *Phyllis Schlafly and Grassroots Conservatism: A Woman's Crusade* (Princeton, N.J.: Princeton University Press, 2005), 8.

7. Klatch, *Women of the New Right*, 22; also McGirr, *Suburban Warriors*, 156.

8. Clyde Wilcox and Carin Larson, *Onward Christian Soldiers? The Religious Right in American Politics*, 3rd ed. (Boulder, Colo.: Westview Press, 2006), 48–49.

9. Klatch, *Women of the New Right*, 23, 122.

10. Wilcox and Larson, *Onward Christian Soldiers?* 59–60.

11. "Americans at Odds Over Gay Rights," May 31, 2006, Gallup poll, available at http://www.gallup.com/poll/23140/Americans-Odds-Over-Gay-Rights.aspx (accessed August 13, 2007).

12. See David E. Campbell and J. Quin Monson, "The Case of Bush's Reelection: Did Gay Marriage Do It?" in *A Matter of Faith: Religion in the 2004 Presidential Election,* ed. David Campbell (Washington, D.C.: Brookings Institution Press, 2007), 120–141. Also see Todd Donovan, Caroline Tolbert, Daniel A. Smith, and Janine Parry, "Did Gay Marriage Elect George W. Bush?" paper presented at the annual meeting of the Western Political Science Association, Oakland, California, March 17, 2005; and David E. Campbell and J. Quin Monson, "The Religion Card: Evangelicals, Catholics, and Gay Marriage in the 2004 Presidential Election," paper presented at the annual meeting of the American Political Science Association, Washington, D.C., September 1, 2005.

13. Klatch, *Women of the New Right,* 146; James A. Morone, *Hellfire Nation: The Politics of Sin in American History* (New Haven, Conn.: Yale University Press, 2003), 484. Or, as Jerry Falwell expressed the point: "God intends the husband to be the decision maker. Wives and children want to follow" (ibid.). This view is not limited to Republicans, of course. An African American woman in South Carolina, pondering whether to support Hillary Clinton or Barack Obama in 2008, told a *New York Times* reporter that she wasn't sure that a woman should be president. "A man is supposed to be the head," she explained. "I feel like the Lord has put man first, and I believe in the Bible." Katharine Q. Seelye, "Clinton-Obama Quandary for Many Black Women," *New York Times,* October 14, 2007.

14. Louis Hartz, *The Liberal Tradition in America* (New York: Harcourt Brace Jovanovich, 1955), 147, 169, 151, 177.

15. Hartz, *The Liberal Tradition in America,* 177, 173; also see 4.

16. See Carl N. Degler, *Neither Black nor White: Slavery and Race Relations in Brazil and the United States* (New York: Macmillan, 1971).

17. Hartz, *The Liberal Tradition in America,* 167–170; Hartz, *The Founding of New Societies: Studies in the History of the United States, Latin America, South Africa, and Australia* (New York: Harcourt, 1964), esp. 17–19, 55–56.

18. Hartz recognizes as much when he notes that ultimately "the Southerners could not remove the Negro from the human category." *The Liberal Tradition in America,* 170. In Hartz's view, southerners who affirmed the humanity of blacks were thereby forced into the untenable position of justifying slavery by assailing Locke and arguing that slavery was good for both blacks and whites. In the years leading up to the Civil War, however, only Fitzhugh advanced this position, and he, as C. Vann Woodward reminds us, "was not typical of anything." "George Fitzhugh, *Sui Generis,*" introduction to George Fitzhugh, *Cannibals All! Or Slaves without Masters,* ed. C. Vann Woodward (Cambridge, Mass.: Harvard University Press, 1960), x. It is worth recalling, too, that with the coming of the Civil War even Fitzhugh "became a convert to the theory of the innate inferiority of the Negro race." Ibid., xi; also see

Hartz, *The Liberal Tradition in America,* 171. Contrary to Hartz, then, southern whites seemed to have little difficulty reconciling their belief that blacks were human beings with their belief that blacks were inferior to whites. There is little evidence that white southerners were tortured souls. Rather, the overwhelming majority appear to have taken for granted a worldview that assigned blacks an inferior place in an ascriptive, stratified social order. Hierarchy based on race is still hierarchy.

19. Kevin M. Kruse, *White Flight: Atlanta and the Making of Modern Conservatism* (Princeton, N.J.: Princeton University Press, 2005), 24, 158; also see 121. Also see Jason Sokol, *There Goes My Everything: White Southerners in the Age of Civil Rights, 1945–1975* (New York: Knopf, 2006), 15.

20. This position is argued in Carol Horton, *Race and the Making of American Liberalism* (New York: Oxford University Press, 2005), chap. 8.

21. Kruse, *White Flight,* 263. Also see Joseph Crespino, *In Search of Another Country: Mississippi and the Conservative Counterrevolution* (Princeton, N.J.: Princeton University Press, 2007).

22. Gary C. Jacobson, *A Divider, Not a Uniter: George W. Bush and the American People* (New York: Pearson Longman, 2007), 4–9.

23. For evidence of the intense partisan polarization in the late nineteenth century, see David W. Brady and Hahrie C. Han, "Polarization Then and Now: A Historical Perspective," in *Red and Blue Nation? Characteristics and Causes of America's Polarized Politics,* ed. Pietro S. Nivola and David W. Brady (Washington, D.C.: Brookings Institution Press, 2006), 119–151.

24. James Davison Hunter, *Culture Wars: The Struggle to Define America* (New York: Basic Books, 1991).

25. Patrick Buchanan, 1992 Republican National Convention speech, August 17, 1992.

26. Hartz, *The Liberal Tradition in America,* 81.

27. Morris P. Fiorina and Matthew S. Levendusky, "Disconnected: The Political Class versus the People," in Nivola and Brady, eds., *Red and Blue Nation?* 51–52. Also see Morris Fiorina with Samuel J. Abrams and Jeremy C. Pope, *Culture War? The Myth of a Polarized America,* 2nd ed. (New York: Pearson Longman, 2007).

28. Alan Abramowitz, "Disconnected, or Joined at the Hip," in Nivola and Brady, eds., *Red and Blue Nation?* 72–85.

29. Dowd is quoted in Fiorina and Levendusky, "Disconnected," 51.

30. Ibid., 52–55.

31. The voting scorecards kept by special interest groups provide a useful measure of this growing elite polarization. The League of Conservation Voters (LCV), for instance, has kept an environmental scorecard since the early 1970s (see http://www.lcv.org/scorecard/). In 1980, the last year of Jimmy Carter's presidency, LCV gave House Democrats an average score of 54 out of 100, meaning that House Democrats sided with the LCV a little over half the time. House Republicans meanwhile averaged 37 out of 100, resulting in a relatively modest 17 percentage point difference between the parties. By 1992, the last year of George Herbert Walker

Bush's presidency, the House Republican average had declined to 17 percent and the Democratic score had inched up to 57, resulting in a 40 percentage point difference between the parties. By 2004, however, the average Democratic score had reached 85 and the average Republican score had sunk to 9, a whopping difference of 76 percentage points. The gap was even more marked among the House leadership, with Democratic leaders averaging 94 percent support and Republican leaders averaging just 4 percent. The story of increasing and sharp partisan polarization is the same no matter what interest group is keeping score, whether it is a liberal group like the American Civil Liberties Union or a conservative group like Focus on the Family. For evidence of the sharply increased polarization between 1980 and 2000 in the South, see David Lublin, *The Republican South: Democratization and Partisan Change* (Princeton, N.J.: Princeton University Press, 2004), 184, 188–89, 205–206. Lublin uses voting scorecards compiled by the Leadership Conference on Civil Rights, the AFL-CIO's Committee on Political Education League, and the National Abortion Rights Action League. Two good recent studies of elite polarization are Barbara Sinclair, *Party Wars: Polarization and the Politics of National Policy Making* (Norman: University of Oklahoma Press, 2006); and Nolan McCarty, Keith Y. Poole, and Howard Rosenthal, *Polarized America: The Dance of Ideology and Unequal Riches* (Cambridge, Mass.: MIT Press, 2006).

32. Unfortunate, among other reasons, because the metaphor of war carries with it the normative implication that the conflict should (hopefully) come to an end at some point and that society can then resume more normal, peaceful relations. But if, as James Hunter has suggested, "culture is, by its very nature, contested," and if part of the purpose of liberal democracy is to enable us "to find a way to live together" in spite of our deep differences, then there is no reason to expect or even hope for an end to the culture wars. James Davison Hunter, "The Enduring Culture War," in *Is There a Culture War? A Dialogue on Values and American Public Life*, ed. E. J. Dionne Jr. and Michael Cromartie (Washington, D.C.: Brookings Institution Press, 2006), 34, 36. Cultural conflict within societies is normal, and the value of liberal democracy is that it enables us to accommodate those differences without anything approaching real war.

33. Alexis de Tocqueville, *Democracy in America,* trans. Arthur Goldhammer (New York: Library of America, 2004), 201–202; part 2, chap. 2, "Parties in the United States."

34. John Gerring, *Party Ideologies in America, 1828–1996* (New York: Cambridge University Press, 1998), 53. The study cited by Gerring is Hans-Dieter Klingemann, Richard I. Hofferbert, and Ian Budge, *Parties, Policies, and Democracy* (Boulder, Colo.: Westview Press, 1994).

35. Gerring, *Party Ideologies in America,* 42, 39.

36. John C. Green and John S. Jackson, "Faithful Divides: Party Elites and Religion," in Campbell, *A Matter of Faith,* 42. Only 3 percent of Democratic delegates were white evangelical Protestants who attended church at least once a week, whereas nearly one-quarter of Republican delegates fit this description (44).

Among the general public, about 5 percent of Democrats and 21 percent of Republicans are white evangelicals who attend church at least once a week (50).

37. Green and Jackson, "Faithful Divides," 46. Three-quarters of Republican delegates described themselves as conservative or very conservative, whereas only about 50 percent of Democratic delegates described themselves as liberal or very liberal. Republicans were more likely to call themselves very conservative (22 percent) than Democrats were to call themselves very liberal (13 percent).

38. E. J. Dionne Jr., "Polarized by God? American Politics and the Religious Divide," in Nivola and Brady, eds., *Red and Blue Nation?* 183, 185, 188.

39. Dionne, "Polarized by God?" 201–203. Gary C. Jacobson, "Comment," in Nivola and Brady, *Red and Blue Nation?* 94–95. Also see John C. Green, "The American Religious Landscape and Political Attitudes: A Baseline for 2004," http://pew forum.org/publications/surveys/green-full.pdf (accessed August 13, 2007).

40. Green, "The American Religious Landscape and Political Attitudes," 39.

41. Barbara Norrander and Jan Norrander, "Stem Cell Research," in Campbell, *A Matter of Faith*, 151.

42. Green, "The American Religious Landscape and Political Attitudes," 45.

43. Marie Gottschalk, *The Prison and the Gallows: The Politics of Mass Incarceration in America* (New York: Cambridge University Press, 2006), 1–3.

44. Ibid., 1–2.

45. Ibid., 3.

46. Ibid., 1.

47. Bureau of Justice statistics, "Number of Persons Executed in the United States, 1930–2008, from Capital Punishment, 2007—Statistical Tables, December 2008, NCJ 224528, available at http://www.ojp.usdoj.gov/bjs/glance/tables/exe tab.htm (accessed October 28, 2009).

48. Gottschalk, *The Prison and the Gallows*, 202.

49. Of the nineteen states Gore carried, Kerry lost two (Iowa and New Mexico). Kerry also carried one state that Gore did not: New Hampshire. Of the states that were carried by Gore or Kerry, only three had more than four executions over the thirty-year span. Delaware led the way with fourteen, followed by California at thirteen and Illinois at twelve.

50. Bureau of Justice "Capital Punishment Statistics," available at http://www .ojp.usdoj.gov/bjs/cp.htm (accessed July 28, 2007).

51. Gottschalk, *The Prison and the Gallows*, 349n20.

52. Race, too, arguably plays a crucial role in explaining policy outcomes that seem more congruent with the Hartzian thesis, such as the status of the United States as a welfare state laggard. In the minds of many white Americans, the color of welfare is as black as the color of crime. The main difference is sex. In the minds of many whites, welfare is associated with black women, the "welfare queen" and her illegitimate children, whereas crime is associated with menacing young black males. The welfare state may be smaller in the United States not simply because Americans

distrust the federal government but because they don't want their tax dollars going to support African Americans. See the empirical evidence presented in Christopher Howard, *The Welfare State Nobody Knows: Debunking Myths about U.S. Social Policy* (Princeton, N.J.: Princeton University Press, 2007), chap. 9, "Race Still Matters." Also see Jill Quadagno, *The Color of Welfare: How Racism Undermined the War on Poverty* (New York: Oxford University Press, 1996); and Martin Gilens, *Why Americans Hate Welfare: Race, Media, and the Politics of Antipoverty Policy* (Chicago: University of Chicago Press, 2000).

53. Barry Adam, "The Defense of Marriage Act and American Exceptionalism: The 'Gay Marriage' Panic in the United States," *Journal of the History of Sexuality* 12 (2003): 259–276.

54. Ibid., 261. Also see "The Right to Privacy in the U.S. pre–*Lawrence v. Texas*" (as of June 25, 2003), http://thetaskforce.org/downloads/reports/issue_maps /sodomymap0603.pdf (accessed August 7, 2007).

55. Adam, "The Defense of Marriage Act and American Exceptionalism," 261; State Nondiscrimination Laws in the U.S. (as of July 2, 2007), available at http://www .thetaskforce.org/downloads/reports/issue_maps/non_discrimina-tion_7_09_color.pdf(accessed August 7, 2007).

56. Josephine Mazzuca, "Gay Rights: U.S. More Conservative Than Britain, Canada," Gallup Poll, October 12, 2004, http://www.gallup.com/poll/13561/gay-rights-us-more-conservative-than-britain-canada.aspx (accessed August 7, 2007). The U.S. poll was taken in May 2004, and the polls in Canada and Great Britain were conducted in September 2004.

57. Julie Ray, "Worlds Apart: Religion in Canada, Britain, U.S.," Gallup Poll, August 12, 2003, http://www.gallup.com/poll/9016/worlds-apart-religion-canada-britain-us.aspx (accessed August 7, 2007).

58. Green, "The American Religious Landscape and Political Attitudes," 15, table 6.

59. Ibid., 45.

60. Morone, *Hellfire Nation,* 24. Of course, as Morone also stresses, religion has powerfully shaped political attitudes and movements on the left as well. There is no better example of this than Martin Luther King Jr. and the civil rights movement. However, there can be little doubt that over the past quarter century of American politics, the morally charged religious commitments of the Right have played a far more politically central role than the religious commitments of the Left. Indeed Morone's historical study of the politics of sin is also a normative plea that the Left rediscover its own moral and religious vision and initiate "a revival from the other side of the Puritan legacy," the Social Gospel side "committed to social justice" and "communal responsibility" (496–497).

61. As Gottschalk points out, the South was also a powerful brake on the development of federal criminal justice institutions. "Federal law enforcement," Gottschalk shows, expanded only after "the South reached détente with the rest of the

country over the racial divide in the postwar decades." Gottschalk, *The Prison and the Gallows,* 75. Anxieties about and restrictions on federal power, in other words, owed at least as much to the South's desire to preserve a way of life built on racial subordination as it did to the power of the Lockean creed. The doctrine of states' rights employed a liberal antistatist vocabulary, but generally in the service of insulating and shoring up hierarchical social relations.

CHAPTER 8

The Case against Arrested Development: Hartz's Liberal Tradition in America Revisited

Carol Nackenoff

Now in print for more than half a century, Louis Hartz's *Liberal Tradition in America* has surely earned a place among the handful of classics in the field of American politics. Hartz's claim about the constraints within which political discourse takes place in the United States remains influential, regardless of the important critiques the thesis has sustained over the years. What is the value of Hartz's "liberal tradition" to twenty-first-century scholars seeking to understand political developments in the contemporary era as well as in the past? I argue that whatever use we can make of Hartz's construct must take into account the historically specific baggage it carries. This baggage poses serious limits to its utility for current and future researchers into domestic politics, law, and policy. My particular concern in this essay will be an attempt to discover, once we determine what can no longer serve well, what remains useful or provocative about the *Liberal Tradition* for students of law, courts, and American political development.

Alexis de Tocqueville reported that, in antebellum America, "there is hardly a political question in the United States which does not sooner or later turn into a judicial one."[1] This tendency is surely more pronounced in the early twenty-first century than it was when Tocqueville wrote. Since struggles over principles, values, and constitutional meaning frequently take place in American courts, it is highly appropriate to examine the place of courts—especially the Supreme Court—in "the liberal tradition." To do so, we need to consider Hartz's contribution to studying the role of law and courts in American political development, and we must also ask how meaningful it is to pose the "liberal tradition" as the context within which constitutional deliberation takes place in the United States.

While a brief review of Hartz's central contentions would seem to point us to certain observable patterns in contemporary constitutional law, the explanation offered for some of these patterns, and especially their assumed imperviousness to change, may prove unsatisfactory. Before we can go much further in thinking about how helpful Hartz is when thinking about American legal traditions, however, we must locate *The Liberal Tradition* in some of its historical and intellectual heritage. Understanding some of the time-bounded elements of the Hartzian thesis can help us recognize what can probably *not* be retained for twenty-first-century political scientists who continue to mine Hartz for insights. We will then be in a somewhat better position to consider how much purchase *The Liberal Tradition* offers us when thinking about the law. We can learn even more about how well Hartz speaks to current scholarship on law, courts, and political development in the United States by drawing on recent developments in law and American political development scholarship to engage Hartz in conversation.

HARTZ AND THE BOUNDARIES OF
AMERICAN POLITICAL DISCOURSE

The core of the liberal tradition entails fear of state power to the point of irrational limitation on governmental power. This fear exists in conjunction with blindness to the exercise of power by nonstate actors that exercise social and economic power. It includes irrational fear of the mob—the propertyless—who might combine and ruin things for the minority, the men of substance who have property. It includes legitimation of unequal material outcomes through the belief that, by playing by the rules of the capitalist game, all can aspire to prosper. The rules include self-help and individualism.

Hartz described the liberal tradition as one of Lockean, atomistic individualism, as Locke was wedded to the Horatio Alger dream of success around 1840.[2] He argued that the American democrat, a peasant-proletarian hybrid, was hoodwinked by the Whig-Hamiltonian-capitalists. Seduced by the materialist dream of equality of opportunity, the American democrat accepted the rules of the game as the Whigs themselves won the economic race. The Whigs had managed to "throw a set of chains around" the American democrat, selling a bill of goods that became an ideological straightjacket. American political thought became fixed in time and intellectually impoverished.[3]

As a result, American politics was inoculated against any serious threat of the cross-Atlantic migration of socialism. In Hartz's America, politics was marked by consensus; truths were self-evident, beyond examination.

What made all this possible was that America lacked a feudal past. Absent the feudal and clerical institutions of the Old World, there was no genuine aristocracy against which an emerging bourgeoisie could react or against which they could constitute a bourgeois class identity. It necessarily followed for Hartz, since he was influenced by the premise of historical materialists, that ideas were the product of relations among social classes, that the peasant-proletariat never developed its own working-class consciousness as the industrial system matured, even if the objective circumstances were akin to those of European working-class counterparts. Having failed to turn to socialism during this key moment, American workers and radicals missed the boat when it left the dock and were subsequently immune to such appeals.

In this narrative, Hartz accorded a special place to "judicial aristocracy" in the successful Whig ensnarement of the American democrat. Hamiltonian yearning for aristocracy was fulfilled, if imperfectly, by the power of fundamental law, which served as a substitute for Europe's "ecclesiastical and civil establishments, venerable from their antiquity."[4]

Locke, then, was the conservative principle in America. That is what Americans conserved and thus became "exceptional" in their immunity to class conflict and what that produced in Europe. Americans, classed though they were, thought they were atomistic individuals.

RECOGNIZING HARTZ IN AMERICAN LAW

When we turn to the law, some of Hartz's characterizations of the liberal tradition seem to ring true, even when they are not especially original. Hartz notes distinctive urges to protect private property, a particular celebration of atomistic social freedom, and determination to limit the power of the federal government. By looking briefly at each of the three aforementioned dimensions of constitutional adjudication—protection of private property, celebration of individual autonomy, and fear of the power of the federal government—we can see that these observations appear sound. Hartz can describe certain patterns that we find at law.

Hartz recognized what many others have also: the centrality of property and the opportunity to acquire it to the U.S. Constitution we framed. Scholars from Charles Beard and Merrill Jensen to Bertell Ollman have argued that the Constitution represents the triumph of economic elites, or propertied elements, over the masses, and Michael Harrington once wrote that "some of the *Federalist Papers* seem to have been written by a Marx of the master class."[5] In Harrington's view, the framers either brilliantly or inadvertently devised a system that would keep the future working class from attaining political power, protect wealth against assault, and limit the kinds of demands that geographically dispersed interests could effectively press onto the political agenda. In all these views, structure limited political prospects—at least for the have-nots. For Hartz, those have-nots did not even think the thoughts or dream the dreams of European working classes.

How core, and therefore sacrosanct, a value property is has become a highly salient question in recent years. In part inspired by natural law proponents who claim that property was one of the values the Constitution was designed to protect and that it was among the fundamental rights existing prior to the Constitution, the U.S. Supreme Court has, in recent decades, ratcheted up the level of protection accorded private property in regulatory takings cases. In lieu of the rational basis scrutiny to which legislation regulating the uses of private property (such as zoning regulation) has been generally subjected, the Rehnquist Court began to demand greater justification for regulation and demand compensation for a wider range of governmental interferences with property use. It is unclear at present, for instance, whether investment-backed expectations require compensation, whether partial restrictions on property use under the Endangered Species Act are compensable takings, and whether states (or the federal government) can act on new scientific information to regulate future uses of private property without running afoul of the Fifth Amendment takings clause. Moreover, the Court's doctrine of standing privileges injuries that can be expressed as discrete (individual) economic losses over injuries that are widely shared, more attenuated, or of a noneconomic sort (for example, some environmental harms).

Hartz's analysis may also help us understand why disparate outcomes based in wealth do not generally trigger strict scrutiny in constitutional law. For example, unequal access to educational resources absent a specific racial (or possibly ethnic) bias has not generally been considered a Fourteenth Amendment equal protection problem. As Justice Lewis Powell wrote for the majority in *San Antonio Independent School District v. Rodriguez,* "the class of disadvantaged 'poor' cannot be identified or defined in customary equal protection terms."[6] Relative deprivation, as opposed to "an absolute deprivation of the desired benefit,"[7] especially when the benefit is not regarded as a fundamental right, does not warrant the highest level (strict) of judicial scrutiny. "At least where wealth is involved, the Equal Protection Clause does not require absolute equality or precise equality of advantages."[8] This is because "a large, diverse, and amorphous class" such as the poor is not a traditional suspect class:

> The system of alleged discrimination and the class it defines have none of the traditional indicia of suspectness: the class is not saddled with such disabilities, or subjected to such a history of purposeful unequal treatment, or relegated to such a position of political powerlessness as to command extraordinary protection from the majoritarian political process.[9]

For Hartz, Americans believed they were all of the same estate.[10] Class was, and became with the Alger myth, even more alien to the American democrat's way of thinking.

Likewise, the Court refused to treat poverty as a constitutional concern when states that participate in the Medicaid program, or when the federal government itself, chose not to fund therapeutic or nontherapeutic abortions. The liberty interest protected in *Roe v. Wade* (1973) was not considered diminished, even though when a law "impinges upon a fundamental right explicitly or implicitly secured by the Constitution [it] is presumptively unconstitutional."[11] Quoting Justice Powell's majority opinion in *Maher v. Roe* (1977), Justice Potter Stewart wrote:

> An indigent woman who desires an abortion suffers no disadvantage as a consequence of Connecticut's decision to fund childbirth; she continues as before to be dependent on private sources for the service she desires. The State may have made childbirth a more attractive alternative, thereby influencing the woman's decision, but it has imposed no restriction on access to abortions that was not already there. The indigency that may make it difficult—and in some cases, perhaps, impossible—for some women to have abortions is neither created nor in any way affected by the Connecticut regulation.[12]

The Court's understanding of the woman's liberty interest is that she has the right to be left alone—not that the state (or the federal government) has any affirmative obligation to help her secure access to that service she seeks. Privacy is respected because liberty is most often understood as the absence of state compulsion or interference with a private choice.[13]

Indeed, these particular abortion cases may mark some of the earliest articulations of the newly emerging government speech doctrine, embodying

the idea that government has wide latitude in choosing how to spend limited public funds. When speaking with its money, government is expressing
preferences entitled to a great deal of deference.[14] What we can certainly
see, however, is that Court majorities have generally seen liberty as freedom
from government dictates. The Court is quite reluctant to impose financial
obligations on the federal government when providing access to nonfunda-
mental services or benefits. Poverty erects no government-imposed barrier
to the enjoyment of an opportunity or right.

Writing at a time when income disparities were far less pronounced
than they were to become by the late twentieth century, Hartz might have
marveled even more at the hoodwinking he believed the Hamiltonian-
Whig-capitalists have accomplished. There is ample evidence that economic gains of the last several decades have gone disproportionately to
those in the top tier in income distribution. A recent study indicates that
major pillars of economic security for Americans—including job stability
and public and private benefits that workers have expected to access
(health care, retirement benefits)—are dangerously eroding.[15] Attitude
surveys suggest it would be difficult to claim that there exists a prevailing
sentiment that rewards are shared or that we are all of one estate, or to
claim that respondents believe their children will be better off than they
are. This is hardly a vindication for the American dream. Even if there is
less upward mobility and greater economic disparity than at the time the
Horatio Alger stories gained popularity, few members of the Supreme
Court have been willing to consider poverty and its disadvantages constitu-
tionally problematic.

The treatment of wealth and poverty is also a constitutional reflection of
Hartz's atomistic individualism. The Court works best at the behest of individuals, not groups. For conservatives such as Antonin Scalia, injuries that
set someone apart from other citizens, particularized and not generalized
grievances, are those most appropriately brought before the Court. Most
groups and certainly majorities should take their policy complaints to the
legislature.[16] In classic complaints where the individual is pitted against the
majority, the Court has the strongest charge to intervene.

The notion that groups or classes of citizens may have rights tends to be
alien to American constitutional law. Even though Justice Felix Frankfurter,
writing for the Court in 1952, sustained a state criminal group libel law that
targeted any publication that "portrays depravity, criminality, unchastity, or
lack of virtue of a class of citizens, of any race, color, creed or religion . . .
[or which] exposes the citizens of any race, color, creed or religion to contempt, derision, or obloquy or which is productive of breach of the peace or

riots," that law, *Beauharnais v. Illinois,* has never served as a precedent in another such decision.[17] As Scalia wrote in *Adarand Constructors, Inc. v. Pena,* "Individuals who have been wronged by unlawful racial discrimination should be made whole; but under our Constitution there can be no such thing as either a creditor or a debtor race. That concept is alien to the Constitution's focus upon the individuals. . . . In the eyes of government, we are just one race here."[18] Moments during which group rights or interests are acknowledged have been fleeting.

Fear of state power, a legacy of our quarrel with the British Empire and of the founding era for Hartz, also helps explain why the American state has few acknowledged affirmative constitutional obligations. To say that a person has a right does not entail correlative obligations beyond the removal of barriers placed there by the state. In the case of abortion, the right is to seek, not even to find, providers, unless providers are willing to offer their services. For Hartz, a more activist and positive state, as in the New Deal, was pragmatic and experimental and not adequately theorized.[19]

Reaction to the New Deal beginning in the late 1970s included movements aimed at rolling back some of the power of the federal government vis-à-vis the states (and the citizens thereof). Interpretations of the Tenth, Eleventh, and Fourteenth amendments and of the commerce clause (Article I, §8) were all marshaled to this purpose. The doctrine of state sovereign immunity, holding that states were, in effect, mini sovereigns who yielded specific powers to the newly established federal government, retaining all others, affected the capacity of citizens to sue states in federal court for failure to enforce federal law.[20] Reviving controversies that dated to the founding era, Supreme Court justices used the same case law, the records of the Constitutional Convention of 1787, and often the same *Federalist Papers* to reach different conclusions about the proper relationship between the federal government and the states.[21] What were the default rules for reading constitutional silences? While it is too early to tell the full consequences of the decisions in *United States v. Lopez* and *United States v. Morrison,* it seems that the Court may be prepared to rein in federal commerce clause regulations that lack discernible economic effects.[22]

Hartz would not likely be surprised if he were to observe the reaction against some of the New Deal legacies and the rolling back of some of the federal government's reach. Hartz wrote of "the experimental mood of Roosevelt, in which Locke goes underground while 'problems' are solved often in a non-Lockian way."[23] So Locke has simply resurfaced—predictably.

And so we can identify certain patterns at law that point toward Hartz's characterization of American politics and political discourse. But are the tendencies we see clearly foreordained by the document through which a Whig-Hamiltonian "judicial aristocracy" has supposedly been enshrined? And is Hartz's explanation for such tendencies adequate? For instance, a number of states have found unequal school funding to violate equal protection clauses in state constitutions, especially where education is specifically mentioned as a right or a fundamental right in those constitutions.[24] While some of these state provisions postdate the Constitution, there is clearly room in American political thought for those who have diverse thoughts on the relationship between education, fundamental rights, and equality. Values have varied with both time and location. Even the Texas District Court found, in *Rodriguez*, that wealth was a suspect classification. So thinking outside the box happens. Are the outcomes of such disagreements foreordained by a liberal tradition? Is the best way to think about such divergent holdings that they are simply a few accidentals in an otherwise pervasively Lockean melody?

THE LIBERAL TRADITION AND ITS HISTORICAL MOMENT

The Liberal Tradition was and remains the product of a particular historical moment. While a number of scholars have joined Hartz in arguing that there are peculiar patterns in the American political experience, it is *The Liberal Tradition in America* that is most closely associated with the notion of American exceptionalism.[25] American exceptionalism as a concept seemed to be particularly well suited to the Cold War era. As the McCarthy era ended but the Cold War burned hot, communism and liberalism were seen as engaged in a pitched battle for the hearts and minds of peoples around the world, and nations allied (or were expected to ally) themselves with one of the two superpowers. At the time Hartz wrote, the meaning of America was forged in opposition to the Soviet Union. In a polarized world, where socialism and communism continued to be seductive, America posed itself as a bulwark against such seduction. The stark polarity between New World and Old provides less purchase in the post-Soviet era.

Hartz wrote during a period in which scholars were attracted to the idea of a single national "character." What united a people was stronger than political bonds, and character had explanatory power in politics. National character and political culture bound a people together, although there could still be sharp disagreements, especially those based on social class, as well as scapegoating on religious or ethnic grounds. In America, the idea of national character was joined to the notion of shared values and the belief that nearly everyone understood words to mean the same thing. There was ostensibly a universe of discourse in which everyone that mattered participated.

Hartz's vision suggested that citizens, who have ostensible interests inherent in their social class, suffered from that disease of his era: "false consciousness." Thus, classes that failed to perform their world-historical roles failed to understand their interests; they had been manipulated or co-opted. Thus, the American peasant-proletariat misunderstood itself and had been sold a bill of goods. And within a few years of *The Liberal Tradition*, sociologist Daniel Bell would proclaim *The End of Ideology*, writing *On the Exhaustion of Political Ideas in the Fifties*. The big "isms" of the past were dead—and perhaps we are, indeed, living in a post-big-ideas world.[26]

At the time of *The Liberal Tradition in America*, there were few extreme liberals or conservatives in Congress. Liberal Democrats and many Republicans accepted the need for new civil rights legislation, and bipartisan support helped pass some social welfare legislation. Parties were perceived as chasing the median voter, offering few substantial choices to the public. John Gerring, who has studied party ideologies in the United States, refers to this period as the "universalist epoch." Party rhetoric was inclusionary beginning in the 1940s and 1950s. By the time of Adlai Stevenson's campaigns, Democrats had stopped attacking their opponents and had stopped distinguishing themselves as "liberals." In fact, even shortly after Franklin Delano Roosevelt's first election, when "liberalism" was used in Democratic campaigns, it was usually used as part of the trilogy including communism and socialism, thus being invoked as an American, rather than a partisan, philosophy.[27] Gerring argues that a universalist postwar Democratic Party delivered a message with "intertwined concepts of consensus, tolerance, compromise, pragmatism, and mutual understanding."[28] This sounds highly consistent with Hartz's liberal tradition. But we do not live in such times now.

It was also an era in which literary texts had discoverable meaning. Many believed this to be true of jointly authored texts, to wit, the Constitution. Although *Brown v. Board of Education* had been decided in May 1954, Hartz did not acknowledge this controversial decision or the reaction it provoked as having any relevance to his vision of basic moral unanimity. A few years later, Herbert Wechsler, troubled by the Court's reasoning in *Brown*, penned an essay that would have a major impact on a generation of legal scholars. Suggesting that *the* meaning of the Constitution was undiscoverable but that there were various principles found therein, Wechsler argued that principled judges must decide which principles were paramount for them and set out to follow wherever those principles led.[29] Judicial restraint was accomplished when justices consistently adhered to these principles, and this neutrality concerning outcomes was the closest to apolitical that constitutional adjudication could get.

All America was John Locke, not Edmund Burke, Hartz contended. The ocean provided a buffer, so that America could pursue its own path of development. In an era before the Internet became available to billions, before diseases could be transported across the earth quickly by mass air travel, before satellite images brought instant new access, before capitalism exported fast food and popular culture around the globe, and before terrorists could fly airplanes into the World Trade Center, that watery buffer may have had greater meaning. Even if America pursued a different path of development from Europe in the past, its capacity to withdraw from the world has become impossible. Whether America could learn how to converse with the world in new ways remained, in ways that Hartz sensed, problematic.[30] The international communication and translation difficulties Hartz identifies may remain among his most important insights about American politics, but it is beyond the scope of this chapter.

What we see is that a number of conditions that made Hartz's vision of America possible have changed. The end of the Cold War surely changed the character of many disagreements with the rest of the world, and Hartz was particularly tone deaf when it came to conflict inspired by religious worldviews, both at home and abroad. Most importantly for our purposes, a vision that minimizes the impact and import of change and of disagreement at home must be revisited and reconsidered. Indeed, we need ways to think about change that Hartz cannot provide.

CHANGE AND AMERICAN POLITICAL DEVELOPMENT

Hartz would have enjoyed hearing some good political arguments. Instead, he claimed to hear small variations on a theme. Hartz understood that new ideas had to have strong, indigenous roots if they were going to be able to grow. He concluded that America was extremely unlikely to become more self-aware or grow new ideas.

Hartz's thesis is that American politics is remarkable for what doesn't happen. The pattern is one of repeated refrains, much ado about nothing (hysteria, especially concerning the Left), and predictable outcomes.[31] The boundary conditions within which disagreements over values and meaning take place were fixed in the past, and as a result, truths became self-evident.

For Hartz, there are limits to intellectual growth and presumptions against significant change in America. Political thought and politics in America are mired in the past.

It is important to underscore here how Hartz understood change, or significant departures in politics. Hartz's America was defined by the fact that we don't experience social revolutions and overthrow the government; all other change paled by comparison. The upheavals other nations have experienced have, in his view, largely passed America by. Struggles in American politics are treated as having relatively low stakes, decidedly not life-and-death ones. Conflicts, including the Civil War, were considered minor by comparison to those wrenching Europe and the rest of the world. This surely leaves Hartz vulnerable. The Civil War and bloody industrial struggles in the Gilded Age have always posed challenges to Hartz's consensus view. And as Sean Wilentz noted a few years ago, "The great weakness of Hartz's approach was that, as a unified field theory of American political thought, it turned politics in a modern liberal polity into fake battles fought with wooden swords."[32]

In one regard, the mention of Hartz in connection with the burgeoning scholarship on "American political development" seems almost nonsensical. As Karen Orren and Stephen Skowronek observe, "Hartz's analysis went far toward rendering the whole idea of American political development an oxymoron."[33] American political development as a field begins with a premise that appears to violate Hartz's central contention. American political development scholars and historical institutionalists "*take time seriously,*"[34] while Hartz tells a story of arrested development.

New efforts are afoot to reconceptualize the dynamics of political change in America as institutions have returned to the foreground in the study of politics.[35] Historical institutionalist scholarship and political development scholarship insist that conflict drives political development. This is true for the Court as well. Conflict must be taken seriously, and consensus demeans conflict. Conflicts between institutions and policies have become focal points, although conflicts between groups and classes remain important. Instead of positing an integrated political system, scholars accept the idea that "relations among political institutions are (at least) as likely to be in tension as in fit and the tension generated is an important source of political conflict and change."[36] Conflicts over rules, norms, and terms of control among different institutions developing in different measures of political time generate opportunities for creative change by actors who can exploit tensions and contradictions in institutional development. If the political universe "is inherently open, dynamic, and contested" and if "existing norms and collective projects, of varying degrees of permanence, are buffeted against one another as a normal condition," then for students of American political development, America cannot be *presumed* to be mired in an ever-recurring drama.[37]

Many scholars are fascinated by the patterning of American politics and with discovering key moments and turning points. The lesson from *The Liberal Tradition* is about inevitability and determinism. Path dependence, an idea that has great currency in historical institutionalist approaches to American politics and political development, is likewise about discerning patterns. As Paul Pierson and Theda Skocpol write, "Outcomes at a critical juncture trigger feedback mechanisms that reinforce the recurrence of a particular pattern into the future," and such processes "can be highly influenced by relatively modest perturbations at early stages."[38] Fateful patterns can be established as a result of changes that may not appear dramatic at the time of their occurrence. "Once actors have ventured far down a particular path, however, they are likely to find it very difficult to reverse course. Political alternatives that were once quite plausible may become irretrievably lost."[39] If "self-reinforcing processes are prevalent in political life," including ways of thinking about the political realm, then formative moments and turning points are vital to the study of politics.[40]

Path dependence, then, is a way of thinking not only about change but also about certain missing changes. Scholars of historical institutionalism and American political development insist that even inertia as a pattern is vulnerable.[41] There is plenty of room to investigate roads not taken. Is it possible that Hartz could be, like Molière's Monsieur Jourdain in *Le Bourgeois Gentilhomme*, a man who simply did not realize he was speaking prose, and morph into an important presence in the scholarship on path dependence? This seems rather unlikely.

Hartz asked provocative questions about the absence of change, but *The Liberal Tradition* neither investigated nor saw institutional or—at least since the 1840s—ideational vulnerabilities. For him, political thought had become unhinged from any kind of institutional dynamic, so there was no need to investigate a dynamic by which words and deeds could reconstitute each other. Hartz's assertion that there were boundary conditions beyond which American politics would not wander may blind scholars to battles that have significant transformative potential. His thesis allowed for too little contingency, foreclosing the outcome of too many conflicts. The questions posed by *The Liberal Tradition* can drive scholarship but do not constitute it.

POLITICAL DEVELOPMENT AND THE COURT

This conclusion is also borne out upon examination of the Court, where Hartz could point to recurring themes and patterns. Indeed, we can grant that legal discourse from the bench has been relatively constrained. However, Hartz is ultimately just a starting point for considering the Court's place in maintaining an ostensibly "liberal tradition" in American politics and political discourse.

In 1941, Robert H. Jackson wrote that "never in its entire history can the Supreme Court be said to have for a single hour been representative of anything except the relatively conservative forces of its day." In the several years prior to his appointment to the Court, Jackson had served successively as solicitor general and attorney general of the United States; his remark was made in the context of Roosevelt's struggle with the Court and against what Jackson saw as "the usurpation, the unwarranted interferences with lawful governmental activities, and the tortured construction of the Constitution" by the conservatives.[42] Jackson thought that the Court was deployed against change. Hartz was sympathetic to Jackson's posture, and it is not surprising that he took note of Jackson. Hartz claimed that Jackson, as solicitor general, had "skirted with the truth without knowing it" when he said that "struggles over power that in Europe call out regiments of troops, in America call out battalions of lawyers." Battles were waged with lawyers, Hartz claimed, because of "an ethical settlement which [the Court's] adjudicative function symbolized."[43]

The notion that we inhabit a bounded liberal tradition posits that Americans (other than fringe elements) participate in a universe of shared discourse even if we speak in slightly different dialects. We understand each other when we speak about constitutional values, even if our perspectives diverge somewhat. For Hartz, discordant notes die out rather quickly, leaving no traces. But to revisit Stanley Fish's question, is it so obvious that there is *a* text in this class?[44] If American law strikes a particular balance between the value of free speech and equal protection—values Herbert Wechsler's principled justices would find in the Constitution—is it the case that those who see matters differently (for example, in the matter of hate speech) nonetheless abide by the winner's rules and don't consider themselves permanent losers?[45] At a minimum, this requires some faith that coalitions are shifting and that openness in the process doesn't rig the game on behalf of some privileged discourses or perspectives. Critical legal scholars and critical race scholars point out that law only looks neutral, objective, and inclusionary from the perspective of the winners of political and constitutional struggles. Mark Tushnet has argued very persuasively that we cannot assume that people are part of a shared community of understanding just because they are using the same words.[46]

Legal discourse is highly patterned—more so than most other secular public discourses in the United States. New institutionalist approaches to the Court recognize that members of the Court are constrained by legal traditions, language, and norms that are specific to the Court as an institution.[47] Institutions can shape principles and purposes; they can "influence the self-conception of those who occupy roles defined by them in ways that give those persons distinctively 'institutional' perspectives."[48]

Justices expect legitimate arguments and legal reasoning to draw on constitutional text and on narratives that make use of case-law precedent. Only when these requirements are followed is an argument likely to be understood or to make sense. Justifications from the bench require references to text and precedent; one could say that establishing, through precedent and previously recognized language, what the pattern *is* vindicates conclusions. Law can function to keep certain political impulses in check by requiring that the very language with which the aggrieved argue be derived from the Constitution and from precedents, tests, and doctrine already cognizable, for the most part, to the Court.[49]

However, even though law is patterned and informed by the history of American case law, it can still take various paths. Precedents are restated and reworked, and, like other texts, they are appropriated differently by different justices and for different purposes. Even those who purport to follow an original public meaning choose their heroes and their historians.

The Court can be understood as an institution where participants interpret and reinterpret texts and legal precedents and where decisions both reflect and shape political thought. Institutional actors and activists outside the Court also participate in constructing constitutional meanings. Not only is the Court's agenda shaped in part by the infusion of money and attention to particular issues by organized groups, but undertheorized decisions invite activists to seek opportunities to participate in doctrinal developments by going to Court.[50] Participants are not simply passive victims of rules, policies, and institutions—as they might have been seen under an earlier "false consciousness" rubric. Through these contestations, both values and institutions have the potential to change.

As Keith Whittington has so well demonstrated, a good deal of the Constitution is constructed by other institutional participants in the federal government—institutions that have different incentives at various periods (during different types of regimes) to contest, alter, or accept the Court's view of the Constitution.[51] Sometimes, other branches of the federal government urge the Court to participate in political conflict by pressing that institution to attempt resolution of contentious issues. *Dred Scott* is a case in point: both legislative and executive branches sought Court intervention. As both Mark Graber and Keith Whittington have shown, the propensity of elective branches to relocate decision making on certain issues to the judiciary is nothing new in American history, even if the Court's claim to have sole responsibility to settle constitutional questions has a much more recent flavor.[52] However, it can hardly be said that the Court forged consensus where it was lacking.

Mark Graber argues that the Constitution is a deliberate compromise over deeply divisive moral issues—and the central divisive issue in the early nineteenth century was slavery. If people sharing civic space cannot engage in constitutional compromises, they are hardly likely to coexist as a people. Graber finds that compromises allow us to agree to disagree. While Robert Wiebe once argued that America consisted of segmented societies in part because the availability of land allowed communities to move away from each other rather than learn how to solve their disagreements,[53] Graber suggests that constitutions can erect certain kinds of barriers between those who cannot agree. When compromises work, each side agrees not to try to compel the other to change. "The continued existence of that constitutional regime depended on the continued satisfaction of each side with that constitutional bargain."[54]

However, if the *Dred Scott* decision restated an earlier constitutional compromise to keep slavery, viewed by segments of the founding generation as a constitutional evil, off the table so that those with very important differences could agree to be governed, it could not sufficiently restore a later generation of Americans to that compromise to avoid bloodshed, followed by an amended constitutional understanding. The best Hartz does here is claim that "the Constitution did not fare very well in the only time any such [fundamental value] struggles did appear in the United States, the time of the slavery controversy in the middle of the nineteenth century."[55] Neither the Constitution nor the Court could keep a divisive issue off the political table when political actors in a subsequent generation chose not to accept the bargain.

In attempting to save *The Liberal Tradition* from the defects of consensus and attendant moral unanimity, J. David Greenstone posited two or more poles of normal American political discourse, each reflecting a different perspective on the relationship between liberal principles. Greenstone understood our culturally conditioned words as Wittgensteinian "tools in a toolbox" that are available for quite different uses. Concepts are ambiguous enough for major conflicts to erupt over their meaning. Nevertheless, Americans encounter "grammatical limits on what we can meaningfully say, think, and perceive."[56] In this account, bipolarity best expressed the way in which different thinkers and groups understood tensions between competing values, such as between liberty and union in the 1850s. Greenstone found marked tension between humanist liberal perspectives (which can largely be equated with the Lockean atomistic individualism of Hartz) and reform liberal perspectives (identified with John Dewey, Jane Addams, and the Progressive era's embrace of the positive state, with government helping assure that all citizens can develop their faculties). American political struggles were, then, quite real, sometimes leading to bloodshed. In this account, the Constitution is a document expressing a complicated but pervasively liberal American political culture. Humanist, reform liberal, and republican perspectives could all be found in law. There were different but patterned ways in which justices resolved tensions over principles.[57]

Agreeing with Greenstone that principle, precedent, and the legal culture establish rules of discourse and liberal bounds within which that discourse takes place, Ronald Kahn nevertheless finds many real, principled disagreements that matter on the Court.[58] He argues that judicial decision making is guided by polity and rights principles, "the basic filters through which doctrines of popular sovereignty and fundamental rights confront each other." Different justices weigh these principles differently, leading to important disagreements, but all are members of an interpretive community in which principle, not instrumentality, rules.

While Kahn and Greenstone find the "liberal tradition" a meaningful designation once these constellations of values and principles are identified and differentiated, it is sensible to ask what explanatory power the terminology retains. If the liberal tradition can explain and predict such a wide variety of contingent outcomes, including civil war and virtually all our constitutional disagreements, how much is it still helping us?

The fact that Americans are heirs of Locke is certainly apparent. But our political heritage is also of David Hume and the Scottish Enlightenment, of Niccolò Machiavelli, and of Thomas Hobbes and the Puritans.[59] While Hartz contended that "Locke dominates American political thought, as no thinker anywhere dominates the political thought of a nation,"[60] the Constitution—like American political discourse—is not pure Locke. These other traditions bring striking potential for tensions.

Rogers Smith has been prominent among those questioning the "purchase" of Hartz's "liberal tradition" because liberalism is not the only political tradition in America. He makes the case that we have a richer (in his view, not better) and wider set of enduring narratives to which American political elites appeal, and these include republican and ascriptive (exclusionary) traditions.[61] As yet another scholar has pointed out, "Articulations of citizenship have always depended upon the exclusion of constructed and ascribed others."[62] Liberal outcomes may be preferable, but they do not predictably win out in political contests and are therefore problematized rather than given.

In a number of respects, we also do ourselves a disservice as comparativists by viewing American legal conflicts as unique. Some patterns and developments are not specific to America. Ran Hirschl has explored how the judicialization of political conflicts—juristocracy—has been developing in various nations, not simply in the United States. Conflicts are displaced from the political arena and constitutionalized; one vehicle for such constitutionalization can be the transformation of political struggles into demands for rights. Hirschl argues that where "judicial empowerment through constitutionalization" occurs, it generally results from "a strategic tripartite pact between hegemonic, yet increasingly threatened, political elites seeking to insulate their policy preferences from the vicissitudes of democratic politics; economic elites who share a commitment to free markets and a concomitant antipathy to government; and supreme courts seeking to enhance their symbolic power and institutional position."[63]

Thinking about judicial power in Machiavellian terms, Rogers Smith further suggests that "if elites have seen the rise of judicial power as a way to complete the construction of modern constitutional democracies, they have done so in part because they feel their core interests are likely to be better protected in democratized regimes through the strengthening of these relatively insulated political institutions."[64] Elites may be especially able, through judicialization of conflict, to preserve and promote the acquisition of wealth.[65] From these perspectives, then, judicialization of conflict represents a strategic attempt to delimit and contain political debate within relatively safe channels for elites as democratization expands. The displacement of conflict allows for its continuation on other terrains and in less threatening ways. But Courts remain important participants in these struggles over democracy.

If we attempt to insist that our legal and political conflicts are preordained liberal, we not only neglect what is not liberal in American politics but lose the contingency in new ideas and circumstances. We make things look alike that may not be alike at all. To say that political outcomes reflect our past is not then to say that politics—or law—lacks dynamism. Hartz is ultimately not going to help scholars explore what is dynamic about politics or law or the way vital struggles may be taking place there.

DIVISIVE ISSUES AND *LIBERAL TRADITION* BLIND SPOTS

The "liberal tradition" has little capacity as a guide to many current political and legal struggles. Hartz was unable to identify the relationship between cultural and religious battles and American liberalism, nor did he offer a good explanation for the deep divisions that can emerge in American politics. For recent generations, these divisions include issues of abortion, immigration, separation of church and state, and gay marriage.

Indeed, religion was not very important to Hartz's secular understanding of American political values.[66] While *Time* magazine could display a bold cover asking "Is God Dead?" in 1966, recent survey data find that religion is of much more importance to Americans than to those living in other prosperous nations.[67] As we follow legal battles over relations between church and state ranging from school prayer to the teaching of intelligent design, funding of faith-based initiatives, and various forms of state aid flowing toward religious education, it is hard to believe that religion can be relegated to a mere footnote in American political development. When we add in struggles over issues of public decency and morality, the list of issues engaging religious convictions becomes quite long.[68] When abortion providers are murdered by those who believe that abortion itself is murder, the struggle is quite literally over life or death. If this particular example represents politics on the fringe (after all, the majority of Americans are somewhere in the center on the abortion debate), it is hard to maintain that faith has not sometimes been quite divisive in either contemporary or former periods of American politics. Cultural and religious values have been vital components of struggles ranging from slavery to immigration, prohibition, women's rights, Progressive era causes, peace making, and civic engagement more generally. For many generations of Americans, the meaning of America is intimately linked to God's design, and the nation and its people must be recalled to its purposes.[69]

Indeed, the Horatio Alger story that Hartz believes seals the deed in American political history cannot reasonably be read as a simple, materialist tale of equality of economic opportunity. This Unitarian-inspired formula can be read to show that the young person's rite of passage was vital to the welfare of the community. If the future of the Republic hinged upon its virtue, then the character of the young and the character of the Republic were inextricably bound.[70] Even with its dream of rising through the ranks, the Alger story was entwined in nineteenth-century culture wars and meant something other than Hartz made of it. Moral issues loom large when character formation is taken as central to the political project.

Other recent scholars have put struggles over morality and virtue at the center of their important accounts of American political thought, conflict, and development. Contending that "liberal political history underestimates the roaring moral fervor at the soul of American politics," Jim Morone argues that "American politics developed from revival to revival." Examining the role that different arguments about sources of sin (systemic versus personal) have played in American political battles, Morone finds that moral crusaders played a vital role in American state building.[71] Jim Block's *Nation of Agents*, offering a very different narrative of American history from Hartz's, places agency rather than liberty at the center in the formation of the American self. Central struggles in American politics pit those who believe liberty requires that habits of virtue be inculcated through institutions, traditions, and authority against those who seek to achieve liberal autonomy without such imposed constraints. Block maintains that "the great theorist of agency civilization" for America was Hobbes, not Locke. Divisions in American politics, then, can best be understood by examining tensions between a sectarian Protestant vision of an exclusive religious community and understandings of agency as natural and not requiring institutional coercion.[72]

Popular accounts of a culture war raging in contemporary American politics are easy to find, although evidence for such a proposition at the level of mass opinion is relatively modest.[73] Even where surveys find that most Americans have moderate views on divisive religious and cultural issues, highly mobilized activists are another matter. Ideology has been found to be a powerful predictor of political participation. And when the Court engages contentious issues, activists target the Court as they seek to achieve their goals. The Court is a part of the struggle over political values, and when issues can be fought out in constitutionalized terms, the Court may become a central focus of activity for several reasons.

Mobilized, highly motivated, and organized interests have pressed their agendas by finding cases and taking them to court. Availability of financial resources helps determine the sustained attention issues receive in the legal arena. Because the Supreme Court is often reluctant to take up new issues before they have a record of litigation in lower courts, there are significant barriers to entry for issues at this level, and surmounting these barriers depends on the "availability of resources for legal mobilization."[74] When the

Court does enter an arena of controversy, decisions—perhaps especially if
they are "minimalist"—often mobilize further legal contestation.[75] While
much has been written about the calculated strategies through which liberal
legal organizations such as the American Civil Liberties Union and the
NAACP Legal Defense Fund developed and pressed their civil rights and civil
liberties agendas in the federal courts, recent attention has also been devoted
to the efforts of more recent conservative groups to regain control of the law,
including the Federalist Society, the Center for Individual Rights, and the Institute for Justice.[76] Funders and think tanks facilitate these developments.

In periods when particular constitutional meanings are contested, both
underdeveloped arguments and new language generated or adopted by the
Court provide fresh opportunities to develop and press arguments by interested activists and members of the legal community. As Thomas M. Keck
has pointed out, "the 'legal' ideas that influence the justices . . . are derived
in large part from ongoing debates in the broader political system, and the
'political' interests that pressure the Court are often constituted by legal
categories created by the justices themselves."[77] Thus, activists turn to the
Court when the Court signals its openness to their issues, and Court decisions also help frame constituencies, advocates, interests, and interpretations of the social world.[78]

Polarization has additional dimensions that may affect the judicial
branch. Congressional voting is more polarized than at any time in the past
century, and party activists are highly polarized.[79] Surveys documented the
deepening political (if not cultural) polarization of the American public.[80]
A number of scholars, including Nolan McCarty, Keith Poole, and Howard
Rosenthal, believe that any such public polarization as has been observed is
occasioned by elite polarization, and not vice versa. According to students
of congressional roll-call voting, propensity for legislative gridlock appears
to rise with party polarization in Congress and reduces the output of significant (as opposed to trivial and narrow) legislation. "Perhaps one of the
most important long-term consequences of the decline in legislative capacity caused by polarization is that Congress's power will decline relative to
the other branches of government."[81] It seems plausible that perceptions of
Supreme Court activism may be rising as Congress is doing less and even
delegating enforcement power to courts, and that such perceptions may
therefore be integrally linked to what is going on elsewhere in the federal
government. If polarization and other factors producing gridlock in Congress indicate that government by other means is becoming the norm, the
Court may continue to be a primary site of conflict and an important source
of policy making.[82]

We are left with the questions of why and under what circumstances the Court engages, or disengages, from deeply divisive issues. Thinking in part about the late years of the Rehnquist Court and the early years of the Roberts Court, Mark Graber has recently made an intriguing suggestion that periods of intense, extreme partisanship may set into motion forces tending to moderate judicial outcomes, especially when the Court decides polarized, contentious issues.[83] Thus, rather than attempting to press an advantage when conservatives (or liberals) dominate the Court at fractious moments, perhaps these Courts seek to moderate tensions.[84] Stepping back from the political fray, they try to forge outcomes competing factions can live with. Yet it seems hardly appropriate to claim that the Constitution settles, or removes from the table, many of the deeply divisive issues in American politics.

Is it possible that some moral grievances can find no language—partly because of the way earlier Courts have set precedents—through which they can capture the attention of the Court? What kind of constructive role can the Court play in mediating such divisive conflicts when the conflicts do enlist constitutional language? These seem to be important questions, but they are questions that *The Liberal Tradition* is not going to help us address well.

Political battles in the United States are likely to be expressed in appeals to time-honored traditions and values and are often expressed in constitutional language. Contemporary Americans do tend to constitutionalize their political struggles, perhaps an indication of the extent to which the Court has become part of a strategic calculus in politics. The Constitution becomes a weapon to fight with; it means different things to different contestants. If we look to American history, we will find plenty of struggles over constitutional meaning.[85] The outcomes of these struggles tell us quite a bit about power, mobilization, political opportunities, and institutional change. We often learn about contingency and possibility rather than inevitability. I do not think we learn very much about these struggles—or even see most of them—by positing a bounded "liberal tradition" in American political or legal discourse. And it may be that by thinking in terms of boundaries and constantly repeated tropes, we also miss opportunities to remain open to new possibilities.

NOTES

Portions of this chapter have appeared in Carol Nackenoff, "Groundhog Day Again? Is the 'Liberal Tradition' a Useful Construct for Studying Law, Courts, and American Political Development?" *Good Society* 16, no. 1 (2007): 40–45. Some of the ideas have also appeared in Nackenoff, "Locke, Alger, and Atomistic Individualism Fifty Years Later: Revisiting Louis Hartz's Liberal Tradition in America," *Studies in American Political Development* 19 (Fall 2005): 206–215. Those portions are reprinted by permission of copyright holders Penn State University Press and Cambridge University Press. Thanks to Swarthmore College students Aaron Strong, 2006; Ian Sulam, 2005; and Joshua Hudner, 2005, for research assistance on these earlier publications, and thanks to Sanford Levinson for comments and suggestions.

1. Alexis de Tocqueville, *Democracy in America,* ed. J. P. Mayer, trans. George Lawrence (Garden City, N.Y.: Doubleday, 1969), 270.

2. It is actually inappropriate to term the Alger myth an antebellum one, despite Hartz's conflation of Alger and the log cabin myth of the William Henry Harrison campaign. Horatio Alger's stories and novels began appearing under his own name in 1864, and the one that would seal his fame, *Ragged Dick,* appeared in serialization in *Student and Schoolmate* in 1867 and in novel form (published by A. K. Loring) in 1868. While Alger had published an anonymous bound poem containing some similar themes in 1857, he was essentially a Gilded Age writer. He continued to produce stories and novels until his death in 1899; additional new titles were completed under agreement by Edward Stratemeyer over roughly the next decade.

3. Louis Hartz, *The Liberal Tradition in America* (New York: Harcourt, Brace & World, 1955), esp. 62–63, 203–205. See my discussion in Nackenoff, *The Fictional Republic: Horatio Alger and American Political Discourse* (New York: Oxford University Press, 1994), 264–266.

4. Hartz, *The Liberal Tradition in America,* 104, quoting Joseph Story.

5. Charles A. Beard, *An Economic Interpretation of the Constitution of the United States* (New York: Macmillan, 1913); Merrill Jensen, *The Articles of Confederation* (Madison: University of Wisconsin Press, 1940); Jensen, *The New Nation* (New York: Knopf, 1950); Bertell Ollman, "Toward a Marxist Interpretation of the U.S. Constitution," *Monthly Review* 39 (December 1987): 18–26. See Michael Harrington's "Comment 1" to Chapter 16, "Pluralism and Political Parties," by Norman Thomas, in *Failure of a Dream: Essays in the History of American Socialism,* ed. Seymour Martin Lipset and John H. M. Laslett, eds. (Garden City, N.Y.: Anchor, 1974), 661–677.

6. Justice Lewis Powell writing for the majority, *San Antonio Independent School District v. Rodriguez,* 411 U.S. 1, 19 (1973).

7. Ibid., 23.

8. Ibid., 24.

9. Ibid., 28.

10. Hartz, *The Liberal Tradition in America,* 108.

11. Justice Stewart, writing for the Court in *Harris v. McRae,* 448 U.S. 297, 312 (1980) and quoting *Mobile v. Bolden,* 446 U.S. 55, at 76 (plurality opinion), http://caselaw.lp.findlaw.com/cgi-bin/getcase.pl?navby=case&court=us&vol=446&invol=55.

12. Justice Powell, writing for the majority in *Maher v. Roe,* 432 U.S. 464, 474 (1977).

13. There have been moments in constitutional jurisprudence when the Fourteenth Amendment was read to offer some small amount of protection for the poor or when it was read to suggest that some version of the welfare state was a constitutional duty. See Sanford Levinson, "When (Some) Republican Justices Exhibited Concern for the Plight of the Poor: An Essay in Historical Retrieval," in *Law and Class in America: Trends since the Cold War,* ed. Paul D. Carrington and Trina Jones (New York and London: New York University Press, 2006), 21–36. On privacy, see Catharine A. MacKinnon, "Privacy v. Equality: Beyond *Roe v. Wade,*" in *Feminism Unmodified* (Cambridge, Mass.: Harvard University Press, 1987).

14. See Carol Nackenoff, "The Dueling First Amendments: Government as Funder, as Speaker, and the Establishment Clause," *Maryland Law Review,* vol. 69, no. 1 (2009), in press.

15. Jacob S. Hacker, *The Great Risk Shift* (New York: Oxford University Press, 2006).

16. Antonin Scalia, "The Doctrine of Standing as an Element of the Separation of Powers," in *Views from the Bench,* ed. Mark W. Cannon and David M. O'Brien (Chatham, N.J.: Chatham House, 1985), esp. 206–208.

17. *Beauharnais v. Illinois,* 343 U.S. 250 (1952), 251, quoting from the Illinois statute.

18. Antonin Scalia, concurring in part and concurring in the judgment in *Adarand Constructors, Inc. v. Pena,* 515 U.S. 200 (1995).

19. Hartz, *The Liberal Tradition in America,* 260, 263, 270, 277, and passim.

20. This line of cases began with *Seminole Tribe of Florida v. Florida,* 517 U.S. 44 (1996).

21. One of the richest expositions of this controversy in case law is *U.S. Term Limits v. Thornton,* 514 U.S. 779 (1995). The Arkansas state constitutional amendment imposing term limits on members of the U.S. House and Senate was struck down in a 5–4 decision.

22. See *United States v. Lopez,* 514 U.S. 549 (1995) and *United States v. Morrison,* 529 U.S. 598 (2000). These cases maintain the New Deal substantial effects test; however, they stipulate that proper Congressional regulation was directed "at the instrumentalities, channels, or goods involved in interstate commerce." One reason the impact of *Lopez* and *Morrison* remains unclear is that *Gonzales v. Raich,* 545 U.S. 1 (2005), upholds federal regulation of medical use of marijuana under the Controlled Substances Act using the "aggregate effects" test, the broadest test the Court used during the New Deal era and one that *Morrison* had seemed to reject; see *Wickard v. Filburn,* 317 U.S. 111 (1942). Ernest Young, however, contends that the Court's foray into protection of federalism through both state sovereign immunity and commerce clause routes looks rather like a failure to date. Ernest A. Young, "Just Blowing Smoke? Politics, Doctrine, and the Federalist Revival after Gonzales v. Raich," *Supreme Court Review,* 2005, ed. Dennis J. Hutchinson, David A. Strauss, and Geoffrey R. Stone (Chicago and London: University of Chicago Press, 2006).

23. Hartz, *The Liberal Tradition in America*, 260.

24. These states include New Jersey, Connecticut, Kentucky, Tennessee, and Texas. See Douglas S. Reed, "Twenty-five Years after *Rodriguez*: School Finance Litigation and the Impact of the New Judicial Federalism," *Law and Society Review* 32, no. 1 (1998): 175–220. By this point, litigation in thirty-six states had yielded some sorts of victories in twenty.

25. Among the most important fellow participants should be counted Werner Sombart, *Why Is There No Socialism in the United States?* (1906; reprint, New York: Sharpe, 1976); Selig Perlman, *A Theory of the Labor Movement* (New York: Macmillan, 1928); and from a different direction, Sacvan Bercovitch, *Puritan Origins of the American Self* (New Haven, Conn.: Yale University Press, 1975). Of course, a good part of Hartz's claim can also be found in Alexis de Tocqueville's work.

26. Daniel Bell, *The End of Ideology: On the Exhaustion of Political Ideas in the Fifties* (Glencoe, Ill.: Free Press, 1960).

27. John Gerring, *Party Ideologies in America, 1828–1996* (Cambridge: Cambridge University Press, 1998), 248–250. Gerring examines party platforms and candidate speeches.

28. Ibid., 250.

29. Herbert Wechsler, "Toward Neutral Principles of Constitutional Law," *Harvard Law Review* 73 (1959): 1–35.

30. I think a case can be made that contemporary U.S. policy in the Middle East is at least an intriguing illustration of Hartz's charge that America's "messianism is the polar counterpart of its isolationism" and that America, lacking experience of a social revolution at home, demonstrates "hampered insight abroad" as it tries to lead other nations and peoples to adopt the American liberal creed. Hartz's skepticism about our ability to export our political tradition seems warranted in a post–Cold War world. However, foreign policy is beyond the scope of this chapter. See Hartz, *The Liberal Tradition in America*, 286, 288, 305–306.

31. This repetition, involving small variations on a theme, is the reason for my use of the title "Groundhog Day Again?" (See the unnumbered note at the beginning of the note section.)

32. Sean Wilentz, "Uses of *The Liberal Tradition*: Comments on 'Still Louis Hartz after All These Years,'" *Perspectives on Politics* 3 (2005): 118.

33. Karen Orren and Stephen Skowronek, "The Study of American Political Development," in *Political Science: The State of the Discipline*, ed. Ira Katznelson and Helen V. Milner (New York: Norton, 2002), 726.

34. Paul Pierson and Theda Skocpol, "Historical Institutionalism in Contemporary Political Science," in Katznelson and Milner, *Political Science*, 695 (emphasis in the original).

35. See Ronald Kahn and Ken I. Kersch, eds., *The Supreme Court and American Political Development* (Lawrence: University Press of Kansas, 2006).

36. Karen Orren and Stephen Skowronek, "In Search of Political Development," in *The Liberal Tradition in American Politics: Reassessing the Legacy of American Liberalism*, ed. David F. Ericson and Louisa Bertch Green (New York: Routledge, 1999), 39.

37. Karen Orren and Stephen Skowronek, "Institutional Intercurrence: Theory Building in the Fullness of Time," in *Political Order,* ed. Ian Shapiro and Russell Hardin, Nomos XXXVIII (New York and London: New York University Press, 1996), 139, 140, and "In Search of Political Development."

38. Pierson and Skocpol, "Historical Institutionalism in Contemporary Political Science," 699.

39. Ibid., 699–700.

40. Ibid., 700.

41. See the discussion in ibid., 701–703.

42. Robert H. Jackson, *The Struggle for Judicial Supremacy* (New York: Knopf, 1941), 187, 189.

43. Hartz, *The Liberal Tradition in America,* 281–282n.

44. Stanley Fish, *Is There a Text in This Class? The Authority of Interpretive Communities* (Cambridge, Mass.: Harvard University Press, 1980).

45. But see Mari J. Matsuda, Charles R. Lawrence III, Richard Delgado, and Kimberlè Williams Crenshaw, *Words That Wound: Critical Race Theory, Assaultive Speech and the First Amendment* (Boulder, Colo.: Westview Press, 1993); Catharine A. MacKinnon, *Only Words* (Cambridge, Mass.: Harvard University Press, 1993).

46. Mark V. Tushnet, "Following the Rules Laid Down: A Critique of Interpretivism and Neutral Principles," *Harvard Law Review* 96 (February 1983): 826, 785. See also Tushnet, *Red, White, and Blue: A Critical Analysis of Constitutional Law* (Cambridge, Mass.: Harvard University Press, 1988).

47. See Cornell W. Clayton and Howard Gillman, eds., *Supreme Court Decision-Making: New Institutionalist Approaches* (Chicago: University of Chicago Press, 1999), esp. the chapters by the two editors.

48. Rogers M. Smith, "Political Jurisprudence, the 'New Institutionalism,' and the Future of Public Law," *American Political Science Review* 82 (March 1988): 95.

49. Austin Sarat, "Going to Court: Access, Autonomy, and the Contradictions of Legal Legality," in *The Politics of Law,* ed. David Kairys, 3rd ed. (New York: Basic Books, 1998), 97–114.

50. See Charles R. Epp, "External Pressure and the Supreme Court's Agenda," in Clayton and Gillman, *Supreme Court Decision-Making,* 255–279; Julie Novkov, *Constituting Workers, Protecting Women* (Ann Arbor: University of Michigan Press, 2001); Carol Nackenoff, "Constitutionalizing Terms of Inclusion: Friends of the Indian and Citizenship for Native Americans, 1880s–1930s," in Kahn and Kersch, *The Supreme Court and American Political Development,* 366–413.

51. Keith E. Whittington, *Political Foundations of Judicial Supremacy* (Princeton, N.J.: Princeton University Press, 2007); and Whittington, *Constitutional Construction* (Cambridge, Mass.: Harvard University Press, 1999).

52. Mark A. Graber, *Dred Scott and the Problem of Constitutional Evil* (Cambridge and New York: Cambridge University Press, 2006); Whittington, *Political Foundations of Judicial Supremacy.*

53. See Robert Wiebe, *The Segmented Society* (New York: Oxford University Press, 1975).

54. Graber, *Dred Scott and the Problem of Constitutional Evil*, 6.

55. Hartz, *The Liberal Tradition in America*, 85. He adds: "For the solution the constitutionalists offered to the frightful conflicts they imagined was a complicated scheme of checks and balances which it is reasonable to argue only a highly united nation could make work at all. Delay and deliberate confusion in government became intolerable in communities where men have decisive social programs that they want to execute."

56. J. David Greenstone, "Political Culture and American Political Development: Liberty, Union and the Liberal Bipolarity," *Studies in American Political Development* 1 (1986): 1–49, esp. 9–17, from which the quotations are drawn.

57. Ibid. Greenstone applies this approach to constitutional law in "Against Simplicity: The Cultural Dimensions of the Constitution," *University of Chicago Law Review* 55 (1988): 428–449. He does acknowledge a republican strain in American political thought, but bipolarity receives most of his attention. See esp. ibid., 446–447. Greenstone also contends that if a culture is to be coherent enough to survive, some of its tenets must be beyond dispute—for example, liberal theory proscribes certain forms of interpersonal domination as illicit.

58. Ronald Kahn, *The Supreme Court and Constitutional Theory, 1953–1993* (Lawrence: University Press of Kansas), 18, 20. See also Kahn, "Liberalism, Political Culture, and the Rights of Subordinated Groups: Constitutional Theory and Practice at a Crossroads," in Ericson and Green, *The Liberal Tradition in American Politics*, 171–197.

59. On Hume and the Scottish Enlightenment, see Garry Wills, *Inventing America* (Garden City, N.Y.: Doubleday, 1978); on Machiavelli, see J. G. A. Pocock, *The Machiavellian Moment: Florentine Political Thought and the Atlantic Republican Tradition* (Princeton, N.J.: Princeton University Press, 1975); on Hobbes and the Puritans, see James E. Block, *A Nation of Agents: The American Path to a Modern Self and Society* (Cambridge, Mass.: Harvard University Press/Belknap Press, 2002).

60. Hartz, *The Liberal Tradition in America*, 140.

61. Rogers M. Smith, *Civic Ideals: Conflicting Visions of Citizenship in U.S. History* (New Haven, Conn.: Yale University Press, 1997).

62. Richard Iton, "The Sound of Silence: Comments on 'Still Louis Hartz after All These Years,'" *Perspectives on Politics* 3 (March 2005): 114.

63. Ran Hirschl, *Toward Juristocracy* (Cambridge, Mass.: Harvard University Press, 2004), 214.

64. Rogers Smith, "Judicial Power and Democracy: A Machiavellian View," in *The Supreme Court and the Idea of Constitutionalism*, ed. Steven Kautz, Arthur Melzer, Jerry Weinberger, and M. Richard Zinman (Philadelphia: University of Pennsylvania Press, 2009), 77.

65. Ibid., 74, citing John P. McCormick, "Contain the Wealthy and Patrol the Magistrates: Restoring Elite Accountability to Popular Government," *American Political Science Review* 100, no. 2 (May 2006): 147–163. For another important argument about the relationship between the national movement toward judicial review and

elite interests, see Tom Ginsburg, *Judicial Review in New Democracies: Constitutional Courts in Asian Cases* (New York: Cambridge University Press, 2003).

66. Following the publication of *The Liberal Tradition in America*, scholars repeatedly pointed to the important place of religious meanings and tropes in American politics and political discourse. Some of the important contributions to this literature include Sacvan Bercovitch, *The American Jeremiad* (Madison: University of Wisconsin Press, 1978); Bercovitch, *Puritan Origins of the American Self;* Garry Wills, *Nixon Agonistes* (New York: New American Library, 1970); Wills, *Under God* (New York: Simon & Schuster, 1990); Michael Kammen, *People of Paradox* (New York: Vintage Books, 1972); John Patrick Diggins, *The Lost Soul of American Politics* (New York: Basic Books, 1984); Robert N. Bellah, *Broken Covenant: American Civil Religion in a Time of Trial,* 2nd ed. (Chicago: University of Chicago Press, 1992); Robert Booth Fowler, *Religion and Politics in America* (Metuchen, N.J.: Scarecrow, 1985); Wilson C. McWilliams, *The Idea of Fraternity in America* (Berkeley and Los Angeles: University of California Press, 1973).

67. *Time* cover story, April 8, 1966. Pew Research Center for the People and the Press, "Among Wealthy Nations . . . U.S. Stands Alone in Its Embrace of Religion," introduction and summary, Pew Global Attitudes Project, report released December 19, 2003, http://people-press.org/reports/display.php3?ReportID=167 (accessed March 7, 2005).

68. Even the battle over an individual right to bear arms goes beyond libertarians, having cultural and possibly religious dimensions. See Katharine Q. Seelye, "Kentucky Pastor Invites Flock to Carry Firearms to Church," *New York Times,* June 25, 2009. The pastor is from the Assembly of God.

69. See Nackenoff, *The Fictional Republic,* esp. 268–269; Bercovitch, *Puritan Origins of the American Self,* 81 and passim; Bercovitch, *The American Jeremiad.*

70. Nackenoff, *The Fictional Republic,* 8 and chap. 3, "Republican Rites of Passage."

71. James A. Morone, *Hellfire Nation: The Politics of Sin in American History* (New Haven, Conn.: Yale University Press, 2003), esp. the introduction and part 5; and 7, 11, 32.

72. Block, *A Nation of Agents,* 3, 5–9, 15–18, 28–30, and chap. 4.

73. The best of these journalistic accounts is probably Thomas Frank, *What's the Matter with Kansas? How Conservatives Won the Heart of America* (New York: Metropolitan Books, 2004). For a demonstration that there is very little to the red state/blue state divide, see Morris P. Fiorina with Samuel J. Abrams and Jeremy C. Pope, *Culture War? The Myth of a Polarized America,* 2nd ed. (New York: Pearson Longman, 2006).

74. See Epp, "External Pressure and the Supreme Court's Agenda," 255–279; quotation on 260.

75. See Cass R. Sunstein, *One Case at a Time* (Cambridge, Mass.: Harvard University Press, 1999) on judicial minimalism. Of course, Sunstein hopes that minimalism will promote returning deliberation about the Constitution's meaning to legislatures and perhaps the people, but there are many reasons why these consequences could be doubted.

76. See Steven M. Teles, *The Rise of the Conservative Legal Movement: The Battle for Control of the Law* (Princeton, N.J.: Princeton University Press, 2008). Also Thomas M. Keck, "From *Bakke* to *Grutter*: The Rise of Rights-Based Conservatism," in Kahn and Kersch, *The Supreme Court and American Political Development*, 414–442.

77. Keck, "From *Bakke* to *Grutter*," 414.

78. See ibid., 416; and also Michael McCann, "How the Supreme Court Matters in American Politics: New Institutionalist Perspectives," in *The Supreme Court in American Politics: New Institutionalist Interpretations*, ed. Howard Gillman and Cornell Clayton (Lawrence: University Press of Kansas, 1999).

79. Keith T. Poole and Howard Rosenthal, *Congress: A Political-Economic History of Roll Call Voting* (New York: Oxford University Press, 2000); Norman Ornstein and Barry McMillion, "One Nation, Divisible," *New York Times,* June 23, 2005, http://www.nytimes.com/2005/06/23/opinion/24ornstein.html?ex=1141102800&en=2bee9cc7a7c8562b&ei=5070. Keith Poole made the point that when Congress was last this polarized, near the turn of the twentieth century, American politics was quite violent and unstable; "Political Polarization and Economic Inequality," Mathematics Department lecture, Swarthmore College, October 19, 2004.

80. Pew Research Center for the People and the Press, "The 2004 Political Landscape: Evenly Divided and Increasingly Polarized," report released November 5, 2003, http://people-press.org/reports/display.php3?ReportID=196 (accessed March 7, 2005). In November 2005, to take just one example, 80 percent of self-identified Republicans approved of President George W. Bush's performance in office while only 7 percent of self-identified Democrats did. See the CNN/USA Today/Gallup telephone poll conducted November 11–13, 2005, reported in "Poll: Bush Approval Mark at All-Time Low," *CNN.com,* November 14, 2005, http://www.cnn.com/2005/POLITICS/11/14/bush.poll/. This is more striking than the partisan division in approval ratings during the administrations of most incumbent presidents.

81. Nolan McCarty, Keith T. Poole, and Howard Rosenthal, *Polarized America: The Dance of Ideology and Unequal Riches* (Cambridge, Mass.: MIT Press, 2006), 178–183; quotation on 186. The authors suggest that Congress may even be choosing to delegate more enforcement activity to the courts rather than to administrative agencies, weakening the other branches relative to the judiciary (citing an unpublished 2003 manuscript); see also chaps. 3 and 6. According to these authors, periods of increasing congressional polarization seem to track increases in economic inequality and rises in immigration-restriction sentiment for most of the twentieth century. There is some evidence that a polarized Congress pays less attention to policies that might narrow income disparities and less attention to social welfare policy for all but the elderly than a less-polarized legislature.

82. The relationship between gridlock and the search for alternative paths for policy making is the central focus of Christopher McGrory Klyza and David Sousa, *American Environmental Policy, 1990–2006: Beyond Gridlock* (Cambridge, Mass.: MIT Press, 2008). They argue that gridlock helps explain the role played by adversarial legalism in environmental policy making (192–193).

83. Mark Graber, "Polarization and the Courts," lecture delivered September 23, 2008, at the Wayne Morse Center for Law and Politics, University of Oregon, reported at http://www.uoregon.edu/~morse/democracy.html. Graber is there quoted as saying, "Rather than understanding courts as the forum of principle in American life, one should also recognize their capacity to provide needed moderation during times of excessive partisanship."

84. See Mark Graber, "Does it Really Matter? Conservative Courts in a Conservative Era," http://www.bsos.umd.edu/gvpt/apworkshop/graber07.pdf (accessed June 19, 2009). Gerald N. Rosenberg, in *The Hollow Hope: Can Courts Bring about Social Change?* (Chicago: University of Chicago Press, 1991), threw down the gauntlet to those who believed the Court could serve as an important force for change even when it attempted to do so.

85. See Ken I. Kersch, *Constructing Civil Liberties: Discontinuities in the Development of American Constitutional Law* (New York: Cambridge University Press, 2004). See also Anne Norton, *Alternative Americas: A Reading of Antebellum Political Culture* (Chicago: University of Chicago Press, 1986).

What's Living, What's Dead, in the Work of Louis Hartz

Mark Hulliung

The essays in the present volume represent a plurality of points of view and do not lend themselves to a definitive conclusion as to the status today of Hartz's famous book. Hence it is best that the editor acknowledge from the outset that the views expressed in this deliberately brief afterword are his and his alone. In setting forth his conclusions about the present-day standing of *The Liberal Tradition in America,* he cannot and does not pretend to speak for the other contributors.

Max Weber once remarked that every book "*asks* to be 'surpassed' and outdated";[1] eventually every book fades into the past. Doubtless Weber was correct, but Hartz's case is the unusual one of a book that lived for several decades and then entered into a nether world suspended somewhere between life and death. It is the peculiar fate of Hartz's book that it still fares well in some academic disciplines but not in others: while historians have by and large abandoned him and political theorists no longer or rarely respond to his work, he is still alive in the world of political science, especially within the ranks of those scholars who congregate under the umbrella of "American political development."

One searches mainly in vain for Hartz in the world of today's historians, largely but not exclusively due to the downgrading of intellectual history and the upgrading of social history during recent decades—a change that has led most historians to ignore Hartz except on those occasions when they chastise him for omitting such topics as race and gender. Even more discouraging for anyone seeking a Hartzian revival, when an intellectual historian such as James Kloppenberg does finally step forward to reconsider *The Liberal Tradition in America,* he rejects Hartz's account of American history as rigidly formulaic and oversimplified. Perhaps the single strongest indication of the disinterest of contemporary historians in *The Liberal Tradition in America* is that Joyce Appleby, in the course of reinstating the notion of an early American "liberal" tradition, in contradistinction to J. G. A. Pocock's "republican" interpretation, treats Hartz as all but irrelevant to her quest.[2]

Dying, yes, but not yet dead, would seem to be the conclusion about Hartz's work that is suggested by the research interests of today's historians. Despite all the signs of his demise, there is one opening for a possible resurgence of his work among their numbers: nowadays historians speak incessantly about studying America in a "transnational" and comparative setting, which may give them reason, sooner or later, to revisit Hartz, whose work was pioneering in its insistence upon studying America in relation to Europe.

If Hartz fares poorly these days with historians, it is not obvious that he does much better with political theorists. Here the obstacle standing in the way of his having a continuing influence is that he was not a card-carrying member of any particular school of thought, whether the "Straussians," the "critical theorists," or any other identifiable intellectual group. Nor did he found a new school made in his own image. Certainly he educated his fair share of graduate students, some of whom sought and occasionally still seek to elaborate his work,[3] but it is far from obvious that an up-and-coming generation has inherited the Hartzian outlook.

His less-than-happy fate with political theorists is perhaps best underscored by noting that after Harvard University showed him the door, his work disappeared at the institution that had housed him throughout his career. It was Judith Shklar who stepped in to fill the departmental void in the teaching of American political thought, and although she refrained from dismissing her former colleague by name in the main body of her publications, Shklar clearly repudiated him when she wrote that "America has not marched single file down a single straight liberal highway." In her endnotes she was more explicit: "I have been very careful not to follow [Hartz's] tendency to even out the discontinuities of America's past, and especially to exaggerate American liberalism." To her mind the scars resulting from the practice of chattel slavery left a deep imprint in America's history, infecting and compromising our very understandings of freedom, and Hartz, she believed, had failed to come to terms with this ugly side of the American past and present.[4]

The one place Hartz's name is still frequently cited is within the field of study termed American Political Development, which is where generalization-seeking political scientists go to harvest the highly contextualized and temporally sensitive findings of historians. An excellent case in point is J. David Greenstone's *The Lincoln Persuasion: Remaking American Liberalism* (1993). In his study of antebellum political culture Greenstone drew upon the writings of historians such as Daniel Walker Howe, who bestowed upon the Whigs of the second party system the nuanced and sympathetic reading that is missing both in Hartz and in Arthur M. Schlesinger Jr.'s earlier book on "the age of Jackson."[5] With the help of Howe and other historians, Greenstone posited not a "liberal consensus" but a "liberal polarity" in American history. Even in the absence of something akin to European socialism and conservatism, Greenstone discovered debates in the American past that were as vital as those depicted by Hartz were mere shadowboxing. Against the "negative liberty" of the Jacksonians, there was the "positive liberty" of the Whigs; against letting people alone, there was the call for moral uplift, the reform of penal institutions, the crusade for temperance, and the outcry of Conscience Whigs against slavery as both a sin and a violation of the Declaration of Independence; and there was the exploration of the positive uses of government to develop the economy and the self. Had he reached beyond the Civil War, Greenstone might have made similar contrasts between New Freedom and New Nationalist Progressives, as opposed to Hartz's misleading conflation of the two at the expense of everything new in the New Nationalism.

Hartz's name also inevitably makes an appearance whenever scholars such as Rogers Smith posit an illiberal tradition in American history, whether by way of suggesting that "ascriptive" ideologies are essentially add-ons to a dominant liberal tradition or by way of arguing that the liberal tradition is more the exception than the rule. Here again political scientists have taken advantage of the research of historians. In 1955, the same year that Hartz published his book, Richard Hofstadter wrote in *The Age of Reform* that the main American intellectual traditions have been "liberal"— "that is, popular, democratic, progressive," which, he argued, made all the more striking the "coexistence of illiberalism and reform" in the Populist and Progressive movements.[6] Also in 1955, John Higham published *Strangers in the Land: Patterns of Nativism, 1860–1925,* the book that arguably began the study of illiberalism in the American past that Rogers Smith pursued on a larger scale decades later.

At this point we must, however, issue a caveat: citations to Hartz by scholars such as Greenstone and Smith do not necessarily demonstrate that

Hartz's mode of analysis is still in play. One might well suggest that their research represents a different way of thinking about American history rather than a revision of Hartz. If Greenstone sees different versions of liberalism in serious contention throughout the past, if he sees ideas as active forces in American history, has he not broken with Hartz? Do not both Greenstone and Smith implicitly reject Hartz's notion that ideas simply reflect social class? Do not the struggles they record between one version of liberalism and another, or between liberalism and illiberalism, amount to a decisive move away from Hartz's manner of thinking about political culture?

Perhaps what has happened is that even though Hartz has faded, the notion of a liberal tradition in America continues to be asserted in new, non-Hartzian ways. Scholars may continue to find useful the notion of an American liberal heritage as one tradition among others, as "a" tradition rather than "the one and only" tradition. Joyce Appleby has filled the emptiness of the Hartzian conception of a liberal society with the gritty content of economic thought in early America.[7] Bernard Bailyn has not spoken about liberalism per se, but one might suggest that his discussion of the Opposition Whig ideology imported by Americans demonstrates historically and in depth how liberal ideas of fear of power, insistence upon checks and balances, and the like became implanted in America—as opposed to Hartz's ahistorical, almost a priori claim that Americans, being middle-class, were necessarily liberals and therefore compulsively demanded excessive checks upon government.[8]

One might argue that many scholars today are busily rescuing the notion of a liberal tradition not only from Hartz but from other thinkers of the 1950s, such as Lionel Trilling, who wrote that "in the United States at this time liberalism is not only the dominant but even the sole intellectual tradition,"[9] or Richard Hofstadter, who suggested as late as 1964 that "it had been our fate as a nation not to have ideologies but to be one"—that one being liberalism.[10] Rather than positing a one-dimensional, repetitive, static liberal tradition, contemporary scholars have retrieved a richer, multifaceted, changing liberalism, responding to challenges and adapting to new circumstances, sometimes succeeding, sometimes failing to face down the forces of illiberalism. It is also worth observing that the intellectuals involved in this process of post-Hartzian reinvention of the idea of a liberal tradition in America are drawn not only from the ranks of the political scientists but from the historians and from historically minded political theorists as well.

There may well be no better example of the need to move beyond Hartz in order to make the case for a liberal tradition than a revisiting of the question of the role of Locke in the American past. In 1963 historian Marvin Meyers published an essay on Hartz's book that has proven to be quite prescient. "The American liberal tradition has more dignity and substance than Professor Hartz's interpretation recognizes," observed Meyers, who expressed frustration that the "Locke" of Hartz is a mere label, having little or nothing to do with John Locke. "I will not be surprised," he added, "if John Locke, proper, holds almost as much significance for the understanding of American political thought as Professor Hartz attributes to the 'Lockeian' ethos."[11]

Recently Meyers's prediction has come true: the reality of Locke's presence in American history and the considerable significance of that presence has been and continues to be spelled out by a number of scholars. We now know, on the basis of painstaking historical research, that Locke failed in England in 1688 but triumphed in America in 1776, a contrast offering us insight into the differences between the political cultures of the two countries. Locke was too radical to hold together a coalition of Whigs and Tories in 1688 but was perfect for the Americans when they chose in 1776 to declare independence. Locke's social contract of natural rights, consent, and popular sovereignty received practical meaning when Americans invented the device of constitutional conventions and popular ratification. America's Revolution, then, was arguably a genuine revolution of abstract theory transformed into living practice, and perhaps the American rather than the French Revolution should therefore be regarded as the beginning of modern history—no matter that Hartz, like Tocqueville before him, treated the American Revolution as a minor event, an affirmation of tradition. The forceful, revolutionary Lockean language of the preamble of the Declaration of Independence distinguishes it from the timid English Declaration of 1689 and links it, by way of a model, with the French Declaration of the Rights of Man and Citizen of 1789.

A focus on Locke in America carries with it the additional advantage of dealing in a better way with two concerns that preoccupied Hartz: the absence in the United States of Burkean conservatism on the right and of Marxian socialism on the left. For Hartz it was simply a given that, with no feudal aristocracy, there could not be an American Edmund Burke; he had his answer as to whether there was a conservative tradition in America before he began his research. If he had bothered to examine American thought, he might have discovered that it was far more clearly the prevalence of Locke's political theory than the absence of an aristocracy that time and again stopped Burke before he could start on this side of the Atlantic ocean, or he might have found that antebellum Southerners were so much under the spell of social contract theory that they turned to the alienable rights of

Hugo Grotius and Samuel Pufendorf to vindicate slavery rather than aligning themselves with Burke's anticontractual thinking.

As for socialism, had Hartz taken Locke seriously he might have noted that both Progressives and socialists in America sometimes acknowledged a debt to Henry George, who was heir to the Lockean-inspired land-reform movement of the nineteenth century. George and the land reformers insisted that each new generation could only be assured of its inalienable Lockean rights if the produce of the land but not the land itself became private property. Socialists in America frequently learned from Henry George this lesson about land and then self-consciously applied it to other forms of property, those of a modern industrial economy.[12]

Having missed Locke's role in American history, Hartz did not realize he might have found something rather like socialism had he delved into the journalism of George Henry Evans and his cohort, union organizers originally, then land reformers who seized on Locke's claim that the land originally belonged to all in common. More radical than Locke, they held that the ideals of the *Second Treatise* could only be sustained by denying Locke's claim that land could ever be legitimately removed from the commons and transformed into private property.

Why was there no socialism in America? Perhaps there was, but in the wheat fields of the West rather than the tenements of New York City, and under the auspices of the *Second Treatise of Government* rather than the *Communist Manifesto*.

Hartz's book may now be history, but the possibility of a liberal tradition in America is still very much in play. Although Pocock thought his classical republican interpretation crushed Hartz, these days it is Pocock who is on the defensive against a post-Hartzian resurgence of liberal interpretations. No one today contends that the liberal tradition is everything in America, but many scholars have been making the case that it is something and not a small thing.

We have all grown accustomed to the insight that Hartz missed what was illiberal in the American past; we should also ponder the thought that he missed liberalism itself. The history of American liberalism is not present in *The Liberal Tradition in America*. One task we might assign ourselves is to write that history.

NOTES

1. Hans Gerth and C. Wright Mills, eds., *From Max Weber: Essays in Sociology* (New York: Oxford University Press, 1958), 138.

2. Joyce Appleby, *Liberalism and Republicanism in the Historical Imagination* (Cambridge, Mass.: Harvard University Press, 1992). In a personal communication, Professor Appleby confirmed my sense that she found Hartz unimportant for her research projects.

3. For example, see James P. Young, *Reconsidering American Liberalism: The Troubled Odyssey of the Liberal Idea* (Boulder, Colo.: Westview Press, 1996); Sanford Lakoff, "Liberalism in America: Hartz and His Critics," *Critical Review of International Social and Political Philosophy* 8, no. 1 (March 2005): 5–30; Philip Abbott, "Still Louis Hartz after All These Years: A Defense of the Liberal Society Thesis, *Perspectives on Politics* 3, no. 1 (March 2005): 93–109.

4. Judith Shklar, *American Citizenship: The Quest for Inclusion* (Cambridge, Mass.: Harvard University Press, 1991), 13, 106, 22–23.

5. J. David Greenstone, *The Lincoln Persuasion: Remaking American Liberalism* (Princeton, N.J.: Princeton University Press, 1993); Daniel Walker Howe, *The Political Culture of the American Whigs* (Chicago: University of Chicago Press, 1979); Arthur M. Schlesinger Jr., *The Age of Jackson* (Boston: Little, Brown, 1945).

6. Richard Hofstadter, *The Age of Reform* (New York: Vintage Books, 1955), 13, 20.

7. Joyce Appleby, *Capitalism and a New Social Order: The Republican Vision of the 1790s* (New York: New York University Press, 1984).

8. Bernard Bailyn, *The Ideological Origins of the American Revolution* (Cambridge, Mass.: Harvard University Press, 1967).

9. Lionel Trilling, *The Liberal Imagination: Essays on Literature and Society* (New York: Harcourt, Brace, Jovanovich: 1950), vii.

10. Richard Hofstadter, *Anti-Intellectualism in American Life* (New York: Vintage Books, 1964), 43.

11. Marvin Meyers, "Louis Hartz, the Liberal Tradition in America: An Appraisal," *Comparative Studies in Society and History* 5, no. 3 (April 1963): 267.

12. Mark Hulliung, *The Social Contract in America: From the Revolution to the Present Age* (Lawrence: University Press of Kansas, 2007), chaps. 3, 6.

About the Contributors

RICHARD J. ELLIS is the Mark O. Hatfield Professor of Politics at Willamette University. Among his books are *Presidential Travel: The Journey from George Washington to George W. Bush* and *To the Flag: The Unlikely History of the Pledge of Allegiance.*

ALAN GIBSON teaches political science at California State University, Chico. He is author of *Interpreting the Founding: Guide to the Enduring Debates over the Origins and Foundations of the American Republic* and *Understanding the Founding: The Crucial Questions.*

MARK HULLIUNG is Richard Koret Professor of History at Brandeis University. His two most recent books are *Citizens and Citoyens: Republicans and Liberals in America and France* and *The Social Contract in America: From the Revolution to the Present Age.*

DESMOND KING is Andrew W. Mellon Professor of American Government at the University of Oxford and Fellow of Nuffield and St. John's Colleges. His recent publications include *Separate and Unequal: African Americans and the U.S. Federal Government* and the coedited *The Unsustainable American State.*

JAMES T. KLOPPENBERG is Charles Warren Professor of American History at Harvard University. He is author of *Uncertain Victory: Social Democracy and Progressivism in European and American Thought, 1870–1920* and *The Virtues of Liberalism* and coeditor of *A Companion to American Thought.*

CAROL NACKENOFF is Richter Professor of Political Science at Swarthmore College. She is author of *The Fictional Republic: Horatio Alger and American Political Discourse* and coeditor of *Jane Addams and the Practice of Democracy.*

ROGERS M. SMITH is Christopher H. Browne Distinguished Professor of Political Science at the University of Pennsylvania and Chair of the Program on Democracy, Citizenship, and Constitutionalism. He is author of *Liberalism and American Constitutional Law* and *Civic Ideals: Conflicting Visions of Citizenship in U.S. History,* among other works.

MARC STEARS is University Lecturer in Political Theory and Fellow in Politics at University College, Oxford. He is author of *Progressives, Pluralists and the Problems of the State* and *Demanding Democracy: American Radicals in Search of a New Politics* and coeditor of *Political Theory: Methods and Approaches.*

Index

abortion, 210–211, 218, 221–222, 241, 243, 254
Abramowitz, Alan, 217
absolute power, 24, 66
absolutism, royal, 3, 22
Adams, John, 101
Adams, Samuel, 101
Addams, Jane, 103–104, 189, 252
Adler, Mortimer J., 18
Adorno, Theodor, 108
AFL-CIO, 33
African Americans, 64, 74, 77, 105, 128, 197, 220, 227
Africans, 65, 68
Alger, Horatio, 94, 103, 129, 150, 184, 238, 241–242, 254–255
American Civil Liberties Union, 233, 256
"American creed," 24, 60, 61
American Enterprise Institute, 37
American exceptionalism, 3, 27, 110, 161, 171, 223, 228, 229, 244
"Americanism," 94, 105, 187, 188, 192, 196, 198, 199
American Medical Association, 33
American Political Development, 1, 56, 76, 78–79, 82, 127, 141–142, 171, 237–238, 246–248, 254, 267, 269
American Political Science Association (APSA), 1, 90
American Revolution, 42, 45, 69, 99–100, 109, 151–152, 154–159, 167, 169, 171, 174–175, 271

ancien régime. See Old Regime
Andrews, George Reid, 106
Anglican church, 100
Anglo-Saxons, 163
Antebellum America, 14, 34, 44–45, 61, 99, 101–102, 104, 131, 134, 237
anticlericalism, 96
antielitism, 184
Anti-Federalists, 101, 168–169
antistatism, 134–135, 142, 160
Appleby, Joyce, 12, 172, 268, 270
Aquinas, Thomas, 112
Arendt, Hannah, 15, 18, 33, 108
Aristotle, 22–23, 113
Aron, Raymond, 20
Asians, 99
Atlantic Republican tradition, 160, 163
Augustine, 112
Auerbach, Eric, 108
Augustinian Christianity, 102
Australia, 4, 30, 228
Austro-Hungarian Empire, 14
authoritarianism, 16, 134, 157
autonomy, 44, 62, 92, 102, 103, 211, 239, 255

Babeuf, Gracchus, 108
Bacon's Rebellion, 69
Bad Godesberg, 106
Bailyn, Bernard, 150, 154–158, 160, 270
Bakunin, Mikhail, 28
Ballance, Pierre Simon, 108

Bancroft, George, 28, 32
Barber, Benjamin, 5
Basson, Lauren, 70–71
Beard, Charles, 1, 20, 28, 32, 91, 137, 149, 166–167, 169–170, 173, 239
Beaumont, Gustave de, 68
Becker, Carl, 167
behaviorism, 93
Bell, Daniel, 39–40, 198, 245
Bell, Derrick, 67, 70–71
Bensel, Richard, 134
Berger, Peter, 37
Berlin, Isaiah, 38–39
Bernstein, Edward, 104, 111
Berryer, Pierre Nicolas, 108
Better American Federation, 192
Beveridge Report, 105
Bible, 211–212
Billington, Ray Allen, 23, 30
Bill of Rights, 100, 105
Bingham, Arthur, 192
blacks, 37, 45, 67, 69, 73, 99, 213–215, 225
Blanc, Louis, 108
Block, Jim, 255
Bolingbroke, Henry St. John Viscount, 157
Bolsheviks, 101
Bonald, Vicomte Louis Gabriel, 108
Boorstin, Daniel, 11, 38–40, 171
Booth, Paul, 199
Bossuet, Jacques Bénigne, 108
Boston Port Act, 156
Boudin, Louis, 108
bourgeoisie, 15, 99, 103, 151, 162, 239
Brandeis, Louis, 42, 103–104, 170
Briand, Aristide, 108
British Americans, 65, 68
British Constitution, 77, 156
British Empire, 243
British Labour Party, 27, 106
Brownson, Orestes, 102
Brown v. Board of Education (1954), 245
Brzezinski, Zbigniew K., 15, 18
Buchanan, Pat, 216
Bull Moose campaign, 187
Burckhardt, Jacob, 16, 17
Burke, Edmund, 28, 37, 151–152, 166, 171, 246, 271–272
Bush, George W., 32, 116, 209, 211–212, 215–217, 220–221, 225–226

Calhoun, John C., 43, 114
Calvinist, 97, 163
Canada, 3–4, 225–228
capitalism, 27, 34–38, 66, 93, 101, 102, 104, 115, 116, 125–143, 150, 161, 172, 188, 207, 208, 213, 246
capital punishment, 223–225, 229
Carnegie, Andrew, 103, 132
Carter, Jimmy, 215
Catholics, 22, 219, 221–222, 227
Center for Individual Rights, 256
Charter of Fundamental Rights, 226
Chase, Stuart, 192
"Christian Sparta," 101
civic republicanism, 76
civic virtue, 12
Civil Rights Movement, 103
Civil War, 2, 13, 42–43, 69, 73, 77, 103, 116, 130–131, 133, 154, 171, 213, 247, 252, 269
Civil War amendments, 103
Chapman, Herrick, 106
Charlemagne, 109
Chartists, 4
China, 23, 112
Chinese Americans, 74
Christianity, Christians, 97, 102, 210, 219–220
Clark, Elizabeth J., 101
classical republicanism, 12, 156, 158
Clinton, Bill, 208, 215–216, 223
Cobbett, William, 4
Cold War, 13, 15–20, 24–26, 32–33, 35, 39–40, 77, 92, 105, 134, 149, 198, 244, 246
collectivism, 95
colonialism, 116
common law, 40, 156
Commonwealth Club, 105
Communist, Communism, 15, 94, 106, 111, 116, 134–135, 193, 197, 199, 245, 272
Communist Manifesto, 272
communitarians, 37, 43
Comte, Auguste, 31, 108
Concerned Women for America, 229
Confucians, 112
Congress, 105, 128, 133, 207, 217, 245, 256

Congress of Industrial Organizations, 194
consensus theory, 57, 198, 200
conservatism, 25, 28, 93, 151, 170, 207, 209–210, 212, 214–215, 269, 271
constitution, constitutionalism, 19, 23, 43, 46, 57, 69, 71, 100, 113–114, 132, 136–137, 152–154, 156, 158–160, 168–170, 173–174, 190, 192, 211, 218, 237–246, 249–253, 255–257, 271
Constitutional Convention (1787), 168, 174, 243
Cooley, Charles, 189, 190
Cooper, James Fenimore, 108–109
"Country Party," 156, 161
courts, 101, 168, 237–238, 252–253, 255–257
Crockett, Davy, 94
Croly, Herbert, 42, 103–104, 137, 188–189, 191
Curti, Merle, 154

Darwinian liberalism, 73–74
Dawson, Michael, 75
Declaration of Independence, 46, 197, 269, 271
Declaration of the Rights of Man and Citizen, 46, 271
Defense of Marriage Act, 266
Democratic party, 5, 26–27, 106, 214, 219, 223, 228, 245
Depression, 116, 127, 192, 197, 200
despotism, 16–17, 21–23, 36
Dewey, John, 103–104, 108–110, 115–116, 192–195, 197–198, 200, 252
Diamond, Martin, 155
Diggins, John Patrick, 114
Dilthey, Wilhelm, 31–32, 94
Disney, Walt, 94
Dowd, Matthew, 217
Du Bois, W. E. B., 67
Durkheim, Emile, 31

education, 102, 105, 109, 128, 210, 240, 244, 254
egoism, 98
Eisenhower, Dwight, 26, 207–208, 215
Ellis, Richard J., 99–100
Ely, Richard, 103
Endangered Species Act, 240

England, 4, 20–24, 26, 29, 30, 36, 45, 46, 104, 105, 151, 156, 160, 224, 271
English Declaration of Rights (1689), 271
English North America, 100, 113
English Whigs, 29, 271
Enlightenment, 4, 41, 111, 156
Equal Protection Clause, 240, 244
Equal Rights Amendment, 211
Ericson, David, 72–75, 81
ethnicity, 42, 91, 96, 100
ethnocentrism, 19
European Union, 226
Evangelicals, 211, 220–222, 227
Evans, George Henry, 272
Exodus, 103
expansionism, European, 74

Fabianism, 104
Fair Deal, 103, 105, 128
Family Research Council, 229
Fascism, 135
FDR. *See* Roosevelt, Franklin Delano
Federalists, 29, 78, 94, 101, 114, 153, 159–160, 166, 168–169, 240, 243, 256
Federalist Society, 256
feminism, feminists, 103, 211–212
feudalism, 22–25, 29, 35, 38, 93–94, 111, 116–117, 130, 140, 150–152, 161, 163, 165, 186, 228
Fifth Amendment, 131, 240
Fiorina, Morris, 216–217
Fish, Stanley, 249
Fitzhugh, George, 43, 139, 150, 213–214
Flax, Jane, 62–53, 65
Fletcher, Andrew, 157
Florence, 36, 160
Focus on the Family, 229
Foner, Eric, 125, 185, 193, 196
Fong, Edmund, 58
Foucault, Michel, 62, 107
founders, American, 100–101, 150, 154–155, 160, 165, 167, 171, 174
Founding, American, 6, 12, 45, 129, 136–137, 140, 150–151, 154–155, 160–161, 163–167, 171–175, 187–188, 243
Fourteenth Amendment, 131, 240, 243
framers, constitutional, 71, 153, 158, 168, 169, 174, 190, 240

France, 3, 22–23, 26, 29, 35, 104, 224, 226, 228
free-markets, 129–132, 253
free speech, 102, 249
Friedrich, Carl J., 15, 18
French Declaration of Rights (1789), 271
French Revolution, 3, 16, 26, 46, 100, 153, 271
French Socialist Party, 106
Freud, Sigmund, 112

Gabriel, Ralph Henry, 94
Gasset, José Ortega y, 16
gay marriage, gay rights, 212, 222–223, 227, 254
Geertz, Clifford, 156–157
gender, 62–63, 76–77, 91–92, 96–97, 99–100, 107, 129, 163, 174, 210–211, 267
Gentz, Friedrich, 45
George, David Lloyd, 104, 170
George, Henry, 272
German Social Democratic Party, 27, 106
Germany, 104, 115, 224, 226
Gerring, John, 219, 245
Gerstle, Gary, 125, 185, 193, 196
G.I. Bill, 105, 128
Gilded Age, 247
Gilman, Charlotte Perkins, 103–104
Gingrich, Newt, 209
Gitlin, Todd, 199
Gleason, Philip, 61
God, 166, 210–212, 220, 254
Goldwater, Barry, 209
Good, Tom, 200
Gordon, Thomas, 157
Gottschalk, Marie, 224
Graber, Mark, 251, 257
Gramsci, Antonio, 107
Grant, Madison, 58
Great Britain, 115, 167, 209, 226, 227
Great Depression, 116, 127, 197, 200
Great Society, 208
Green, Donald P., 113
Green, John, 220–221, 227
Green, T. H., 104
Greenstone, J. David, 57, 72, 251–252, 269–270
Gross Domestic Product (GDP), 228

Grotius, Hugo, 272
Guizot, François, 17
Gunnell, John, 58, 170–171

Habermas, Jurgen, 114
Halèvy, Élie, 3
Hall, David, 97
Hamiltonian, 170, 238–239, 242, 244
Hamlet, 101
Harrington, Michael, 240
Hartz, Louis
    Economic Policy and Democratic Thought, 1–2, 5, 13, 43–44, 101, 130
    The Founding of New Societies, 2–5
    The Necessity of Choice, 6, 17, 31, 43
Harvard University, 2–3, 90–91, 108, 268
Haskell, Thomas L., 111
Hayden, Tom, 199
health care, 223, 228, 242
Hegel, Georg Wilhelm Friedrich, 16, 32, 41, 112–113
Heidegger, Martin, 15–16
Hercules, 101
Higham, John, 41–42, 269
Hirschl, Ran, 253
Hispanics, 99
historicism (German), 31–32
Hitler, Adolf, 18
Hoadly, Benjamin, 157
Hobbes, Thomas, 15, 153, 252, 255
Hobhouse, L. T., 104
Hochschild, Jennifer, 57, 59–62, 69
Hoffmann, Stanley, 20
Hofstadter, Richard, 11, 103, 155, 269–270
Holland, Catherine, 79
Holmes, George, 139
Holmes, Oliver Wendell, Jr., 18
Holton, Woody, 167, 174
homosexuality, 226–228
Hoover, Herbert, 26, 209
Horkheimer, Max, 108
Horton, Carol, 57, 72–75, 126, 185
Howe, Daniel Walker, 269
Hughes, Henry, 139
Hume, David, 252
Hunter, James, 216
Huntington, Samuel, 163
Hurricane Katrina, 116

iconoclasm, 96
illiberalism, 16, 72, 213, 269–270
immigrants, 192
immigration, 106, 140, 254
imperialists (European), 65, 75
independent voters, 217
Indian removal, 102
Indians (American), 99
individualism, 62, 98, 101, 104, 110, 114,
    171, 189, 191, 193, 200, 208, 238,
    242, 252
Institute for Justice, 256
intelligent design, 254
isolationism, 14
Iton, Richard, 61–62

Jackson, Andrew, 29, 34, 42, 269
Jackson, Robert H., 249
Jacksonians, 36, 43, 78, 101–102, 269
Jacobins, 93, 101
Jaffa, Harry, 95
James, William, 110
Janara, Laura, 67
Jaurès, Jean, 104
Jefferson, Thomas, 28, 34, 42, 58, 101–
    102, 109, 166, 195
Jeffersonians, 36, 43, 78, 112, 166, 168,
    170
Jensen, Merrill, 167, 239
Jews, 97, 99, 219, 222
Jim Crow, 74, 77
Johnson, Lyndon, 106, 208–209
Johnson, Tom, 191
judicial decisions. *See* courts
July Charter (France), 29
Justice Felix Frankfurter, 242
Justice Lewis Powell, 240
Justice Potter Stewart, 241

Kahn, Ronald, 252
Katznelson, Ira, 128, 163
Keck, Thomas M., 256
Kellogg, Paul, 189–190
Kennan, George, 14
Kerry, John, 220–221, 226
King, Desmond, 77, 82, 185
Klatch, Rebecca, 210–211
Klingemann, Hans-Dieter, 219

Klinkner, Philip, 77
Kloppenberg, James, 126, 149, 185, 268
Knights of Labor, 103
Koch, Adrienne, 95
Kohn, Margaret, 67
Kramnick, Isaac, 172
Krieger, Leonard, 95
Kruse, Kevin, 215
Ku Klux Klan, 78

labor movements, labor unions, 13
La Follette, Robert, 192
laissez-faire, 2, 14, 28, 73, 101, 103, 116,
    129–130, 132–133, 208, 210
Laslett, Peter, 19
Latin America, 4
Lawrence v. Texas (2003), 226
Lewis, John L., 194–195
liberal mythology, 58
libertarianism, 210
liberty, 3, 22, 43, 57, 64, 94–95, 98, 100,
    141, 155–156, 158, 160, 184, 186,
    193, 210, 241–242, 252, 255, 269
Limbaugh, Rush, 209
Lincoln, Abraham, 72, 102–103, 109, 195,
    269
Lincoln's Second Inaugural, 102
Lippmann, Walter, 18, 189, 191
Lipset, Seymour Martin, 33, 39–40
Lively, Richard, 134
localism, 37, 38, 107, 112
Locke, John. *See Second Treatise of*
    Government
Louis XIV, 3
Lovett, Robert Morss, 192
Luther, Seth, 1, 13
Lutz, Donald S., 113
Lynd, Staughton, 167

Macaulay, Thomas Babington, 17
Machiavelli, 252–253
MacPherson, C. B., 171
Main, Jackson Turner, 167
Maistre, Joseph de, 28, 128
Mann, Arthur, 94
Mannheim, Karl, 25–26, 29, 39, 41–44
Marcuse, Herbert, 114
Marvell, Andrew, 157

Marx, Karl, 25, 28, 45, 65, 67, 93, 104, 106–109, 111, 113–114, 125, 149, 162, 210, 240, 271
Marxist, 4, 11, 16, 27, 111, 125, 130, 162–163, 172, 222
Matthew (Bible), 103
Mayflower, 95
McCarthyism, 13, 15–16, 18, 24, 104
McDonald, Forrest, 174
Mead, George Herbert, 110
Medicaid, 241
Mehta, Uday, 63–65, 68, 75
Meyers, Marvin, 94–95, 271
Middle Ages, 22, 29
militarism, 16
Mill, James, 29
Mill, John Stuart, 30, 41, 102, 114
Mills, Charles, 74–75
Mills, C. Wright, 199
modernity, 15, 58, 61, 75, 80, 157
Molière, 248
Montesquieu, 20–25, 30, 112
Moral Majority, 229
Morgan, Edmund, 69–70, 154
Morgenthau, Hans, 31
Morone, James, 229, 255
Morrison, Toni, 62
Mowry, George, 94
Murray, Charles, 58
Mussolini, Benito, 16
Myrdal, Gunnar, 60–61, 71–72, 163, 197

NAACP, 78, 103
NAACP Legal Defense Fund, 256
Napoleon, 16
National Association for Constitutional Government, 192
National Security League, 192
Native Americans, 77, 163–165, 167
Nazism, 134
neoconservatives, 37
Neuhaus, Richard John, 37
Neville, Henry, 157
New Deal, New Dealers, 2, 13–14, 26, 36–38, 99, 103, 105, 128, 194, 198, 208, 243
New Left, New Left intellectuals, 5, 37–38, 40, 199–200, 209
New Politics, 5

New Right, 37, 107
Nietzsche, Friedrich, 16, 109, 112
nihilism, 15, 19
Nixon, Richard, 214
Nott, Josiah, 58
Novak, William J., 101

Obama, Barack, 185
Offe, Claus, 106
Oglesby, Carl, 199–200
Old Regime, 3, 21–23, 26, 93, 110
Ollman, Bertell, 239
Olson, Joel, 70–71
Oriental despotism, 22
Orren, Karen, 247
Ortega y Gasset, José, 16

Paine, Thomas, 43, 166
Palmer, A. Mitchell, 104, 140
Palmer, R. R., 23
Palmer Raids, 15
Parrington, Vernon, 20, 91
participatory democracy, 37
patriotism, 186, 188, 191, 195
Patten, Simon Nelson, 189
Peirce, Charles Sanders, 110
per genus et differentiam, 22
Pew Research Center, 221
Philadelphia, 168
Pierson, George W., 23
Pierson, Paul, 248
Plato, 18–19, 23, 113–114
Plessy judgment, 128
pluralism, 19, 33–34
Pocock, J. C. A., 12, 38–39, 150, 155, 158, 160–163, 268, 272
Poland, 22, 114
Polanyi, Karl, 125
polygamy, 102
Pope John Paul II, 211
Popper, Karl, 18, 108
popular sovereignty, 18, 44, 92, 102, 116, 137, 252, 271
Populist Party, Populists, 103, 269
positivism, 31–32
postmodern, 62
pragmatism, 18, 108–110, 115, 245
primogeniture, 100
Progressive Party, 103, 187, 192

Progressivism, Progressives, Progressive
historians, 1, 11, 14, 20, 24, 27–28,
42, 45, 97, 99, 103–106, 109, 116,
125, 130, 134, 137, 149–150, 154,
156, 166–170, 173–175, 187–193,
195, 198, 200, 252, 254, 269, 272
New Freedom, 42, 187, 189, 269
New Nationalism, 42, 269
prohibition, 254
property, 4, 29, 57, 72, 97, 99, 101, 105,
114–115, 129–130, 132, 135–136,
150, 167–168, 184, 238–240, 272
property rights, 65, 81, 92, 155, 164
Protestant, Protestants, 22, 166, 219–222,
227, 255
Pufendorf, Samuel, 272
Puritan, 150, 229, 252
Putnam, Robert, 32, 37

race, racism, 4–5, 37, 42, 57–59, 61–64,
66–82, 91–92, 96, 100, 128–129, 141–
142, 163–164, 166, 174, 197, 210,
212–215, 225–226, 228, 242–243,
249, 267
radicalism, 3–4, 6, 28, 159, 169, 185–187,
192–194, 196, 198
rational choice theory, 93, 113
Rauschenbusch, Walter, 103
Rawls, John, 1, 113–114, 142
Reagan, Ronald, 208–209, 215
Reconstruction, 77, 131
Red Scare, 15, 93, 104, 140, 192
Reform Act (England), 29
Rehnquist Court, 240, 257
relativism, moral and cultural, 19, 211
religion, 5, 22, 38, 42, 91, 94, 96–97, 100,
129, 152–153, 161, 163, 210–211,
219–222, 226–227, 229, 242, 254
republicanism, 12, 62, 69–70, 76–77, 92,
100–102, 114, 117, 126, 137, 150,
154–161, 163, 166, 171–175, 228,
252–253, 268, 272
Republican Party, 26, 78, 116, 128, 133,
135, 168, 192, 207–209, 211–212,
214–220, 222, 225, 227–228, 245
Revolution (French), 3, 16, 26, 46, 100,
152–153, 171, 271
Revolution, Revolutionaries (American),
2, 11–13, 42, 45, 69, 71, 77, 99–100,

109, 130, 151–152, 154–159, 167,
169, 171, 173–175, 196, 271
rights
alienable rights, 45, 271
inalienable rights, 45, 60, 272
natural rights, 12, 38, 44–45, 64, 77,
157, 160, 163, 271
rights of man, 46, 55, 166, 271
social rights, 44
Riker, William, 113
Riley, Patrick, 5
Ritter, Gretchen, 134
Roazen, Paul, 5–6, 17, 38, 94, 96
Roberts Court, 257
Roche, John P., 31
Roe v. Wade (1973), 241
Rodgers, Daniel, 155–156, 167, 173
Roosevelt, Franklin Delano, 13, 26, 38,
103, 105–106, 128, 208, 243, 245, 249
Roosevelt, Theodore, 42, 187, 191
Rorty, Richard, 185–186, 196
Rousseau, Jean-Jacques, 96, 108–109, 113–
114, 153
Royer-Collard, Pierre Paul, 17
Ruggiero, Guido de, 3
Russia, 23, 151–152, 171, 224

sabbatarianism, 102
salus populi, 101
Sanders, Elizabeth, 134
Scalia, Antonin, 242–243
Scandinavia, 106, 223
Schlesinger, Arthur M., Jr., 11, 20, 269
Schmalhausen, Stephen, 195
scientific racism, 61
Scott, Dred, 251
Scottish Enlightenment, 252
Second Treatise of Government, 44, 272
segregated state, 127–128
segregation, 127–128
September 11, 2001, 116, 215
serfs, 114
Shalhope, Robert, 155
Shannon, David A., 23
Shapiro, Ian, 113
Shaw, George Bernard, 110
Shays, Daniel, 168–169
Shklar, Judith, 63, 68, 91, 198, 268
Sidney, Algernon, 157

Skocpol, Theda, 248
Skowronek, Steven, 79–80, 126, 247
slavery, 4–5, 42, 59, 62, 65, 68–70, 72–73,
      77–78, 94, 102, 139, 150, 163, 166,
      213, 251, 254, 268–269, 272
Slavs, 99
Smith, Adam, 43
Smith, James Allen, 20, 169–170
Smith, Rogers M., 126, 150, 163–167, 174,
      185, 213, 253, 269–270
social class, 15, 25, 34, 39, 41, 43, 45, 239,
      244–245, 270
social contract, 12, 38, 44–45, 74–75, 157,
      160, 271
Social Democrats, 27, 103–107, 109–110
social equality, 57, 125, 150, 185–186, 188,
      193, 200
socialism, 25, 92–94, 105–106, 110, 129–
      130, 151, 170–171, 209, 219, 239,
      244–245, 269, 271–272
social science, 31, 91, 93, 95
Social Security, 13, 104, 128
Sombart, Werner, 105
Soule, George, 137, 192, 194–195, 201
South Africa, 2–4
Southern Baptist Convention (1998), 212
Southern colonies, 69
Soviet Union, 198, 244
Spain, 22, 224, 226, 228
Stalin, Joseph, 18
Stamp Act, 156
State, the, 14, 31, 57, 125–143, 153, 184,
      193, 208, 211, 224, 226, 243
state governments, 2, 36, 101, 131, 158
State of the Union Address (1944), 105
Stears, Marc, 57, 81
stem-cell research, 221–222
Stevenson, Adlai, 207, 245
Strauss, Leo, 108, 113
Strong, Josiah, 58
Supreme Court, 131, 133, 190, 237, 240,
      242–243, 249, 253, 255–256
Sweden, 115, 219, 226

Talmon, J. L., 16
Tead, Ordway, 192
temperance, 102, 269
Tenth Amendment, 243
Texas District Court, 244

Third Estate, 29
Third World, 15
Thucydides, 31
Time magazine, 254
Tocqueville, Alexis de, 3, 12–13, 17, 20–
      21, 24–26, 29–30, 32–38, 41, 45, 68,
      94, 97–99, 102, 115, 135–136, 164,
      218, 237, 271
   Democracy in America, 3, 12, 17, 20–21,
      24, 32, 35, 37, 97
   The Old Regime and the French Revolution,
      3
Tories, English, 101, 271
Tory estates (in America), 100
totalitarianism, 15–19, 35, 198
trade unionism, 194
Trenchard, John, 157
Trilling, Lionel, 270
Trotskyite, 23
Truman, Harry, 26, 105–106
Turner, Frederick Jackson, 20, 30, 32, 91
Tushnet, Mark, 250

Union, federal, 36, 101, 105, 131–132
Unitarian, 254

Vietnam, 107
Virginia, 35, 69, 166, 225
Voltaire, 112

Wald, Lillian, 103
Wallerstein, Immanuel, 66
Walzer, Michael, 196
Washington, George, 35
Webb, Beatrice, 104
Webb, Sidney, 104
Weber, Max, 31, 58, 97, 112, 125, 267
Webster, Noah, 107
Wechsler, Herbert, 245, 249
Weldon, T. D., 19
Wells, H. G., 189
West, Cornel, 196
Weyl, Walter, 137, 189, 191
Whigs (American), 36, 78, 94, 101–102,
      112, 166, 238
   Conscience Whigs, 269
   Opposition Whigs, 270
white-supremacist, 73, 75, 128, 213
Whitman, Walt, 116–117

Whittington, Keith, 250–251
Wiebe, Robert, 251
Wilde, Oscar, 110
Wilentz, Sean, 247
Wilson, Woodrow, 1, 14, 42, 79, 90, 103, 170, 189
Wittgenstein, Ludwig, 58, 252
women, 42, 45, 63, 77, 94, 103, 163–167, 211, 212, 229, 241, 254

Wood, Gordon, 150, 157
Woodrow Wilson Prize, 1, 90
Woodward, C. Vann, 23, 27
World War I, 14, 15, 104, 127, 187, 192
World War II, 39, 77, 127, 128, 195, 196

Zuckert, Michael, 156